(WHERE IS)

THE PROMISE

OF

CHRIST'S

APPEARING?

What you have not been told!

Bob Anderson

Gregory Gilmore

Israel Gilmore

Duane Klebs

(WHERE IS)

THE PROMISE

OF

CHRIST'S APPEARING?

What you have not been told!

Copyright © 2013 by Bob Anderson, Gregory Gilmore,
Israel Gilmore and Duane Klebs

ISBN - 13   978-0615863658
ISBN - 10   0615863655

All Scripture quotations are from the King James Version of the Bible unless otherwise specified in the quote.

****

All Scripture quotations are *italicized*. Where Scripture text is **boldfaced**, an emphasis has been added. Square parentheses in the Scripture quotations show [additions for explanatory purposes.]

We have used Capital Letters for pronouns and certain nouns that relate to God to eliminate confusion about Who is being referred to in Scripture quotations.

****

Printed in the United States of America

Table of Contents

Introduction

Wars, wars and rumors of wars, plus extreme weather like flooding, earthquakes and tsunamis in diverse places are in store for our near future. Just pick up a newspaper or turn on the TV and you will read about or see another conflict, earthquake or devastating storm somewhere in the world. Christ said these would be some of the signs before His return. Like a woman in travail, all these things are like birth pangs that intensify in frequency and duration.

However, how do we know that we are any closer to Christ's return today than we were 50 years ago? Everyone was sure that the time for Christ's return was near when Israel fulfilled prophecy by becoming a nation again after 2000 years of exile. Do you know that the Bible has predicted with uncanny accuracy certain political alignments that precede the Tribulation period? These political alignments did not exist 50 years ago.

While many theologians would have you believe that no further prophecy need be fulfilled before Christ returns, this book delves into identifiable prophetic events that are to happen before the Tribulation period and before Christ returns. The sheer number of prophecies being fulfilled since the turn of the century is exciting, yet the world seems oblivious because it has turned away from God and the Bible.

Did you know that the Bible predicted that in the end of days good would be promoted as evil and vice versa? This has to do with the mirror image of God. Evil always imitates Truth, just in reverse like a mirror image. We will show you examples of how evil prospers using the mirror image of God. A great falling away from Christ's teachings in the end of days will be one of these prophecies. People will not accept the truth. The notion that all the world's major religions have the same god has taken like wild fire. People are already accepting the lie that there are many pathways to God. God tells us that there is a right and a wrong, that there is the Truth and there is the lie. Satan is the father of all lies but Jesus said, *"I Am The Way, The Truth, and The Life: no man cometh unto the Father, but by Me"* (John 14:6). The world says Christianity is intolerant because Christ claims He is the only way to God the Father. While the world rejects this basic

5

tenant of Christianity in favor of the lie, a charismatic prince will like a court jester get the whole world to worship the supposed one true god. When the time is right, he removes that god from the temple and he stands there in its place, demanding to be worshipped. Will Christians still be here to witness this prophecy? Together we will learn what the Bible says about this prophecy and the timing of the Gathering of the Bride to Christ.

War is coming to Israel and no, it is not Armageddon. It seems the whole world is against Israel and soon, before the Tribulation period begins, a nuclear war will ensue. You will never guess the outcome.

Speaking of Armageddon, why is everyone so quick to say the next Great War will be Armageddon? There is a whole lot of prophecy that has to be fulfilled before Armageddon comes. Also, who fights in that last great battle on the earth, all nations against each other right? Read it again, because that is not what Armageddon is really about. The Armageddon passage in Revelation is a typical example of how the Bible is misinterpreted. You will learn that Scripture is precise and one needs to read every line carefully. Go back and read Revelation 19 again and you might be surprised that the whole world is not in battle against one another, but united against something else.

This book gets into what happens to all the people who are left behind after Christ comes for His Bride and why no other generation before us could have seen Christ's return. Also, is it possible that Christ's crucifixion occurred in the middle of Daniel's seventieth week? As you read your Bible alongside this book, you will discover all the prophetic passages relevant to our times. Guess what is in the news lately, some of those very prophecies.

Chapter 1

Rightly Dividing the Word of God

In order to understand the Holy Bible, the Apostle Paul told Timothy to *"study to show thyself approved unto God, a workman that needeth not to be ashamed, **rightly dividing the Word of Truth"*** (2 Tim. 2:15). To rightly divide God's Word one must have an overall understanding of God's plan and how Scripture is to be interpreted as it relates to different time periods. One brings about erroneous doctrine if individual Scriptures of God's Word are not properly interpreted, not properly applied, or not placed in the proper timing. We will show you from the Scriptures how we have arrived at our conclusions and the methods we have used. We will start with the big picture of God's overall plan and move to the more detailed.

God's Law

God's Law was present in Creation and will always exist even into the eternity future. God's Law is what holds everything in Creation together and makes it orderly. It is seen in science in all the physical laws that exist, such as the law of gravity, the law of thermodynamics, the law of aerodynamics, etc. God's Law controls the physical dimension of our universe, as well as the spiritual dimension, where God and the angels reside under God's Authority.

God's Law is very much in affect for humanity today (Rom. 3:31, 4:16). All humankind is condemned to death under the moral and legal requirements of this Law (Rom. 3:10-12, 3:19-20, Heb. 10:1-4). God's Law is a heavy yoke that none can measure up to, for all have sinned and fall short of meeting the Law's requirements (John 3:15-20, Rom. 3:23). All are naturally disobedient to the Ten Commandments of God's Law because of our inherited human sin nature. But Christ says,

> *Come unto Me, all ye that labour and are heavy laden, and I will give you rest. Take My yoke upon you, and learn of Me; for I am meek and lowly in heart: and ye*

> *shall find rest unto your souls. For My yoke is easy, and My burden is light* (Matt. 11:28-30).

It is only by being conceived by the Holy Spirit and brought to new life in your spirit through Jesus Christ that one can spiritually escape the bondage and yoke of God's Law. Christians can live in peace with God by closely following the Holy Spirit's leading and are thereby obeying God's Law. However, when we break God's Law, consequences in the flesh arise. If we commit adultery, we will have failed marriages. If we worship things instead of God, we should expect the blessings of those things, which are tarnish and rust instead of God's blessings. If one cheats the next in business dealings, one should expect a bad reputation and one should expect their business to suffer accordingly. God does not reward sin. Do you see how God's Law has not been suspended? The things we do in the flesh have consequences. Just because we are forgiven in our spirit does not take away the consequences in the flesh. When we bring our flesh into line with our spirit filled walk with God, only then can we be at peace with God and lead fulfilled happy lives.

God's Will and Testament

God's Law governs everything, including His sovereign and legal Will and Testament. God's Will and Testament became necessary when iniquity was found in Lucifer and God has brought about a wonderful plan for bringing His Creation back to a perfect state. Part of that plan is that through God's Son, Jesus Christ, one can be restored back to perfect relationship with his or her Creator, God the Father. God's Will and Testament also reverses death, destruction and chaos that were brought about by Lucifer, also known as *"that old serpent, which is the Devil, and Satan"* (Rev. 12:9, 20:2).

God has progressively revealed His Will and Testament throughout the whole of Scripture. God's Will and Testament is a legal contract with all of His Creation. Every change He makes to His Will and Testament is a legal codicil or is like an addendum to a contract.

For instance, if there is an open-ended contract and at some point in the future one wants to place an addendum to said contract, then the addendum would take effect at the appointed time. Everything prior to the addendum may or may not be covered as determined by the new addendum. When Christ, being fully God and fully human, fulfilled the legal and moral requirements of God's Law and the Mosaic Law with the New Covenant of Grace, He put into effect a legal codicil to God's Will and Testament. This new addendum through Jesus Christ covers the provision for atonement of all of humanities' past, present and future sins.

> *For it pleased the Father that in Him* [Jesus] *should all fulness dwell; And, having made peace through the blood of His cross, by Him* [Jesus] *to reconcile all things unto Himself* [God]; *by Him, I say, whether they be things in earth, or things in heaven* (Col. 1:20).

Jesus Christ is testator of God's Will and Testament (Heb. 9:15-17) and the central focal point of all Scripture.

However, Satan's counterfeit systems are always coming against God's Will and Testament. Satan has attempted to keep God's Will from coming to completion throughout the Earth Ages.

Earth Ages

Many present theologians interchange the word "Age" when they are really talking about Dispensations. The reason that we define an Age as an Earth Age is to eliminate as much confusion as possible and to make it clear that an Age is not equivalent to a Dispensation. Clarence Larkin says,

> An "Age" in Scripture is from one "cataclysmic" or "climatic" change to another in the earth's surface or condition. This corresponds to what is called in Geology an "Age." So we see that Science and the Bible agree as to the meaning of the word "Age."[1]

We agree with this definition as being true and accurate. There were "cataclysmic" and "climatic" changes that took place on the earth during the flood of Noah's time. We know this from the fact that *"the same day were all the fountains of the great deep broken up"* (Gen. 7:11). Geology also points to a tremendous change to the rock

9

strata that took place at some point in our history. Also, the human life span was reduced from about 900 years to about 120 years due to the change in atmospheric conditions brought about by God's judgement on a rebellious creation.

At the end of the Tribulation period there will be another "cataclysmic" and "climatic" change to the surface of the earth. Once again, God brings righteous judgement on a rebellious creation that worships the Antichrist and Satan's systems. Zechariah 14:4 says that the Mount of Olives will split in two and create a great valley when the Lord's feet shall stand on it at the end of the Tribulation period.

> *And every mountain and island were moved out of their places* (Rev. 6:14).

> *And there was a great earthquake, such as was not since men were upon the earth, so mighty an earthquake, and so great. And the great city was divided into three parts, and the cities of the nations fell* (Rev. 16:18b - 19a).

> *And every island fled away, and the mountains were not found* (Rev. 16:20).

There will indeed be "cataclysmic" and "climatic" changes at that time. Isaiah 65:20 also tells us that a person who is a hundred years old is considered to be a mere child. It says that men will live to be very old, perhaps as old as Methuselah. This is a reversal of what took place at the flood.

Many believe that after the White Throne Judgement at the end of the millennial reign of Christ, there will be a new heaven and a new earth. This will be another Earth Age.

Please look at our chart on the next page to see how an addendum to God's Will and Testament may affect an Earth Age, a Covenant, or a Dispensation that the change occurred in. When looking at the chart, notice that the Earth Ages, Covenants and Dispensations do not all line up. The point is that they cannot be synonymous even though they may fall into line occasionally. They are clearly different from one another. Also note that at the Garden of Eden, at the Flood, and at the beginning of the Millennium are the only times all three line up (Earth Ages, Covenants and Dispensations).

God's Plan for the Earth Ages

In the begining it was God's Will to restore His creation back to perfection ──────→ to the All in All

God's Will and Testament Governs All

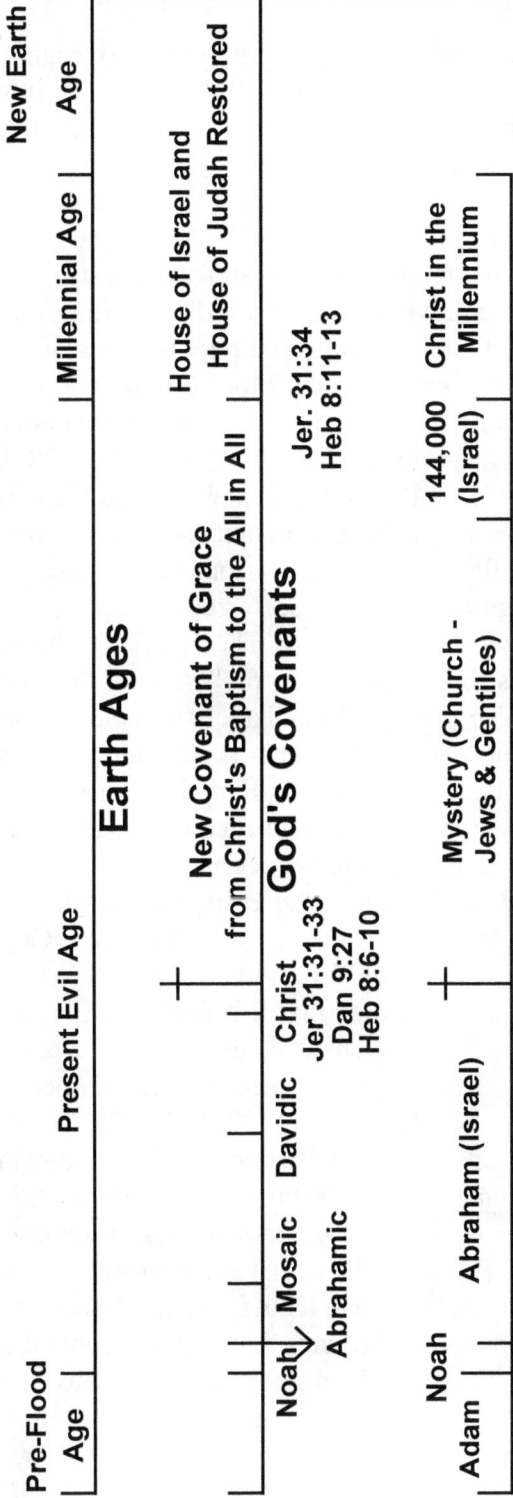

Earth Ages

| Pre-Flood Age | Present Evil Age | Millennial Age | New Earth Age |

New Covenant of Grace
from Christ's Baptism to the All in All

House of Israel and
House of Judah Restored

God's Covenants

Christ
Jer 31:31-33
Dan 9:27
Heb 8:6-10

Jer. 31:34
Heb 8:11-13

Noah   Mosaic   Davidic
        Abrahamic

Mystery (Church - Jews & Gentiles)

144,000 (Israel)   Christ in the Millennium

Dispensations

Noah
Adam   Abraham (Israel)

The All in All

(There are some Covenants and Dispensations not shown here)

Satan has also interfered with God's Covenants and has brought about much confusion, even to this day, as to how Covenants and Dispensations relate to one another. Let us look at these in an attempt to dispel the confusion.

New Covenant of Grace

God's Law, given to Moses and written down in the Pentateuch, governs how and when animal sacrifice is done for the atonement of sin under the Old Covenant. The requirements of animal sacrifice for the atonement of sin under the Mosaic Law as it was before the Christ addendum will never be required again. Christ ended that at the cross once and for all, forever (Dan. 9:27, Heb. 7:27-28, Heb. 9:12, 26-28, Heb. 10:10, 12, 14). God will never again ask Israel to sacrifice animals in the temple for the atonement of sin. However, Israel begins animal sacrifice during the Tribulation period, but God is not directing them to do so. In fact, Israel makes a covenant (Isa. 28:15, 18) with *"that man of sin"* (2 Thess. 2:3-4), the false prince (Dan. 9:26), who is the mirror image of *"Messiah the Prince"* (Dan. 9:25). When the false prince allows Israel to begin animal sacrifice in the rebuilt temple, Satan deceives Israel into thinking that they are helping God restore His Earthly Kingdom for the Jews. This is Satan's attempt to provide an alternate means of salvation other than Jesus Christ, as far as the Jews are concerned.

After the Gathering of the Bride of Christ, the need for animal sacrifice will not revert to the way it was before God's legal codicil, a legal amendment to His Will and Testament. Whosoever believes in Jesus Christ shall have eternal life from the Christ addendum. God's New Testament or Covenant confirmed with many (Dan. 9:27) was delivered by Jesus Christ, *"even the Messenger of the Covenant"* (Mal. 3:1; also see, Heb. 8:6, 10:29, 12:24, 13:20).

Christ did not come to abolish the Ten Commandments of God's Law or suspend the Old Testament Covenants. *"Think not that I am come to destroy the law, or the prophets: I am not come to destroy, but to fulfill"* (Matt. 5:17). Christ came to fulfill their legal and moral requirements, as only He could! Jesus Christ, as God and fully human, was the only Mediator that could become the pure and perfect sacrifice for humanities' sin because no sin was found in Him (Heb. 4:15, 7:26-28, 9:14). By Jesus Christ's once and for all blood sacrifice for humankind's sin, the *"ordinances of divine service"* (Heb. 9:1) were no longer needed. Animal sacrifice was abolished with all the ceremonial offerings for the atonement of sin.

Note: Israel will be asked to perform animal sacrifice as a memorial under the new theocracy during the Millennial Dispensation. However, this animal sacrifice is not for the atonement of sin, but to honor God's fulfillment of His promises and Covenants with Israel (Jer. 31:31-34, Heb. 8:6 - Heb. 9:10, Heb. 10:14-18). It is much like partaking of communion in this present Dispensation, commemorating the shed blood and the breaking of Christ's body on the cross until Christ returns for His Bride.

This means that to now do animal sacrifice for the atonement of sins would be an abomination to God. Hebrews 9:15-17 tells us,

> *And for this cause He* [Jesus] *is the Mediator of the new testament* [New Covenant], *that by means of death, for the redemption of the transgressions that were under the first testament* [Old Covenant], *they which are called might receive the promise of eternal inheritance. For where a testament is, there must also of necessity be the death of the testator* [Jesus Christ]. *For a testament is of force after men are dead: otherwise it is of no strength at all while the testator liveth* (Explanation added).

Since no man was worthy under the Ten Commandments of God's Law given to Moses (Rom. 3:19-20, 4:13-14), Christ brought grace into the world, forever. The Christ addendum is found in John 3:16. God declares Christ's death as the appropriate and designated sacrifice for our sin. Jesus stands in our place having paid the penalty of death for our sin, and He completely satisfies God's demands morally and legally. If we believe in God's provision for salvation, Christ's sacrifice under the New Covenant brings about a total expungement of our sins and we become a new creation in Christ (2 Cor. 5:17).

We see the Mosaic Law being simplified by Christ, with rewards much greater than under the old Mosaic Law. People were required to be obedient and perform works with perfection to the letter of the

Mosaic Law. Salvation through Christ is a gift from God under the New Covenant of Grace. *"For by grace are ye saved through faith; and not of yourselves: it is the gift of God: not of works, lest any man should boast"* (Ephes. 2:8-9). Works have nothing to do with obtaining salvation. Works are however the proof of our love for God. Works are not out of necessity, but out of love (1 John 5:3). What is really important is that we mature in our relationship with God. If we focus on maturing in our love for God, our personal relationships with humanity will also change for the better.

The Christ codicil is twofold: First, the Christ addendum fulfilled the legal and moral requirements of the Ten Commandments under God's Law unconditionally because Christ was without sin (Heb. 4:14-15, 7:26). Jesus Christ's ultimate sacrifice as the Lamb of God also replaced animal sacrifice for the atonement of sin. Secondly, the Christ addendum allows Gentiles to be included as heirs to the Kingdom of God.

Christ did not abolish the Ten Commandments of God's Law. In fact, Jesus reaffirmed the legal and moral obligations of God's Law given to Moses by giving us two commandments of the New Covenant: 1) Love God with all your heart, 2) Love your neighbor as yourself. When Christ gave us these two condensed commandments of the New Covenant, He reaffirmed the original Ten Commandments of the Old Covenant. How then can anyone say that Christ suspended the Law?[2] These two commandments of the New Covenant cover all Ten Commandments of God's Law under the Old Covenant, that the LORD wrote down in the Mosaic Law (Exo. 24:12, Deut. 4:13, 5:22).

The Christ addendum replaced the ordinances of divine service in an earthly temple concerning most of the ceremonial aspects of the Mosaic Law, especially animal sacrifice for the atonement of sin (Heb. 9). Christ's once and for all time blood sacrifice has already made atonement for all of humanities sin. If anyone accepts Christ, either Jew or Gentile, then God's Law is fulfilled spiritually (Rom. 5:12-17, 8:1-4). If anyone rejects Christ's pardon, under God's Law one stands condemned already (John 3:18).

Stewardship Change at New Dispensations
This section is a closer look at Dispensations, their Administration, and their purpose. According to Clarence Larkin,

A Dispensation stands for a "moral" or "probationary" period in the world history. The form of "Administration" is different in each Dispensation.[3]

This Administration is governed by God's Will and Testament. Each time God wants to deal with His Creation in a different manner, He starts a new Dispensation. The purpose of a Dispensation is to govern who is given ward or stewardship over the message of salvation. It is either God teaching man or man teaching man about the good news of God's salvation plan. Each Dispensation has a distinct beginning and ending point. God has used different forms and methods to present His good news to all His Creation throughout all the Dispensations since iniquity was found in Satan.

> *God, who at sundry times and in divers manners spake in time past unto the fathers by the prophets, Hath in these last days spoken unto us by His Son, Whom He hath appointed Heir of all things, by Whom also He made the worlds* [Earth Ages] (Heb. 1:1-2).

If present theologians would just understand that the legal and moral requirements of God's Law as written down in the Mosaic Law were fulfilled by Jesus Christ through the New Covenant of Grace, they would stop trying to segregate how God deals with Jews and Gentiles into dispensational fragments! Salvation is a free gift to anyone who will accept it under the New Covenant of Grace. God does not limit the gift among peoples or nations. When we are born again in the Spirit, we are branches that are grafted into the root, which is Jesus. We become part of the olive tree. Part of the *"Mystery"* is the bringing together of Jew and Gentile as one new body under the New Covenant of Grace through the Christ Addendum to God's Will and Testament (Ephes. 3:3-11).

At this moment in history, the Gentiles through *"the Mystery of God"* (Rev. 10:7) are given the stewardship over the message of salvation. *"This is a great mystery: but I speak concerning Christ and the church"* (Ephes. 5:32).

15

> *Whereof I* [Paul] *am made a minister, according to the dispensation of God which is given to me for you, to fulfill the Word of God* (Col. 1:25).

> *For this cause I Paul, the prisoner of Jesus Christ for you Gentiles, if ye have heard of the dispensation of the grace of God which is given me to you-ward* (Ephes. 3:1-2).

Paul goes on to talk about how the Mystery was hidden from the Earth Ages (Rom. 16:25-27, Col. 1:25-28). Because Israel rejected Jesus' message of salvation and rejected Him as the Messenger of the Covenant, the Gentiles were given the stewardship of the message of salvation through the Mystery until the mid-Trib Gathering. Then the stewardship of the *"Everlasting Gospel"* (Rev. 14:6) is given to Israel through the 144,000 Jews until the Millennium. In the Millennium the message of God comes directly from His lips to man through Jesus Christ. Each one of these changes in stewardship of the message of salvation is a different Dispensation.

The Symphonic View of Scripture

The best way to explain the Symphonic View of Scripture is to compare it to a symphony created by a composer. The composer has an overall idea of the music he wants preformed from the beginning. By using individual instruments or various sections of the symphony orchestra such as string, wind and percussion, he brings about all the sounds he wants to achieve. The melodic theme is played throughout the entirety of the symphony along with many harmonic accompaniments.

The "master score" of the symphony has the individual staffs for each of the different sections within the orchestra on each page. These staffs are divided horizontally with lower notes at the bottom and the higher notes at the top of the staffs. These staffs are divided vertically delineating bars of time. The conductor of the symphony orchestra uses the "master score" to direct the individual musicians to play the notes "in the proper key" and "on time" to bring together a wonderful harmonious sound. However, if the musicians play off key or at the improper time, the sound they make will not be harmonious. Have you ever heard an orchestra warming up or a group of individual musicians playing at random? The sounds they make are not harmonious at all and are more like noise.

God is the composer and conductor of this symphony of Scripture. Each Scripture is related to all other Scriptures in the Bible. Although many men wrote the 66 Books in the Bible, they were only God's pencils. God is the true Author of all Scripture (John 1:1, 1:14; 2 Tim. 3:16). Throughout the "master score" there is a melodic story line from Genesis to Revelation. The bars of time tell **when** events happen in the story line. Each staff of the conductor's sheet has all the Scriptures that sound in the appropriate bar. The chorus tells the main theme of the score, which is salvation through the coming Messiah. Whenever the bars come back around to the message of the coming Messiah, the chorus repeats. The accompaniment is the harmonious witness of all the other Scriptures supporting the melodic line.

Theologians that take stand-alone verses and hold them up as proof of their premises are missing the symphonic aspect of Scripture. All individual Scriptures need a double witness, even as Christ needed a double witness; it is part of God's Law (Deut. 17:6, 19:15; John 8:16-18, 2 Cor. 13:1). Sometimes it is not easy to find the double witness in Scripture, but it is there! Keep looking, you will find it. On more important issues it is common to have many witnesses or accompaniments to the truth. This is why there are four Gospels to give witness to the things Christ did and said. This quadruple witness means that it is important for us to understand this concept. Another example, John was told four times in the Book of Revelation that God is the *"Alpha and the Omega"* (Rev. 1:8, 1:11, 21:6, 22:13).

Symphonic Method of Scriptural Study

The Symphonic Method of Scriptural Study is a method of studying the Bible to arrive at the Symphonic View, which is the view of the score that has at least a double witness and is without conflict of any other Scriptures. If we could see the entire score that God composed, we would see that all Scripture is inseparably intertwined together. When you study the Bible always try to find where the Scripture fits on the melodic line and which bar of time it belongs in. Do not be surprised if it fits in more than one place. Keep changing the bar of time until you can find no further conflicts within the whole of Scripture. You must have a faith that the Scriptures do not conflict, even when they appear to. Know that the only reason the Scriptures may appear to conflict is a lack of understanding on our part. Go back to the root word in the original language and check your Bible's interpretation of the word against what you have researched. Learn the history and customs of the period when the Scripture was written in. Usually all that needs to happen to dispel the conflict is to change your pre-conceived notions on the subject matter.

The Bible is too complex for us to actually spread out the whole score from beginning to the end. The score would be miles long and have hundreds of staffs of accompaniment. For God this is easy stuff, but for us maybe it is enough to know it exists. We can see small pieces of it and hear the beautiful music it brings together. Here is a small section of the Bible's Score:

The music we hear is the story told. It is the melody.

	John the Baptist	Messiah comes	Christ's Baptism	Christ begins His ministry	Miracles of Christ	Teachings of Christ
Staffs						
	Isaiah 40:3	Isaiah 61:1-2	Isaiah 60:1	Isaiah 60:3	Matt 8-9	Matt 5-7
Staffs						
	Malachi 3:1	Matt 3:13-14	Matt 3:15-17	Matt 4	Luke 4	Luke 6-7
Staffs						
	Matt 3:1-12	Dan 9:24-25	Dan 9:24	Dan 9:27	Mark 1:21-34	Mark 2-4
Staffs						
	Mark 1:2-7	Luke 4:18	Luke 3:21-22	Luke 5		
Staffs						
	Luke 3:1-6	Mark 1:8	Mark 1:9-11	Mark 1:16-17		

Christ said that the whole Bible was written about Him. *"Then said I, Lo, I come (in the volume of the Book it is written of Me,) to do Thy will, O God"* (Psalms 40:7, Heb. 10:7). When reading the Old Testament always try to find the story of Jesus. It is there! We find that there is much more about Christ in the Old Testament than most people are aware of. Do not forget the types that point to Christ.

Types of the True

Look for the double meaning in Scripture verses of the Old Testament that points to Christ. One example is found in the Scriptures describing Moses while the Israelites were in the wilderness. The Scripture describes two events that have a type of relationship to the true. First, in Exodus 17:6 God told Moses to strike the rock to get water for Israel. Then some time later when Israel was in need of more water, God told Moses to speak to the rock, but Moses did not listen to God. He struck the rock instead and nothing happened. So Moses struck the rock again, then the water came out abundantly. Moses was not allowed to bring Israel to their Promised Land as a punishment for not listening to God (Num. 20:8-12).

Here is the true representation of the Old Testament type. The rock represents Christ in 1 Corinthians 10:4 and God said to *"strike the rock"* to get life giving water in Exodus 17:6. Christ said that the water He gives will spring up into everlasting life in anyone who drinks it (John 4:14). Now that is life-giving water! The second time, God told Moses *"to speak ye unto the rock"* (Num. 20:8) to get life giving water; but Moses did not understand the *"Mystery of God"* (1 Cor. 2:7-8). By striking the rock again, it was like crucifying Christ all over again. Jesus only needed to be struck once for all eternity. This was a prelude of things to come. Israel still does not understand that Christ is the Rock and He gives freely to anyone that asks for His life giving water. Perhaps Israel would have understood, if only Moses had understood. Do not be too hard on Moses though; remember that the *"Mystery"* was kept hidden from humanity and Satan until after Christ's resurrection (1 Cor. 2:7-8, Ephes. 3:1-11, Col. 1:24-28).

The Mirror Image

Try this experiment. Stand in front of a mirror with your right hand raised. The image in the mirror is in the exact image of you with one exception; the left hand is raised in the mirror image. This mirror image looks like you, but it is not the true you; it is only a reflection of your image that has been twisted by 180 degrees.

The Godhead as Creator of the entire Universe is the True Image, whereas Satan and his systems always display **a reflection** of that Truth that is **twisted**, thus a "mirror image." The Godhead is the Absolute Truth, but Satan is a created being that only tells half-truths. Satan uses these elements of truth to make it appear as if it is true, but it still is a lie! This is how Satan deceived Eve; he twisted God's Word. Satan even tempted Jesus by questioning His authority as the Son of God and by twisting the written Word of God (Matt. 4:1-10, Luke 4:1-13).

Satan, as a created being, desires to usurp God's rightful authority as Creator to govern His Creation and thus, Satan is a mirror image of God. The false prince will be the mirror image of Jesus Christ as *"Messiah the Prince"* (Dan. 9:25) from the beginning to the middle of the Tribulation period. This false prince who is killed near mid-Trib and appears to rise from the dead is the mirror image of Jesus Christ as *"the Prince of Life, whom God hath raised from the dead"* (Acts 3:15). This Satan-indwelt-man then becomes the Antichrist, who is the mirror image of Jesus Christ as King. The Antichrist usurps Jesus Christ's rightful role to rule over the kings of the earth from the middle to the end of the Tribulation period. The false prophet will bring about signs and wonders as the mirror image of the Holy Spirit. These are the primary examples of the "mirror image" that will be explained in more detail throughout this book. However, there are many other examples of the mirror image contained in the Scriptures. Have fun finding them!

Summary of the Big Picture of God's Plan

God's Law has always existed and will never cease to exist. It is what holds all God's creation together. Lucifer, also known as Satan, has attempted to usurp God's authority and has brought about chaos, destruction, death, and eternal separation from God. Therefore, God chose to put a plan into place whereby He would restore His creation back to a perfect state, morally and legally. This plan is called God's Will and Testament and its contents are found in the Holy Bible, from the beginning of Genesis to the end of Revelation. Everything from Genesis through Malachi is pointing to God coming in the form of a man, Jesus Christ, to provide a way for humanity to be restored to perfect life in and with God eternally. The Old Testament patterns are a type of and foreshadow events that have been and will be fulfilled by Jesus in Heaven and on Earth. Jesus Christ is the focal point of God's Will and Testament.

The New Testament explains the purpose for Christ's death, burial, resurrection and provision for our immortal bodies when we are Gathered to Him. Jesus Christ is the Mediator of the New Covenant in Hebrews 9. However, it was God's plan from the beginning to provide the free gift of salvation through His Son, Jesus Christ. This is what we call the "Christ addendum", a legal codicil to God's Will and Testament. This addendum could not take effect until Jesus Christ, who is the Testator of God's Will and Testament (Heb. 9:11-17), had died without sin. God the Father and the Holy Spirit are the two witnesses to the Will, thereby providing the legal means to offer Jesus Christ as the only acceptable gift of eternal salvation from God to humanity. That is why Jesus said, *"I am The Way, The Truth, and The Life: no man cometh unto the Father, but by Me"* (John 14:6).

Each time God makes an addendum to His Will and Testament, the addendum never weakens the original Will. An addendum to God's Will and Testament can affect a change in Earth Age, Covenant or Dispensation, as God sees fit. All the unconditional Covenants given in the Old Testament of the Holy Bible are still in effect and will be fulfilled by God's Will and Testament. The addendum of grace through Jesus Christ was added to fulfill the moral and legal requirements of God's Law. Jesus Christ was the one and only perfect sacrifice for sin for all time under the New Covenant of Grace. This Covenant addendum and the entirety of God's Law will never end.

There was a transitional period after Israel rejected the message of Jesus Christ during His earthly ministry. The Anointed One of God was offering a Kingdom and a King, but Israel rejected Christ because of unbelief. This transitional period lasted about 40 years; from the time that the veil of the Holy of Holies in the Temple was torn in two at Christ's death, burial, and resurrection until the Romans destroyed Jerusalem and the temple complex. The nation of Israel was still holding on to the traditions of Mosaic Law, like animal sacrifices and ordinances of divine service in an earthly temple. This 40 year probationary period very closely parallels the children of Israel at the time of the Exodus in the Old Testament. Because of their unbelief, that generation died in the wilderness and was never allowed to enter the Promised Land. Because of the unbelief of the Jews during Christ's earthly ministry, that generation did not enter into the kingdom that Jesus was offering, either.

However, Jesus Christ revealed to the Apostle Paul that salvation is through grace by faith. What actually changed regarding dispensations was that the stewardship of the message of salvation passed from Israel to the Gentiles through the Mystery. After the Gathering of the Bride to Christ, the Mosaic Law with all its animal sacrifice for the atonement of sins will not revert back as it was before the Christ addendum.

Even though Israel broke their first Covenant with God, the LORD promised to make a New Covenant with Israel, established upon better promises through Jesus Christ (Jer. 31:31-34, Heb. 8:6 - Heb. 9:10, Heb. 10:14-18). The provision of this New Covenant of Grace was confirmed when Jesus Christ died on the cross as the Passover Lamb for the whole world. Jesus was put in the tomb, resurrected the third day, and ascended to the Father in Heaven. Jesus Christ became our Kinsman-Redeemer and He will redeem us when God the Father says it is the proper time. After *"the Mystery of God"* is *"finished"* (Rev. 10:7), the stewardship of Christ's message of salvation will transfer back to Israel through the 144,000 Jews at the dispensation change. They will then begin preaching the message of the *"Everlasting Gospel"* (Rev. 14:6) during the last half of the Tribulation period. In the Millennium, God's message of salvation comes directly from God to man through Jesus Christ.

Chapter 2

Daniel's Seventieth Week

Many Bible scholars believe that Daniel's sixty-nine weeks ended with Christ's crucifixion, thereby ending the Jewish dispensation. They believe that the last and seventieth week of the Jewish dispensation has not started yet and it will not start up again until the beginning of the Tribulation period.[4] *"And he shall confirm the covenant with many for one week: and in the midst of the week he shall cause the sacrifice and the oblation to cease..."* (Dan. 9:27). Because Daniel says *"he shall confirm the covenant"* for *"one week,"* seven years, it is believed that this is the whole seven years of Tribulation period. One of the main reasons this is believed by so many is because both are seven years long. It is also commonly believed that the *"he"* is the Antichrist who makes a seven-year peace treaty or covenant.[5] This Antichrist is the one that allows animal sacrifice and temple worship to begin and then causes it to cease when he breaks that treaty three and one half years later.

Popular belief is that Daniel's seventieth week has not yet begun. These Bible scholars believe that the Age of Law was suspended at the cross and replaced by the Age of Grace.[6] Many of them believe that after the sudden and sign-less Rapture, the Age of Law will return for the entire seven years of the Tribulation period.

Parenthetical View of Daniel's Seventieth Week

John Darby was one of the Fathers of dispensationalism in the mid-eighteen hundreds. Darby's theory segregates Jews, Gentiles and Christians from one another. To this day, his view is controversial. We would like to dispense with the whole concept of Dispensations, but we cannot. There is an element of truth in Darby's theory. However, many dispensationalists today are no longer exactly certain of the defining tenants of Darby's theory. Clarence Larkin sees the "Ecclesiastical Dispensation" as "Grace" which parallels the "Davidic Covenant."[7] However, Covenants or Earth Ages are not synonymous with Dispensations.

John Darby and Clarence Larkin's teachings live on in the traditions of men to this day. It is common among current theologians to describe Dispensations using the Age of Law and the Age of Grace as defining terms. These traditions of men hold that the Mosaic Law, the Age of Law, was suspended when Christ died on the cross. Then, the Church Age or Age of Grace began. After the Rapture of the church, it is believed by many that the Dispensation of Mosaic Law, the Age of Law, will revert back. Hal Lindsey refers to this as "the great parenthesis."[8]

Others have evolved the word Dispensation into "economy." Teachers, like Hal Lindsey, believe there is a distinct difference between and with respect to the economy of Law and the economy of Grace. Lindsey says, "The seven-year period called the Tribulation by theologians is actually the completion of the Dispensation of Israel under Law."[9]

Larkin supports this by introducing the idea that "soon the Holy Spirit will no longer strive with men" during this tribulation period.[10] Where is Larkin getting the idea that the Holy Spirit will be removed from the earth? He does not show his Scriptural witnesses or proofs. Dispensational theorist's according to the traditions of men today advocate that the Holy Spirit is the great restrainer. 2 Thessalonians 2:6-7 clearly means that the restrainer is an obstacle to *"the mystery of iniquity"* until the restrainer is taken out of the way. From this, dispensationalists' make the mental leap that the Holy Spirit must be removed from the earth before the Satan-indwelt-Antichrist can be revealed. Clearly that is not what Scripture says.

It is not that dispensationalists are all wrong on everything. While we agree that the Holy Spirit probably is the great restrainer, we do not agree that the Holy Spirit will ever be removed from the earth. Think about this for a moment. The Holy Spirit entered Christ at His baptism and then Christ went into the wilderness and was tempted by Satan. Satan can indeed be in the presence of the Holy Spirit. The Holy Spirit being part of the Triune Godhead is omnipresent and can indwell believers on the earth while restraining Satan in Heaven until it is time to release him (Rev. 12:10). So the notion that the Holy Spirit and the believers He is indwelling must be removed from the earth before the Antichrist is revealed is baseless in Scripture. Furthermore, all those who are left behind at the Gathering and will accept the free gift of salvation still need the Holy Spirit after the Bride has been given her reward at the Gathering.

In Larkin's defense, he clearly believed in the Dispensations of "Law, Grace, Judgment, and Millennial."[11] Although Larkin never went as far as saying, "Age of Law, Age of Grace, Age of Law;" that came later as the traditions of men built one precept upon another until there is an evolutionary understanding of the "Parenthetical Dispensation." There is a mountain of evidence to suggest that this line of dispensational thinking may be flawed.

Symphonic View of Daniel's Seventieth Week

We think that dividing the "Mosaic Law" into Ages with a parenthetical view of the "Church Age" in the middle is erroneous thinking, as well as creating much conflict with Scripture. What Larkin did not see is that after the Bride of Christ is Gathered, grace continues because of the New Covenant; for *"whosoever believes"* in Christ (John 3:16) shall have the justification by His blood. Grace came about as a Covenant change, not a dispensational change. Grace will not be removed for the Mosaic Law to revert to animal sacrifice the way it was before the cross. Christ was the sacrificial Lamb for all humanity, forever. God's grace is not taken to Heaven at the Gathering. His grace will never end, ever! Neither is the Holy Spirit removed to make way for the Antichrist, as too many believe.[12] God will still be offering salvation through the Holy Spirit to those who accept Him after the Gathering of the Bride of Christ.

The dispensationalists have it partially right in that there was a dispensation change after Christ's death. The Bible also tells us in plain language there will be another dispensation change mid-Trib. It says that when the seventh trumpet begins to sound *"the Mystery of God should be finished"* (Rev. 10:7). Pre-Trib dispensationalists have the timing wrong by placing a dispensation change before the Tribulation period begins because of the Pre-Tribulation Rapture Theory.

Theologians are missing *"that from the going forth of the commandment to restore and build Jerusalem **unto** the Messiah the Prince shall be **seven weeks, and threescore and two weeks"** (Dan. 9:25 - Emphasis added). At Jesus Christ's baptism, God *"anointed"* Jesus (Acts 4:27, 10:38) as *"the Most Holy"* (Dan. 9:24). Therefore, the seven weeks and the 62 weeks were completed at Jesus' baptism. From that point the seventieth week started immediately. Christ's crucifixion was three and one half years later. One half of Daniel's seventieth week was completed at the cross. The last half of the seventieth week will be a 42-month period, or 1260 days, at the end of the Tribulation Period. The time period between the first half of the seventieth week and the last half of the seventieth week is the Mystery of God Dispensation. See our chart below:

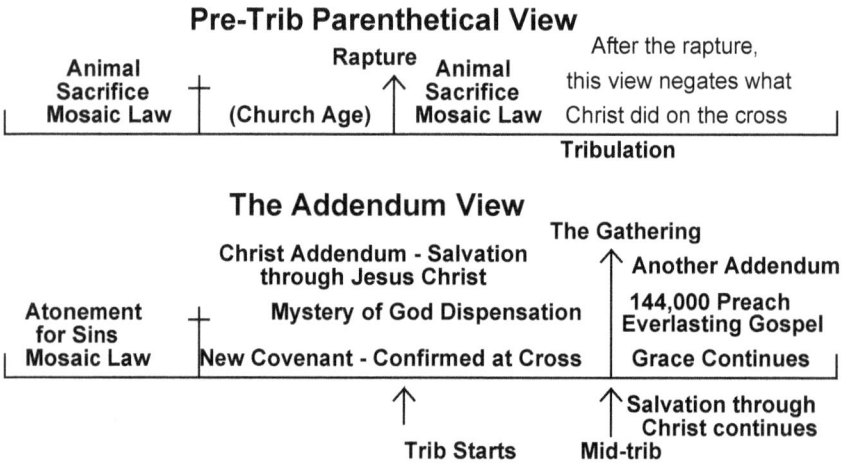

Pre-Trib Parenthetical View

Animal Sacrifice Mosaic Law	(Church Age)	Rapture ↑ Animal Sacrifice Mosaic Law	After the rapture, this view negates what Christ did on the cross

Tribulation

The Addendum View

		The Gathering ↑ Another Addendum
	Christ Addendum - Salvation through Jesus Christ	
Atonement for Sins Mosaic Law	Mystery of God Dispensation	144,000 Preach Everlasting Gospel
	New Covenant - Confirmed at Cross	Grace Continues

↑   ↑ Salvation through Christ continues
Trib Starts   Mid-trib

The Pre-Trib Parenthetical View totally misses the change in Covenant. Jesus Christ has already confirmed *"the Covenant with many"* (Dan. 9:27 - Emphasis added), thereby completing the first half of Daniel's seventieth week. A Scriptural witness is, *"So Christ was **once offered** to bear the sins of **many"*** (Heb. 9:28 - Emphasis added). They are also missing that *"Messiah the Prince"* caused *"the sacrifice and the oblation to cease"* in *"the midst"* of Daniel's seventieth *"week"* (Dan. 9:25, 27) and how this affects Israel after the Gathering of the Bride to Christ. It is not God's desire for animal sacrifice for the atonement of sins to take place after Christ became the perfect sacrifice for sin **once** and **forever**. These dispensationalists are segregating Jews and Gentiles into dispensational fragments using "The Parenthetical View of the Church Age." Finally, returning to animal sacrifice under the "Age of Law" after the Rapture negates Christ's ultimate sacrifice on the cross.

Daniel's Split Week

We have compiled considerable evidence that Daniel's seventieth week was split. Daniel's seventieth week began with Christ's baptism and was cut in half at the cross. The other half of Daniel's seventieth week will begin again when Christ reveals himself to Israel mid-Trib. This is the time of Jacob's trouble during the last three and one half years of the Tribulation period. Let us look at the evidence:

Exhibit A - What Time was Fulfilled and When?

This exhibit will show that the fullness of time was come at Christ's baptism. We will show that the time that ended at His baptism was the sixty-nine weeks and that there was no gap of time between the sixty-ninth and seventieth weeks. Because of this, the seventieth week was half over when Christ died on the cross.

What *"time"* did Jesus fulfill? Mark makes it clear that some mysterious time was fulfilled, but what time was He referring to?

> *Now after that John was put in prison, Jesus came into Galilee, preaching the gospel of the kingdom of God. And saying,* ***"The time is fulfilled****, and the kingdom of God is at hand: repent ye, and believe the gospel"* (Mark 1:14-15 - Emphasis added).

We believe that the time that was fulfilled is the sixty-nine weeks spoken of by the Prophet Daniel. In the seventieth week Christ is to accomplish several things: *"to make an end of sins, to make reconciliation for iniquity, to seal up the vision...and to anoint the most Holy"* (Dan. 9:24). According to Daniel 9:27, Christ is to *"confirm a Covenant with many for one week."* The sixty-ninth week was fulfilled and Christ has already fulfilled some things meant for the seventieth week. *"But when the fulness of time was come"* (Gal. 4:4), God the Father brought forth Jesus as *"the Messenger of the Covenant"* (Mal. 3.1) to *"whosoever believeth"* (John 3:15-16). Christ began to confirm that Covenant at His Baptism three and one half years before the cross.

> *But when* ***the fulness of time*** *was come, God sent forth His Son, made of a woman,* ***made under the law, to***

redeem them that were under the law, that we might receive the adoption of sons. And because ye are sons, God hath sent forth the Spirit of His Son into your hearts, crying, Abba, Father. Wherefore thou art no more a servant, but a son; and if a son, then an heir of God through Christ (Gal. 4:4-7 - Emphasis added).

Jesus came when the *"fulness of time was come"* (Gal. 4:4) and began Daniel's seventieth week. The stewardship of the message of salvation was still through Israel. Christ came to redeem them that were under the law that they might receive adoption as sons. *"He came unto His own, and His own received Him not. But as many as received Him, to them gave He power to become the sons of God, even to them that believe on His name"* (John 1:11-12 - Emphasis added). Christ was preaching to Jew and Gentile alike in Jerusalem, Judea, Samaria and Galilee that the Kingdom of God was at hand. At the baptism of Jesus Christ there was a **change in Covenant**, but not a change in dispensation.

When Jesus was on His way to Galilee, He stopped in Samaria at Jacob's well and had a conversation with the Samaritan woman. This conversation with the Samaritan woman was early on in Christ's ministry.

Ye [Samaritans] *worship ye know not what: we* [Jews] *know what we worship: for salvation is of the Jews. But the hour cometh, and now is,* [This *"hour"* denotes a change before the cross] *when the true worshippers shall worship the Father in spirit and in truth: for the Father seeketh such to worship Him. God is a Spirit: and they that worship Him must worship Him in spirit and truth. The woman saith unto Him, I know that Messias* [Messiah] *cometh, which is called Christ: when He is come, He will tell us all things. Jesus saith unto her, I that speak unto thee am He* (John 4:22-23a, 25-26 - Emphasis added).

Time fulfilled said another way is *"the hour cometh, and now is"* (John 4:23). Jesus was telling her and us, that from that hour everyone was to worship God in spirit and truth. From this clearly God the Father was bringing about a change in Covenant through the Christ addendum, but not a change in dispensation. The stewardship of the message of salvation was still through Israel. However, Christ confirmed a Covenant that day with Gentiles, the Samaritans, fulfilling that part of Daniel 9:27's prophecy, *"and He shall confirm a Covenant with **many** for one week..."* Jesus was preaching to Jew and Gentile alike because of that Covenant change.

> *Even so we, when we were children, were in bondage under the elements of the world. But when **the fulness of time** was come, **God sent forth His Son**, made of a woman, **made under the law** (Gal. 4:3-4 - Emphasis added).*

At Jesus' baptism He was *"anointed"* (Luke 4:18, Acts 10:38) as that *"prophet"* raised up from the Jews, that is spoken of in Deuteronomy 18:15, 18 and Acts 3:22-23. Jesus was still operating under the Legal Dispensation with all the ordinances of divine service of the Old Covenant and the stewardship of the message of salvation through the Jews. His disciples were told to go only to the lost sheep of Israel (Matt. 10:34). They were not to go to the Gentiles. Only Christ went to the Gentiles before He went to the cross (Matt. 15:21-28, John 4:4-42).

> *I the LORD have called Thee in righteousness...**and give Thee for a Covenant of the people,** for a light of the Gentiles (Isa. 42:6 - Emphasis added).*

> *It is a light thing that Thou shouldest be My Servant to raise up **the tribes of Jacob**, and to restore **the preserved of Israel**: I will **also** give Thee for a light to **the Gentiles, that Thou mayest be My salvation unto the end of the earth** (Isa. 49:6 - Emphasis added).*

> *Thus saith the LORD, In an acceptable time have I heard Thee, and in a day of salvation have I helped Thee: and I will preserve Thee, **and give Thee for a***

> *Covenant of the People*, *to establish the earth, to cause to inherit the desolate heritages* (Isa. 49:8 - Emphasis added).

> *Behold,* **the days come***, saith the LORD, that I will make* **a New Covenant** *with the house of Israel, and with the house of Judah: Not according to the Covenant that I made with their fathers in the day that I took them by the hand to bring them out of the land of Egypt; which My Covenant they brake, although I was an husband unto them, saith the LORD: But this shall be* **the Covenant** *that I will make with the house of Israel;* **After those days***, saith the LORD,* **I will put My law in their inward parts, and write it in their hearts***; and will be their God, and they shall be My people* (Jer. 31:31-33 - Emphasis added. Quoted in Hebrews 8:8-10, 10:16).

> *And to* **Jesus the Mediator** *of* **the New Covenant***, and to the blood of sprinkling, that speaketh better things than that of Abel* (Heb. 12:24 - Emphasis added).

> *And He* [Messiah the Prince] *shall confirm the Covenant with many* [Jew and Gentile] *for one week...* (Dan. 9:27 - Explanation added).

We see from Isaiah, Jeremiah, Daniel and Hebrews that God the Father through Jesus Christ confirmed the Covenant with many, meaning Jew and Gentile alike. Christ was the Messenger of the Covenant *"after those days"* (Jer. 31:31-33). The Scriptural witness is that Jesus was baptized *"when the fulness of time was come"* (Gal. 4:4). The question is, when was this Covenant confirmed?

Daniel denotes that there is a distinction of time concerning the seven weeks, the sixty-two weeks and the one-week. We can find no Scriptural witness showing any lapse of time between the sixty-ninth and seventieth week. In fact, a gap between the sixty-ninth and seventieth week conflicts with Scripture. Malachi is a Scriptural witness that there is not any time elapsed between the weeks. *"And the Lord, whom ye seek,* **shall suddenly come** *to His Temple, even* **the**

Messenger of the Covenant, *whom ye delight in"* (Mal. 3:1 - Emphasis added). Jesus started His earthly ministry suddenly or immediately after His baptism by picking His disciples. Christ came suddenly to the Temple and fulfilled these Scriptures without a gap of time between the sixty-ninth and seventieth week. Daniel 9:25 states that *"from the going forth of the commandment...**unto** the Messiah the Prince shall be seven weeks, and threescore and two* [sixty-two] *weeks."* Symphonically, Daniel's sixty-ninth week was already fulfilled at Jesus' baptism. The Messiah was *"cut off"* in the *"midst"* of the *"one week"* (Dan. 9:26-27), also known as Daniel's seventieth and final week! The gap of time is not between the sixty-ninth and seventieth week, but between the two halves of the seventieth week.

Since the seventieth week had already begun before the cross, then we can say with earnest that Daniel's seventieth week is not synonymous with the entire seven-years of the Tribulation. This line of reasoning supports the premise that the time of Jacob's trouble is a forty-two month period. The Mystery of God is finished just before that forty-two month period and the True Church will escape God's wrath during that same forty-two month period.

Symphonic View of Daniel's Split Week

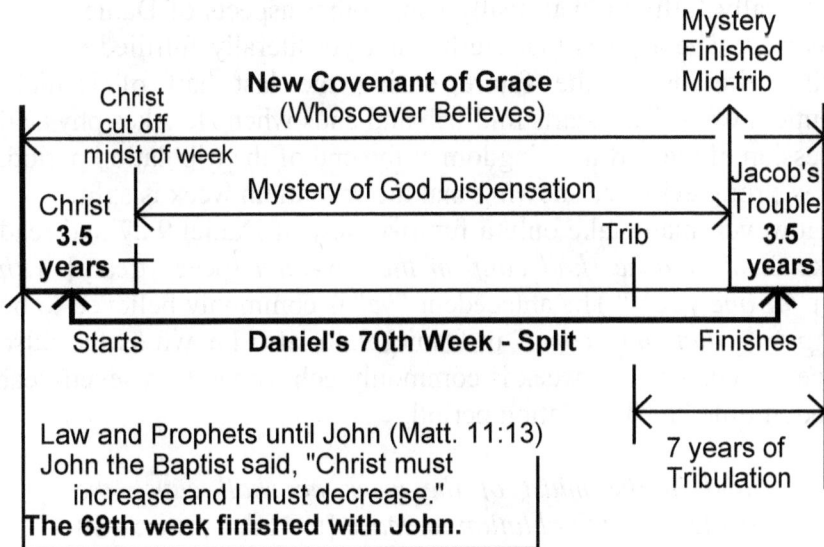

Exhibit B - Breaking Down Daniel 9:27

The antecedent *"He"* in Daniel 9:27 is *"the Messiah the Prince"* of Daniel 9:25 and He has already confirmed *"the Covenant with many."*

> *And **He** [Messiah the Prince] **shall confirm the Covenant with many** [Jew and Gentile alike] for **one week**: and **in the midst of the week** He [Messiah] shall cause the sacrifice and the oblation to cease [because Jesus was the ultimate Passover Lamb], and for the overspreading of abominations He shall make it desolate [Israel continued animal sacrifice after Christ's resurrection causing an abomination to the LORD], even until the consummation [temple was destroyed in 70 AD], and that determined shall be poured upon the desolate [Israel dispersed throughout the nations] (Dan. 9:27 - Emphasis added).*

If this verse is read and understood like this then God's *"anointed"* One (Acts 10:38, 4:27, Heb. 1:9), *"Messiah the Prince"* (Dan. 9:25), split Daniel's seventieth week two thousand years ago. This is a historical view of what Messiah the Prince has already literally fulfilled in the first half of Daniel's seventieth week. Jesus Christ has also literally fulfilled historically some other aspects of Daniel 9:24-27 as well. The aspects that He has not yet literally fulfilled will be fulfilled literally in the future during the last half of Daniel's seventieth week. This starts mid-trib and ends when He takes physical possession of the earthly Kingdom at the end of the tribulation period. This is strong evidence showing that the seventieth week is split.

However, many take only a futurist view of Daniel 9:27 and read it like this: *"And he shall confirm the covenant* [peace treaty] *with many for one week."* The antecedent *"he"* is commonly believed to be *"the prince that shall come"* in Daniel 9:26, also known as the false prince of evil. The one-week is commonly believed to be a seven-year period of time, the Tribulation period.

> *...and in the midst of the week he shall cause the sacrifice and the oblation to cease [the false prince will cause the sacrifice to cease], and for the overspreading*

> *of abominations he shall make it desolate* [by desecrating the temple], *even until the consummation* [full end of the abomination that causes desolation is when the son of perdition sits in the Holy of Holies of the rebuilt temple declaring to be God], *and that determined shall be poured upon the desolate* [the wrath of God] (Dan. 9:27).

The interesting thing about this verse is that it can and should be read both ways. All the things that the false prince/Antichrist will do is in the futurist view and have not yet been accomplished as of this writing. Daniel 9:27 has a dual meaning. Some Scriptures do this, especially concerning Satan acting through the false-christ in the mirror image of Christ. The false-christ will copy Christ in every way, even unto confirming a covenant with Israel and ceasing sacrifice as Christ did, but for different reasons. Christ ended the sacrifice by offering Himself as the supreme and final sacrifice for all humankind's sin debt, while the false-christ will end the sacrifice in the future so people can worship him instead of God.

Mirror Image Examples:
- The false prince as the false-christ has a false covenant with Israel, likely reinstating animal sacrifice and temple worship. It must be remembered however, after the cross it is an abomination to offer any animal sacrifice to God for the atonement of sin because of the New Covenant of Grace. Only Christ's blood washes away all past, present and future sins, forever.
- The false prince as the false-christ has a three and one half-year ministry, like Christ.
- The false prince as the false-christ claims falsely to be God.
- The false prince as false-christ dies and is raised from the dead, probably on the third day like Christ, but different at the same time. There is something seriously wrong with his reanimation.
- This Satan-indwelt-man becomes the Antichrist at that time and has a 42-month kingdom on earth, claiming it will be forever. During the second half of the Tribulation period this Antichrist, as the false king, usurps Jesus Christ's rightful role as KING OF KINGS to rule over the kings of the earth.

Exhibit C - Jesus Cut Off

This exhibit is closely related to the previous one, but we feel it is a stand-alone point. Daniel 9:27 comes right out and says that Christ split the week in plain language. Jesus started Daniel's seventieth week at His baptism and was *"cut off"* in the *"midst of the week"* (Dan. 9:26-27). What week has the Christ split if not Daniel's seventieth week?

By now many of you are thinking, what about Daniel 9:26? *"And after threescore and two weeks shall Messiah be cut off"* (Dan. 9:26). We realize that most of you have always been taught that this means that Christ was crucified and died at the end of the sixty-nine weeks. However, is this an accurate interpretation when compared to the whole of Scripture? Scripture symphonically tells us that Christ was not crucified at the end of the sixty-ninth week, but some time after the sixty-nine weeks were completed. How long after the sixty-nine weeks were completed we have to learn from the whole of Scripture. We learned from our first exhibit that the sixty-nine weeks were completed when the *"Messiah the Prince"* (Dan. 9:25), God's Son Jesus Christ, was baptized at the *"fullness of time"* (Gal. 4:4). From Jeremiah 31:33 we learned that *"After those days, saith the LORD, I will put My law in their inward parts, and write it in their hearts."* We also learned that Jesus Christ, as *"the Messiah"* that was to come, appeared unto the woman at the well in Samaria (John 4:22-26) and that the Messiah began to confirm *"the Covenant"* with many (Dan. 9:27, Isa. 42:6, 49:8, Jer. 31:31-33, Mal. 3:1). Christ was *"cutoff"* (Dan. 9:26) **after** He was presented as *"the Messenger"* (Mal. 3:1) of the *"New Covenant"* (Jer. 31:31, Heb. 8:8, 8:13) and rejected by Israel, resulting in His death on the cross. We learn from Daniel 9:27 that *"in the midst of the week He* [Messiah the Prince] *shall cause the sacrifice and the oblation to cease"* because He became the Supreme Sacrifice. The context of this Scripture is clearly the *"midst"* of the *"one week"* (Dan. 9:27), also known as Daniel's seventieth and final week! That means that Daniel's seventieth week was half completed at the cross.

> *And He* [Messiah the Prince] *shall confirm the Covenant with many for* **one week: and in the midst of the week He shall cause the sacrifice and the oblation to cease**

[Messiah ended God approved animal sacrifice in the earthly temple at the cross, once for all], *and for the overspreading of abominations He shall make it desolate* [continued animal sacrifice after Christ became the Supreme Sacrifice], *even until the consummation* [temple was destroyed in 70 AD], *and that determined shall be poured out upon the desolate* [Israel dispersed throughout the nations] (Dan. 9:27 - Emphasis added).

The second half of Daniel's seventieth week will start at the change in dispensation that begins at the middle of the Tribulation period. An angel told Daniel that *"for a time, times, and an half"* the false prince/Antichrist will *"have accomplished to scatter the power of the holy people, all these things shall be finished"* (Dan. 12:6-7). Also, that the saints *"shall be given into his hand **until** a time and times and the dividing of time"* (Dan. 7:25 - Emphasis added). The false prince also takes away the daily sacrifice and sets up an abomination 1290 days before the end of the Tribulation period (Dan. 12:11). All these things place this event in the middle of the Tribulation period, which is when the Mystery of God is finished, as He declared by the prophets (Rev. 10:7).

It is clear from Revelation 10:6 that there is a change in dispensation by the words, *"that there should be time no longer."* Does that mean that there is no more time left in the world? No, it means that there is no more time left in the Mystery Dispensation at the seventh trumpet. The Mystery of God is finished at the mid-Trib Gathering of the Bride of Christ into the Heavenly Kingdom. The Scriptural witness to this is found in Revelation 14:13, *"Blessed are the dead which die in the Lord from henceforth:"* This Scripture also denotes a change in dispensation with the words *"from henceforth."*

Christ's ministry to and for Israel begins again when Christ appears as a King at the mid-Trib Gathering of the Elect and with the 144,000 Jews beginning to preach the Everlasting Gospel. These 144,000 are *"the firstfruits unto God and to the Lamb"* (Rev. 14:4) under a new dispensation during the last three and one half years of the Tribulation period, that ends at the battle of Armageddon.

This new dispensation is the second half of Daniel's seventieth week and is *"the time of Jacob's trouble; but he shall be saved out of it"* (Jer. 30:7). Those faithful Jews who recognize Jesus as the Messiah at the mid-Trib Gathering of the Bride will be protected for 1260 days or 42 months (Rev. 12:6 and 12:14). This is the same 42 months that the Antichrist rules on earth and also the same time that God pours out His wrath on the Antichrist and his followers. Once again, when is the change in dispensation? It is mid-Tribulation and all these things support why Daniel's seventieth week is split.

Exhibit D - *"Covenant"* of Daniel 9:27 is in the New Testament!

The words of Christ, the words of Paul and all of the New Testament are Scriptural witnesses to the fact that the *"He"* in Daniel 9:27 applies to Christ as *"Messiah the Prince"* of Daniel 9:25 and that He has already confirmed *"the Covenant with many"* (Dan. 9:27).

First, let us look at the words of the Messiah, Jesus Christ, at the Last Supper. When Jesus gave His disciples the cup after supper He said, *"Drink ye all of it;* **for this is My blood of the New Testament** [**the** (New) **Covenant**; see Note below], *which is* **shed for many** *for* **the remission of sins."** (Matt. 26:27-29 - Emphasis and explanation added). At the Lord's Supper Jesus was telling the twelve disciples and us that He was about to consummate the (New) Covenant by the shedding of His blood for many. This would provide *"the remission of sins"* (Matt. 26:28) for *"whosoever believeth in Him"* (John 3:15). Jesus' words are just like Daniel 9:24-27, *"Messiah the Prince"* shall confirm *"the Covenant with many"* and *"make an end of sins."*

Note: (Both *"testament"* and *"covenant"* are translated from the same Greek word, *"diatheke"* (Strong's # 1242), in the Greek Dictionary of the New Testament in the Strong's Exhaustive Concordance. It is unfortunate that the King James Version Bible translated this as *"testament"*, especially when the manuscripts and the other translations say *"covenant."*)

> *And He took the cup, and when He had given thanks, He gave it to them: and they all drank of it. And He said unto them, "This is* **My blood** *of the* **New Testament** [New Covenant], *which is* **shed for many"** (Mark 14:23-24 - Emphasis added).

Likewise also the cup after supper, saying, "This cup is the New Testament [New Covenant] *in My blood, which is shed for you"* (Luke 22:20 - Emphasis added).

The choice of words that Jesus used at the Last Supper is very interesting. He said that His *"blood"* was *"shed for many"* for *"the remission of sins"* (Matt. 26:28-29). The use of blood in the whole of Scripture is confined to two purposes: (**1**) the making of a Covenant (Exodus 24:6-8, Heb. 8:6-10, 9:11-22), and (**2**) atonement for sin (Lev. 17:11, Heb. 9:22). From these Scriptures we see that *"the Messiah the Prince"* (Dan. 9:25) confirmed *"the Covenant with many"* (Dan. 9:27) and He provided the way to *"make an end of sins"* (Dan. 9:24) by the shedding of His own *"blood"* (Matt. 26:28, Mark 14:24, Luke 22:20, Heb. 9:12, 14, 10:19). Jesus Christ Himself said that He was confirming the Covenant with many as predicted in Daniel 9:27.

While the Apostle Paul was not at the Lord's Supper with the Twelve, He reaffirmed that the cup after supper was *"the New Testament in My* [Christ's] *blood"* (1 Cor. 11:25). Paul's words are saying that *"the Covenant"* (Dan. 9:27) was confirmed by Christ's blood sacrifice and that we should take communion in remembrance of His sacrificial *"death till He come"* (1 Cor. 11:26). Paul *"received"* this by direct revelation *"of the Lord"* (1 Cor. 11:23) some time after his conversion. This is yet another Scriptural witness signifying the shedding of Christ's blood on the cross for the atonement of our sins and the confirming of *"the everlasting covenant"* (Heb. 13:20).

At the Lord's Supper Jesus went on to say, *"But I say unto you, I will not drink henceforth of this fruit of the vine, until that day when I drink it new with you in My Father's kingdom"* (Matt. 26: 29 - Emphasis added). From the word *"henceforth"* (Matt. 26:29) we see that Christ was changing His role from *"Prophet"* (Deut. 18:15, 18, Acts 3:22-23) to *"High Priest"* (Heb. 4:14, 5:6, 8:1, 9:11, 10:21).

But Christ being come an High Priest of good things to come, by a greater and more perfect tabernacle, not made with [human] *hands, that is to say, not of this building; Neither by the blood of goats and calves, **but by His own blood He entered in once into the holy***

37

place, having obtained eternal redemption for us (Heb. 9:11-12 - Emphasis added)

*For **Christ** is not **entered** into the holy places made with* [human] *hands, which are the figures of the true; but **into heaven itself**, now to appear in the presence of God for us* (Heb. 9:24 - Emphasis added).

*So Christ was **once offered** to bear the sins of **many*** (Heb. 9:28a - Emphasis added).

*...but now **once** in the end of the world* [age] *hath He* [Christ] *appeared to **put away sin** by **the sacrifice of Himself*** (Heb. 9:26b - Emphasis added).

*And that **He*** [Christ] *might reconcile **both** unto God in **one body by the cross**, having slain the enmity thereby: And **came and preached peace** to you which were **afar off*** [Gentiles]**, and to them that were nigh** [Jews]**.** *For through Him **we both** have access by one Spirit unto the Father* (Ephes. 2:16-18 - Emphasis added).

*This is **the Covenant** that I will make with them **after those days**, saith the Lord, I will put My laws into their hearts, and in their minds will I write them; And their sins and iniquities will I remember no more.* (Heb. 10:16-17 - quoted from Jeremiah 31:33, 34b - Emphasis added).

*In that He saith, **"A New Covenant,"** He hath made the **first*** [Covenant] ***old*** (Heb. 8:13 - Emphasis and explanation added).

Christ confirmed a *"New Covenant with the house of Israel and with the house of Judah"* (Jer. 31:31, Heb. 8:8, 8:10, 8:12 10:16). He became the Supreme *"sacrifice"* (Heb. 9:26, 10:12) *"once"* (Rom. 6:10, Heb. 7:27, 9:12, 26, 28, 10:10, 1 Peter 3:18) and *"for ever"* (Heb. 10:12, 14).

> *But this Man,* **after He had offered one sacrifice for**
> **sins for ever,** *sat down on the right hand of God; From*
> **henceforth** *expecting* **till** *His enemies be made His*
> *footstool* (Heb. 10:12-13 - Emphasis added).

Jesus Christ as Testator of God's Will and Testament (Heb. 9:16-17, 10:9) brings about this *"New Covenant"* (Heb. 8:8, 8:13). Jesus Christ will forever be the Lamb of God and the only One that can take away the sins of the entire world! Likewise, He will forever be a High Priest (Heb. 7). Both of these roles are a result of the shed blood of the New Covenant of Grace that Jesus Christ has already historically confirmed. Question; if Jesus Christ has not already confirmed *"the Covenant with many"* (Dan. 9:27), when or how could He do so in the future? He has already become the sacrificial victim by experiencing death on the cross and He has already shed all His blood that would be needed to make a legal covenant.

Therefore, we see that during Christ's earthly ministry He was *"the Messiah the Prince"* (Dan. 9:25) that has already confirmed the *"Covenant"* (Dan. 9:27, Jer. 31:31-34, Ezek. 37:26) with the Jews, as well as the Gentiles. God had the Romans destroy the temple and the city as a result of Israel's continuous rejection of the perfect *"sacrifice"* (Heb. 7:27, 9:26, 10:12) offered to and for them. This fulfills the requirement that the first half of Daniel's seventieth week was *"determined* **upon thy people** *and* **upon thy holy city"** (Dan. 9:24 - Emphasis added). Because Christ became the only God approved sacrifice (Heb. 9:12, 9:26, 10:14, 12:24, 13:20-21) in the *"midst"* of the *"one week"* (Dan. 9:27), He has split Daniel's seventieth week by historically completing the first half of the week at the cross.

Exhibit E - Thy Kingdom is at Hand

John the Baptist came preceding Christ *"in the spirit and power"* of Elijah (Luke 1:17), announcing the Messiah as the Lamb of God. *"Behold the Lamb of God, which taketh away the sin of the world"* (John 1:29).

> *In those days came John the Baptist, preaching in the*
> *wilderness of Judaea, and saying, Repent ye: for the*
> *kingdom of heaven is at hand* (Matt. 3:1-2).

> *From that time Jesus began to preach and to say,*
> *Repent: for the kingdom of heaven is at hand* (Matt.
> 4:17).

A Scriptural witness is when Jesus went all around Galilee teaching in the synagogues and *"preaching the gospel of the kingdom"* (Matt. 4:23). Another Scriptural witness is when Jesus sent out the twelve, *"And as ye go, preach, saying, The kingdom of heaven is at hand"* (Matt. 10:7). From these Scriptures we know the kingdom message was being preached during Christ's ministry on earth.

> *The law and the prophets were until John* [the Baptist]:
> *since that time the kingdom of God is preached, and*
> *every man presseth into it* (Luke 16:16).

> *For all the prophets and the law prophesied until John.*
> *And if ye* [Israel] *will receive it, this is Elias* [Elijah],
> *which was for to come* (Matt. 11:13-14).

The earthly Kingdom promised to Israel could have come at the end of Daniel's seventieth week if only Israel would have received Christ, but they rejected Christ as King and the Kingdom He was offering. Since Israel did not receive Christ as the Messiah, the Anointed One, the earthly Kingdom did not come at that time; so Christ began the Mystery Dispensation instead. However, Elijah will still precede Christ, fulfilling the prophecies of Malachi 4:5 and Matthew 17:11 before Christ returns for His Bride.

John the Baptist announced the coming of the Lamb of God, but Christ did not fulfill His role as the Lamb until three and one half years later, at the cross. Elijah will precede Christ announcing Him as the Lion of the tribe of Judah at the beginning of the Tribulation period, and it will be three and one half years after Elijah's ministry begins that Christ will come as the Messiah, revealed to Israel at the mid-Trib Gathering. The Mystery Dispensation started at the cross and ends mid-Trib when the seventh and last trumpet begins to sound according to Revelation 10:7.

We are still patiently waiting for both the Heavenly and Earthly Kingdoms to come. The Bride of Christ will be brought to the

Heavenly Kingdom mid-Tribulation. Three and one half years later Christ brings about the Earthly Kingdom promised to Israel. He installs Israel as the head of the nations and Jerusalem as the capital of the world. All these things point to the fact that Daniel's seventieth week has been split into two parts. (Please refer to "Symphonic View of Daniel's Split Week" chart on Page 31).

Exhibit F - *"That Prophet"* Comes Suddenly

If the Law and the Prophets were until John the Baptist turned his ministry over to Christ, what is that time between John and the cross, if not the first half of Daniel's seventieth week?

In Daniel 9:24-25 it makes it clear that there were sixty-nine weeks until *"the Messiah the Prince."* From the time God fulfilled the prophecy *"to anoint the most Holy"* (Dan. 9:24) at Christ's baptism to Christ beginning Daniel's seventieth week was sudden. There is no indication that any time elapsed between the sixty-ninth and the seventieth week.

> *Behold, I will send My messenger* [John the Baptist], *and he shall prepare the way before Me:* **and the Lord, Whom ye seek, shall suddenly come to His Temple, even the Messenger of the Covenant,** *whom ye delight in: behold He shall come, saith the LORD of hosts* (Mal. 3:1 - Emphasis added).

When Jesus came to the Temple, He came suddenly like Malachi said He would. Christ came to Israel as the Messiah when *"God anointed Jesus of Nazareth with the Holy Ghost and with power"* (Acts 10:38; also see Acts 4:27). That is when John the Baptist told everyone to follow Jesus and not himself anymore. John said of Jesus, *"He must increase, but I must decrease"* (John 3:30). After being anointed with the Holy Spirit, Christ went into the wilderness to be tempted of the devil. He then started His Ministry in Galilee (Acts 10:37). Some time after that, He entered suddenly into the Temple in Jerusalem on the Passover (John 2:13-25). Three years later He again entered Jerusalem and was crucified as the Passover Lamb for the entire world, thus ending His three and one half-year ministry. The Law and the Prophets ended with John the Baptist when he baptized Christ and the sixty-ninth week ended then also. The seventieth week then started when Christ was baptized and John handed over his ministry to Christ. This being true, then Daniel's seventieth week is half over and was divided by Christ on the cross. A new dispensation started at the cross and ends at the mid-Trib gathering of the Bride of Christ. This is also related to Daniel's *"dividing of time"* at mid-Trib (Dan. 7:25).

Exhibit G - Jesus Split the Week

This exhibit will show that Jesus split the seventieth week when He addressed the synagogue in Nazareth. Jesus split the verse at the comma when He stood and read from Isaiah 61:1-2.

> **The Spirit** *of the Lord God is upon Me; because* **the LORD** *hath* **anointed Me** *to preach good tidings unto the meek; He hath sent Me to bind up the broken-hearted, to proclaim liberty to the captives, and the opening of prison to them that are bound;* **to proclaim the acceptable year of the LORD,** ... (Isa. 61:1-2 - Emphasis added).

When Christ sat down after reading these verses, He said to the Jews in that synagogue, *"This day is this Scripture fulfilled in your ears"* (Luke 4:21). Jesus was telling those Jews and us that God had already *"anointed"* Him to preach, heal and *"to proclaim the acceptable year of the LORD"* (Isa. 61:1-2, Luke 4:18-19) early on in His earthly ministry. The rest of the verse in Isaiah 61:2 talks about *"...the day of vengeance of our God."* Christ stopped short of saying the vengeance part of this Scripture. Jesus split Daniel's seventieth week by splitting Isaiah 61:2 and placing the *"day of vengeance"* two thousand plus years after Jesus fulfilled the first half in Luke 4:21.

We know that the wrath of God and His vengeance is during the second half of the Tribulation, during the time of Jacob's trouble. This time of Jacob's trouble is three and one half years long. In fact, the wrath of the Lamb and the wrath of God are poured out together at the very end of the Tribulation period, as *"double"* portions (Rev. 18:6).

We believe that Daniel told us to separate the sixty-ninth and seventieth week not by two thousand years, but by a moment. When Jesus proclaimed in the very beginning of His earthly ministry that this was the *"acceptable year of the LORD"* (Isa. 61:2, Luke 4:19), He fulfilled the Scriptures. He fulfilled the beginning of Daniel's seventieth week when God the Father and the Holy Spirit anointed Jesus at His Baptism. Jesus became the Christ or Messiah, meaning the Anointed One, because of the New Covenant of Grace. He came to preach the Gospel, heal the sick, proclaim liberty to the captives of this world and open the prison door of death. Therefore, Christ's earthly ministry completed the first half of Daniel's seventieth week at the cross, thereby splitting Daniel's seventieth week.

Exhibit H - When the Seventy Weeks Actually Started

We will show in this exhibit that the widely held theory that Daniel's sixty-ninth week ended at the cross is controversial. What if the theologians have it wrong and Christ's baptism fulfilled Daniel's 483-year prophecy three and one half years earlier, prior to the crucifixion. By calculating the years from the king's decree to rebuild the Temple until the cross, is speculation. Many scholars cannot even agree which king issued the decree.

The consensus among theologians is that Daniel's seven sevens and sixty-two sevens equal 483 years. Another way of saying it is seven weeks of sevens and sixty-two weeks of sevens.

$$(7x7) + (62x7) = 483$$

Everyone seems to agree on the math, but it is controversial when those 483 years actually started. Because of this, it is debatable when the 483 years ended. Some of the most highly esteemed scholars cannot agree on Christ's actual birth date;[13] some say 4-2 BC, others say 6-4 BC. Our point here is that theologians have used Daniel's prophecy in an attempt to prove that the seventieth week has not started yet, implying that the whole Tribulation period is the seventieth week. We are pointing out the error in that belief. The error is we do not really know what year it is right now for sure.

We find no Scriptural support that any time elapsed between the sixty-ninth and seventieth week. Then calculating the 483 years to prove that all seven years of the Tribulation is Daniel's seventieth week is futile. Why are so many theologians looking to the cross for the fulfillment of the 483 years, when they should be looking to when *"Messiah the Prince"* was anointed or baptized? It clearly states in Daniel 9:25 that *"from the going forth of the commandment to restore and to build Jerusalem* **unto** *the Messiah the Prince shall be seven weeks, and threescore and two weeks."* The sixty-ninth week ended three and one half years before the cross. The first half of the seventieth week started immediately when Christ was baptized and became the Anointed One (Luke 4:18, Acts 10:38, Heb. 1:9). It was literally and historically fulfilled by His death on the cross as the Sacrificial Lamb for all humankind in the *"midst"* of the *"one week"* (Dan. 9:27).

Exhibit I - Mystery of God

In this exhibit we will show the significance of the Mystery Dispensation being finished mid-Trib and why this must split Daniel's seventieth week.

For three and one half years during Christ's earthly ministry He was saying to Israel, I am *"that Prophet"* (Deut. 18:15, 18-19; Acts 3:22-23). Moses told you that I would come. But, Israel rejected Christ and cut Him off. As a result, Christ broke off some of the natural branches of the olive tree, Israel, so that the Gentiles might be grafted in (Rom. 11:17-21). Gentiles became partakers of the root of the olive tree through Jesus Christ under the Abrahamic Covenant.

God began the Dispensation where the message of salvation is through the Mystery. The Mystery Dispensation goes from the cross until the middle of the Tribulation period. Revelation 12 tells us Sion is in travail just prior to mid-Trib. After the mid-Trib Gathering of the Bride of Christ, then it is the time for Jacob's trouble to begin during the last three and one half years of the Tribulation period. The time of Jacob's trouble cannot extend into the Millennium because of Jeremiah 30, when God's promise to restore Israel is completely fulfilled.

"But in the days of the voice of the seventh angel, when he shall begin to sound, **the mystery of God should be finished**, *as He hath*

declared to His servants the prophets" (Rev. 10:7 - Emphasis added). After the mystery of God is finished mid-Trib, the message of salvation will again be through Israel.

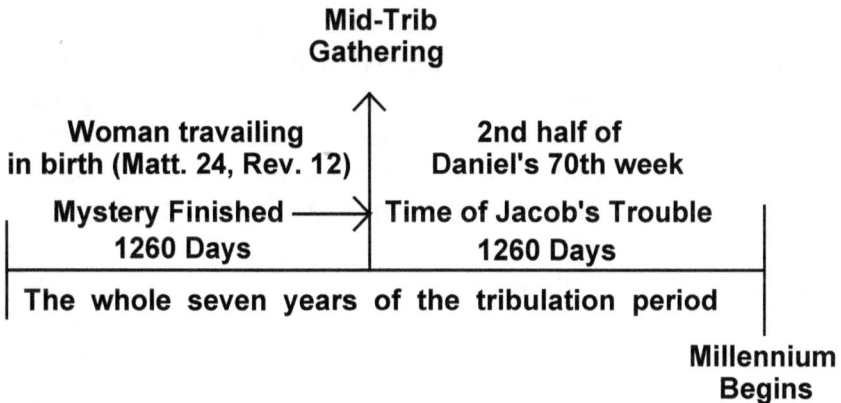

**Mid-Trib
Gathering**

Woman travailing in birth (Matt. 24, Rev. 12)	**2nd half of Daniel's 70th week**
Mystery Finished ⟶	**Time of Jacob's Trouble**
1260 Days	**1260 Days**

The whole seven years of the tribulation period

**Millennium
Begins**

If Christ died and ascended to Heaven at the changing of the dispensation in the middle of Daniel's seventieth week about two thousand years ago, why wouldn't He come for His Bride mid-Trib at the changing of the dispensation just before the beginning of the second half of Daniel's seventieth week? The Mystery of God being finished mid-Trib, just when the faithful of Israel are protected for 1260 days, is very strong evidence that Daniel's seventieth week is split.

Exhibit J - Messiah's Dual Role

This exhibit will show that the 144,000 that are sealed from the twelve tribes of Israel (Rev. 7:1-8) will finish the second half of Daniel's split week because Christ died after only completing the first half of the week.

Jesus had a multiple roles when He came to us. First, He came as *"Messiah the Prince"* for Israel (Dan. 9:25). Secondly, He was stricken for the Jewish transgressions (Isa. 53:8). He came to

> *...finish the transgression, and to make an end of sins, and to make reconciliation for iniquity, and to bring in everlasting righteousness, and to seal up the vision and prophecy, and to anoint the most Holy* (Dan. 9:24).

45

We know that His role as King over the nation of Israel in a literal and physical earthly sense did not come to pass at that time. As a result, it is apparent just from this, that there is a work as of yet unfinished. Jesus was anointed most Holy at His baptism and He made reconciliation for sin by His death on the cross as the final sacrifice. According to Hebrews 9:26, *"...He appeared to put away sin by the sacrifice of Himself."* He also sealed up the vision and prophecy of the seven year Tribulation period in the sealed book in Heaven, but He did not complete the other things listed in Daniel 9:24. Christ has not yet finished the transgression or brought in everlasting righteousness. Since His ministry was three and one half years long before He was *"cut off"* (Dan. 9:26), and Scripture suggests that a full week is seven years, it seems evident that what was left unfinished for Israel takes another three and one half years to complete. One of the messages in Christ's ministry was that the message of salvation was originally intended to be spread through the stewardship of Israel (Isa. 59:20-21, Matt. 10:5-6, 15:24). However, Israel as a nation rejected Him and cut Him off in the middle of His ministry (John 19:15). When Christ becomes King mid-Trib, He continues His ministry for Israel through the 144,000. These 144,000 Jews preach that salvation through Christ is available to both Jews and Gentiles alike during the time of Jacob's trouble (Rev. 10). Yes, salvation is still available after the Bride of Christ is removed from the earth. This is because of the Covenant change that started at Jesus' baptism.

> *And I saw another angel fly in the midst of heaven, having the everlasting gospel to preach unto them that dwell on the earth, and to every nation, and kindred, and tongue, and people* (Rev. 14:6).

This angel teaches the 144,000 a new song that only they could learn. This new song is the *"Everlasting Gospel."* These 144,000 Jews are given the stewardship of this Everlasting Gospel in the second half of the Tribulation period.

Jesus is promising a Heavenly Kingdom for His Bride, and the 144,000 having the Everlasting Gospel are promising salvation for the believers in Jesus after the Gathering. The Everlasting Gospel is the final Gospel of man teaching man about God's plan of salvation. Like every dispensation, this new dispensation is an addendum to God's Will, not the abolition of our current Gospel, but an addendum to it. Grace does not end!

The Everlasting Gospel is different from the Gospel we now have. The difference is that the Bride of Christ is promised to escape God's wrath, which is our *"blessed hope"* (Titus 2:13). The Everlasting Gospel will not save anyone from living through the time of God's wrath. Obviously the offer to be Christ's Bride is past after the Gathering and one may be martyred for Christ's namesake. However, God in His sovereignty has the power to keep you through this time. If you have been left behind, do not worry. God loves you and wants you to love Him. If you are an overcomer during this period and physically survive, you will be part of the Earthly Kingdom in the Millennium. If you are killed and have not denied Christ, you will obtain eternal life.

Both the Heavenly and the Earthly Kingdoms are given by grace. However, works seem to matter somehow for the Earthly Kingdom; *"...henceforth: Yea, saith the Spirit, that they may rest from their labours; and their works do follow them"* (Rev. 14:13). We think those who are still alive and do good works will be rewarded in the Earthly Kingdom, as the Bride will be in the Heavenly Kingdom. Faithful works are not an entry fee, but they are rewarded.

After the Gathering, one must worship God or Satan. Satan will attempt to kill all that refuse to worship him through the false prophet and the Antichrist. There will not be a fence to sit on anymore during the great Tribulation period of God's wrath. Both God and Satan require a decision. God offers life eternal; Satan offers life in the here and now, only Satan cannot deliver.

Exhibit K - Israel Blinded to The Covenant Change

This is the final exhibit and is the symphonic view of the Mystery Dispensation and why Israel was blinded to the Covenant change. We will show that the dispensation changed at the cross, will change again mid-Tribulation, and how all this relates to the split week.

In Malachi 3:1 we learned that the Lord is the Messenger of the Covenant. We learned in earlier exhibits that Jesus began to confirm the New Covenant of Grace with the Jews and Gentiles at the beginning of the seventieth week. Because the Jews rejected Jesus as

47

God's Son and His message of salvation, they crucified the Lord Jesus Christ. He was cut off in the midst of the week, thus completing the first half of Daniel's seventieth week.

> *And so all Israel shall be saved: as it is written, There shall come out of Sion the Deliverer, and shall turn away ungodliness from Jacob: For this is My Covenant unto them, when I shall take away their sins* (Rom. 11:26-27).

Jesus is the only one who can take away Israel's sin. Just because the Jews did not accept Jesus before the cross does not mean that God's Covenant of Grace for Israel is null and void. The Covenant from Romans 11 will become effective at the beginning of the second half of Daniel's seventieth week. This happens at the middle of the Tribulation period when Israel recognizes that Jesus is the Messiah they have been looking for. Remember that God never breaks any of His Covenants!

We know that the nation of Israel was blind to whom Jesus was because they crucified their Messiah. This rejection of Jesus and His message of salvation brought about a change in stewardship. The stewardship of the message of salvation was through Israel (John 4:22), but Israel rejected the Son of God. Then the stewardship of the message of salvation passed to the church through the Mystery. To understand what this Mystery is, when it starts and when it ends, we will look at what takes place in the Mystery Dispensation.

> *For I would not, brethren, that ye should be ignorant of this mystery, lest ye should be wise in your own conceits; that blindness in part is happened to Israel, **until the fulness of the Gentiles be come in*** (Rom. 11:25 - Emphasis added).

From this Scripture we learn several things:
- That there is blindness that has happened to part of Israel. Not all Jews were blinded to the truth, especially the apostles and their converts, even to this day.

- This blindness remains until the fullness of the Gentiles is completed, when the Mystery of God is finished mid-Trib.
- Paul tells us that all this is a Mystery.

The Symphonic View of Times of the Gentiles

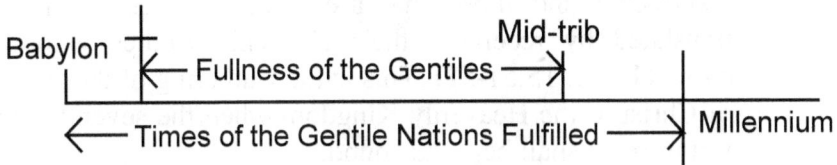

The Mystery of God involves the grace of God; whosoever believes in Jesus shall have everlasting life. Prior to Christ's death, salvation was unattainable; one could only atone for one's sin through animal sacrifice. Atonement of sin had to be done through the stewardship of Israel.

After Christ's baptism, salvation is attainable only by faith in Christ. The stewardship of God's message of hope was given to the body of Christ after Christ died and rose again. The body of Christ consists of all people, whosoevers that believe in Jesus Christ as their personal Savior.

What does all this have to do with Daniel's split seventieth week? The way we see it is, Christ started Daniel's seventieth week when the Holy Spirit anointed Him at His baptism to be the Messenger of the New Covenant of Grace to both the Jews and Gentiles. Then in the middle of that seventieth week, He was cut off by His crucifixion on the cross because of the blindness of Israel. This brought about the Mystery Dispensation.

This Mystery Dispensation goes from the cross until the Gathering of the Bride of Christ, when the Mystery is finished. This brings us to an important point. *"But in the days of the voice of the seventh angel, when he shall begin to sound, the Mystery of God should be finished"* (Rev. 10:7).

What does it mean when it says, *"the Mystery of God shall be finished"?* There is a two-part answer for this question.

1) Part one is from the perspective of the Bride of Christ, the faithful of the True Church and it means several things:
    - The stewardship of the message of salvation by the Bride of Christ is finished.
    - According to Revelation 10:6 there is *"time no longer"* in the Mystery Dispensation.
    - The Two Witnesses and the dead in Christ shall be resurrected and those that are alive in Christ will be translated by receiving their Heavenly Bodies without dying (1 Cor. 15:51-52). This is the Gathering of the Bride of Christ to the Heavenly Kingdom when the seventh and last trumpet shall begin to sound.
    - All these events take place mid-Trib.

2) Part two is from the perspective of Israel. When we talk about the Mystery of God being finished as it relates to Israel, it also means several things:
    - There is a change in the stewardship from the message of salvation through the Bride of Christ to the *"Everlasting Gospel"* taught by the 144,000 Jews during the second half of the Tribulation period, which is the second half of Daniel's seventieth week. This is also known as the time of Jacob's trouble.
    - Israel's blindness will be removed. *"Blindness in part is happened to Israel, **until** the fulness of the Gentiles be come in"* (Rom. 11:25 - Emphasis added).
    - Israel will recognize Jesus as the Messiah at the Gathering of the Bride of Christ. *"And they shall look upon Me whom they have pierced, and they shall mourn for Him"* (Zech. 12:10). Matthew 24:30-31 says that all the tribes of the earth will mourn when they see the Son of man coming in the clouds with a great sound of a trumpet. We will show later in this book why the seventh trumpet must be blown 42 months before the end of the Tribulation period.
    - All these events happen at the middle of the Tribulation period!

The Mystery Dispensation is how God administers the message of salvation through the Bride of Christ made up of foreigners, Gentiles that are grafted into the olive tree as branches (Rom. 11:19).

This is the Symphonic View of the Mystery of God

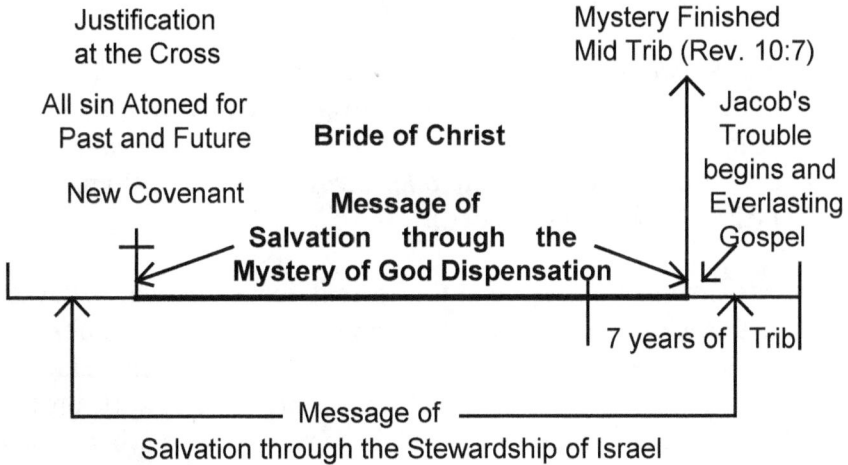

Justification
at the Cross

Mystery Finished
Mid Trib (Rev. 10:7)

All sin Atoned for
Past and Future

Bride of Christ

Jacob's
Trouble
begins and
Everlasting
Gospel

New Covenant

**Message of
Salvation through the
Mystery of God Dispensation**

7 years of Trib

Message of
Salvation through the Stewardship of Israel

Israel is still the olive tree including the root, which is in Christ; the Gentiles are branches grafted into that root. The tree and the branches in Christ are one body together. This one body in Christ is known as the Mystery. Are the branches greater than the tree? If God was willing to cut off some of the natural branches, which is Israel, then how much more willing is He to cut off some of the wild branches that were grafted into the tree (Rom. 11:17, 21, 24). Just because the church is grafted into the tree does not mean that the church is greater than Israel. Both receive their nourishment from the root, which is Jesus Christ!

No Replacement Theology!

All of "Exhibit K" is really strong evidence against Replacement Theology. A resurging movement in the Christian community is a belief that because Israel rejected Christ, Israel has no place in the Kingdom of God. The belief is that the church is the new spiritual Israel and God has dispensed with Israel forever. Whenever the Bible speaks about Israel, they replace Israel with the church as if the words are synonymous, hence Replacement Theology. According to Hal

Lindsey, "Augustine taught that the Church had taken Israel's place."[14] Hopefully by now you have figured out that Replacement Theology is erroneous teaching.

The LORD God promised David that his seed would sit upon the throne and rule all Israel again. *"Yet have I set My King* [Jesus] *upon My holy hill of Zion"* (Psalms 2:6 - Explanation added).

> *And so all Israel shall be saved: as it is written, There shall come out of Sion the Deliverer, and shall turn away ungodliness from Jacob:* **For this is My Covenant unto them, when I shall take away their sins** (Rom. 11:26-27 - Emphasis added).

Christ's Covenant of Grace at the cross is for whosoever believes, however, that Covenant has yet to become totally effective for the nation of Israel because of their unbelief. Individual believers can now have a relationship with God because of Christ's work on the cross, but all Israel being saved will become effective when Israel sees and believes in the true Messiah at the Gathering of the Bride of Christ mid-Trib. All of the other Covenants of the Old Testament shall be completely fulfilled in the Millennial Period, after the Tribulation period is finished. This is when king David regains his throne (Jer. 30:9, Hosea 3:5) and Jesus Christ is *"KING OF KINGS AND LORD OF LORDS"* (Rev. 19:16).

Whenever you hear Replacement Theology being preached, remember the promises God has made to Israel in His Will and Testament. If His promises to Israel are not honored, then our hope of salvation is also in vain.

Chapter 3

World War III
or is it Armageddon?

Obviously the Bible does not say "World War III" anywhere. But it does mention a war that clearly takes place before the Tribulation period in Ezekiel 38 and 39. The Bible talks about three different major conflicts in the Middle East in the end of days. And this is where so many people get confused. We hear that "Armageddon is coming" from almost everywhere: movies, tabloids, even Christians are saying it. But should we be expecting Armageddon every time a major conflict erupts in the Middle East? We will show that the answer for this question is unequivocally no. There is a catastrophic short nuclear war in our near future, but it is not Armageddon. There will be another conflict in the middle of the seven-year Tribulation period and then the final battle is Armageddon, where all the world's armies meet in the Middle East to square off against an unusual enemy. We will shed some light on the battle of Armageddon that heretofore to best of our knowledge has never been published.

Interpretation of Scripture

When we say the Bible must be interpreted literally, it means that we must take an exegesis approach to the Scriptures. Magog is not a symbolism for a government system; it is the area that Magog settled in. When the Bible says the earth was flooded, it was flooded. When the Bible prophets tried to describe weapons from the twenty-first century, they used terms they understood, hence bows and arrows. An exposition approach to the Scripture is then used to understand what the author meant when he said arrows. Ezekiel was definitely talking about an end times war for the reasons listed above, so when he says "arrows" he definitely did not mean wooden sticks with feathers because he definitely described a battle that has not happened yet, and nobody uses bow and arrows anymore.

The First War: Pre-Tribulation

First, let us examine the evidence of when Ezekiel's war takes place. God restores Israel for His glory and not for their sake. The valley of dry bones spoken of in Ezekiel 37 is definitely an end time prophecy that God started to fulfill in 1948 and will be consummated at the setting up of the Earthly Kingdom after the end of the Tribulation period. Ezekiel 40 - 42 is the description of the new Temple in the Millennium and is obviously end time prophecy Scripture. If Ezekiel 37 and 40 - 42 are end time prophecies, then Ezekiel 38 and 39 are end time prophecies as well.

Ezekiel 38-39 describes the whole Gog-Magog war and the repercussions of it. *"Son of man, set thy face against Gog and the land of Magog, the chief prince of Meshech and Tubal..."* (Ezek. 38:2).

Some people think Gog is the Antichrist, the leader of Turkey and the southern parts of Russia, perhaps Kazakhstan and maybe the Ukraine as well, because the Bible says that Gog is the *"chief prince."* However, Gog cannot be the Antichrist or any fleshly man because the Antichrist is cast into the lake of fire forever just before the Millennium (Rev. 19:20). In Revelation 20:8, Gog and Magog appear together again. If Gog is truly the *"chief prince"* and appears again at the end of the Millennium, then Gog must be supernatural in nature. If not, then Gog must be something that can exist, be defeated and exist again after a thousand years.

Gog is a mystery. It is not likely that Gog is a religious leader because he would have to live through the Tribulation period, receiving the mark, etc. and somehow not die when Christ returns. Gog could possibly be a false religion or worship of something or someone other than God. Some speculate that Gog is Satan himself because Gog will rise again in Magog at the end of the Millennium and cause the final uprising against God before the Great White Throne Judgment. However, Satan is restrained in Heaven until mid-Trib and could not be Gog on earth during the first war before the tribulation period and still be our accuser in Heaven at the same time. Satan is not omnipresent and is thereby limited physically to being in one place at a time. Opinions vary greatly on the identity of Gog.

Known combatants: This war has clearly defined combatants. We will discuss who these nations of people are and where they come from to attack Israel. This is a list of all the known combatants that come against Israel in the first war.

"Magog" = Land of Russia. Magog was the son of Japheth. Magog settled in southern Russia, including the Ukraine and Kazakhstan. His sons settled in the lands from southern Russia to Western Turkey, over to Greece and Italy, all the way up to and including Germany.

Note: *"Rosh"* as found in NAS Bible does not mean Russia. "Rosh" is a Hebrew word which means: chief, head or beginning. (**Rosh** Hashanah is the first of Tishri, the **beginning** of the Jewish New Year). Rosh is the *"chief prince"* of Meshech and Tubal.

"Meshech" = land of Turkey and part of southern Russia.
"Tubal" = parts of eastern Turkey. Some theologians surmise that *"Meshech"* is Moscow and Tubal is *"Tubalsk,"* two cities in Russia. Given the migration of the families, this is true to the best of our understanding.

Ezekiel 38:5-6 also adds Persia, Ethiopia, Libya, Gomer and Togarmah:
"Persia" = land of Iran.
"Cush" = land of Ethiopia-Cush the son of Ham. The land of Cush is south of Egypt in the Sudan and Ethiopian areas.
"Libya" = Libya of today, but is ancient Phut or Put.
"Gomer" = may mean Germany, but historical facts are unclear as to whom Gomer really is. Some say Gomer is Spain.
"Togarmah" = Turkey / Armenia.

The first war is a short one, but the outcome of it is that five-sixths of the attacking armies are annihilated (Ezek. 39:2). When reading Ezekiel 39:6, *"And I will send fire on Magog"*, the level of destruction upon the northern armies suggest that nuclear weapons are used. Nothing on earth could cause such devastation except nukes. However, it is possible that near Israel, smaller bombs known as Neutron bombs are used. These bombs do not have the same heat blast as a traditional nuclear weapon. A neutron bomb destroys flesh while not destroying tanks and weapons because it is a flash of radiation similar to a x-ray. Imagine an entire army being cooked by neutron bombs. Ezekiel goes on to say that they who dwell in the cities of Israel burn the weapons of this war for seven years (Ezek. 39:9). If regular conventional nukes were used, there would be nothing left to burn for seven years and this is the reason the Gog-Magog war is before the Tribulation period. People will be *"continually employed"* to bury the dead from this battle (Ezek. 39:14-15). People that come across the bones of the dead are to place markers by them and leave them for the professionals to move and bury. If neutron bombs were used, then the bones would be full of radiation. Israel would need specialists trained to dispose of the bodies and bones.

Ezekiel 38 also speaks of God's direct involvement and the world will know that *"I am the LORD"* (Ezek. 38:23). It will be obvious that God intervened with this battle and defeated the enemies of Israel.

Other Possible Combatants Not Specifically Mentioned

It is hard to imagine a battle with the whole Russian-Muslim confederate armies invading Israel without the United States defending Israel. Ezekiel 39:6 is an ominous Scripture showing that this war has far reaching consequences; *"and I will send fire on Magog, and among them that dwell carelessly in the isles: and they shall know that I am the LORD."* It is interesting to note that Iraq was not on the list of known combatants. It is probable that Iraq is not involved in the battle because of the United States' involvement there. If the Gog-Magog war happened in 1990, Iraq most certainly would have joined in the battle against Israel. Do you remember all the missiles fired in hate toward Israel from Iraq?

The six-day war in 1967 took the Muslims by surprise when Israel defeated them in a quick counter strike. With the whole Russian army coming to join the battle, the Muslims will feel pretty confident that victory will be at hand this time. Their half-brother, Israel, whom they have hated for so long, will finally be dead, or so they think. Ezekiel 38 and 39 says Russia and its Muslim allies ignore thousands of years of prophecy about this battle. Russia and its allies provoke God's white-hot anger upon themselves. We thought the 1967 war was short. May the Lord have mercy on them! Few will survive on that day and God will give *"Gog a place there of graves in Israel"* (Ezek. 39:11).

Ezekiel 38:4 says that God will *"put hooks into thy jaws"* and draw them into this war. The Scripture infers politics. Something will happen to draw Russia into war that is influenced by God.

Evidence that Gog-Magog war is before the Tribulation period:

1) The Lord God defeats the armies from Magog while they attempt to destroy Israel (Ezek. 38:1-6). Israel burns the war materials for seven years (Ezek. 39:9) and the Tribulation period is seven years long before the millennium begins.

2) Israel will bury the dead for seven months (Ezek. 39:12). They bury them in the valley of Hamon-gog in Israel to cleanse the land so the rebuilt the temple can be sanctified.

3) This Gog-Magog battle must be pre-Trib because Israel is victorious. When the Antichrist leads an attack against Israel mid-Trib, Israel is defeated. Revelation 12 has the woman fleeing from the Antichrist to Edom, Moab and Ammon over the mountains into the wilderness. How can Israel be victorious in the north and be running for their lives in the south at the same time? Obviously these are two separate events and all theologians who place the Gog-Magog battle during the Tribulation period must be mistaken.

4) How can Magog and its allies attack the land of unwalled villages (Ezek. 38:11) when everyone is talking peace and is unsuspecting if Israel is on the run from the Antichrist mid-Trib? Obviously the war cannot be mid-Trib. A pre-Tribulation battle is the only way the Scripture makes sense when reading Ezekiel 38:11.

5) Does the false prince or the Antichrist lead these armies against Israel? There is a common belief among theologians that the man of sin is supposed to come from the revived Roman Empire.[15] Why aren't any European nations mentioned in Ezekiel 38? Perhaps because Western Europe is not in this war against Israel. However, Israel defeats the ex-super power Russia, who is allied with Iran, Turkey, Ethiopia and Libya. Israel will probably get a little help from someone, perhaps the United States. Yes, God delivers Israel from a certain defeat, but God often uses weapons that are man-made to do His bidding. God will also use natural disasters to defeat the armies that go against His will. Then after this war, what is left of Israel will desire a covenant with the false

prince (Job 41:1-4). If the false prince was leading these armies against Israel pre-Tribulation, why would Israel follow him and look at him as someone they can trust a few months later? Therefore, the false prince cannot be the one leading these armies in the first battle.

6) When is that man of sin revealed to Israel? He is revealed when the Satan-indwelt-man claims to be God in the middle of the Tribulation period. That is when he becomes the *"son of perdition"* (2 Thess. 2:3). This is the *"consummation"* of abominations (Dan. 9:27). Our point of all this about the false prince is timing. The false prince rises to power from the ashes of this pre-Tribulation battle. Then after the false prince is killed mid-Tribulation, he is raised from the dead as the Antichrist. This war will be past history when the Antichrist comes on the scene. One needs to understand the timing of all these Scriptures with the symphonic view.

How is it Possible for Israel to Bury the Dead From the Gog-Magog War for Seven Months if this War Occurs Mid-Trib?

It is believed by many that the Gog-Magog war occurs mid-Trib. Look at the evidence:

> *And seven months shall the house of Israel be burying of them, that they may cleanse the land. Yea, all the people of the land shall bury them; and it shall be to them a renown the day that I shall be glorified, saith the Lord God* (Ezek. 39:12-13).

It goes on to say that when the house of Israel sees a human bone, they place a marker by it so the gravediggers can easily find the bones. This is being done in the valley of Hamon-gog. We believe the reason they are marking the human remains is because of radiation from the nuclear weapons or neutron weapons that are used. Israel is cleansing the land in preparation for the new temple and the restoration of Israel to its former glory, they hope.

Let us look at mid-Trib events for a moment using the Symphonic Method. Satan was just cast down from heaven. The Gathering of the Bride to Christ takes place as represented by the woman giving birth.

The faithful of Israel flee to the wilderness, to a place prepared for her by God, where God takes care of her for 1260 days. The Satan-indwelt-Antichrist pursues Israel with his armies to kill them (Rev. 12:1-17). Only a third of Israel escapes from the Antichrist (Zech. 13:8-9). There will then be another holocaust for the ones who could not escape. The Antichrist or beast that rises out of the pit is in control of Jerusalem, and gives power to his ten kings for *"one hour"* or *"42 months"* (Rev. 17:12 & Rev. 13:5). One third of Israel is now hiding in the desert, out of reach from the dragon. The dragon-indwelt-Antichrist sends his armies like a torrent of water after Israel, but God swallows up his armies just like He swallowed up Pharaoh's army in the Red Sea; except this time, the earth swallows up the armies with a great earthquake. Imagine being swallowed up by quicksand shaking and vibrating until you are many feet below the surface. How horrible it will be for anyone foolish enough to serve in Satan's army on that day.

How can Israel bury the dead of the fallen armies of Gog and Magog for seven months in Israel, while God is protecting them from the Antichrist for 1260 days? After reading the last paragraph the answer should be obvious, they cannot! The Symphonic Method has eliminated the possibility for the Gog-Magog war to be mid-Tribulation. So one must move that war to pre-Tribulation or post-Tribulation and look for conflicts in the Scriptures. Obviously the burning of war materials for seven years eliminates the post-Tribulation possibility as well. The symphonic view places this war before the Tribulation period begins.

Israel Burns the Spoils of War for Seven Years

After God causes Israel to win this Gog-Magog war, Israel burns the weapons for seven years.

> *And they that dwell in the cities of Israel shall go forth, and shall set on fire and burn the weapons...and they shall burn them with fire seven years* (Ezek. 39:9).

The whole Tribulation period is divided by two halves of 1260 days each. You do the math. Israel will not have the freedom to move about if all this is happening during the middle of the Tribulation period.

We have heard some wide-ranging theories about when the Gog-Magog war happens. Dr. Jack Van Impe is a well-respected theologian and is good intentioned when he places the war where it does not belong. We heard him make the argument that Israel must burn the war materials after the Tribulation is over, when Christ reigns from Jerusalem during the millennial period.[16] In his reasoning for this he explains that they burn the weapons from that war for seven years and since Israel does not start to burn them until mid-Trib, then they must burn them into the Millennium. We think the real reason Israel burns the war materials for seven years as opposed to 20 or so, is that the Tribulation period is only seven years long.

In summary, Israel defeats an overwhelming army, thus the reason for burying so many bodies as to take seven months to do so. Israel cannot drive around in 4x4's looking casually for the bones of their fallen enemies while the dragon is pursuing them into the desert. Scripture suggests that the war with Gog and Magog is the last war Israel fights as a nation, because in the next conflict at mid-Trib, the Antichrist's armies are already within Jerusalem. Many theologians would have us believe that this war with Gog is not until after the abomination that causes desolation, mid-Trib. Yet, for this to be true, Israel could not burn the war materials for seven years like Ezekiel prophesied. Many people get the timing all wrong because they put the "revealing" of Antichrist at the beginning of the Tribulation and the Gog-Magog war at the middle, and the Rapture before any of it begins. We hope this clears up the issue of when God through Israel defeats Russia and the Islamic armies.

Why isn't the War with Gog-Magog Mentioned in the Book of Revelation before the Millennium?

The reason the Gog and Magog war is not mentioned in the Book of Revelation is because the war is in the past when the Tribulation period begins. The great battle that defeats Russia and its allies will happen before the Tribulation period. Read Job 41:8; keep in mind that God is the author of all Scriptures through divine inspiration. God is saying, *"remember the battle,"* meaning I delivered you from certain defeat. And God also said, *"will he make a covenant with thee?"* (Job 41:4). This covenant is made with Israel at the beginning of the Tribulation period. God is inferring in Job 41:4 that the false prince makes a covenant with Israel. It is entirely possible that this covenant is the same covenant mentioned in Daniel 9:27. What is the purpose of this covenant? The false prince is allowing Israel to rebuild the temple and start animal sacrifice, which is an abomination to God. We think it will also allow the Sanhedrin the prime opportunity to regain their power in an attempt to restore Israel to its former glory. If *"the battle"* in Job 41:8 were during the Tribulation period, none of this would make sense. The Scriptural witness says that the Gog-Magog war is before the Tribulation period begins.

We always say, "Where are the Scriptural supports or witnesses for every premise?" Any position we take has multiple Scriptures supporting the premise, otherwise the premise is without witnesses, and without witnesses, there is only partial truth. There also must not be any conflicting Scriptures in your premise or you do not have the whole truth either. These are fundamental truths that must be learned to properly interpret the Scriptures. Do we believe we have the only truth? No, we do not. We pray the Holy Spirit will give you wisdom and understanding beyond what He has given us.

The Second Conflict: Mid-Tribulation

The second conflict is against Israel and the remnant of Israel. There will be no outright war against Israel like before when the Russian and Islamic nations attacked Israel. This time Israel has invited the enemy inside the borders and allowed Jerusalem to be encompassed. Israel allows the false prince to have troops in Jerusalem with legal authority. By this time the false prince will have the world broken into ten regions and on the brink of every nation giving up their national sovereignty. This new world government will have its own army, not unlike United Nations troops now. These troops will desecrate the new temple. The country of Israel will fall from within and their flag will come down. Then the worst Jewish holocaust will ensue. The Jews that fear God, which is the woman in Revelation 12:6 and 12:14, will have escaped into the wilderness and will have God's protection for 1260 days. The Antichrist will hunt Israel in the wilderness, but he will fail. The Antichrist then settles for going after the remnant of Israel, the 144,000, all around the world. This holocaust is a continuation of the second conflict and it lasts for 42 months until Christ's Triumphal Return at Armageddon.

The Symphonic View of the Second Conflict

"And when ye shall see Jerusalem compassed with armies, then know that the desolation thereof is nigh" (Luke 21:20). Whose armies surround Israel and when does Daniel's prophecy of the *"abomination that causes desolation"* happen?

The beast that rises out of the sea in Revelation 13 is the false prince and still just a man. This false prince will bring his armies to Jerusalem and encompass the city. This is when he places an abomination in the temple by military force and ceases animal sacrifice at the same time (Dan. 11:31). Isaiah 44:13-20 talks about a statue being made of wood. This abomination happens 30 days prior to mid-Tribulation (Dan. 12:11). During this 30-day window of time the false prince claims he is God (Ezek. 28:2, 2 Thess. 2:4). Sometime shortly after this, the false prince is killed with a *"mortal wound"* (Ezek. 28:9 & Rev. 13:3). Satan is cast down from Heaven *"to the sides of the pit"* (Isa. 14:15) in the middle of the Tribulation, and Satan indwells the false prince. Upon the false prince's miraculous healing, he becomes the Antichrist, *"the son of perdition"* (2 Thess. 2:3) and commits *"the abomination of desolation"* (Matt. 24:15, Mark 13:14) or *"consummation"* of abominations that cause desolation (Dan. 9:27). Desolation is the key word because it places the *"armies"* (Dan. 11:31, Luke 21:20) at Jerusalem in the middle of the Tribulation. After becoming the Antichrist, he enters the temple and proclaims himself to be the God of the universe, God above all others (2 Thess. 2:4, Rev. 13:4). He then kills the Two Witnesses (Rev. 11:7, Dan. 12:7).

Those in Judea in southern Israel flee into the wilderness (Matt. 24:16, Mark 13:14). The false prince already has his armies in Jerusalem, preventing everyone from escaping when he becomes the Antichrist. There is battle for the control of Jerusalem, but it will be quick. We are not saying that the Israeli government will not put up a fight. However, it is hard to launch jet fighters when your enemy controls the runways. Whatever resistance Israel musters will not be enough. God allows Judah and Jerusalem to be again in captivity.

This captivity starts mid-Tribulation and continues until Armageddon is finished at the end of the Tribulation period.

These same armies are used by the Satan-indwelt-Antichrist to pursue the *"woman,"* Israel, into the wilderness after giving birth. Hal Lindsey agrees that the woman in Revelation 12 is Israel.[17] The flood is the army of the Antichrist, which is swallowed up by the earth. The Antichrist is pursuing the woman into the desert because she is fleeing from him. The woman goes into hiding at the beginning of the second half of the Tribulation period with God's protection for 1260 days.

Third Battle: Armageddon, Christ's Triumphal Return

It seems everyone teaching eschatology (the branch of theology dealing with death, resurrection, judgment, immortality, end times) has missed that the battle of Armageddon is not man against man or nation against nation, but the kings of the earth show up in the Middle East to fight Jesus. The Antichrist has control over all ten regions of the earth and he knows he has a short time before Christ's Triumphal Return, so he masses all his armies for the final standoff against the King of Kings and Lord of Lords. The sword from Jesus' mouth, His spoken Word, will kill every one of the Antichrist's followers. Everyone who is alive and overcomes the Antichrist by refusing to worship him or take his mark will be allowed to enter the earthly Kingdom in his or her flesh and blood body during the Millennium.

The Battle of Armageddon

And I saw heaven opened, and behold a white horse; and He that sat upon him was called Faithful and True, and in righteousness He doth judge and make war. His eyes were as a flame of fire, and on His head were many crowns; and He had a name written, that no man knew, but He Himself. And He was clothed with a vesture dipped in blood: and His name is called The Word of God. And the armies which were in heaven followed Him upon white horses, clothed in fine linen, white and clean. And out of His mouth goeth a sharp sword, that with it He should smite the nations: and He shall rule them with a rod of iron: and He treadeth the winepress *of the fierceness and wrath of Almighty God. And He hath on His vesture and on His thigh a name written, KING OF KINGS, AND LORD OF LORDS. And I saw an angel standing in the sun; and he cried with a loud voice, saying to all the fowls that fly in the midst of heaven, Come and gather yourselves together unto the supper of the great God; That ye may eat the flesh of kings, and the flesh of captains, and the flesh of mighty men, and the flesh of horses, and of them that sit on them, and the flesh of all men, both free and bond, both small and great. **And I saw the beast, and the kings of the earth, and their armies, gathered together to make war against Him that sat on the horse,** and against His army. And the beast was taken, and with him the false prophet that wrought miracles before him, with which he deceived them that had received the mark of the beast, and them that worshipped his image. These both were cast alive into a lake of fire burning with brimstone. And the remnant were slain with the sword of Him that sat upon the horse, which sword proceeded out of His mouth: and all the fowls were filled with their flesh* (Rev. 19:11-21 - Emphasis added).

The Triumphal Return and Entry into Jerusalem

And Enoch also, the seventh from Adam, prophesied of these, saying, behold, the Lord cometh with ten thousands of His saints, to execute judgment upon all... (Jude 1:14-15).

Christ will return with ten thousands of His saints at the Triumphal Return. Not just 10,000, but many, many 10,000's, a limitless number. He will ride a white horse (Rev. 19:11). Christ returns to the earth at the end of the Tribulation with His *"armies which were in heaven"* (Rev. 19:14) to defeat Satan and his army of malcontents at the battle of Armageddon. He separates the sheep nations from the goat nations. Jesus will then reign as KING OF KINGS AND LORD OF LORDS here on the earth, not just from Heaven. This is when He begins to rule all nations with a rod of iron.

After the battle of Armageddon has ended Christ sits on the throne of His glory in Jerusalem. This is known as His Triumphal Entry into Jerusalem. Two thousand years ago Christ entered the east gate of Jerusalem on a donkey showing His meekness. After the Tribulation period is over and Satan is defeated at Armageddon, Christ will enter the east gate in Jerusalem on a white horse showing His Glory. This is His real Triumphal Entry into Jerusalem.

We cannot describe these events any better than the Bible does. Here are some Scriptures that describe the events leading up to His Triumphal Return:

When they therefore were come together, they asked of Him, saying, Lord, wilt Thou at this time restore again the kingdom to Israel? And He said unto them, It is not for you to know the times or the seasons, which the Father hath put in His own power. But ye shall receive power, after that the Holy Ghost is come upon you: and ye shall be witnesses unto Me both in Jerusalem, and in all Judaea, and in Samaria, and unto the uttermost part of the earth. And when He had spoken these things, while they beheld, He was taken up; and a cloud received Him out of their sight. And while they looked steadfastly toward heaven as He went up, behold, two men stood by them in white apparel; Which also said, Ye men of Galilee, why stand ye gazing up into heaven? **This same Jesus, which is taken up from you into heaven, shall so come in like manner as ye have seen Him go into heaven.** *Then returned they unto Jerusalem from the mount called Olivet, which is from Jerusalem a sabbath day's journey* (Acts 1:6-12 - Emphasis added).

Behold, the day of the LORD cometh, and thy spoil shall be divided in the midst of thee. For I will gather all nations against Jerusalem to battle; and the city shall be taken, and the houses rifled, and the women ravished; and half of the city shall go forth into captivity, and the residue of the people shall not be cut off from the city. Then shall the LORD go forth, and fight against those nations, as when He fought in the day of battle. And His feet shall stand in that day upon the mount of Olives, [Triumphal Return] *which is before Jerusalem on the east, and the mount of Olives shall cleave in the midst thereof toward the east and toward the west, and there shall be a very great valley; and half of the mountain shall remove toward the north, and half of it toward the south. And ye shall flee to the valley of the mountains; for the valley of the mountains shall reach unto Azal: yea, ye shall flee, like as ye fled from before the earthquake in the days of Uzziah king of Judah: and the LORD my God shall come, and all the saints with Thee. And it shall come to pass in that day, that the light shall not be clear, nor dark:* [Still Triumphal Return] *But it shall be one day which shall be known to the LORD, not day, nor night: but it shall come to pass, that at evening time it shall be light. And it shall be in that day, that living waters shall go out from Jerusalem; half of them toward the former sea, and half of them toward the hinder sea: in summer and in winter shall it be. And the LORD shall be King over all the earth: in that day shall there be one LORD, and His name one* [Triumphal Entry into Jerusalem] (Zech. 14:1-9).

More Scriptural Witnesses For The Symphonic View Concerning These Three Conflicts

Chronology of events according to Zechariah:

- (Zechariah 11) The rejection of the King during Christ's earthly ministry.
- (Zechariah 11:12) Jesus betrayed for 30 pieces of silver.
- (Zechariah 12) Israel [already a nation] is being attacked. God will cause blindness and confusion on their enemies. In the day when they are in siege against Judah and Jerusalem, the Lord will prevail (Zech. 12:2-4). Even though the whole world is against it, Jerusalem falls into the hand of Israel. *"And Jerusalem shall be inhabited again in her own place, even in Jerusalem"* (Zech. 12:6). This happened in 1967.

- (Zechariah 12:8) *"In that day shall the Lord defend the inhabitants of Jerusalem."* Verse 6; Jews take Jerusalem [1967]. Verse 8; Jews are protected defending Jerusalem [future war]. This is the first conflict in the end times, the Gog-Magog war. God will destroy all the nations that come against Jerusalem. This is a pre-Trib event.
- (Zechariah 12:10-11) Christ revealed, *"and they shall look upon Me whom they have pierced, and they shall mourn for Him, as one mourneth for his only son..."* The prophets will be ashamed and say I am no prophet. I am no husband to the Lord (Zech. 13:4-5). *"And one shall say unto Him, What are these wounds in thine hands?"* (Zech. 13:6). This is a mid-Trib event.
- (Zechariah 13:8) Two thirds of Israel cut off. Only 1/3 will be brought through the fire. We believe this is the 1/3 that escape to Judea and flee into the wilderness for protection for 1260 days. This is when the Antichrist's armies encompass Jerusalem. It is the second conflict. This is a mid-Trib event.
- (Zechariah 14:1-2) Armageddon! All the nations come against Israel to do battle there. This is at the end of the Tribulation period.
- (Zechariah 14:3-5) The Triumphal Return of the Lord! He will place His feet on the Mount of Olives. And the Lord my God will come, and all the saints with thee.
- (Zechariah 14:6-7) Evening time will be like daytime. This could mean two things: 1) a comet hits the earth and knocks the earth out of its place. 2) Jesus is the light of the world. At the Triumphal Return it is neither light nor dark. Remember that at the Gathering the sun and moon have darkened and it is dark all the time (Isa. 13:10, Matt. 24:29, Rev. 6:12).
- (Zechariah 14:8). Jesus said that the water He offers us would cause us to thirst no more. *"And it shall be in that day, that living waters shall go out from Jerusalem."* It also means actual water springing forth from Jerusalem. This is at the end of the Tribulation period and the beginning of the Millennium.
- (Zechariah 14:12) This verse is finishing the Armageddon thought. All flesh that came against Jerusalem will be consumed by fire while they are still standing on their feet. Their eyes are

consumed in the sockets; their tongues shall be consumed in their mouth. This is at the end of the Tribulation period.

- (Zechariah 14:16-19) All the survivors of the nations who came against Israel will be required to come to Jerusalem to worship the King, the Lord of hosts. If they refuse, there will be drought in their land.

Chapter 4

The Tribulation

What is the Tribulation Period?

The Tribulation period is a seven-year time span with two halves of 1260 days each. Jesus called the beginning of the Tribulation period the *"beginning of sorrows"* (Matt. 24:8, Mark 13:8) and likened it to birth pangs. The Mystery Dispensation is finished at the end of the first half and God's wrath is poured out during the entire second half of the Tribulation period. However, the ending of the Tribulation period is not the end of the world. The world will be transformed and there will be no false religions that remain; all other gods will have been proven to be false. Everyone sees Christ in all His glory and every knee shall bow to worship Him. The earth will be similar to the days before the flood, where people live up to a thousand years before they die.

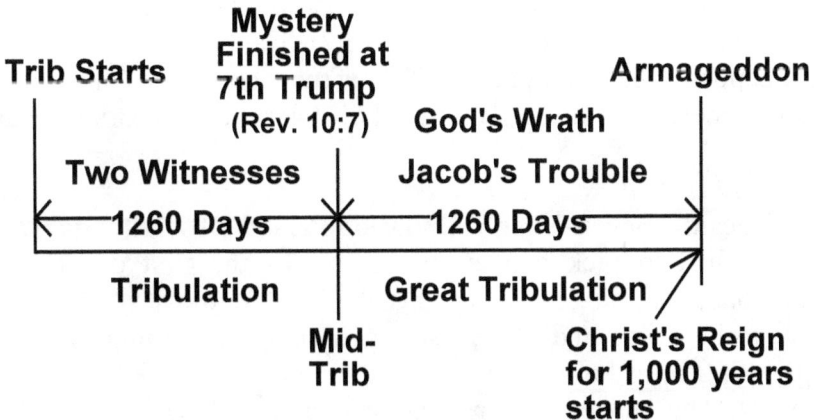

The First 1260 Days:

The temple construction is completed within seven months after the Tribulation period begins. The Two Witnesses start their ministry at the beginning of the Tribulation and it is 1260 days long (Rev.

11:1-3). The Two Witnesses will appear as people among us and will prophesy about Christ's soon return. It is not likely that we will know the exact first day of the Tribulation period, because then one could easily calculate the exact day when Christ will come. However, that does not mean we are not to know what season He should come. He gave us specific signs to watch for in the days just prior to when He will return for His Bride. Example: The sun and moon will darken and not give off their light. When this happens, then and only then is His return imminent.

The first 1260 days is when the great outpouring of the Holy Spirit happens. We believe miracles of faith and healing occur in the first 1260 days. Old men will have dreams sent by God and young men will see Godly visions (Joel 2:28). False miracles will also occur in an attempt to deceive the whole world, even true Christians if it were possible. A supernatural time will exist on earth, as well as progressively worsening apostasy. In much of the world it will be illegal to preach true Christianity, something most of the world now takes for granted. There will also be a time of great persecution of all believers.

The first 1260 days of the Tribulation period is the final days of the Mystery Dispensation. The pregnancy of the woman (Rev. 12) will end with the birth of the Bride of Christ when *"the Mystery of God"* is accomplished mid-Trib (Rev. 10:7). The birth of the Bride of Christ happens when the faithful of the True Church are Gathered in the air to meet the Lord at His mid-Trib Glorious Appearing in the sky.

When Does the Seven-Year Tribulation Period Officially Start?

If we had to pick one event that marks the first day of the Tribulation, it would be the day that the Two Witnesses, whom we believe to be Elijah and Moses, start preaching. Their ministry lasts exactly 1260 days before they allow themselves to be killed by the Antichrist. The end of the Tribulation period will be another 1260 days after their death. However, this is precisely why we think their first days will be controversial, so no man knows the exact hour the Lord will come. Based on a Jewish calendar year of 360 days, we come up with three and one half years of trials and tribulations, and three and one half years of God's wrath, totaling seven years.

Two Witnesses present in the First Half of the Tribulation Period

It is significant that Elijah and Moses are present in the first half of the Tribulation period because of what these men represent. Jesus promised that Elijah would come to announce His return. Christ's Glorious Appearing and Gathering of His Bride cannot happen before Elijah comes (Mal. 4:5, Matt. 17:11). We believe that Elijah represents the Prophets and the living in Christ at the Gathering because Elijah never died. We think that Moses represents the Law and the dead in Christ. In Revelation 11:4, *"these are the two olive trees"* representing Israel and they are also *"the two candlesticks"* representing the faithful of the True Church (Rev. 1:20), which is the Bride of Christ. Both of these groups of people are grafted into olive tree root, which is Christ through the Abrahamic Covenant (Rom. 11:17-19, Gal. 3).

It is interesting that Israel hears the Two Witnesses, but does not like what they have to say because of their testimony of Jesus. Doesn't that sound familiar? The world also hates the Two Witnesses because of their message to repent before Christ comes to establish the Heavenly Kingdom. They hold to the commandments of God and the faith of Jesus (Rev. 14:12) until the Antichrist kills them mid-Trib (Rev. 11:7). Three and one half days after the Two Witnesses are killed, they are raised from the dead. We believe they are resurrected along with the Bride of Christ. At mid-Trib the *"mystery of God"* is finished (Rev. 10:7).

The Purpose of the First Half of the Tribulation Period

The purpose of the first half of the Tribulation period is to bring humanity to a decision, to choose whom they will serve (Joshua 24:15). It is a time of testing. One must choose God or reject God. Read all seven letters to the churches in the Book of Revelation. In these letters it is made crystal clear that if you want to see the crystal sea in Heaven, you must never deny your faith in Jesus Christ, even unto death. Those that fear for their lives and try to save them, will lose them (Luke 9:24). Those that do not fear to die will receive the crown of Life, the resurrection at the Gathering. Those who seek to keep or attain wealth during this time of testing will have to work around the mark of the beast and his economic system. In their time of testing, many humans let the cares of world come between them and God. *"For what shall it profit a man, if he shall gain the whole world, and lose his own soul? Or what shall a man give in exchange for his soul?"* (Mark 8:35-36). A true Christian seeks first the kingdom of God and carries their cross daily for the Lord. During the Tribulation period a true Christian will refuse to take the mark of the beast and refuse to deny Christ's name. They are overcomers!

God uses earthly birth pangs to get our attention and to remind us He is coming soon. The very heavens and the earth groan with earthquakes, volcanic activity and extreme hurricanes. Possibly even a comet may hit the earth during the second trumpet (Rev. 8:8). If an asteroid or comet hit the Pacific Ocean, it could easily kill a third part of the sea life and destroy a third part of the ships. It could cause tidal waves like never seen before. It could cause the volcanic ring of fire to erupt whereby the volcanoes would throw so much ash into the atmosphere that the sun and moon could be partially blotted out from the earth. In Revelation 8:12 it says that only a third part of the sun and moon goes dark when the second trumpet sounds. Whether a third part of the earth goes dark or third part of the affected area goes dark, we do not know. However, just prior to the Gathering of the Bride of Christ, the sun and moon will be darkened. When you see these things come upon the earth, then lift up your head because your redemption draws very near. Matthew 24:29-30 claims that immediately after the tribulation of those days, Christ comes in His Glorious Appearing in the sky with His angels to collect the Bride of Christ.

The Second 1260 Days

Satan is cast down from heaven just prior to the start of the second 1260 days. He kills the Two Witnesses and claims to be God in Holy of Holies of the rebuilt temple. These days are known as *"the time of trouble, such as never was since there was a nation even to that same time"* (Dan. 12:1). This is *"the time of Jacob's trouble; but he shall be saved out of it"* (Jer. 30:7). The Antichrist pursues the woman Israel into the wilderness, where God protects her for 1260 days (Rev. 12:6, 12:14). The second half of the Tribulation period is also known as *"the hour of temptation"* (Rev. 3:10) during the 42-month reign of the Antichrist (Rev. 13:5) with the ten kings of the earth (Rev. 17:12-13). This is the same time period that God's wrath is poured out upon those that worship the Antichrist and his political, economic and religious system. It is a period of *"great tribulation"* (Matt. 24:21, Rev. 7:14).

A battle called Armageddon is at the end of this 42-month period. It is not clear who the combatants are except to say that all combatants turn their weapons on Christ when He returns to end all wars. Almost everyone assumes that Armageddon is the final battle of man against man, but that is not inferred in the Scriptures. The battle is man against God.

> *And I saw the beast, and the kings of the earth, and their armies, gathered together to make war against Him that sat on the horse, and against His army* (Rev. 19:19).

When Christ returns to the earth at the battle of Armageddon it will be His Triumphal Return. Out of His mouth comes a sword, His spoken Word. The beast and his false prophet are thrown alive into the lake of fire.

When Christ returns to Jerusalem it will be His Triumphal Entry into Jerusalem, after defeating the beast and serving His revenge on those who persecuted Israel. This is when God honors all of His Covenants with Israel. This is when God has the Temple rebuilt or He brings the Temple down from Heaven to Jerusalem. Either way, Israel begins animal sacrifice (Ezek. 40:42, 44:11) ceremonially in remembrance of God's Covenants, which will have been fulfilled by that point. These animal sacrifices will not be for the atonement of sin. Israel will be restored as a Nation and will never go into captivity again.

The fact that Israel exists today does not mean God has restored Israel, not in the sense that we just described. Israel as we know it today will again go into captivity mid-Trib. Part of Israel will be protected by God in the wilderness. The rest of Israel is trapped and is slaughtered. Only in the Millennium will God's promise to restore Israel be completely fulfilled.

The Purpose for the Second Half of the Tribulation

The purpose of *"Great Tribulation"* is many things. The stewardship of the *"Everlasting Gospel"* is given to Israel through the 144,000 and repentance toward God is still being offered. These

144,000 are Messianic Jews from the twelve tribes of Israel who continue to have the testimony of Jesus and preach the Everlasting Gospel. Imagine 144,000 Jewish Billy Grahams in the world preaching salvation through the grace and blood of Jesus Christ.[18] These 144,000 will preach for the remainder of the Tribulation period.

It also brings the wrath of God to punish those who have persecuted the Jews and the True Church. There will be an ultimate showdown between God and evil at Armageddon and all those who will take the mark or worship the beast shall be destroyed. Christ physically comes to separate the sheep nations from the goat nations (Matt. 25:31-46) and to cleanse the earth for the promised Earthly Kingdom to come. Christ Jesus will be established as the world leader, the *"KING OF KINGS AND LORD OF LORDS"* (Rev. 19:16). This will end all wars for 1,000 years and restore the Kingdom to Israel (Acts 1:6).

Is All of the Tribulation Period the Wrath of God?

The Book of Revelation talks about seven seals, seven trumpets and seven vials. There are some theologians that believe that all of the Tribulation period is the wrath of God.[19] They believe that when the first seal is opened, the wrath of God begins with the four horseman of the apocalypse. We do not believe this to be true. We believe that the breaking of the seals are the *"beginning of sorrows"* (Matt. 24:8) or birth pangs of the coming Heavenly Kingdom (Rev. 12).

Christ said He would keep us from the hour of His wrath (Rev. 3:10). What and when is that hour? It is a period of immense tribulation when the vials of God's wrath are poured out against the Satan-indwelt-Antichrist and his subjects. This period is 42 months long (Rev. 13:5), the time that Satan is on the earth (Rev. 12:7-12). The combination of Satan being on the earth indwelling the Antichrist and God's wrath at the same time is what makes this 42 month period the time of trouble like the world has never seen before. This period is also known as the *"time of Jacob's trouble; but he* [the faithful of Israel] *shall be saved out of it"* (Jer. 30:7) during these 42 months.

In the Scriptures, Christ promised to keep us from the hour of His wrath. It is true that we are exempt from God's entire wrath. The first and every subsequent occurrence of God's wrath in the Book of Revelation are all symphonically after the mid-Trib sounding of the seventh trumpet and the Gathering of the Elect. We believe that God's wrath is not until the second half of the Tribulation period.

Wrath is first mentioned within the sixth seal in Revelation 6:16-17. However, this is the only Scripture in the New Testament that associates wrath with the Lamb of God; every other time wrath is mentioned it is always associated with God the Father. In order to determine the timing of when this sixth seal happens, you must understand where the action is taking place. All the seals are broken in Heaven, and John sees spiritually in Heaven what will physically happen on earth at a future time. If you interpret the timing of events in the Book of Revelation symphonically, you will understand that some of the physical effects of the sixth seal take place as signs just before the Gathering of the Elect. The sun turns black, the moon becomes as blood, stars fall from heaven and the powers of heavens are shaken (Matt. 24:29-31, Rev. 6:12-14a). Satan and his dark angels will have just been expelled from heaven at this point (Rev. 12), making it possible for the Gathering of the Bride to Heaven. The remainder of the physical events of the sixth seal take place on earth symphonically when Jesus comes to take physical possession of the earth at His Triumphal Return. These physical events of the sixth seal, which are the great earthquake, the mountains and islands moving out of their places, and the wrath of the Lamb are described under the seventh vial in Revelation 16:18-20. The timing of *"the wrath of the Lamb"* in Revelation 6:16 is described when Christ comes with *"the armies which were in heaven"* (Rev. 19:14).

> *And out of His mouth goeth a sharp sword, that with it He should smite the nations: ...and He* [Christ] *treadeth the winepress of the fierceness and wrath of Almighty God* (Rev. 19:15).

Where else in the Book of Revelation is the treading of the winepress talked about? In Revelation 14:19-20. Where is that action taking place? The angel came out of the Temple in Heaven. When does that action happen on Earth? It happens at Armageddon in Revelation 19:15. Why do we ask these questions? It is to show you a pattern of how to determine the timing of events throughout the Book of Revelation. If the action is taking place in Heaven, it is spiritual in nature; somewhere else in the Book of Revelation it will show you symphonically when that event will physically happen on Earth. If you attempt to read the Book of Revelation chronologically, it will make no sense. Please understand that the action goes back and forth from Heaven to earth. The spiritual always manifests itself before the physical.

Also understand that the trumpets are clearly sounded in the first half of the Tribulation period. When you do your research, you will find no mention of wrath given symphonically until after the Gathering of the Elect at the seventh trumpet. This means that no wrath is mentioned in the first half of the Tribulation period. After the Two Witnesses are resurrected mid-Tribulation, then the wrath of God is mentioned. We believe that the first half of the Tribulation is to get the world's attention through birth pangs. Then the wrath of God begins in the second half of the Tribulation period to punish Satan, the beast's world system and those who refused Christ's invitation.

The church will go through three and one half years of trials and tribulations. Find comfort in knowing that as long as you hold fast to your faith in Jesus and not deny His name, you will have eternal life in Heaven. Find comfort in knowing that we will not be persecuted by the Antichrist for three and one half years because Satan is restrained in heaven and will continue to be until he is cast down just before mid-Trib. The false prince will not become the Satan-indwelt-Antichrist until the middle of the Tribulation period, just days before the Gathering. Also find comfort in knowing that man of sin, the false prince, gains power through peace and deception, not war. This means the first half of the Tribulation period will likely have a short reprieve from all the war that led up to the beginning of the Tribulation period. We are referring to Christ's *"wars and rumors of wars"* (Matt. 24:6, Mark 13:7).

In the first half of the Tribulation during the birth pangs and when the sun and moon have darkened, many Christians will likely be told, "see, there wasn't any sudden Rapture; it is all a lie." Christ is not coming and many other false teachings about Christianity will abound. There are already a great number of "so called" Christians who do not believe in the deity of Christ and who believe many other false teachings. However, we do not believe it is possible for the true

Christian to be deceived. Many so-called Christians may lose their faith during this period of progressively worsening apostasy of the church. Let no man deceive you, *"a falling away"* from the faith or great apostasy comes as a result of the revealing of *"the son of perdition"* just **before** Christ Gathers His Bride (2 Thess. 2:3). Be watchful for these things and hold fast to your faith in Him.

The Bride of Christ will not endure the wrath of God, but it will endure its fair share of trials during the first half of the Tribulation period. The trials and tribulations that the Bride of Christ will endure are in part, faith oriented. Even today in America, if your child brings a Bible into school or wears a pennant with the cross on it, you may find out how quickly you and your child will endure faith trials. Court case upon court case is being brought against Christianity in an attempt to expunge God and Jesus Christ from every public place. It seems some people cannot expunge all references to God fast enough. They do not seem to care about offending us Christians. This is just a prelude of much worse things to come.

Will Christians Suffer Before the Gathering?

There will be much suffering, even before the Tribulation period begins. It is possible that a billion people could die during Gog-Magog war before the Tribulation period starts. People will say it is "Armageddon" or it is the "wrath of God," but it will not be. Christ said there will be *"wars and rumours of wars... but the end is not yet"* (Matt. 24:6).

In the first half of the Tribulation period there is progressive apostasy in the church. People will probably ask, how could God allow such suffering to happen? Many could lose their hope because they have been told Christians will not suffer through any part of the Tribulation period and that they will escape all such suffering. Even now there is a gradual falling away from Christ's teachings in parts of the world that have been traditionally strong Christian societies.

Another likely cause for this progressive apostasy is that church members are not reading their Bibles and do not have the knowledge of these things in advance. Perhaps a new apostate church leader will lead many Christians astray who do not know *"The Word of God"* (Rev. 19:13). The Scriptures say that in the end times *"people will be willingly ignorant"* of these things (2 Peter 3:5). Jesus told us that He has *"foretold you all things"* (Mark 13:23). Only the true Christians who are studying God's Word will not be fooled or deceived.

However, we believe that there will be an event called the great apostasy. Something happens that makes weak believers stop believing in the true Christ. It might be a combination of both the willing ignorance of the people and the mirror-image resurrection of the false prince. We believe that Satan indwells the false prince when he rises from the dead and he becomes the Antichrist. Also, the false prophet causes the worship of that risen Antichrist. All these reasons could cause the great apostasy. It is important to understand that it is the false prince and not the Antichrist that comes in the first half of the Tribulation period. The Satan-indwelt-Antichrist comes in the middle of the Tribulation and continues for 42 months.

The Scriptures also talk about the false prince bringing a foreign god into the rebuilt temple. We know that a one-world religion will come during the Tribulation period. One that Muslims, false Christians and all the world's religions can agree on (Rev. 13:15). This false prince will say that all the world's religions have a basis of the one true God. When the world follows, he switches out that false god and elevates himself in its place. It seems impossible now but there is evidence that the world is ripe for such a religion. Even now the people are saying that current world religions are the problem. Religious people are haters of people who are not like them. They cite Muslims killing Christians and Christians killing Muslims, Protestants killing Catholics and Catholics killing Protestants. We should all just learn how to get along and accept that there are many paths to "Heaven." **This is not our belief!**

Christianity has become offensive to people. Businesses recently have refrained from saying "Merry Christmas" and acknowledging Christ because it might offend someone. In America, the freedom to express one's religion is acceptable unless one is a Christian or a Jew, then it is offensive.

> *Then shall they deliver you up to be afflicted, and shall kill you: and ye shall be hated of all the nations for My name's sake. And then shall many be offended, and shall betray one another, and shall hate one another. And*

78

many false prophets shall rise, and shall deceive many
(Matt. 24:9-10).

These false prophets will deny the virgin birth, resurrection of the body and mostly deny the deity of Christ. All these false teachers in the church will deceive many and will enable this new world religion to prosper through confusion of what the Scriptures really say. *"Many will be offended"* means people will be offended by Christianity, like what is beginning to happen in America even now. Another possibility is that people may be offended in the Lord because they believe it has all been a lie when no sudden Rapture came to save them from this severe suffering.

The masses will believe what they see on TV. They will see false miracles and wonders to believe in. Only the people that have a love of the truth will not be fooled (Matt. 24:24 & 2 Thess. 2:10). Jesus said, *"I Am The Way, The Truth, and The Life: no man cometh unto the Father, but by Me"* (John 14:6). It does not matter what all the heathen say about us. Our faith is based on truth. The truth is that Jesus is the only man in history who claimed to be God, died and was resurrected by the Holy Spirit, and will come again. No other religion is based on this premise. God came down to walk among us and suffer that we might live with Him forever. The Creator became His creation, to save it!

Summary of the Tribulation Period

The birth pains begin when the Tribulation period starts. Dominion of the earth is still in Satan's possession until God divests him of it and gives it to the Lord Jesus Christ. This does not happen until the Heavenly Court sets and the sealed book in Heaven is opened. The false prince rises to power on earth. The Two Witnesses begin their ministry by warning people on earth that Christ is coming soon. The false prince becomes the Satan-indwelt-Antichrist just before the mid-Trib Gathering of the Elect. When the Bridegroom comes for His Bride mid-Trib, it is the birth of the Heavenly Kingdom.

Jesus Christ takes physical possession of the earth three and one half years later, at the end of the Tribulation period. Only after Christ returns to earth at the battle of Armageddon will the Earthly Kingdom come about. It will last for one thousand years. The earth will be transformed quite suddenly. People will once again live up to a thousand years like they did before the flood. The beasts of the field will not eat each other and the earth will produce abundantly, all because Jesus broke the curses that were put on the earth at the fall of Eden. Jesus became a curse on the cross so creation could be brought back to a perfect state.

Chapter 5

The Antichrist

What is the Difference between the false prince and the Antichrist?

The false prince is a mere man. 2 Thessalonians 2:3 gives two descriptions for this same man calling him *"that man of sin"* and then there is a comma, *"the son of perdition."* By rightly dividing the word at the comma, one may deduce that there is a difference between the two names. First *"that man of sin"* is a mere man, and secondly *"the son of perdition"* is *"that man of sin"* indwelt by Satan.

> *Let no man deceive you by any means: for **that day** [our gathering to Christ] **shall not come, except** there come a falling away **first**, and that man of sin **be revealed, the son of perdition** (2 Thess. 2:3 - Emphasis added).*

The false prince and the Antichrist is one man. However, we need to make a distinction between the false prince and the Antichrist. *"The prince that shall come"* (Dan. 9:26-27) is born a mere man. This false prince comes to power at the beginning of the Tribulation period and is killed just prior to mid-Trib. This is when Satan is banished from heaven, indwells the man of sin's mortally wounded body and they rise out of the bottomless pit. He then becomes the *"son of perdition"* (2 Thess. 2:3), better known as the Antichrist.

Let us look at the Scriptural witness to the fact that Satan indwells the son of perdition. Jesus said these words concerning the eleven disciples and Judas Iscariot,

> *Jesus answered them, **Have not I chosen you twelve, and one of you is a devil?** He spake of Judas Iscariot the son of Simon: for he it was that should betray Him, being one of the twelve (John 6:70-71 - Emphasis added).*

> *And when He had dipped the sop, He gave it to Judas*

> *Iscariot, the son of Simon. And after the sop **Satan entered into him*** (John 13:26b, 27a - Emphasis added).

> *...those that thou gavest Me I have kept, and **none of them is lost**, but **the son of perdition***; *that the Scripture might be fulfilled* (John 17:12 - Emphasis added).

From this we see that after Satan had entered Judas, Jesus called him the *"son of perdition"* (John 17:12). Judas was a type of the future *"man of sin."* When Satan indwells this future *"man of sin,"* he will become the *"son of perdition"* (2 Thess. 2:3).

To further illustrate the differences between the false prince and the son of perdition, better known as the Antichrist, look at our chart illustrating the symphonic view on the subject. There are many staffs we missed in this small section of the score. Have fun finding them on your own. Now that is Bible study!

The Symphonic View of the Coming Antichrist

FP the man	Claims to be God	Is killed	Raised again	Son of perdition	Reigns 42-months
2Thess 2:3	Ezek 28:2	Ezek28:8-10	Rev 17:8	2 Thess 2:3	Rev 13:5
Job 41:1	Isa 14:14	Isaiah 14:15	Rev 17:11	2 Thess 2:8	Rev 17:12
Rev 13:1	Dan 11:31	Rev 17:8	2Thess2:11	Dan 8:23	Rev 12:6
	Matt 24:15	Rev 17:11	Rev 11:7	Ezek 28:12	Rev 12:14
	2 Thess 2:4				Rev 14:7

False prince - the man

He has many names throughout Scripture: *"Prince of Tyrus"* (Ezek. 28:2), *"the Assyrian"* (Isa. 14:25, Micah 5:5), *"vile person"* (Dan. 11:21), *"the prince that shall come"* (Dan. 9:26), *"that man of sin"* (2 Thess. 2:3) *"beast that rises out of the sea"* (Rev. 13:1).

Antichrist - the man indwelt by Satan

Once indwelt by Satan, he has different names: *"king of Tyrus"* (Ezek. 28:12), *"the king of Babylon"* (Isa. 14:4), *"the wicked"* (Isa. 14:5), *"little horn"* (Dan. 7:8, 8:9), *"king of fierce countenance"* (Dan. 8:23), *"And the king...shall exalt himself, and magnify himself above every god"* (Dan. 11:36), *"the son of perdition"* (2 Thess. 2:3), *"that Wicked"* (2 Thess. 2:8), *"antichrist"* (1 John 2:18, 2 John 1:7), *"the beast that ascendeth out of the bottomless pit"* (Rev. 11:7) and *"the beast that was, and is not, and shall ascend out of the bottomless pit, and go into perdition... and yet is"* (Rev. 17:8).

The Unholy Trio

Revelation 16:13 names the false trio as: *"the dragon," "the beast,"* and *"the false prophet."* We like to call them the "unholy trio" because Satan's house is divided, unlike the triune Godhead of the Father, Son and Holy Spirit. The unholy trio each has their own role to play in the end times. Satan's counterfeit system is always copying God and is a mirror image of what God docs.

The false prince will pose as and copy Jesus Christ, the Messiah the Prince, during the first half of the Tribulation. The Antichrist as false king over the ten kings of the earth is the "mirror image" of Jesus Christ as the KING OF KINGS AND LORD OF LORDS over everything.

The Dragon

The dragon is *"that old serpent, called the Devil, and Satan, which deceiveth the whole world"* (Rev. 12:9. Also see Rev. 20:2). The great restrainer is preventing Satan from walking on the earth like he did with Jesus. However, that does not limit Satan's ability to influence the principalities of the air and powers on earth. The dragon (Satan) while in heaven gives power to the false prince on earth during the first three and one half years of the Tribulation period. Once Satan is cast from heaven *"to the sides of the pit"* (Isa. 14:15), he recovers the soul of that man of sin, the false prince who was killed, and together they return to the body back on the surface. The false prince is that man Satan indwells and he becomes the Antichrist when it appears that Satan raises the false prince from the dead.

The False Prophet - Beast from the Earth
Revelation 13 has this to say,

> *And I beheld another beast coming up out of the earth; and he had two horns like a lamb, and he spake as a dragon. And he exerciseth all the power of the first beast before him, and causeth the earth and them which dwell therein to worship the first beast, whose deadly wound was healed. And he doeth great wonders, so that he maketh fire come down from heaven on the earth in the sight of men, And deceiveth them that dwell on the earth by the means of those miracles which he had power to do in the sight of the beast; saying to them that dwell on the earth, that they should make an image to the beast, which had the wound by a sword, and did live. And he had power to give life unto the image of the beast, that the image of the beast should both speak, and cause that as many as would not worship the image of the beast should be killed* (Rev. 13:11-15).

The false prophet is the beast that rises out of the earth and is able to perform miracles on behalf of the false prince/Antichrist. The false prophet has two horns like a lamb. We think this means he will be a so-called prominent religious leader. He claims he is a godly man, but he speaks like the dragon. By his fruit we will know he is not a Christ follower. He has an image of the Antichrist made and then forces everyone to worship that image. He causes the image to be able to speak. Anyone who refuses to worship this image is killed (Rev. 13:15). The false prophet will cause all men to take a mark in the right hand or in the forehead and worship the beast or his image in order to buy or sell. We will go into more detail about the "mark of the beast" later.

*If there arise among you **a prophet, or a dreamer of dreams**, and giveth thee a sign or a wonder, And the sign or the wonder come to pass, whereof he spake unto thee, **saying**, Let us go after other gods, which thou hast not known, and let us serve them; **Thou shalt not hearken unto the words of that prophet, or that dreamer of dreams: for the LORD your God proveth you,** to know whether ye love the LORD your God with all your heart and with all your soul. Ye shall walk after the LORD your God, and fear Him, and keep His commandments, and obey His voice, and ye shall serve Him, and cleave unto Him. And that prophet, or that dreamer of dreams, shall be put to death; because he hath spoken to turn you away from the LORD your God...* (Deut. 13:1-5 - Emphasis added).

The Antichrist

The Antichrist is so often confused with the false prince, so be careful when reading Scripture and look for the differences between them. Please read all of Ezekiel 28 for a full understanding of the difference between the false prince and the Antichrist. The prince of Tyrus is a type of the false prince and the king of Tyrus is a type of the Antichrist.

Ezekiel 28:3 says that this false prince is wiser than Daniel is and that there is no secret that can be hidden from him. The false prince gets so prideful over something as petty as wealth, coupled with his seemingly supernatural ability to know secrets that he starts to think of himself as being God. This infers that the dragon gives him some help along the way. Then God mocks him as he is killed. *"Wilt thou yet say before him that slayeth thee, 'I am God?' But thou shalt be a man, and no God, in the hand of him that slayeth thee"* (Ezek. 28:9).

After these verses, the king of Tyrus is spoken of. The king of Tyrus is clearly a type of the Antichrist; the false prince indwelt by Satan. It says Satan was in the Garden of Eden, he was perfect in his creation until iniquity was found in him and *"thou art the anointed cherub that covereth"* (Ezek. 28:12-15). *"...thou hast sinned: therefore I will cast thee as profane out of the mountain of God"* (Ezek. 28:16). As we write this book, Satan is presently being restrained in heaven (John 16:11). Satan will be cast out of heaven as stated in Revelation 12 and this will be just before mid-Trib.

The Rise of the Antichrist

1290 days before the end of the Tribulation period (Dan. 12:11) the false prince's army places a statue by force in the temple (Dan. 11:31). This is when the armies encompass Jerusalem (Luke 21:20). Isaiah goes on to explain in detail all the abominations that the false prince performs, as well as the Antichrist, in Isaiah 44:6-20. After the abominations begin to happen, the false prince starts lifting himself up in his own mind to think he is God. This is the abomination that will lead up to the death of the false prince. After the false prince dies he is not buried and his soul is thrown into the bottomless pit (Ezek. 28:8). Satan loses the war in heaven and is cast down from heaven into the earth (Rev. 12:9). Furious, he goes straight to the bottomless pit and collects the soul of the false prince from the pit (Isa. 14:19). When the false prince is raised from the dead, he is now indwelt by Satan and becomes the Antichrist (Rev. 13:3 and 17:8). Because Christ rose on the third day, the Antichrist will probably also be raised on the third day to complete the mirror image of Jesus as *"the Prince of Life, whom God hath raised from the dead"* (Acts 3:15).

> *And when they* [the Two Witnesses] *shall have finished their testimony,* **the beast that ascendeth out of the bottomless pit** *shall make war against them, and shall overcome them, and kill them* (Rev. 11:7 - Emphasis added).

Please notice that the false prince is called the beast that rises *"out of the sea"* (Rev. 13:1), while the Antichrist is called the beast that rises *"out of the bottomless pit"* (Rev. 11:7, 17:8).

When is the Antichrist Revealed?

Many Bible scholars believe that the Antichrist comes before the Tribulation period begins primarily because of their belief that all seven years are the wrath of God.[20] These same people are not seeing the delineation of the false prince becoming the Antichrist years later. It is the false prince that rides the white horse and comes to conquer during the first seal (Rev. 6:2). However, in the beginning of the Tribulation period the false prince comes masquerading as a great leader promising peace and safety. When he decides to turn on Israel his armies are already inside the city of Jerusalem. Israel finally recognizes who he is and flees into the wilderness. If the Antichrist is truly revealed at the beginning of the Tribulation period, why doesn't Israel flee to the wilderness right then, and not wait until the middle of the Tribulation?

Here is where most people get confused. They believe the *"man of sin"* (2 Thess. 2:3) is the Antichrist. However, Satan does not indwell him at the beginning of the Tribulation period. Satan indwells the *"man of sin"* in the middle of the Tribulation, after being cast out of heaven (Rev. 12:3-9). When the body of the *"man of sin"* is brought back from the dead, Satan indwells him at that time (Rev. 13:3-5). Then that *"man of sin"* is called the *"son of perdition"* or better known as the Antichrist.

The Antichrist starts by killing the Two Witnesses, then goes into the temple and proclaims himself to be God above all others. This is known as the *"consummation"* of abominations (Dan. 9:27). This very act is the revealing of the *"son of perdition"* (2 Thess. 2:3). Why do many believe this man is revealed before or in the beginning of the Tribulation? It is simple; he must be because the church must be suddenly raptured before the Tribulation, according to pre-Trib theorists.

We do not want to get in-depth into this subject here because we do so later in this book, but what does this Scripture mean?

> *Let no man deceive you by any means: for that day shall not come, **except there come a falling away first**, and that man of sin be revealed, the son of perdition* (2 Thess. 2:3 - Emphasis added).

The context of this Scripture is the coming of our Lord Jesus Christ and our being gathered to Him. This Scripture says that the Gathering is not until after the *"son of perdition,"* the Antichrist, is revealed.

What does it mean to reveal him? *"And now ye know what withholdeth that he might be revealed in his time"* (2 Thess. 2:6). This verse speaks of the great restrainer. Theologians like Hal Lindsey teach that it is the Holy Spirit indwelling individual believers and all these believers must be removed from the earth before the Antichrist can be revealed.[21] Some believe that it is the Holy Spirit that holds back the Antichrist. Others think it is the Archangel Michael and his angels that cast Satan out of heaven in Revelation 12. The point here is that the Antichrist is revealed when he commits *"the abomination of desolation, spoken of by Daniel the prophet"* (Matt. 24:15). Matthew 24:16 and Mark 13:14 go on to say; then those in Judea should flee into the mountains. In Revelation 12, the woman, Israel, flees to the wilderness where she is protected from the Antichrist for a period of 1260 days or *"a time, and times, and half a time"* (Rev. 12:14).

The question is, which prophecy of Daniel's was Christ referring to in Matthew 24:15; Daniel 8:11, 9:27, 11:31, 11:36 or 12:11? Many theologians believe Christ must have been referring to Daniel 9:27.

The prophecy in Daniel 11:22-35 was partially fulfilled as a type in about 168-170 BC. Antiochus IV plundered the Temple in Jerusalem and he placed an abomination in the Temple, but he did not *"destroy the city and the sanctuary"* (Dan. 9:26).

"And from the time that the daily sacrifice shall be taken away, and the abomination that maketh desolate set up, there shall be a thousand two hundred and ninety days" (Dan. 12:11). Daniel 12:11 is a Scriptural witness that tells us **when** *"the overspreading of abominations"* of Daniel 9:27 begins. Israel is promised in Daniel 9:27 and many other Scriptures that the man who confirms the covenant, likely allowing Israel to rebuild the temple, is the man who commits the abominations that cause desolation in that same temple. Yet, what we find amazing is that Israel does not recognize him until he consummates *"the abomination"* that causes desolation (Dan. 9:27, Matt. 24:15, Mark 13:14). He stands in the temple and proclaims himself God above all others (2 Thess. 2:4). This fact is what makes us think that most in Israel may believe this man is the coming messiah they have been waiting for.

Do not be so sure you will be able to recognize this man at first. What if this false prince comes on the scene real smooth and gentle? What if he comes in peace posing as a great and holy man of God? What if he is a member of a council who's deciding vote confirms the covenant with Israel? Israel, who believes they are in the end times even now, does not run to the wilderness for protection when the *"man of sin,"* the false prince, appears on the scene. No, they wait until the middle of the Tribulation period, even after the sacrifices are abolished because they still do not recognize that *"man of sin"* until he claims to be God and the false prophet demands their worship (Rev. 13).

It may not be as easy to recognize this man as many Christians would believe. What if there is no peace treaty? Daniel 11:22-35 also suggests that some of Israel do look upon the false prince as a messiah figure and some do not. That does not mean the rest of the world will not see him as a savior or messiah of some sort though. The truth probably lies in the middle. Israel may not see the false prince as a messiah at first, but when the false prophet is his witness perhaps many Jews will follow him for a short time, until he desecrates the temple. Certainly after the false prince returns from the dead, claims he is God above all others, and demands their worship, about one third of Israel recognizes who he really is. This group becomes the woman of Revelation 12 who flees to the wilderness and is protected for 1260 days during the last three and one half years of the Tribulation period.

Then, just when all this is going on and the Antichrist's armies encompass Jerusalem, Jesus appears in the air with all the saints who have just received their new Heavenly Bodies. Can you imagine how Israel will feel at that moment, knowing that they pierced their own Messiah all those years ago and have profaned His name all these years? Just imagine the horror they must experience (Ezek. 7:10-19).

> *They shall also gird themselves with sackcloth, and horror shall cover them; and shame shall be upon all faces, and baldness upon all their heads* (Ezek. 7:18).

While he is the false prince, Israel does not recognize that this is the man they were warned about by the Prophets. Although, they know something is wrong with him when the false prince begins to desecrate all the stations of the temple in Isaiah 44:15-20 and takes away the daily sacrifices in the temple (Dan. 8:11-13, 9:27, 11:31, 12:11). Only when he becomes the Antichrist that is raised from the dead is it that they recognize him as the one spoken of by Daniel.

They fear him because no one can make war against him; they think he is immortal. When he comes back to life, he goes into the Holy of Holies and claims to be God in Jerusalem; this is *"the consummation"* of abominations that cause desolation (Dan. 9:27).

According to pre-Trib chronological thinking, you may have already noticed that the beast comes out of the bottomless pit in Revelation 11 before Satan is cast out of heaven in Revelation 12. Let us end the confusion.

How long do the Two Witnesses have? They have 1260 days from the beginning of the Tribulation period to the middle. Satan is cast down from heaven and descends to the *"bottomless pit"* to collect the *"man of sin's"* soul. They ascend to the surface again and restore the body that died from a fatal wound just prior to the middle of the Tribulation period. Revelation 12:6 and 12:14 says that the woman is protected from the Satan-indwelt-Antichrist for 1260 days, until the culmination of the Tribulation period. Do you understand why the Book of Revelation is not in chronological order? It keeps repeating the story over and over again from different viewpoints. This example was from the viewpoint of the Two Witnesses. Then it is from the viewpoint of the woman, then Satan being cast down from heaven into the earth; but all three of these are talking about the same event. Furthermore, after the false prince is raised from the dead, *"power was given unto him* [the Antichrist] *to continue forty and two months"* (Rev. 13:5).

While we are on the subject of chronology, let us look at Revelation 11:2,

> But the court which is without the temple leave out, and measure it not [first half of the Trib]; for it is given unto the Gentiles: and the holy city shall they tread under foot forty two months [second half of the Trib].

This verse covers both halves of the Tribulation period. The first half of the Tribulation period is when temple worship is taking place. This continues until the false prince - Antichrist declares himself to be God in the temple mid-Trib. Then the Gentiles tread on the holy city in the second half of the Tribulation period until times of the Gentile Nations are fulfilled at the battle of Armageddon (Luke 21:24).

Satan will be cast down from heaven just prior to mid-Trib and *"knows he has but a short time"* (Rev. 12:12). He is very busy. The man of sin comes back to life, and he becomes the *"son of perdition,"* the Antichrist. He kills the Two Witnesses, Elijah and Moses. He tries to devour the Bride of Christ before it can be born into the Heavenly Kingdom, before it can be Gathered to Christ out from among the four winds that are striving on the earth. The Antichrist consummates the abominations that cause desolation by revealing himself to Israel and the world by saying, "I am God" in the temple. Now Israel finally sees the man for whom he is and recognizes that this is the man they were warned about. The Antichrist will already have armies surrounding Jerusalem because the false prince brought them there before his death. *"Then let them that which be in Judaea flee into the mountains"* (Matt. 24:16). We need to clarify why Jesus said that only those in Judea should flee as opposed to all of Israel should flee. The reason is that the Antichrist's armies do not surround those in Judea. Most of those who live in Jerusalem are not able to escape.

> *And it shall come to pass, that in all the land, saith the Lord, two parts therein shall be cut off and die; but the third shall be left therein. And I will bring the third part through the fire, and will refine them as silver is refined, and will try them as gold is tried...* (Zech. 13:8-9).

The third part that is refined is the woman of Revelation 12 and they flee into Edom, Moab and Ammon.

Satan is a slow learner though, he did not learn from Pharaoh's mistake. Days later, the dragon pursues Israel into the desert. His armies are like a torrent of water but the earth swallows them up (Rev. 12:13-16), like the Red Sea swallowed up Pharaoh's army.

Chapter 6

The New World Government

The Rise of the Antichrist over Ten Regions on Earth

When the false prince is killed, he already has the world divided into ten kingdoms. It will be a New World government comprised of ten world regions. However, these regions have not yet fully given their power and authority over to the false prince when he is killed. The kingdoms of the earth still have their doubts about this man before he is killed. When the false prince comes back from the dead as the Antichrist, everyone agrees out of fear saying, *"who is able to make war with him?"* (Rev. 13:4) This is when and how the ten kings give the their authority over the ten regions to the Antichrist for 42 months, which is the same as the *"one hour"* in Revelation 17:12.

Breakdown of the Antichrist's rise to power:
- (Rev. 12:3) The dragon has the seven heads and seven crowns on his heads in heaven. This shows that Satan has legal authority over the earth. Notice that the dragon also has the ten horns with no crowns on his horns. This is the false prince rising to power. Revelation 13:2 tells us that *"the dragon gave him his power, and his seat, and great authority."* This is an exact description symphonically of the feet and toes of the fifth kingdom of the statue dream in Daniel 2:41 and the beginning of the dreadful and terrible beast with ten horns in Daniel 7:7 and 7:23-24. The ten toes and the ten horns are the ten kings who have no kingdoms as of yet (Rev. 17:12).
- (Rev. 13:1-5) When Satan has indwelt the false prince to become the Antichrist he still has the seven heads, but now Satan has no crowns on his heads. The ten horns or kings now have the crowns, not Satan. Satan had the dominion over the whole earth because he offered it to Jesus when he tempted Christ on the exceeding high mountain (Matt. 4:8-10, Luke 4:5-8). Now these crowns are on fleshly kings and are nothing like the crowns Satan had before

he was cast out of heaven. These earthly kings only have the color of Law without any real lasting authority of God. All the nations of earth yield their sovereignty, power, and authority unto the ten kings under the authority of the Antichrist *"until the words of God shall be fulfilled"* (Rev. 17:17).

- (Rev. 11:15, 12:10) Jesus Christ, the legal King, receives the power and authority over the kingdoms of this world that Satan once had and abused.

- (Rev. 17:12) This Scripture confirms that the ten horns are indeed kings, which are given power over the ten regions or kingdoms for one hour, the same 42 months that the Antichrist reigns over the entire earth. Note: These are not likely ten countries in the European Union. They are more likely ten regions dividing the entire earth. Perhaps, something like this: Regions: 1. North America, 2. South America, 3. East Asia, 4.West Asia, 5. Indonesia and so on.

King's Dream and Daniel's Visions

So many expositors think the Antichrist's dominion will come out of Daniel's fourth kingdom of king Nebuchadnezzar's statue dream. They refer to this kingdom as the revived Roman Empire. This belief is based upon the premise that Daniel's visions in Chapter 7 are synonymous with the king's dream in Daniel 2, meaning the statue dream is explained by the vision of the four beasts. This view is so prevalent that the 2002 King James Version Study Bible depicts a chart with Daniel's statue of kingdoms and compares it to the four beasts of the end times. Theologians say that the vision of the four beasts is synonymous with kingdoms of past human history. We believe this is erroneous thinking. One of the reasons this is erroneous is that the king's statue of Daniel 2 has seven kingdoms and there are only four beasts in Daniel 7.

Something else we noticed in contrast between the statue dream and the vision of the four beasts is that the statue's kingdoms started with Babylon approximately five hundred years before Christ. King Nebuchadnezzar started the beginning of *"the times of the Gentiles"* (Luke 21:24) with the first captivity of Jerusalem. The dream of the statue in Daniel 2 covers the entire span of *"the times of the Gentiles"* or perhaps better understood as the domination of the Gentile

Nations. However, the vision of the four beasts in Daniel 7 is about the final years of the times of the Gentile Nations. The vision of the four beasts does not span thousands of years like so many believe.

Let us take a fresh look at the dream and controversial visions in the Book of Daniel. There are three sets of Scriptures describing them. The king's dream of the statue of kingdoms is found in Daniel 2:31-45. Secondly, the vision concerning the four beasts in Daniel 7:1-27. The vision of the dreadful and terrible beast in Daniel 7 also connects the little horn to the vision in Daniel 8. First, let us look at the king's dream.

The King's Dream with Daniel's Interpretation

The statue dream that the king had has a total of seven kingdoms that represent *"the Times of the Gentiles"* from Babylon to when Christ's Kingdom is set up on earth. Technically *"the times of the Gentiles"* (Luke 21:24) will end with Christ's Triumphant Entry into Jerusalem during the battle of Armageddon.

1) **Head of Gold:** The first kingdom was Babylon. King Nebuchadnezzar was said by Daniel to be *"this head of gold"* (Dan. 2:38).

2) **Chest and Arms of Silver:** According to the king's dream, the second kingdom is the Medo-Persian kingdom in past history. The angel Gabriel interprets Daniel's vision in Daniel 8:20 as the ram with two horns that are the kings of both Media and Persia. The longer of the two horns and the one that came up last represents Persia, which was the predominant force.

3) **Belly and Thighs of Bronze:** The third kingdom is Greece. The rough goat of Daniel 8:21 is Greece and the horn between his eyes is Alexander the Great because history shows that he conquered the Medo-Persia Kingdoms.

4) **Legs of Iron:** This fourth kingdom is obviously the Roman Empire as proven by history. This kingdom had dominion over Jerusalem during Jesus Christ's ministry here on earth and continued on until the feet and toes of clay came in to existence.

5) **Feet and Toes of Clay Mixed with Iron:** This is the fifth kingdom and is the present kingdom. Satan's mirror image of God's plan brought about the United Nations as a type of the one-world government that is to come. This is the kingdom in which the false prince rises to power. The false prince is a mere man rising to power under demonic influence of Satan in heaven. *"And I stood upon the sand of the sea, and saw a beast rise up out of the sea...and the dragon gave him his power, and his seat, and great authority"* (Rev. 13:1-2). This kingdom will be divided into ten pieces. This is describing the feet and the toes of the fifth kingdom of the king's statue dream in Daniel 2 and the vision of the fourth beast in Daniel 7:7 and 7:12, before the little horn subdues the dominion of the three other kings reigning at the same time. The first three beasts of Daniel 7 are present in this fifth kingdom and last until mid-Trib (Rev. 13:2).

6) **Toes of the Feet - Part Iron and Part Clay:** This sixth kingdom begins mid-Trib when Satan is cast down from heaven and indwells the false prince after his death. This false prince then becomes the Antichrist. Symphonically this is when the ten kings receive their power to reign for one hour (Rev. 17:12), the same 42 months that the Antichrist reigns on earth (Rev. 13:5). The Antichrist is the *"little horn"* of the dreadful and terrible beast with ten horns in Daniel 7:8.

7) **Christ's Kingdom:** In the end of the days of the ten kings under the Antichrist, God in Heaven sets up the seventh kingdom that lasts forever. He will break into pieces the statue representing the Gentile kingdoms of the earth at His Triumphal Return at the end of the Tribulation period. *"Then was the iron, the clay, the brass, the silver, and the gold, **broken to pieces together**..."* (Dan. 2:35 - Emphasis added). *"...and the Kingdom shall not be left to other people, but it shall break in pieces and consume all these kingdoms, and it shall stand for ever"* (Dan. 2:44). This is when Christ takes physical possession of the earth and sets up His Earthly Kingdom for one thousand years.

The Four Beasts of Daniel 7;
Not the Same as the King's Dream!

When the Antichrist comes to power, all four beasts are present on the earth at the same time (Dan. 7:7, 7:12, Rev. 13:2), unlike the statue of the king's dream where one kingdom replaces the previous. The dreadful and terrible beast with ten horns could not be the "Revived Roman Empire" as it does not have the attributes of the Roman Empire, and the fourth beast of Daniel 7 divides the entire earth into ten regions. The Roman Empire never came close to doing that.

Moreover, Daniel does not link the dream of the statue with the vision of the four beasts, so why do so many people try to do so? Unlike *"the ram"* and *"the goat"* that are defined in Daniel 8, the four beasts of Daniel 7 are not linked to specific governments or kingdoms in past history.

The third kingdom in Nebuchadnezzar's dream was Greece. After Alexander the Great died, his kingdom was divided into four kingdoms (Dan. 8:21-22). Because Alexander's kingdom was divided into four and there are four heads on the third beast, we see why many try to link the leopard beast in Daniel 7 to the third kingdom of the statue dream in Daniel 2. We think this is a coincidence and not proof that the third beast is the same as the third kingdom from Nebuchadnezzar's dream. Even if the third beast in Daniel 7 was Greece, what part of the fourth beast would lead someone to think it must be the revived Roman Empire? The four beasts have nothing to do with ancient kingdoms, but represent political forms of governments that exist now.

The relationship of the four beasts in Daniel 7 and the kingdoms of the king's statue dream in Daniel 2 are a witness to one another that the Antichrist's dominion comes chronologically before Christ's Kingdom. We believe that the three beasts will have been completely established and the fourth is on the brink of having world dominion when Christ returns for His Bride.

Let us look at the four beasts. We are speculating as to what each beast represents based upon our research and current political scenarios.

Lion with Wings of an Eagle: The lion represents England or the United Kingdom. Her wings as an eagle represents the United States. We are taken from the UK and the United States are made to stand without England. So in looking at earth's history, we find the lion to be well represented by the Royal Lion of England. It has been said that the sun never set on the Lion's empire.

Bear: The bear represents Russia in the end of days. This beast will consume much flesh. It cannot be denied that when Russia became the Soviet Union, Stalin became a mass murderer and consumed much flesh.

Leopard with Wings of a Fowl: The leopard represents a form of government that as of yet does not exist or only exists now in an immature form. The World Court and the World Banking systems are part of what we think may be the beginnings of the Leopard government. This government will be divided into four heads, and dominion is given to the leopard. We as authors are not sure what the wings represent yet. The leopard is unknown currently. Who or what is the leopard? The leopard is the next government in our near future. A leopard has many spots. Perhaps this means many nations comprise the totality of the leopard, but ultimately the leopard will have four heads. The European Union has the heads of every nation that is a member, yet all those nations elect one head. The leopard could evolve out of the European Union, but it clearly must have four heads worldwide. The European Union of today does not exactly fit the prophecy concerning the four heads, however it may be the beginning of the four heads politically, economically, religiously and judicially.

There was talk about a North American Union comprised of Canada, the United States, and Mexico. If the world joined nations in small groups like this, we could have four heads of government, which could later become ten with the next beast. Like the "Euro" of today, each of the nations keeps their individual sovereignty, but shares a common currency.

Economic chaos would be necessary for this third beast to come about. The United States dollar would have to plummet in value. Right now the dollar is propped up too high and is not backed by the gold standard. Economists are talking about the potential collapse of the dollar and if it does collapse, a logical solution would be a new currency backed by gold and silver. If all the nations of the world would go on a system that is backed by the gold and silver standard, then in theory, all nations would be on an even playing field economically. This could be very enticing and a major motivation if some of the world economies collapse.

This leopard government could be an economic alliance of countries. The leopard precedes the next dominion, where the whole world is divided into 10 regions prior to the false prince becoming the Antichrist. We do know that the Antichrist will rule over a one-world government comprised of ten kingdoms or regions. We know the Antichrist will have economic control over people through his mark system. However, the leopard beast is not the ten-region government that will exist when the false prince returns from the dead. So the third beast does not yet exist in its entirety or is unrecognizable at this time.

Dreadful and Terrible Beast with Ten Horns: The fourth beast is diverse from the rest of the beasts. It will divide the world into ten regions. The false prince will lead this divided kingdom. The fourth beast subdues three of the horns as it comes to power (Dan. 7:24). This means that the *"little horn"* of the dreadful and terrible beast assumes the dominion of the three beasts that coexist with it in Daniel 7. However, the nations do not totally give up their sovereignty and power to the fourth beast until the false prince is killed and comes back to life. Then the entire world fears him; so much so, that they give their sovereignty to him and his ten kings. When Satan raises the false prince from the dead, the entire world is amazed and fears this Antichrist. *"Who is like unto the beast? Who is able to make war with him"* (Rev. 13:4)? This is when the world submits to him and his will that they must worship the Antichrist. All the nations through the ten kings will then give power and authority to this *"little horn"* (Dan. 7:8) of the terrible beast. The little horn of the fourth beast persecutes the saints *"until the Ancient of days came, and the judgment was given to the saints of the Most High; and the time came that the saints possessed the Kingdom"* (Dan. 7:22). The fourth beast will *"wear out the saints of the Most High...until a time, times and dividing of time"* (Dan. 7:25), mid-Trib.

What Do We Know About the Fourth Beast?

Let us look at Daniel 7:21-25:

- *"...and shall devour the whole earth, and shall tread it down, and break it to pieces"* (Dan. 7:23). Rome was far from conquering the entire known world. The fourth beast could not be the revived Roman Empire because the fourth beast divides the earth into ten regions. Daniel 7:11-12 tells us that when the fourth beast is destroyed, the three other beasts had their dominion taken away, but their lives were prolonged for a season and time. The fourth beast initially co-exists with the other three beasts of Daniel 7 and it is clearly an end-time kingdom.

- The fourth beast shall be diverse from all the beasts that were previous to it. Rome does not qualify. Their form of government had roots from Greece and their culture too. We believe that the diversity of the fourth beast will be the beginning of acceptance of a worldwide leader, as indicated by the ten horns.

- The fourth beast will wear out the saints of the Most High until a time, times and dividing of time (mid-Trib).

- The little horn of the fourth beast, also known as the Antichrist, persecutes the saints until the Ancient of days comes to give judgment in favor of the saints. That means that the Gathering of the Bride to Christ cannot happen until the Antichrist is revealed.

Let us look at Revelation 13,

> *And I stood upon the sand of the sea, and saw a beast rise out of the sea* [false prince], *having seven heads and ten horns* [fourth beast], *and upon his horns ten crowns* [crowns upon ten kings], *and upon his heads the names of blasphemy. And the beast which I saw* [fourth beast of Daniel 7] *was like unto a leopard...* (Rev. 13:1-2).

There is nothing here saying it is the revived Roman Empire. Then the verse goes on to explain that this leopard beast has feet like a bear, and a mouth like a lion. This is where we get the idea that all four beasts of Daniel 7 are present in the Tribulation period. The leopard is Daniel's third beast true, but Daniel's fourth beast is still the leopard with attributes of the other two beasts as well (Rev. 13:2). The fourth beast is of the three that precede it. Our Scriptural witness to this premise is found in Revelation 17:10-13, 17. These ten kings give their kingdom unto the beast, until the words of God shall be fulfilled.

The seventh king rises to Power as the false prince and the eighth king as the Antichrist in Revelation 17

Revelation 17 has this to say about this false prince and the Satan-indwelt-Antichrist,

> ***The beast that thou sawest was, and is not; and shall ascend out of the bottomless pit, and go into perdition:*** *and they that dwell on the earth shall wonder, whose names were not written in the Book of Life from the foundation of the world,* ***when they behold the beast that was, and is not, and yet is*** (Rev. 17:8 - Emphasis added).

> *And there are seven kings: five are fallen, and one is, and the other is not yet come; and when he cometh, he must continue a short space* (Rev. 17:10).

The five kings that have fallen are all Gentile kingdoms that have put Israel into servitude: Egypt, Assyria, Babylonia, Medo-Persian, and Alexander the Great's Greece. The Roman Empire was in power when John wrote *"and one is"* (Rev. 17:10). The false prince represents the seventh kingdom that *"is not yet come."* After the death of the false prince, the Antichrist becomes the eighth king. *"And the beast that was, and is not, even he is the eighth,* ***and is of the seven,*** *and goeth into perdition"* (Rev. 17:11 - Emphasis added). His kingdom is not the revived Roman Empire. It is a composite of all the seven kings or seven kingdoms, all Gentile Nations.

Read Revelation 17:10, *"...when he cometh, he must continue a short space."* The false prince dies and when he continues he is the Antichrist (Rev. 13:3). When he continues for a short space, he is given power to reign for *"forty and two months"* (Rev. 13:5). When he is the seventh king he is killed as a mere man (Ezek. 28:1-10) and he continues to become the eighth king (Rev. 17:10) when *"his deadly wound was healed"* (Rev. 13:3). 42 months later he goes into perdition (Rev. 19:20).

Many people do not realize Satan is in heaven right now and has seven heads and seven crowns on his heads (Rev. 12:3). These crowns on Satan's heads are the kingdoms of this world. Christ receives legal dominion over these kingdoms when the sealed book in Heaven is opened and He takes these crowns away from Satan at the sounding of the seventh trumpet. *"The kingdoms of this world are become the kingdoms of our LORD, and of His Christ; and He shall reign for ever and ever"* (Rev. 11:15). However, it is not until Christ returns to the earth three and one half years later as *"KING OF KINGS, AND LORD OF LORDS"* that He exercises His authority on earth by taking physical possession over those earthly kingdoms (Rev. 19).

What is the "Mark of the Beast"?

We cannot say it better than the Bible:

> *And he had power to give life unto the image of the beast, that the image of the beast should both speak, and cause that as many as would not worship the image of the beast should be killed. And he causeth all, both small and great, rich and poor, free and bond, to receive a mark in their right hand or in their foreheads: And that no man might buy or sell, save he that had the mark, or the name of the beast, or the number of his name. Here is wisdom. Let him that hath understanding count the number of the beast: for it is the number of man; and his number six hundred threescore and six* [666] (Rev. 13:15-18).

The beast is known by many names. He is known as the Antichrist, false-christ, the little horn of the dreadful and terrible beast with ten horns and many others. He believes that he is God and he attempts to be the antithesis of God, doing everything Christ did, but in a demented way. As Christ is the type, the Satan-indwelt-Antichrist is the counterfeit type or mirror image. God created Lucifer as an angel of light until iniquity was found in him (Ezek. 28:15). Imagine him being in the presence of the God, but that is not good enough for him. Satan had to try to be God. Now called Satan or the dragon, the devil is the father of all lies.

The mark of the beast is a prime example of how Satan attempts to be like God. The Holy Spirit seals all Christians. Just prior to the Gathering, God seals the 144,000 from the twelve tribes of Israel in their foreheads with His Name. The Antichrist seals his followers with the name of the beast, the number of his name or with his mark on the right hand or forehead. The point is that you will be sealed by whomever you give your allegiance. Your eternal destination is determined by that allegiance, to God's Paradise or to Satan's eternal punishment.

What we think the mark is and is not, and what it does:
- It is not a bar code.
- It will probably be a computer chip implanted under the skin with a visible mark as well. In some parts of the world the mark will be put in or on the forehead and other parts of the world the mark will be put in or on the right hand. It will cause a skin rash or irritation that will not heal, called a grievous wound, probably caused by lithium in the chips.
- It renders cash currency obsolete.
- It inhibits the underground economy. Without cash who can sell drugs?
- It will protect one from identity theft.
- It will severely limit the free movement of terrorists and their funds. No one will be able to fly commercially without the mark.
- Eliminates the need for credit cards or picture ID's.
- The world government will be able to track anyone who has the mark at all times, wherever they may be.
- The world computer monitors spending habits and every transaction one makes. No one may buy or sell anything without it.
- No one will be able to work without it.
- The chip only works while in living flesh.
- After the Antichrist rises to power, one must deny Christ and worship the beast to receive it.
- One may not enter the kingdom of Heaven if one has the mark.

- It will be said that one will receive protection by receiving the mark, but it is a lie. One will receive horrible suffering because of the mark, as well as spiritual death.

A version of the mark that could become the standard already exists today. A computer chip not much larger than a grain of rice is being used on pets and people around the globe. The United States Food & Drug Administration has approved the use of this technology in humans.[22] This chip is only being used as an identity tag now and it contains name, address and medical records, but it has far more potential. Remember way back in the seventies when bar code scanners first came out and were being used in grocery stores? We knew then that it was possible for the mark to exist as soon as we heard that it was technologically possible to pass an item under a machine and the machine knew what the item was. Some Christian leaders are still saying that it will be a bar code, but use some common sense. Technology is far beyond a simple bar code.

Even now, there are microchips that run on the bodies electrical energy and the interactive part of the chip will shut down when the flesh dies. The chip will also be burned with hard data for identifying bodies after death. We believe that the technology is just around the corner for a radio-frequency identification (RFID) chip that can be tracked, so the whereabouts of the chip can be monitored at all times. Talk about George Orwell's *1984; Big Brother is Watching.*

What do we mean by interactive RFID chips? An interactive chip is one that communicates with other computer devices. For example, let us go to the grocery store and make a purchase. You would pass your hand under this new scanning device and the chip would tell the device what your identification number is and that it is in living flesh, making it impossible to steal your identity. You would be given a choice to put this on credit or debit. This scanning device is linked to the world computer banking system, which handles every transaction in the world, all from one location via the Internet. Parts of this technology already exist. Several super computers around the world are capable of monitoring every transaction in real time. Wikipedia claims, "As of June 2013, China's Tianhe-2 supercomputer is the fastest in the world at 33.86 petaFLOPS."[23] A computer this fast is capable of computing thousand of pieces of information on every human being on the planet in a single second. The Internet is full of claims that the European Union has super computer named "the Beast". While it is great stuff for a book like this, that story seems to be a hoax.[24] With that being said, this technology could be the next evolutionary step where a chip in your hand works much like a credit card does today, however it is much safer to use and much less hassle. The chip cannot be lost or stolen and no picture ID or electronic signature is required. A World Bank will absolutely know it is you making the purchase. There are already pre-Tribulationists that believe the mark is a RFID chip.[25]

Think about this technology for one moment. It makes so much sense to have this in place. Identity theft is on the rise. Every time we use our credit cards or write a check, even purchase something on the Internet, we risk having our identity stolen. This microchip technology would virtually eliminate identity theft. It would not even take that much to implement this new technology.

Look how fast checkout counters change. One week they have the old system in place and the next week they have a check out where the consumer does everything, no cashier. So it is not a stretch of the imagination to predict that our entire economic system could change in a very short time. These hand scanners may be along side of the card swiping machines at first, but credit cards will disappear as people switch to the chip.

We believe people will volunteer to have this chip implanted under their skin when the scanners first come out. Take credit cards for example; credit card fraud and identity theft cost credit card companies billions each year. "Don't worry if your card is lost or stolen, we will refund the losses" says the credit card companies. But with the arrival of the new chip technology, the credit card companies will make that guarantee only if one uses the microchip instead of plastic credit cards. The chip allows the credit companies to know with certainty it is you that are making the purchases. In the beginning it will be voluntary to have the mark. When the Antichrist comes to power, it will be required. According to Revelation 13, the false prophet causes this to be established. Clearly the mark exists before the Gathering. There is Scriptural evidence in Revelation 15:2 that it will be. The good news is that Scripture suggests that the Antichrist will only have a few days to kill the Two Witnesses and persecute the

Elect. And this is yet another prophecy that must be fulfilled before Christ comes for His Bride.

Chapter 7

Israel

The covenant, the temple, the abomination of desolation, and the Antichrist are woven into a scenario surrounding the people of Israel in the end times. The nation of Israel plays a pivotal role. Just prior to the Tribulation period, an overwhelming army attacks Israel. God Himself will intervene to save Israel. We believe that after this Gog-Magog war, an exodus of Jews to Israel will occur from all countries around the world. They will seek their homeland, their religion and their temple. In this chapter we will explore past, present and future prophecies concerning God's chosen people and the restoration of Israel as a nation. We will also explore the identity of the Elect, which are both the faithful of Israel and faithful of the True Church.

Ezekiel's Prophecies Concerning Israel

Ezekiel 38 prophesies that when the peaceful and unsuspecting people of Israel are living in *"the land of unwalled villages,"* the enemies of Israel will take notice of it and will come from the north to plunder the land. The former Iranian president Mahmoud Ahmadinejad has repeatedly called for the destruction of Israel. One of the things Mahmoud Ahmadinejad has said is that if Iran were to wage war on Israel that it would make the way for the appearance of the twelfth Imam, the Mahdi. It is the Muslim version of the Second Coming.[26] This sudden attack against Israel could be the Gog-Magog war. The world will probably say this nuclear war is Armageddon, but it is not. Out of the ashes of this short war comes the seven years of the Tribulation period, during which the real battle of Armageddon happens at the end of the seventh year. This Gog-Magog war is yet another prophecy that must be fulfilled before Christ Gathers His Bride in the sky. The mainstream church would like you to believe Christ's return is right at the door. Maybe, what is at the door right now is a false sense of peace in Israel.

When Israel became a nation in 1948, this was the beginning of the fulfillment of Ezekiel 37. There will be further fulfillment of

Ezekiel 37 mid-Trib, when Israel sees the resurrection of the dead at the Gathering to Christ.

> *And ye shall know that I am the LORD,* **when I have opened your graves,** *O My people,* **and have brought you up out of your graves** (Ezek. 37:13 - Emphasis added).

We believe this Scripture is not metaphoric. When Christ comes for His Bride, the graves of all the dead in Christ are emptied. This is when Israel will recognize the true Messiah from the false one claiming to be God. This is when they mourn for Jesus whom they have pierced.

Israel as a present-day country with a government and a flag are not the fulfillment of God's promise to restore the nation. It is just the beginning of the promise. The national flag will be brought down by the Antichrist within the borders of Jerusalem and those trapped in Jerusalem will be brought into captivity for another holocaust starting mid-Trib. Those that flee into the wilderness will escape Satan's wrath. The people of Israel will carry their flag into God's protection for three and one half years. Then with Christ's Triumphal Entry into Jerusalem after Armageddon, Christ and the nation of Israel will return to Jerusalem to establish it as the new capital of the world.

> *And shall put My spirit in you, and ye shall live, and I* **shall place you in your own land**: *then shall ye know that I the LORD have spoken it,* **and performed it,** *saith the LORD* (Ezek. 37:14 - Emphasis added).

The final fulfillment of Ezekiel 37 will be when the Earthly Kingdom is set up after the end of the Tribulation period at the beginning of the Millennium. Please notice that it is God that promises to perform the act of bringing Israel into the land, not some treaty by a country or by a mere man.

What is the Peace Treaty We Keep Hearing About?

It is believed by many in the Christian community that Israel will sign a seven-year peace treaty with the Antichrist, marking the beginning of the seven-year tribulation period.[27] Their source for the seven-year peace treaty comes from Daniel 9:27, *"he shall confirm the covenant with many for one week,"* and "one week" equals seven years. However, it is really the false prince, not the Antichrist, who *"shall confirm the covenant"* (Dan. 9:27). Also, do not count on being able to pinpoint a specific peace treaty to mark the beginning of the Tribulation period.

Christ has already historically confirmed *"the Covenant with many"* (Dan. 9:27) when He came *"to proclaim the acceptable year of the Lord"* (Isa. 61:2, Luke 4:19, 21). Then in the midst of His week He was cut off at the cross, ending God's sanctioned animal sacrificing. Christ is now our Sacrificial Lamb, our Prince and our High Priest. However, Daniel 9:27 is also referring to the *"prince that shall come"* (Dan. 9:26) as a mirror image of *"Messiah the Prince"* (Dan. 9:25). The false prince will also need the false prophet to act as the priestly part of this counterfeit-christ mirror image.

This false prince confirms a covenant. His actual title or position is unknown, although he may actually be a prince. And this covenant allows the false prince to have a military force available to him in Jerusalem. This military force will *"pollute the sanctuary of strength"* 30 days before mid-Tribulation, thereby ending animal sacrifice in the rebuilt temple (Dan. 11:31 and 12:11).

Do not count on being able to point to a significant event that would fulfill one's imagination of some supernatural monster signing a peace treaty with Israel. If a treaty is to be confirmed, it must be confirmed by a mere-mortal-man. In order to fully comprehend the significance of what we just said, we need to scrutinize a few Scriptures. Obviously one is Daniel 9:27 and the others are in 2 Thessalonians 2;

> *And now ye know what withholdeth that he might be revealed in his time* (2 Thess. 2:6).

> *And then shall that Wicked be revealed...* (2 Thess. 2:8).

The great restrainer is what holds back *"that Wicked"* until the time is right for him to be revealed.

As discussed many times in this book, Satan is cast down from heaven mid-Trib. Because Israel does not recognize this man until the middle of the Tribulation period, this means the great restrainer is not removed until mid-Tribulation. The great restrainer is not taken out of the way until it is time for the Antichrist to be revealed (2 Thess. 2:1-12). This is when the abomination of desolation happens. So how could there be a peace treaty signed by "the Antichrist" three and one half years before the false prince is indwelt? It does not fit symphonically.

Many theologians interpret Daniel 9:27 to mean the Antichrist confirms a peace treaty with Israel.[28] And maybe there is a seven-year peace treaty, but our point is, Daniel is not talking about just a peace treaty. Daniel in fact, may not be talking about a peace treaty at all. It is possible the covenant that is mentioned in Daniel 9:27 is a covenant that allows the temple to be rebuilt and animal sacrifice to begin again. It is like a mirror image of God's *"Holy Covenant"* (Dan. 11:28 30) through Jesus Christ, only this one is evil. Furthermore, the premise that the Antichrist would sign such a treaty is a misnomer for the reasons previously described.

Will Israel Rebuild the Temple?

Scoffers have openly laughed in our face with the idea that the temple will be rebuilt on the Temple Mount. Yet prophecy is filled with such a prediction. The people who would deny the possibility simply do not believe the prophecies or do not know about them. Let us examine how far along the temple's reconstruction is underway.

In David Allen Lewis' book, he dedicated a whole chapter to the efforts in rebuilding the temple.[29] Lewis even has a drawing of a survey done showing the actual temple location on the Temple Mount being 100 yards north of the Dome of the Rock.[30] He has laid out all the efforts being done to begin temple construction and re-institute temple sacrifice, as well as breeding a pure red heifer, making garments and temple artifacts.[31] Lewis is adamant that sacrificing of animals will begin during the Tribulation period.[32]

"The 2004 attempt to re-establish the Sanhedrin was an attempt to setup a revived national rabbinical court of Jewish law in Israel which began in October 2004. The organization heading this attempt refers to itself as the nascent Sanhedrin or developing Sanhedrin, and regards itself as a provisional body awaiting integration into the Israeli government as both a supreme court and an upper house of the Knesset, while the Israeli secular press regards it as an illegitimate fundamentalist organization of rabbis. The organization, which is composed of over 70 rabbis (similar to the composition of the original Sanhedrin), claims to enjoy recognition and support from the entire religious Jewish community in Israel, and has stirred debate in both religious and secularist circles."[33]

Many artifacts have been found and recreated, but the one thing that the Jews think they need is the Ark of the Covenant, which contains among many things, the stone tablets of the Ten Commandments written by God. Israel can rebuild the temple without the Ark, but they believe the temple can never be restored to its former glory without it. A few people believe Israel knows where the Ark is and is just waiting for the right time to go get it. It is exciting stuff when you think about it. To find the infamous lost "Ark of the Covenant" reminds one of a Hollywood film with Indiana Jones, *"Raiders of the Lost Ark."* That is the same Ark we are talking about. It is not known if the Ark will ever be found for sure. Revelation 11:19 says that when the Temple in Heaven is opened, the Ark is there. Is this a duplicate Ark? Or is this the Ark Israel carried? If it is, God brought the Ark to Heaven. It is fun to think about.

It is possible that Israel zealously wanting to rebuild the temple will do anything it takes to accomplish this goal. They are not willing to wait for God to completely fulfill His Covenant with Israel in the Millennium, so they try to do this without God's directive. They think they are helping God by speeding along what they think God wants, just like Abraham did when he had his child Ishmael through the bondwoman. Look at all the problems that that has caused Israel. Granted, Israel will be overwhelmed with confidence thinking that God is on their side. God delivers Israel from the whole northern army and they know God did this. Israel will have a new sense of pride that God is on their side. They will see this as an opportunity to regain their power as they attempt to restore Israel to its former height and glory by rebuilding the temple.

Most likely the temple will not be rebuilt until the Islamic nations are taken out of the way. Something has to happen politically for the temple to be rebuilt. Maybe a war or something else that would pave the way for Israel to be able to rebuild the ancient temple where it stood two thousand years ago. The chess pieces of the world need to be moved or taken out of the way for the temple to be rebuilt. War has a tendency to clear many chess pieces off the board. This makes perfect sense in today's understanding of global politics.

The Islamic nations wish Israel would die and go away, but that will never happen. The Muslims want this so much that they have even redrawn maps that exclude Israel, as somewhat wishful thinking. The only maps that will need to be redrawn though are the maps of countries that are enemies of Israel. Any country foolish enough to attack Israel can expect God's intervention. God is protecting Israel from now on. Woe to any country that smites Israel; blessed is any country that gives aid and comfort to Israel. As Islamic nations and Russia gear up for war against God's chosen people, they should keep all the prophecies of Ezekiel in mind because they are doomed to certain death when they attack Israel. God promises to *"leave but a sixth part of thee…upon the mountains of Israel"* (Ezek. 39:2). *"There shall they bury Gog and all his multitude…and seven months shall the house of Israel be burying of them, that they may cleanse the land"* (Ezek. 39:11c, 12). The prophecies are written with such perfection that the whole world will know that God is in charge.

The Muslims around the world would protest the temple being built next to the Dome of the Rock, but after such a military defeat and God being on the side of Israel, if there were ever a time to build the temple it would be then. Besides which Muslim army would be left to defend their position? Plus this is the moment when the man of sin, the false prince, makes a covenant with Israel (Dan. 9:26-27).

The thinking that Daniel 9:27 is talking about a peace treaty is based on the belief that the world thinks a treaty is necessary. It is because of world politics, as we know it. Also a covenant is a contract, oral or written. What if the world power base would change overnight, thus making it unnecessary for a peace treaty? If nuclear weapons and war destroyed most of the Islamic world, Israel would no longer be surrounded by enemies like it is now. Islam is worldwide, and the pressure from Muslims on Israel not to build the temple will never go away. However, many in Israel today are eager to build it anyway, despite what the Muslims want. If God miraculously defeats a super power in defense of Israel, those voices in Israel that desire the temple will no longer be silenced. The fear of reprisals would be lessened by their belief that God is protecting them. This would take a miracle like God provided Israel in defense against Pharaoh's army at the Red Sea. Imagine the pride Israel will have after such a victory. Already in the last century, God has shown His willingness to protect Israel, even in the Six-Day War. As long as God is protecting Israel, the nations of the world could mount the largest army ever seen on earth and they would still lose against Israel. Israel would not need a peace treaty after defeating their enemies, but Israel will seek a covenant.

Job 41 suggests that Israel will seek *"a covenant"* (Job 41:4) with this false prince right after *"the battle"* (Job 41:8). We think this is the Gog-Magog war. Maybe this covenant Job speaks of is the same as Daniel 9:27. Maybe there is a so-called peace treaty that the false prince confirms. Our point is that too much emphasis by too many theologians has been placed on looking for this peace treaty. We should not be looking for a seven-year peace treaty as the clear sign of the beginning of the Tribulation period. We should be looking for signs of this upcoming war, signs that would cause Israel to let down their guard. We should be looking for a sudden war against Israel. After this war, the Tribulation may begin.

With Hamas being in power, we believe Hamas would only do such a thing as to give peace and safety to Israel if Hamas has longer term plans to aid in a sudden coordinated attack against Israel. Ezekiel 38:10 proclaims that the enemies of Israel will hatch an *"evil plan"* of attack against the *"land of unwalled villages."*

Ezekiel 38:14 promised that *"In that day, when My people Israel are living in safety"* the Gog war begins. When this happens, destruction shall come to Russia and its Islamic allies, including Iran and Turkey. These allies will get support from Libya, Sudan, and Ethiopia. It is amazing that Ezekiel does not mention Iraq. Could it be that the United States' involvement has something to do with that? If the U.S. involvement has something to do with Iraq being omitted, then it also means that Gog battle could not have happened until after the United States had invaded Iraq.

What does all this have to do with the temple? Israel will not risk losing peace with Hamas by building the temple now. There is nothing in the Scriptures to suggest that the temple is built prior to the

Gog-Magog battle. But Scripture does suggest that the Gog-Magog war will pave the way for rebuilding the temple. Ezekiel says Israel will cleanse the land of the bones of their enemies for seven months. We think they are cleansing the land in preparation for beginning animal sacrifices in the rebuilt temple.

From the time the Gog-Magog battle ends, it takes Israel seven months and ten days to build the temple, cleanse the land and begin temple worship (see *Appendix - Chart A*). Then animal sacrificing will begin again after almost two thousand years. We think the Tribulation period begins immediately after this battle, when Israel begins cleansing the land. When the Two Witnesses start to preach in Israel, we will know for sure that the Tribulation period has begun.

Most theologians believe when Israel rebuilds the temple that this is the beginning of Daniel's seventieth week, which is a continuation of the original covenant between God and Israel. By now you know this is not so. Daniel's seventieth week is split and does not start up again until mid-Trib. The time of Jacob's trouble also starts mid-Trib and this is when the Antichrist is persecuting Israel.

Israel's Messiah

Israel is still waiting for the Messiah. What is interesting about this is that they are not sure who He is, or even what He is. Is He God? Is He a man, or an angel? They really do not know how to answer that question, but one thing that is for sure, Israel is still waiting for the Messiah. When the false prince confirms the covenant with Israel likely allowing them to rebuild the temple in Jerusalem, it may be possible that some in Israel could look upon the false prince as possibly being the Messiah. When he confirms the covenant for himself though, he is acting in accordance with the will of Satan. Jesus, the one and only true Messiah proclaimed,

> *I am come in My Father's name, and ye receive Me not:*
> *if another shall come in his own name, him ye* [Israel]
> *will receive* (John 5:43).

We have not been able to find supporting Scripture that Israel believes the false prince is the Messiah except John 5:43, but it is logical. However, without Scriptural witness, we may not have the full truth yet. We may only be seeing a piece of it. Always keep this in mind when you are interpreting Scripture. And just because we did not find the double witness to this notion does not mean it doesn't exist. Maybe you can find where Israel looks upon the false prince as their messiah in your studies.

What is the Abomination of Desolation?

It is several things. It is doing something repugnant to God, like sacrificing unclean animals in the temple. It is the defiling of the Holy of Holies. Placing a statue to a foreign god in the temple of God is also an abomination.

"...and for the overspreading of abominations he shall make it desolate, even until the consummation" (Dan. 9:27). Scripture suggests that there will be many abominations performed during the Tribulation period. However, there is a *"consummation"* of abominations (Dan. 9:27) that is *"the abomination of desolation"* (Matt. 24: 15, Mark 13:14) that reveals the *"son of perdition"* (2 Thess. 2:3-4) as the king who exalts himself above God (Dan. 11:36).

The only way to explain this with clarity is to give you the sequence of events concerning the abominations. Isaiah 44:12 says that the blacksmith crafts an idol. The false prince will *"set up"* (Dan. 12:11) this statue of a god in the temple in Jerusalem 1290-days before the end of the Tribulation period. If we back up 1290 days from the end of the Tribulation period, we know when the daily sacrifice is abolished. There are a series of abominations that are done between the 1290-day mark and the exact middle of the Tribulation, which is 1260-day mark. Isaiah 44 goes into detail about the setting up of all these abominations by the false prince. The Antichrist, the Satan-indwelt false prince who becomes *"the son of perdition"* (2 Thess. 2:3), performs the final act in the series of those abominations. It is crucial that you understand that the *"consummation"* of abominations (Dan. 9:27) is when the Antichrist says he is God above all others and the false prophet demands that everyone worships the Antichrist as God. All of this is called *"the abomination of desolation,"* spoken of by Daniel the prophet and quoted by Jesus in Matthew 24:15 and Mark 13:14. *"The consummation"* of abominations (Dan. 9:27) is performed about the exact middle of the Tribulation, on or near the 1260-day mark.

Daniel's Timeline of Abominations

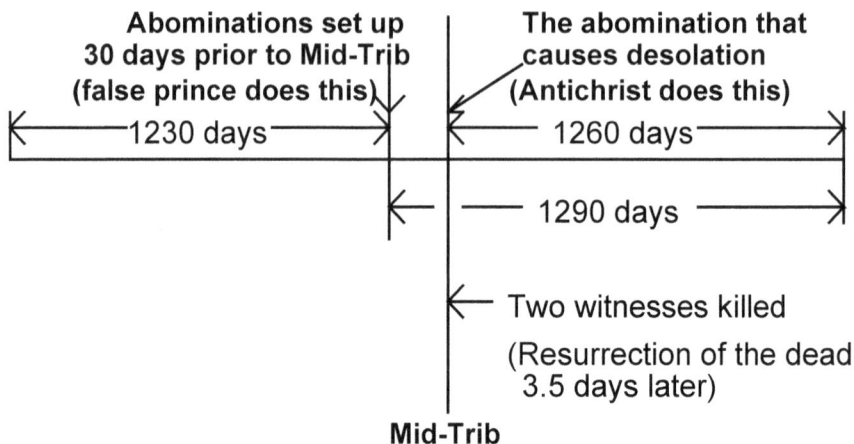

When *"that man of sin"* (2 Thess. 2:3), the false prince, has an image of himself made and placed in the temple as if he were God (Isa. 44:9-20), he is killed shortly thereafter. After his death, he is raised from the dead and then indwelt by Satan. It is now approximately the 1260-day mark. He then enters the temple and commits the consummation of abominations. He is now the *"son of perdition"* (2 Thess. 2:3). This is when all the earth fears him and wonders after him saying, *"who is able to make war with him"* (Rev. 13:4)? The false prophet causes the image of the beast to speak on behalf of the beast. We are guessing here, but it is probably a computer image available through the Internet. It most likely will be interactive with the viewers. This helps the beast be somewhat omnipresent like God.

In summary, the Gathering of the Elect is not until after the *"son of perdition"* is revealed to Israel. This Antichrist is not revealed until the exact middle of the Tribulation period when he kills the Two Witnesses (Rev. 11:7) and declares himself to be God in the temple (2 Thess. 2:4). When you see this world leader come back from the dead, you only have a few days to share the Gospel with the multitudes of the spiritual dead. Therefore, the Antichrist is revealed just days prior to Christ being revealed to entire world at the mid-Trib Gathering of the Elect.

Who are the Elect?

While it is accurate to say that Israel is the Elect, it is not the whole truth. The Elect are both the faithful of Israel and the body of whosoevers, anyone who believes in Christ. Here is a partial list of verses that say who the Elect are:

- *"What then? Israel hath not obtained that which he seeketh for; but the **election** hath obtained it, and the rest were blinded"* (Rom. 11:7). Israel did not obtain, but another group did, the Elect.
- Paul in chains like a criminal stated, *"Therefore I endure all things for the Elect's sakes, that they may also obtain the salvation which is in Christ Jesus with eternal glory"* (2 Tim. 2:10).
- *"Paul, a servant of God, and an apostle of Jesus Christ, according to the faith of God's Elect..."* (Titus 1:1).
- Mark 13:20 is explaining that we will be persecuted in the name of Jesus, *"...but for the Elect's sake, whom He hath chosen, He hath shortened the days."*
- *"Peter, an apostle of Jesus Christ, to the strangers scattered throughout Pontus, Galatia, Cappadocia, Asia, and Bithynia, Elect according to the foreknowledge of God the Father, through sanctification of the Spirit, unto obedience and sprinkling of the blood of Jesus Christ"* (1 Peter 1:1-2). Obviously the Elect is not just Israel! It must also include the Bride of Christ.

Who is Christ warning when He says, *"Wherefore if they shall say unto you, Behold, He is in the desert; go not forth: behold, He is in the secret chambers; believe it not"* (Matt. 24:26)? He is warning the Elect that the false-christ and the false prophet will appear first before the Gathering. He is saying that before the Gathering there will be people saying they have seen Christ and claiming to be Christ.

Even today, people see an image that looks like the image of Christ and thousands of people flock to the site. These are Christians who do not read their Bibles, because if they did, they would not go looking for Christ somewhere. When Christ comes, it will be without fanfare and no one will need to announce it. However, we are not saying His Gathering is a sign-less event. *"For as the lightning cometh out of the east, and shineth even to the west; so shall also the coming of the Son of man be"* (Matt. 24:27). *"But ye, brethren, are not of darkness, that that day should overtake you as a thief"* (1 Thess. 5:4). This is because we are children of the day and we are not ignorant of the signs of the Gathering.

The Persecution of the Elect

The Elect are both the faithful of Israel and the Bride of Christ, who is the faithful of the True Church. And for the Elect's sake, God will shorten the days. What does it mean that God shortens the days? What is shortened is the time that the Elect would have to endure Satan's wrath through the false prince - Antichrist (Rev. 12:12) or the Elect's flesh would not survive (Matt. 24:22).

> *Fear none of those things which thou shall suffer: behold, the devil shall cast some of you into prison, that ye may be tried; and ye shall have tribulation ten days: be thou faithful unto death, and I will give thee a crown of Life* (Rev. 2:10).

> *Though the number of the children of Israel be as the sand of the sea, a remnant shall be saved: For He will finish the work, and cut it short in righteousness: because a short work will the Lord make upon the earth* (Rom. 9:27-28).

At the Gathering Satan is trying to devour the man-child, as it is being born (Rev. 12:4). The man-child is the Bride of Christ who will rule with Christ on the earth three and one half years later, during the Millennium. As soon as this child is born, it is *"caught up unto God, and to His throne"* (Rev. 12:5).

> *And he that overcometh, and keepeth My works unto the end, to him will I give power over the nations: And he shall rule them with a rod of iron; as the vessels of a potter shall they be broken to shivers: even as I received of My Father* (Rev. 2:26-27).

> *And hast made us unto our God kings and priests: and we shall reign on the earth* [the man-child rules the nations with a rod of iron with Jesus Christ] (Rev. 5:10).

During the time that the woman is *"travailing in birth"* (Rev. 12:2) before the man-child is born, the dragon begins killing the faithful of the True Church and the faithful of Israel (Matt. 24:9). *"And it was given unto him* [the false prince - Antichrist] *to make war with the saints, and to overcome them"* (Rev. 13:7). We will be brought before rulers and kings for Jesus sake and be a testimony against them (Mark 13:9, Luke 21:12). When we are delivered up as Christians to be persecuted for Christ's namesake, we are not to *"premeditate"* what we will say in our defense (Mark 13:11). The Holy Spirit will speak through us in our defense in this time of tribulation. But God snatches us away from the Antichrist like a thief in the night. This is our blessed hope, and Satan is defeated again.

> *And they overcame him by the blood of the Lamb* [Christ], *and by the word of their testimony; and they loved not their lives unto death* (Rev. 12:11).

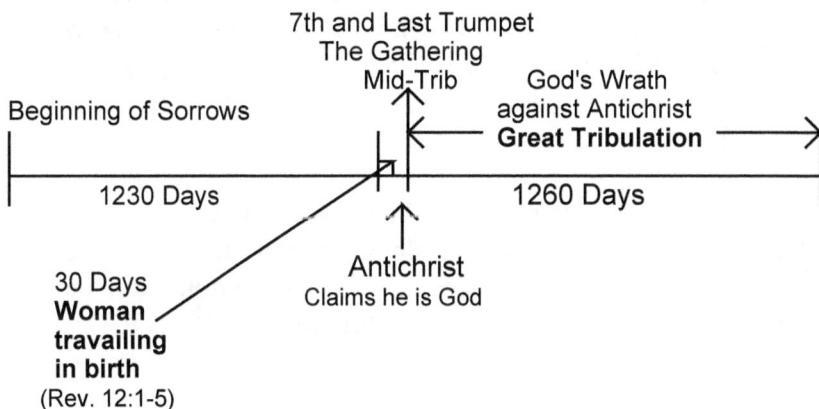

It is important that you understand that the Bride of Christ may have to endure up to 30 days while the woman is *"travailing in birth"* (Rev. 12:1-2). These are the extreme labor pains just prior the Gathering. *"These are they which came out of great tribulation..."* (Rev. 7:14). The great white robed multitude of saints will come out of great tribulation as witnessed in both Revelation 7:9-17 and Matthew 24:21. The tribulation is great because *"the devil is come*

down unto you, having great wrath... " (Rev. 12:12). This great wrath happens through the three woes (Rev. 8:13). Symphonically, the third woe begins just prior to the sounding of the seventh and last trumpet, because that is when Satan is cast out of heaven. Satan's wrath continues for three and one half years until the end of the great Tribulation period.

There is only one Gathering and all these Scriptures in the Book of Revelation depict the event when the saints are caught up to Heaven at about the middle of the Tribulation period (Rev. 7:9-17, 11:11-12, 15-19, 12:5, 14:12-16, 15:2-5).

> *When ye therefore shall see the abomination of desolation, spoken of by Daniel the prophet* [Dan. 12:11], *stand in the Holy place, (whoso readeth, let him understand...)* (Matt. 24:15).

> *For then shall be great tribulation, such as was not since the beginning of the world to this time, no, nor ever shall be. And except those days should be shortened, there should no flesh be saved: but for the Elect's sake, those days shall be shortened* (Matt. 24:21-22).

For the Elect's Sake, What Time Was Shortened?

God promised to shorten the days for the Elect sake. Does that mean that the actual number of days of the Tribulation period is shortened? We do not think so. According to Daniel 12:11,

> *And from the time that the daily sacrifice shall be taken away, and the abomination that maketh desolate setup, there shall be a thousand two hundred and ninety days* [1290 days].

There are a fixed number of days given to Daniel by God. So, what is shortened? God shortens the time that Satan has physical dominion over the Elect by Gathering the Elect out of Satan's physical dominion. This is a huge mid-Trib Gathering point. The Elect are both the faithful of the True Church, who are Gathered to the Heavenly

Kingdom, and the woman, the faithful of Israel, who are Gathered to *"a place prepared of God"* for 1260 days (Rev. 12:6, 14). God showed that there are 1290 days from the time the daily sacrifice is taken away to the end of the Tribulation period (Dan. 12:11). The woman is protected for 1260 days, after she has finished *"travailing in birth"* (Rev. 12:2) *"and her child was caught up to God, and to His throne"* (Rev. 12:5). So, that leaves a thirty-day window that the false prince - Antichrist will persecute the Elect. This dominion has the ability *"to make war with the saints, and to overcome them"* (Rev. 13:7) physically on earth. Satan through the false prophet will attempt to deceive people into worshipping the false prince - Antichrist as if he was God. Satan through the false prince - Antichrist will attempt to kill the Elect's flesh and blood bodies. However, we are promised that nothing can separate us from the love of God, which is in Christ Jesus our Lord (Rom. 8:35-39). Not even death or principalities!

> *And he* [false prince - Antichrist] *shall speak great words against the Most High, and shall wear out the saints of the Most High, and think to change times and laws: and they* [the saints] *shall be given into his hand until a time and times and the dividing of time* [new dispensation, mid-Trib]. *But the judgment shall sit* [God, twenty-four elders and the angels as witnesses in Revelation 4 and 5, Daniel 7:9-10, 13-14, 18, 22], *and They* [the Judgment] *shall take away his dominion, to consume and destroy it unto the end* (Dan. 7:25-26 - Explanations added).

We know from Revelation 11:15 that *"the kingdoms of this world are become the kingdoms of our LORD, and of His Christ; and He shall reign for ever and ever"* at the sounding of the seventh trumpet. Christ is crowned King at the sounding of the seventh trump. Therefore, Satan loses his legal dominion and is banished from heaven just prior to the sounding of the seventh and last trumpet mid-Trib.

During the thirty-days that the woman is *"travailing in birth"* (Rev. 12:2) on the earth, the false prince - Antichrist has power to make war against the Elect. A Scriptural witness to this thirty-day period where everyone will be forced to worship a person other than

Christ Jesus is found in Daniel. King Darius of the Medes and Persians issued a decree that everyone must worship him and him only as god. Anyone found worshipping any other god or man within thirty-days would be thrown into the lion's den (Dan. 6:7-12). We believe that this is a type of what the false prince - Antichrist will do. Immediately after that thirty-days, Christ comes like lightning and removes the Elect to their places of protection.

> *Immediately after the tribulation of those days* [thirty days that the woman is travailing in birth, mid-Trib] *shall the sun be darkened, and the moon shall not give her light, and the stars shall fall from heaven, and the powers of the heavens shall be shaken* [Satan and his angels expelled]: *And then shall appear the sign of the Son of Man in heaven: And then shall all the tribes of the earth mourn, and they shall see the Son of Man coming in the clouds of heaven with power and great glory. And He shall send His angels with the great sound of a trumpet, and they shall gather together His Elect from the four winds, from one end of heaven to the other* (Matt. 24:29-31).

When Does Israel Mourn for Christ Like an Only Son?

The question is, when does Israel mourn for Christ? *"And they shall look upon Me whom they have pierced, and they shall mourn for Him, as one mourneth for his only son..."* (Zech. 12:10). Does this mourning happen before the beginning of the Tribulation period? Does it happen in the middle of the Tribulation at the beginning of the time of Jacob's trouble? Or does Israel mourn for Christ through the entire millennial period?

Before we can go any further discussing when Israel will mourn for Christ, we must first discuss what it means when it says, *"And then they shall see the Son of man coming in a cloud with power and great glory"* (Luke 21:27). Christ was referring to the Gathering of the Bride. Christ is crowned at the seventh and last trumpet of God and not at His Triumphal Return.

Scripture tells us that when all the tribes of the earth shall see the Son of man coming in a cloud, that this event is synonymous with

Christ being revealed to Israel. The Scriptural witness to this is in Revelation 1:7; *"Behold, He cometh with clouds; and every eye shall see Him, and they also which pierced Him: and all kindreds of the earth shall wail because of Him. Even so, Amen."*

Revelation 14:14 is talking about the same mid-Trib event. At the Gathering of the Bride of Christ, one like the Son of man sits on a cloud with only one golden crown on His head. Matthew 24:30-31 is not the Triumphal Return. It is the first of two glorious appearances! The first Glorious Appearing with one crown is at the Gathering, immediately after Christ has received all legal dominion over created things in Heaven and on earth once given to Satan. All the Kingdoms of Heaven and earth will be Christ's forever and ever. Then when Christ comes again at His second Glorious Appearance and Triumphal Return at the end of the Tribulation period, He comes with many crowns to take physical possession of the earth (Rev. 19, Matt. 25:31-46). Jesus is then physically KING over all the Kings of the earth.

Israel mourns for Christ when He is revealed, but when is that?
- If Israel recognizes Jesus and mourns for Him before the Tribulation period begins; they would not build the temple and establish animal sacrifice, would they? Animal sacrifice is an abomination to Jesus. It would be like spitting on Jesus while He was on the cross. If they truly recognize Him and mourn for Him whom they have pierced, then they would not begin animal sacrifice. The Scriptures say that Israel does restore animal sacrifice, so that means they do not recognize Him until sometime after the Tribulation period begins.
- If Christ is revealed to Israel when He returns with many crowns to end the battle of Armageddon, does it make any sense that Israel would mourn for someone they can see and touch anytime they want? When He returns at His Triumphal Return He is staying for one thousand years and will sit on His throne. Every knee shall bow and everyone will worship Him. They worship Him freely, so it does not make any sense at all for the Millennium to be the time when Israel should be mourning Him whom they have pierced.

- Could it be that Israel mourns for Him when Christ returns for the Elect in the middle of the Tribulation? This is more likely when Israel mourns for Jesus because they will have time to do so after finally recognizing Him for whom He really is, *"the Son of man"* (Matt. 24:30). Christ will have taken His Bride to Heaven, and Jesus will not be on the earth for Israel to see anymore until His Triumphal Return three and one half years later. This gives Israel time to mourn.

> *And Jesus said unto them, Can the children of the bridechamber mourn, as long as the bridegroom is with them? But the days will come, when the bridegroom shall be taken from them, and then shall they fast* (Matt. 9:15).

The Remnant of Israel, the 144,000

Who are the 144,000? It is clear from the Book of Revelation that the 144,000 are 12,000 individuals from each of the twelve tribes of Israel. Not one of the 144,000 is a Gentile. It would be intellectually dishonest to read Revelation 7 and say that it implies a meaning that includes Gentiles. However, we cannot believe the number of theories presented of who these 144,000 are. The Bible is written clearly and it says the 144,000 are represented by each of the twelve tribes of Israel, literally.

Revelation 14:3 says that the 144,000 will learn a new song. *"And in their mouth was found no guile: for they are without fault before the throne of God"* (Rev. 14:5). If we go back to Zephaniah 3 it confirms who the 144,000 are:

> *The remnant of Israel shall not do iniquity, nor speak lies; neither shall a deceitful tongue be found in their mouth: for they shall feed and lie down, and none shall make them afraid* (Zeph. 3:13).

> *And the dragon was wroth with the woman, and went to make war with **the remnant of her seed**, which keep the commandments of God, and have the testimony of Jesus Christ* (Rev. 12:17 - Emphasis added).

The 144,000 are sealed by God in or upon their foreheads and have no fear of the Antichrist because God protects them. They are a group of people with Israelite heritage and are the remnant of Israel.

They are spoken of in the same manner in both Old and New Testaments. We believe that Zephaniah 3:11-15 is talking about end time events, *"In that day"* and *"the King of Israel, even the Lord, is in the midst of thee: thou shalt not see evil anymore."* Obviously the events in Revelation are end time events, so Scripture suggests that all these verses are in the same context of time, else Zephaniah's verse would be past history.

Who is the remnant of the woman's seed in Revelation 12:17? We believe the woman is "the faithful of Israel" that flee to a place prepared for her by God in the middle of the Tribulation period. This is because Christ was just revealed to them in the sky when He came for His Bride, and Israel is *"mourning Him whom they have pierced"* (Zech. 12:10). The man-child is the True Church, the Bride of Christ that was just caught up in the air to meet the Lord.

If the remnant of her seed is not the 144,000, then who are they? What are they? The remnant of the seed of the woman will be those who are the first fruits of the new dispensation unto God and the Lamb (Rev. 14:4). The remnant is sealed in or upon their foreheads (Rev. 7:3).

> *And the LORD said unto him, 'Go through the midst of the city, through the midst of Jerusalem, and set a mark upon the foreheads of the men that sigh and that cry for all the abominations that be done in the midst thereof'* (Ezek. 9:4).

Ezekiel 9:1-4 describes the sealing of Jews in Jerusalem. They are sealed by the man clothed in linen, just like in Daniel 12, which has the writer's inkhorn by his side. Then God tells this *"man clothed in linen to set a mark"* (seal) upon the foreheads of those who sigh and that cry for all the abominations going on in Jerusalem in the temple.

It is not certain whether these Jews from Ezekiel 9:4 are the 144,000, but Scripture sure suggests it. One thing is for certain; they are a group of people that are sealed in or upon their foreheads with the name of God for their protection, just like the 144,000. We do not think this is a coincidence. Further, if the remnant of Israel is not the 144,000, then who are they? They cannot be the faithful of Israel, the woman who is protected from the Antichrist in the wilderness because the Antichrist fails in his attempt when he goes after them in Revelation 12. In his fury he goes after *"the remnant of her seed"* (Rev. 12:17). Symphonically these Jews fit the melodic line as the 144,000. Otherwise they must be another group who could be considered the seed of Israel. There is no scriptural evidence to support that premise.

When Satan is cast from heaven mid-Trib, he pursues the remnant of Israel for 42 months. Because of this we know the remnant is present in the second half of the Tribulation. The 144,000, which are the remnant of Israel, are to spearhead the spreading of the *"Everlasting Gospel"* described in Revelation 14. Their ministry encompasses the whole second half of the Tribulation period. This is crucial because the Bride of Christ as the instrument of the Gospel is no longer on the earth after mid-Trib. In the last three and one half years of the Tribulation period it is up to the remnant of Israel to fulfill the mission that would have been Israel's all along, had they accepted Jesus Christ during His earthly ministry.

The remnant of Jacob, which is the 144,000, will be sealed with the name of God in or upon their foreheads. This is a seal of protection. Notice that the mark of the beast is the mirror image of God's seal in or on the foreheads of His followers. Satan will require a mark or seal on his followers as well.

Still not convinced as to what or who the 144,000 are? Let us go to Micah 5:3; *"Therefore will He give them up, until the time that she, which travaileth hath brought forth:* [Or in other words, as the woman gives or gave birth (Rev. 12)] *Then the remnant of his brethren shall return unto the children of Israel."*

Micah 5:5, *"And this man shall be the peace, when the Assyrian shall come into our land: and when he shall tread in our palaces"*... The Assyrian is the Antichrist when he treads in the palaces defiling everything in the rebuilt temple and proclaiming he is God. This is when Jerusalem is encompassed by armies and the desolation thereof is nigh (Luke 21:20) mid-Trib.

Micah 5:6 speaks of the war against the Assyrian in the middle of the Tribulation, because the woman has just travailed in Micah 5:3.

The remnant is delivered from the Assyrian when he comes into the land of Israel.

Then in Micah 5:7, *"And the remnant of Jacob* [144,000] *shall be in the midst of many people"... "And the remnant of Jacob shall be among the Gentiles in the midst of many people..."* (Micah 5:8). But why would God put the remnant of Jacob in the midst of many nations? Could it be they are the 144,000 who *"keep the commandments of God and have the testimony of Jesus"* (Rev. 12:17)? They would be ministering the message of Jesus to the world, because the Bride of Christ is gone and so are the Two Witnesses. It is now the job of the 144,000 to spread the *"Everlasting Gospel"*, as they would have done 2,000 years ago had Israel not rejected Christ. The earthly Kingdom could have come then. Jesus began to preach, and to say, *"Repent: for the kingdom of heaven is at hand"* (Matt. 4:17). By the way, some might say that the 144,000 are in heaven learning the new song, yet Micah 5:7-8 places them ministering on earth. Using the symphonic view of Scripture, there can be no conflict in Scripture. If anyone says the 144,000 are in Heaven in the second half of the Tribulation then there is a conflict with Micah 5:7-8.

How to use the Symphonic Method to Determine Which Half of the Tribulation Period the 144,000 Start Their Ministry

Lets look at the timeline of events in what will be the last seven years of modern history as we see it. The Two Witnesses of Revelation 11 minister in the first half of the Tribulation period for 1260 days or three and one half years. At the point of their death and resurrection, *"the woman"* of Revelation 12 will have God's protection for another 1260 days. Around the time of the Two Witnesses' death, the 144,000 are sealed and begin their ministry. Their ministry lasts until the Millennium. All this happens near the sounding of the seventh trumpet, which is mid-Trib.

Some might argue that the church is suddenly raptured before the Tribulation and at that time a new dispensation occurs, bringing back the Mosaic Law, ending grace. But we can find no evidence that grace will ever end. The symphonic view of the *"Everlasting Gospel"* being learned by the 144,000 (Rev. 14:3) and *"blessed are the dead which die in the Lord henceforth"* (Rev. 14:13) are two strong Scriptural witnesses for a new dispensation mid-Trib. We can find no such evidence for a new dispensation when the Two Witnesses come on the scene at the beginning of the Tribulation. If one is to believe the church is gone before the seven-year Tribulation period, then who is given the stewardship of the message of salvation in the first half of the Tribulation period? It cannot be the 144,000 because they do not learn the new song of the *"Everlasting Gospel"* until the seventh trumpet blows during mid-Trib. The Two Witnesses are not given the *"Everlasting Gospel"* to preach. *"These are the two olive trees and the two candlesticks"* who are ministering to Israel and the church, respectively. Again, there is no evidence that a new dispensation begins prior to mid-Trib. Would God give the stewardship of the message of salvation to the nation of Israel, a nation that does not believe in Jesus? It is obvious Israel does not believe in Jesus during the first half of the Tribulation because they build the temple and begin animal sacrifice, which is repugnant to Christ.

The Symphonic Storyline of 144,000 as we see it

When using the Symphonic Method of Scriptural Study to determine the timing of events, always check your theological storyline against Scripture. If there are conflicts between your understanding of the storyline and Scripture, then you do not yet have the whole truth. You need to keep changing your understanding of the storyline until it no longer conflicts with Scripture. For Example: Where are the 144,000 during the Tribulation period? Let us say your storyline places them in Heaven before the throne of God (Rev. 14). Ask yourself, is this an accurate presumption?

First, we need rightly to divide the Word of God found in Revelation 14:1-6:

* The Lamb stood on mount Zion with the 144,000 (Rev. 14:1). In Ezekiel 9 the man dressed in linen was told to seal them upon their foreheads. This man was searching to place a mark upon the forehead of any man who was crying because of the abominations and animal sacrifices Israel will be doing in the Tribulation period. Animal sacrifices are an abomination to the Lord because of what Christ did on the cross. In other words, Christ is looking for Christian Jews. These 144,000 Jews will not be part of the Bride of Christ, but rather will be the first fruits of a new

dispensation unto God and to the Lamb (Rev. 14:4). Just like the Apostles that were hand picked by Jesus to minister for Israel during the first half of Daniel's seventieth week, these 144,000 will minister for Israel during the second half of Daniel's seventieth week.

- *"And they sung as it were a new song before the throne, and before the four beasts, and the elders"* (Rev. 14:3). Many expositors say the 144,000 are singing in this verse, but that cannot be. The 144,000 are men from Israel on earth, not souls in Heaven. Who are *"they"* that sang? They are the overcomers that are standing on the sea of glass before the throne *"having the harps of God. And **they** sing the song of Moses the servant of God, and the song of the Lamb... "* (Rev. 15:2-3 Emphasis added).

- The harpers are singing the song in Heaven so that the 144,000 could learn it on earth.

- Verse 6 describes an angel flying in the midst of Heaven having the Everlasting Gospel. When has an angel, as the primary agent of its delivery, ever spread the Gospel? This angel has the Everlasting Gospel to preach. This Gospel is the one given to the 144,000 to be preached unto them that dwell on the earth, to every nation and kindred, and tongue, and people. It may be part of the new song that only the 144,000 can learn as *"being the first fruits unto God and to the Lamb"* (Rev. 14:4).

- Since the 144,000 are the first fruits of God and to the Lamb, why would they be in Heaven? Wouldn't the first fruits of a new dispensation for the nation of Israel be on earth?

Take a close look at Revelation 14:1, *"a Lamb stood on mount Sion."* The Lamb is Jesus. He is not yet a King. In Revelation 14:1, Christ has not yet received the *"Kingdoms"* He receives in Revelation 11:15 and 12:10. This means the 144,000 are sealed a short time before the Gathering. Revelation 7 is a Scriptural witness to this. In Revelation 14:13 there is a change in dispensation. This is why He is *"the Son of man, having on His head a golden crown... "* (Rev. 14:14). Christ is in His glorious state when He comes for His Bride as a King, no longer only the Lamb. He will forever be the Lamb, but He takes on His new role as King just before He comes to Gather His Bride at the seventh trumpet mid-Trib.

These 144,000 men having just been sealed are standing on mount Zion. They learn a new song, which is *"the Everlasting Gospel"* from Heaven being sung by the harpers and taught by the angel. Then in Micah 5:7 it appears that they will be scattered throughout the whole world *"as a dew from the Lord"* and *"as the showers upon the grass."* This would fulfill the original purpose meant for Israel, had they not rejected their Messiah. God knew all along that Israel would reject Jesus, so His plan all along was that through the Mystery His Gospel would be preached. The stewardship of the Gospel was given to the Gentiles. When the Bride of Christ is removed from the earth, the stewardship goes back to Israel through the 144,000. This will complete Israel's role of stewardship of the Gospel during the second half of Daniel's seventieth week, from mid-Trib until the Millennium.

Chapter 8

The Church

The church in the last days has numerous promises and warnings given to it by God. There are also many questions that need to be answered concerning the church. Not the least of which is, what is the church and who comprises it? Secondly, what are those promises and warnings given to the church? Furthermore, will the church be kept from the whole seven years of the Tribulation period, just part of it or none of it?

For clarity sake, we need to define a few things that we constantly hear Christians saying that are not entirely accurate. We hear people say that everyone who calls himself or herself a Christian is part of the Bride of Christ. People often interchange the Bride of Christ and the church, as if they are synonymous with each other.

The Bride of Christ is part of the church, but the Bride is not synonymous with the meaning of the word church; not all of the church will be the Bride of Christ! Being included in the Bride of Christ is a reward; one will receive the crown of righteousness (2 Tim. 4:8). The Bride of Christ only includes those who have a close personal relationship with God through Jesus Christ by the Holy Spirit.

Understanding the Parables

Of the parable of the Sower (Matt. 13:1-23, Mark 4:1-25, Luke 8:1-18), the Ten Virgins (Matt. 25:1-13), the Unfruitful Fig Tree (Luke 13:6-9), the Wheat and Tares (Matt. 13:24-43), the key parable is the parable of the Sower. Jesus said this concerning the Sower and the four soil types, *"Know ye not this parable? And how then will ye know all parables?"* (Mark 4:13).

The seed is the Word of God. The Word of God is cast upon all types of soil and all humanity has the Word spread upon it. Please read John 1:1-14.

Wayside soil:

This soil comprises the majority of the world. These people are not generally part of the church. They are non-believers.

> *Those by the way side are they that hear; then cometh the devil, and taketh away the word out of their hearts, lest they should believe and be saved* (Luke 8:12 - Emphasis added).

The seeds are blown to the wayside, where the devil takes away the Word before these people could believe and be saved. God created us and we all have a purpose for being on the earth. Our first and most important purpose for being here is to go through the filter of life. God is separating the wheat from the tares or weeds. Imagine living an entire lifetime never having dealt with the issue of God. This person lived their entire life ignoring God's Word or maybe they followed a false god. These people hope that because they feel they are "good people" they will be given a free pass to Heaven. Being a good person without accepting God's gift of salvation through Jesus Christ only gets you eternal separation from God.

Rocky soil:

These people hear the Word of God and embrace it with joy. They have no roots in Christ though. For a while they listen, but when trials or temptations come, they fall away. These people have no lasting salvation to look forward to and will be left behind at the Gathering. An example would be someone attending a Christian concert and at the altar call goes forward to receive Christ in their mind but not their heart; days or months later, it is as if the concert never happened.

> *They on the rock are they, which, when they hear, receive the word with joy; and these have no root, which for a while believe, and in time of temptation fall away* (Luke 8:13).

These people will likely become part of the apostate church. Besides having no root in Christ, they also bear no fruit. These are the people who deny that Christ is the Messiah, God in human flesh.

Some of these people may even blaspheme the Holy Spirit by taking the mark of the beast or worshiping the Antichrist during the Tribulation period. Their salvation is lost, as if they ever had it to begin with. One can embrace God with joy and not be sealed by the Holy Spirit. Having head knowledge of God doesn't equate salvation. After acknowledging God's existence one can turn from God and walk away. God is not going to make one love Him. He only wants those people in the Kingdom of God that does love Him.

Thorny soil:

The thorny soil type represents people that are part of the church. They also hear the Word of God and embrace it with joy. They appear to have roots in Christ and they are in soil and not on hard rocks.

> *And that which fell among thorns are they, which, when they have heard, go forth, and are choked with cares and riches and pleasures of this life, and bring no fruit to perfection* (Luke 8:14).

Luke 8:14 implies that these so-called Christians could bear fruit, but they *"bring no fruit to perfection."* These are the ones whose faith is choked by the cares and pleasures of the world. The Holy Spirit is drawing these people to Himself, but they are resisting being indwelt by the Holy Spirit and being in union with Jesus Christ. These people are like the five foolish virgins. These people represent the members of the church that are unprepared when Christ comes for His Bride. They are cut off from the reward of the Gathering. They are neither hot nor cold (Rev. 3:16), so Jesus will spit them out into great tribulation. All seven churches have thorny soil types as members. These lukewarm Christians most closely resemble the Laodicean church members whom Christ was rebuking. These people are all around us. Occasionally we see them on Sunday morning, when they show up for church.

Good soil:

This soil type represents people that are members of the True Church. They are the five wise virgins. These people will become the Bride of Christ.

> *That if thou shalt confess with thy mouth the Lord Jesus, and shalt believe in thine heart that God hath raised him from the dead, thou shalt be saved. For with the heart man believeth unto righteousness; and with the mouth confession is made unto salvation* (Rom. 10:9-10).

> *But that on the good ground are they, which in an honest and good heart, having heard the word, keep it, and bring forth fruit with patience* (Luke 8:15).

> *Because thou hast kept the word of My patience, I also will keep thee from the hour of temptation, which shall come upon all the world, to try them that dwell upon the earth* (Rev. 3:10).

They are prepared when Christ comes for His Bride. They have endured patiently, working for the Lord Jesus Christ and exhibit mature fruit before Him at the Gathering.

What is the Church and Who Comprises It?

For our purposes, we are not talking about a building, an organization, or an individual congregation. The church is the collective body of all people who say they are Christians. As far as the church goes, there are three separate groups within the church at the time of the Gathering.

The True Church: These are those true Christians who have a close personal relationship with God through Jesus Christ by the Holy Spirit and will become the Bride of Christ. This group is part of *"the mystery of God"* that is finished when the seventh angel begins to sound mid-Trib (Rev. 10:7). They will be included in the reward known as the Gathering. These are the five wise virgins whose fruit of patience is mature. *"And they that were ready went in with Him to the Marriage: and the door was shut"* (Matt. 25:10).

The unprepared church: This group suckles on the milk and does not think that they have need of the meat of God's Word that God offers to all believers. They are like the Laodicean Church.

> *So then because thou art **lukewarm**, and neither cold nor hot, **I will spue thee out of My mouth**. As many as I love, I rebuke and chasten: be zealous therefore, and **repent** (Rev. 3:16, 19 - Emphasis added).*

They do not have a close personal relationship with nor are they in union with the Lord Jesus Christ. The Holy Spirit is drawing them to Himself but they have not yet surrendered to Him. They are left behind because they are unprepared at the time of the Gathering of the Bride. These are the five foolish virgins.

> *Afterward came also the other virgins, saying, "Lord, Lord, open to us." But He answered and said, "Verily I say unto you, **I know you not"** (Matt. 25:11-12 - Emphasis added).*

Individuals of the unprepared church will either become apostate or become a true Christ follower during the last 42 months of the Tribulation period. Yes, one can have eternal salvation in the new dispensation that starts mid-Trib. However, those converts will not be part of the Bride of Christ.

The apostate church: These are people who say they are Christians and may even go to church, but they do not truly believe. They put money in the offering plate and many are accepted as Christians in the church. They do all the right things and they say all the right things, yet they lack faith. The Holy Spirit does not seal these people. These are attempting to obtain salvation by works or through false conversions. They say the words without conviction. They hear the Word and accept it as head knowledge, but do not apply it in their hearts. We cannot deny that these people are among us. These people have no fruit at all because they have no roots, meaning they have no true faith. These people are not only left behind, but they have no eternal salvation. What does it profit a man to confess Christ with the lips, but not have Him in his heart? None!

> *Not every one that saith unto Me, Lord, Lord, shall enter into the kingdom of heaven; but he that doeth the will of*

*My Father which is in heaven. Many will say to Me in that day, Lord, Lord, have we not prophesied in Thy name? And in Thy name have cast out devils? And in Thy name done many wonderful works? And then will I profess unto them, **I never knew you**: depart from Me, ye that work iniquity* (Matt. 7:21-23 -Emphasis added).

There will be *"a falling away first"* in the church as a whole when *"the son of perdition"* is revealed (2 Thess. 2:3). We as Christians are troubled by the notion that we could lose our salvation after having been sealed by the Holy Spirit and being in union with Christ. True Christians do not fall away or forsake the truth, but rather non-believers claiming to be Christians are looking to this man, the false-christ, as if he were Christ. Could it be that millions of churchgoers are deceived and follow him in an apostate church because they do not have Christ in their heart to begin with? When the false prince, *"that man of sin,"* rises from the dead and becomes the Satan-indwelt *"son of perdition,"* he claims to be God in the temple (2 Thess. 2:3-4). We believe this is the event that causes the great apostasy in the church. The True Church will not believe the *"lie"* (2 Thess. 2:11), but non-believers will believe in the false-messiah or Antichrist. We say "will" because except for the Elect, the whole world will be deceived (Matt. 24:24). The Scriptural witness is,

*And **all that dwell upon the earth shall worship him** [the Antichrist], **whose names are not written in the Book of Life** of the Lamb slain from the foundation of the world* (Rev. 13:8 - Emphasis added).

What is the Mystery of God?

The Mystery of God was kept hidden from the ages and from the generations of Adam to Christ, until Christ Himself revealed the Mystery under the New Covenant of Grace. However, that mystery still is not understood by humanity even today. In John 3:16 it states that *"whosoever believeth in Him* [the Son of God, the Messiah] *should not perish, but have everlasting life."*

In Ephesians 3:1-12, Paul talks about a further revelation of *"the mystery of Christ"* that was revealed to him by Christ.

> *That the Gentiles should be fellowheirs, and of the same body, and partakers of **His** [God's] **promise** in Christ by the gospel* (Ephes. 3:6 - Emphasis added).

Part of this Mystery is Gentiles are to be included as heirs of salvation through Christ, the Anointed One.

> *For the scripture saith, **Whosoever believeth** on Him shall not be ashamed. **For there is no difference between the Jew and the Greek**: for the same Lord over all is rich unto all that call upon Him. For **whosoever** shall call upon the name of the Lord shall be saved* (Rom. 10:11-13 - Emphasis added).

These believers are eligible to be the Bride of Christ. As a group, true Christians are members of Christ's Body with Christ as the Head (Ephes. 1:22-23, Col. 1:18). But there is more to the Mystery.

> *And as we have borne the image of the earthy, we shall also bear the image of the heavenly. Now this I say, brethren, **that flesh and blood cannot inherit the kingdom of God**; neither doth corruption inherit incorruption. Behold, I show you **a mystery; we shall not all sleep, but we shall all be changed,** In a moment, in the twinkling of an eye, at the last trump: for the trumpet shall sound, and **the dead shall be raised incorruptible, and we shall be changed** (1 Cor. 15:49-52 - Emphasis added).

It is no coincidence that Christ chose this word *"mystery"* in telling this prophecy to Paul. All 1 Corinthians 15 is a great explanation of why God needs to change our flesh and blood bodies at the Gathering. The spiritual aspect of the Kingdom of God in Heaven stands in stark contrast to the physical flesh and blood Kingdom on the earth that was presented to Israel throughout the Old Testament. Jesus told the Samaritan woman at the well that God is Spirit and *"true worshippers shall worship the Father in spirit and in truth"* (John 4:23-24). When we are born again, the very presence of God in the form of the Holy Spirit then resides in our spirit, which is a human Temple, and no longer inside the Holy of Holies in an earthly temple or church. At the point that we are *"born again"* (John 3:3), we are in spiritual union with God through Jesus Christ by the Holy Spirit. On earth we live in flesh and blood bodies, spiritually indwelt by the Holy Spirit and betrothed to Christ as His Bride. However, our flesh and blood bodies are not fitted to live in the spiritual realm of the Heavenly Kingdom. We must be changed into our glorified bodies that will live forever. Therefore, the dead in Christ will resurrect and all those who are in Christ that are alive and remain at the Gathering of the Bride of Christ will be changed into their glorified bodies without experiencing death. This is the consummation of the Mystery.

The very relationship between Christ and the members of His Body is also a Mystery (Ephes. 5:23-32). At the Gathering our old flesh and blood bodies will be changed and we will receive our new glorified eternal bodies of flesh and bone like Christ has (Luke 24:39, Ephes. 5:30). Paul speaks of this Mystery as a marriage union, *"and they two shall be one flesh"* (Ephes. 5:31, which is quoted from Gen. 2:24). After the Gathering, the Marriage will occur and then the Bride will become the Wife of Christ (Rev. 19:7).

Also, part of the Mystery is *"that blindness in part is happened to Israel"* (Rom. 11:25). Because Israel rejected the message of the King and the offer of the Earthly Kingdom, God went to the Gentile Nations to present the message of salvation to the world (Acts 28:28, Rom. 11:11). This blindness for Israel as a Nation will continue until the Gathering. However, individual Israelites can have salvation through the promises in Christ during the Mystery Dispensation.

So far we have been talking about the Mystery of God from God's plan or a Holy perspective. However, there is an unholy aspect or mirror image to God's plan of "the mystery" as well. This counterfeit or copycat mystery is spoken of in 2 Thessalonians 2:7 as *"the mystery of iniquity."* Paul said that this mystery of iniquity was already at work in his day. Satan and his principalities and powers are responsible for this iniquity, which continue to the present. A future world leader will rise to power, as a mere man influenced by Satan, that will become the false prince described in Daniel 9:26-27. The pinnacle of this iniquity will be when this *"man of sin"* becomes *"the son of perdition,"* better known as the Satan-indwelt-Antichrist that sits in the temple declaring to be God (2 Thess. 2:3-4).

Satan, through the apostate church, the false prophet, and the Antichrist, will begin to rule over the kings of the entire earth shortly before the mid-Trib Gathering of the Elect. This is the mirror image of God's plan for the Lord Jesus Christ to rule over the kings of the earth, which takes place three and one half years later, at the beginning of the Millennium.

Another part of this mirror image mystery of iniquity is *"MYSTERY, BABYLON THE GREAT, THE MOTHER OF HARLOTS AND ABOMINATIONS OF THE EARTH"* (Rev. 17:5). This is Satan's counterfeit political, economic, and religious system. *"And the woman which thou sawest is **that great city**, which reigneth over the kings of the earth"* (Rev. 17:18 - Emphasis added). Satan's temporary great city on earth, Jerusalem, stands as a mirror image reflection of *"mount Sion...the city of the living God, the heavenly Jerusalem"* (Heb. 12:22) that lasts to the ages of the ages. Once again, Satan's mirror image of the True.

When is the Mystery of God finished?

It is important for us to understand that in the end of this Earth Age there are two Kingdoms brought about by Jesus Christ (Ephes. 1:10, Col. 1:13-20). A spiritual Heavenly Kingdom offered to the Bride of Christ and three and one half years later a physical flesh and blood Kingdom promised to Israel as the head of all Nations and ruled by the Lord Jesus Christ during the Millennium.

Part of the mystery that was hidden from Israel because of her unbelief was the many-membered Body of Christ. When Christ Gathers His Bride to Himself, Christ will also be revealed to Israel. In order for Israel to recognize the Lord Jesus Christ as their true Messiah, the Gathering of the Bride of Christ cannot be sign-less. Israel and all the tribes of the earth shall see Jesus whom they have pierced and they shall mourn for Him (Zech. 12:10, Matt. 24:30, Rev. 1:7). Besides that, the Scriptures say that the Antichrist must be revealed before our Gathering to Christ (Matt. 24:15-31, Mark 13:14-27, 2 Thess. 2:1-4). The Antichrist is revealed when he rises from the dead and declares to be God in the temple. This begins *"the time of Jacob's trouble; **but he** [faithful of Israel] **shall be saved out of it"***

(Jer. 30:7 - Emphasis added). The ones who do mourn for Christ are protected in the wilderness for 1260 days or *"for a time, and times, and half a time"* (Rev. 12:6, 14), making this a mid-Trib event.

"But in the days of **the voice of the seventh angel**, *when he shall* **begin to sound**, **the mystery of God should be finished**, *as He hath declared to His servants the prophets"* (Rev. 10:7). Daniel confirms that this is a mid-Trib event because the false prince, and very briefly the Antichrist, *"will wear out the saints of the Most High...until a time and times and the dividing of time"* (Dan. 7:25). We believe this means not only three and one half years, but also a changing of dispensation mid-Trib by the words *"the dividing of time."* Satan's mirror image of God's plan at present still has seven years of the Tribulation period to be fulfilled. However, from God's perspective, Jesus Christ, The Anointed One has already fulfilled three and one half years of Daniel's seventieth week to and for Israel. Thus we have a mid-Trib change in dispensation from the Gentiles to Israel through the 144,000.

The *"mystery"* of the resurrection of the dead and the translation of the living saints *"at the last trump"* (1 Cor. 15:49-52) connects this event to *"the mystery of God"* that is finished when the seventh trumpet begins to sound mid-Trib (Rev. 10:7). Symphonically, not only is this the seventh trumpet and last trump, it is also *"the trump of God"* (1 Thess. 4:16) that causes the dead in Christ to rise first and the living to be caught up together with them. The *"great sound of a trumpet"* (Matt. 24:31) that shall Gather together Christ's Elect is also part of this same event. The Bride of Christ is taken to Heaven and the faithful of Israel are taken to their place of protection for 1260 days. All these Scriptures are talking about the one and same event, the mid-Trib Gathering of the Elect! It causes great conflict within the Scriptures if you place the timing of the Gathering of the Elect anywhere else other than mid-Trib.

Summary of the Mystery of God

The Bride of Christ that is betrothed to the Bridegroom, Jesus Christ, is a mystery that was not revealed in the Old Testament. This Heavenly Kingdom is in the spiritual realm and is the mystery form of the Kingdom of God offered through the Abrahamic Covenant.

Primarily what was promised in the Old Testament was a physical flesh and blood kingdom on earth. *"But when **the fullness of the time was come, God sent forth His Son, made of a woman,** made under the law, **to redeem them that were under the law**, that we might receive the adoption of sons"* (Gal. 4:4-5). Jesus Christ, as the Son of God and Son of man has already fulfilled the first half of Daniel's seventieth week to and for Israel during His earthly ministry. According to God's plan for Israel, this only leaves three and one half years for the 144,000 of Israel to minister during the last half of the Tribulation period. However, Satan has a mirror image to God's plan for Israel that lasts the entire seven years of the Tribulation period.

Paul tells us that *"the mystery of iniquity"* was already at work in his day (2 Thess. 2:7). This iniquity by Satan and his principalities and powers are present in the world now and will continue to be, bringing about the false *"prince that shall come"* (Dan. 9:26). This false prince is a mirror image of *"Messiah the Prince"* in Daniel 9:25. The false prince is a mere man that is killed and indwelt by Satan to become the Antichrist just prior to mid-Trib. As a mirror image of Christ, the Antichrist usurps Christ's rightful place to rule over the kings of the earth during the last three and one-half years of the Tribulation period.

Satan also brings about the apostate church by people pledging their allegiance to the world's political, economic and religious system of the Antichrist. This apostate church is the mirror image of the True Church, which will become the Bride of Christ.

When the Body of Christ was revealed to the Apostle Paul under the New Covenant of Grace, it was a *"revelation of the mystery, which was kept secret since the world began, but now is made manifest... according to the commandment of the everlasting God"* (Rom. 16:25-26). This "Body" with Christ as its "Head" is compared to husbands and wives, thus making Christ the Bridegroom and the True Church the Bride of Christ. Paul goes on to tell us, *"for we are members of His body, of His flesh, and of His bones...and they two shall be one flesh. This is a great mystery: but I speak concerning Christ and the church"* (Ephes. 5:30-32). This is speaking of the consummation of our union with Christ in Heaven. Our physical, flesh and blood bodies must be changed into our spiritual, glorified, forever bodies fitted for that realm (1 Cor. 15:49-52). If we are in Christ and alive at the time of the Gathering, we will never die (John 11:26, 1 Cor. 15:51-52 and 1 Thess. 4:13-18). This is also part of the mystery that was revealed to Paul.

"For I would not, brethren, that ye should be ignorant of this mystery... that blindness in part is happened to Israel, until the fullness of the Gentiles be come in" (Rom. 11:25). God's promises are now extended to the Gentiles as well as Israel (Ephes. 2:1-22). The preaching of the message of salvation through Jesus Christ was transferred to the Gentiles through the mystery of God, which ends when the seventh trump begins to sound (Rev. 10:7). Therefore, *"the fullness of the Gentiles"* ends at the dispensation change at the mid-Trib Gathering of the Elect. When the Bride of Christ is caught up to Heaven at the Gathering of the Elect, the faithful of Israel recognize Jesus Christ as their true Messiah that they have been waiting for. God supernaturally protects the faithful of Israel, who is represented by *"the woman"* in Revelation 12, for 1260 days, thereby bringing their flesh and blood bodies into the Millennium.

The True Church is Mentioned in Revelation after Chapter 4

Some theologians are trying to say that because the word "church" is not mentioned after Revelation 4:1 that this is strong evidence the church is not present during the Tribulation period.[34] But, this is a false premise because the True Church is mentioned many times in other ways.

1) The church is written seven letters guiding it through the first half of the Tribulation period. All seven letters have a promise to those *"that overcometh"* (Rev. 2 - 3). The great multitudes clothed in white robes are the saints who came out of great tribulation. We believe this to be the Bride of Christ (Rev. 7:9-17 and Matt. 24:21-31). The ones left behind at the mid-Trib Gathering of the Bride of Christ will need to seek out the 144,000 and the *"Everlasting Gospel"* message they minister with in the new dispensation.

2) When the seventh angel is about to sound the seventh and last trumpet, the Mystery of God is finished (Rev. 10:7); the Bride of Christ is Gathered. If the Mystery being finished is not the Bride of Christ, the True Church, then what is it? Since we know the Mystery

is a dispensation whereby the Church, which is the Bride of Christ, is given stewardship of the message of salvation until mid-Trib, how can one earnestly say the Church is not mentioned after Revelation 4:1?

3) At the sounding of the seventh trumpet thy servants the prophets, the saints (including the Two Witnesses), and them that fear Thy Name are rewarded (Rev. 11:18). The Bride of Christ, which are the saints, are Gathered up in their glorified bodies and rewarded with this group in Revelation 11:18.

4) The woman and the dragon... The True Church is the child that the woman brings forth and *"her child was caught up unto God, and to His throne"* (Rev. 12:5). All those who would say the man-child in Revelation 12:5 is Jesus Christ in the past tense are taking that verse out of context. *"Before she travailed, she brought forth; before her pain came, she was delivered of a man-child* [Jesus]*"* (Isa. 66:7). Christ was delivered before the woman travailed, before her pain came. Revelation 12:1-6 tells us when Zion travails. The woman is *"travailing in birth, and pained to be delivered"* (Rev. 12:2) just before she flees to the wilderness for 1260 days (Rev. 12:6).

> *Who hath heard such a thing? Who hath seen such things? Shall the earth be made to bring forth in one day? Or shall a nation be born at once?* ***For as soon as Zion travailed, she brought forth her children*** [the Elect] (Isa. 66:8 - Emphasis added).

Daniel confirms this premise by saying that the archangel Michael stands up for the *"children of thy people"* during times of trouble or travail (Dan. 12:1). Notice that the man-child is caught up *"before the throne of God, and serve Him day and night in His Temple"* (Rev. 7:15). This is the description of the Bride of Christ being Gathered in preparation for the union between Christ and His Bride, making way for the Marriage Supper of the Lamb. Where else in Revelation does it mention the sounding of the last trumpet and someone being caught up to Heaven to serve God other than mid-Trib? It certainly is not in Revelation 4:1, nor is it at the end of the Tribulation. Even if post-Tribulation theorists try to place the seventh trumpet at the end of the

Tribulation, the child is caught up 1260 days before the end of the Tribulation. This is hard-hitting evidence against post-Trib thinking.

5) If any man takes the mark of the beast, he shall experience *"the wrath of God"* (Rev. 14:9-11). Then it says, *"Here is the patience of the saints"* (Rev. 14:12). Just a few sentences later, Jesus is crowned King (Rev. 14:14). The Gathering happened between Revelation 14:12 and 14:14. Who are these *"saints"* if not the True Church? This is clearly shown in Revelation 14:13 by *"blessed are the dead which die in the Lord from henceforth."* The word *"henceforth"* denotes a changing of dispensations. Those that die from henceforth are not part of the Bride of Christ, but are resurrected at the end of the Tribulation.

We would like to point out here again, that there is only one Gathering of the Bride of Christ. Throughout this book we cite different Scriptures that point to the Gathering. This is where multiple Rapture theories come from. It is because people do not understand the symphonic view of the Scriptures and do not rightly divide the Word of Truth, especially in Revelation. Many Scriptures that are spread out over several chapters are all talking about the same event, like a symphony all playing notes in the same bar of music.

6) Here is the biggest point of all about the premise that the church is not mentioned in Revelation after 4:1. The word church is used to talk about the entire body of people that believe in Jesus Christ. We know people are left behind! Obviously the unprepared church is still here in the Tribulation period, all seven years. No matter which Gathering theory one believes in, the church is present in the Tribulation period. Not everyone is Gathered. Read what Luke says,

> *Watch ye therefore, and pray always, that ye may be accounted worthy to escape all these things that shall come to pass, and to stand before the Son of man* (Luke 21:36).

Only the ones who are accounted worthy to escape are pulled out. One cannot divorce the True Church from the Mystery of God. The Mystery is mentioned after Revelation 4:1; so how can anyone say the church is not mentioned after Revelation 4:1? Simply pointing out that the word "church" does not appear after Revelation 4:1 does not prove that the church is absent from the Tribulation period.

Here is more on the relationship between the church of "whosoevers" and the Mystery.

> *Even the mystery which hath been hid from ages and from generations, but now is made manifest to His saints: To whom God would make known what is the riches of the glory of this mystery among the Gentiles; which is Christ in you, the hope of glory* (Col. 1:26-27).

> *There is one body, and one Spirit, even as ye are called in one hope of your calling; one Lord, one faith, one baptism, one God and Father of all, who is above all, and through all, and in you all* (Ephes. 4:4-6).

We are all members of the body of Christ, and He lives in us through the Holy Spirit. This is equally applicable to the Jews as well as the Gentiles. Those Jews that accept Jesus before the Gathering to Christ are eligible to be part of the Bride of Christ. God promises Israel that He will prove that Jesus is the Messiah at the resurrection mid-Trib and He shall put His Spirit in them. Those Jews that recognize Jesus as their Messiah at the Gathering will be protected for 1260 days and go into the Millennium as flesh and blood bodies. With this understanding, most theologians will have a difficult time saying that the church is not present in the first half of the Tribulation period.

Who is the Great Restrainer in 2 Thessalonians 2?

We really do not know what the restrainer is or who it is, but we do know it is spiritual in nature. Most believe that the restrainer is the Holy Spirit and others believe it is Jesus himself. Still others think it might be Michael, the archangel.

What is the Great Restrainer restraining?

The issue that is more important than the identity of the restrainer is what or whom the restrainer is holding back, Satan's *"son of perdition"* (2 Thess. 2:3). We hear so many Bible scholars expounding their theories about whom the restrainer really is, but very little time is spent on what the restrainer is restraining.

> *And now ye know what withholdeth that he might be revealed in his time. For the mystery of iniquity doth already work: only he who now letteth will let, until he be taken out of the way. And then shall that Wicked* [the Antichrist] *be revealed...* (2 Thess. 2:6-8).

This was written two thousand years ago and the restrainer was busy restraining even back then. Because of this, we know that the great restrainer is not restraining a mere mortal man for two thousand years. Only Satan could have that level of iniquity over a two thousand-year time span. The restrainer is restraining Satan from indwelling the *"son of perdition"*.

> *Let no man deceive you by any means: for that day* [the day of the Lord Jesus Christ and our Gathering to Him (vs. 1-2)] *shall not come, except there come a falling away first,* [war in heaven and a spiritual apostasy here on earth] *and that man of sin be revealed, the son of perdition* (2 Thess. 2:3 - Explanation added).

We want to point out again, that there is a difference between the *"man of sin"* and the *"son of perdition."* The *"man of sin"* is a mere mortal man whom Satan gives secret power to. The *"son of perdition"* is this same man who appears to come back from the dead when Satan indwells him. In 2 Thessalonians 2:1-4, the coming of the Lord Jesus Christ to Gather the saints unto Himself will not happen until there is a great falling away in the church first and *"the son of perdition"* be revealed by declaring to be God in the temple. When the sudden and sign-less Rapture before the beginning of the Tribulation period does not happen, this could cause many in the church to lose their faith. Is this what is meant by *"a falling away first"* in 2 Thessalonians 2:3?

Many believe that the *"strong delusion"* in 2 Thessalonians 2:11 could be the false prince appearing to be raised from the dead as *"the son of perdition."* For this to be true, Satan must indwell this man. But Satan is fighting a war in heaven and is not thrown out of heaven until the middle of the Tribulation period (Rev. 12:9). He is not omnipresent like God is, so he cannot be fighting a war in heaven in Revelation 4:1 through Revelation 12 and also indwelling a body on earth during the first half of the Tribulation period. He can only indwell the false prince after he is cast out of heaven at mid-Trib. God can be in all places and be in the past, present and future all at the same time, but Satan cannot. Satan may think he is God, but he was a creature created by God and is restrained until the proper time.

Symphonically Satan indwells the *"man of sin"* immediately after losing the war in heaven, after being *"cast out into the earth"* (Rev. 12:9). This places the revealing of the *"son of perdition,"* the Satan-indwelt-Antichrist, just prior to the middle of the Tribulation period because the Antichrist is revealed when he rises from the dead and claims to be God in the temple (2 Thess. 2). 2 Thessalonians 2:9 says that Satan is to blame for the son of perdition's workings of iniquity.

However, let us not forget what 2 Thessalonians Chapter 2 is all about; *"now we beseech you, brethren, by the coming of our Lord Jesus Christ, and by our gathering together unto Him..."* The Gathering cannot happen until the *"son of perdition,"* the Satan-indwelt-Antichrist, is revealed. Therefore, the son of perdition will be revealed just a short time before the Mid-Trib Gathering of the saints to Christ.

What is the Church of Philadelphia Promised to be Kept From?

It is being preached by many that Christians will not suffer through any part of the Tribulation period. But where does it say that in the Bible? It doesn't. Pre-Trib preachers are telling us that Christ can come at any moment, but where have we seen the great apostasy caused by the revealing of the Antichrist or Christians being betrayed? Read what the Bible says in Matthew 24:9-10, Mark 13:9, Luke 21:12 and 1 Peter 3:14. Many of you are thinking that we were promised not to suffer during the Tribulation period because of the promise in Revelation 3:10, but that is not exactly what it says. It promises to keep faithful Christians of the Philadelphia church from the hour of temptation. Once again, we point out that the hour is 42 months, not seven years. We get this hour premise from linking Revelation 17:12's *"one hour"* with Revelation 13:5's *"forty and two months"*.

> *Because thou hast kept the word of My patience, I also*
> *will keep thee from **the hour of temptation**, which shall*
> *come upon all the world, to try them that dwell upon the*
> *earth* (Rev. 3:10 - Emphasis added).

We know the Tribulation period is divided into two halves. During the first half, God is allowing man's evilness to come to its full measure so humanity will have to choose either Christ or Antichrist. During the second half of the Tribulation period, God is pouring out His wrath on those who have chosen to follow the Antichrist. We believe that *"the hour of temptation"* (Rev. 3:10) and the ten kings receiving *"power as kings one hour with the beast"* (Rev. 17:12) happens during a three and one half-year period that encompasses the whole second half of the Tribulation period. God pours out His wrath during this timeframe.

Read Revelation 14:7, *"for the hour of His judgment has come."* Scripture suggests that the Gathering happens when the hour has come in the middle of the Tribulation period.

> *Here is the patience of the saints: here are they that*
> *keep the commandments of God, and the faith of Jesus.*
> *And I heard a voice from heaven saying unto me, Write,*
> *Blessed are the dead which die in the Lord from*
> *henceforth…* (Rev. 14:12-13a).

Our Scriptural witness is found in Revelation 3:10, *"Because thou hast kept the word of My patience"* and Revelation 3:8, *"I know thy works…. Thou hast kept My word, and not denied My name."* We believe all these verses are speaking of the same event. The saints, who have been patiently waiting for Christ's promise to deliver them from Satan's wrath, have not denied the name of Christ or lost their faith. Secondly, the hour of wrath has come. Thirdly, from now on, blessed are the dead that die in Christ during the last three and one half years of the Tribulation period. And finally, a new dispensation starts with Revelation 14:13, *"from henceforth."* The stewardship of the *"Everlasting Gospel"* is given back to Israel through the 144,000. Although, many Bible scholars use the Philadelphia church as the poster child for why they believe the church will not see any of the seven year Tribulation period, we have clearly shown the error in that thinking. Furthermore, we want to point out that all the true believers from the seven churches are promised to be spared from the hour of temptation, including the Laodicean church.

> *Behold, I stand at the door, and knock: if any man hear My voice, and open the door, I will come in to him, and will sup with him, and He with Me* (Rev. 3:20).

Even the members of the Laodicean church have the opportunity to be part of the Bride of Christ.

> *Behold, I* [Jesus] *come quickly: hold that fast which thou hast, **that no man take thy crown**. Him that overcometh will I make a pillar in the Temple of My God, and he shall go no more out: and I will write upon him the name of My God, and the name of the city of My God, which is new Jerusalem, which cometh down out of heaven from My God: and I will write upon him My new name* (Rev. 3:11-12 - Emphasis added).

> *That the trial of your faith, being much more precious than of gold that perisheth, though it be tried with fire, might be found unto praise and honour and glory at the appearing of Jesus Christ: Receiving the end of your faith, even the salvation of your souls* (1 Peter 1:7, 9).

The Gathering is a reward; it is a crown to lay at the Lord's feet. Only the people who are Gathered get this crown. If you lose your crown by denying His name, you will miss the Gathering. The Gathering is a reward and is guaranteed to those who are part of the True Church, which is Bride of Christ. The unprepared church, which is typified by the five foolish virgins in Matthew 25 or the thorny soil type in the Gospels, will have to choose to follow Christ or Antichrist because they are unprepared at the time of the Gathering. Why else is the Lord saying to the church of Philadelphia, let no man take away your crown? Why else would Jesus say in Luke 21,

> *Watch ye therefore, and pray always, that ye may be accounted worthy to escape all these things which shall come to pass, and to stand before the Son of man* (Luke 21:36).

> *Blessed is the man that endureth temptation: for when he is tried, he shall receive the crown of Life, which the Lord hath promised to them that love Him* (James 1:12).

Faith put into action has a role in earning this crown; the prize is being included in the Gathering of the saints in the air to meet Jesus. In addition, the church of Philadelphia is promised to be kept from the hour of temptation, which shall come upon the entire world, because of their faithful works.

> *I know thy works: behold, I have set before thee an open door, and no man can shut it: for thou hast a little strength, and hast kept My word, and hast not denied My name* (Rev. 3:8).

They were patiently enduring and waiting for Jesus. While waiting for the Gathering, they remembered God's promise by keeping His Word, and they did not deny the name of Jesus. God said to the church of Pergamos in Revelation 2:13, *"I know thy works... and thou holdest fast My name, and hast not denied My faith."* In fact, all seven letters tell the reader that the overcomers will receive blessings for being an overcomer. Read all seven letters and see what it takes to be an overcomer. Some things are clear. Never renounce Christ, never lose faith in Him, watch for His coming and pick up your cross daily. These are some of the faithful works that are necessary for keeping the crown. We get into this in more detail in the *"Salvation"* Chapter.

The church of Philadelphia will keep *"the word of My patience"* (Rev. 3:10), but what are they enduring or patiently waiting through? Could it be they are enduring the first half of the Tribulation period? If not, then they must be enduring something before the Tribulation period. The point here is, they are enduring tribulations of some kind and it affects the whole church. The pre-Tribulation theorists like to use the Philadelphia church as evidence for the sudden and sign-less

Rapture happening prior to the Tribulation period because of the promise to be kept from the *"hour."* We understand their interpretation, but the *"hour"* may not be seven years long and therefore there is an inherent problem in their view.

Keep in mind though that the remnant of the church of Philadelphia is still here now, as well as remnants from all the seven churches. The seven letters are letters to the actual churches in the past, but they are also written to us in this time as well. Many times Scripture has a partial near fulfillment and a total future fulfillment. When one reads a verse it means what it says in plan language, yet it may also have a dual meaning symphonically within the whole of Scripture. We find this again and again concerning prophecy throughout both the Old and New Testaments.

Getting back to the seven letters to the seven churches, each church is told to overcome and is given blessings for doing so. We do not think it is a coincidence that the church is said to have overcome later in Revelation 12:11; this verse is mentioned right after Satan is cast down from heaven, after losing his battle there. To endure is to overcome, and it hits our spirit to mean, live through a time of Tribulation when the *"son of perdition"* or Antichrist is revealed without becoming backslidden or losing patience because Jesus did not come when most thought He should. We must keep the faith, and the testimony of Jesus. We must never deny His name. *"And they overcame him by the blood of the Lamb, and by the word of their testimony; and they loved not their lives unto death"* (Rev. 12:11). All this happens before the Gathering. Does this Scripture sound like there will be a sudden and sign-less pre-Trib Rapture to you?

Do Not Be Offended in the Lord

John the Baptist, while in the dungeon waiting to have his head cut off was puzzled because Jesus did not come for him to save his life. In Luke 7:19 John asked of Jesus, *"art thou He that should come? Or look we for another?"* John has not lost his faith in Jesus. He is facing death and is asking Jesus for an affirmation. He is asking for comfort from the Lord. Jesus replied,

> *Go your way, and tell John what things you have seen and heard; how that the blind see, the lame walk, the*

> *lepers are cleansed, the deaf hear, the dead are raised,*
> *to the poor the gospel is preached. And blessed is he*
> [John the Baptist]*, whosoever* [all believers] *shall not be*
> *offended in Me* (Luke 7: 22-23).

Jesus is telling John and all of us that we are not to lose faith in Him, even unto death. If any of us find ourselves imprisoned because of our faith in Jesus, we are not to deny His name, even if it means death for us.

> *Then shall they deliver you up to be afflicted, and shall*
> *kill you: and ye shall be hated of all nations for My*
> *name's sake. And then shall many be offended, and shall*
> *betray one another, and shall hate one another* (Matt.
> 24:9-10).

We believe that the Scripture says many Christians will be disillusioned and lose faith in the promise of Christ's Appearing. True Christians will not lose the guarantee of salvation. However, the unprepared church may lose the reward of the Gathering. Search your heart. If the Lord does not come before the Tribulation period and we see all kinds of signs and wonders, Christians who are not strong in their faith will begin to wonder and question their faith. Scripture says, *"God shall send them strong delusion, that they should believe a lie"* (2 Thess. 2:11). We believe that the revealing of the son of perdition by appearing to rise from the dead is that great delusion and it is not meant to, nor does it deceive the Bride of Christ.

We Are to Know When Christ Will Come

What about the verses that say we are not to know what day or hour that Jesus will come. Sitting here today we cannot tell you what day Christ will come for the church. We do not know. Only the Father in Heaven knows when the clock will start. It starts when the first seal is opened in Heaven and the Two Witnesses start preaching. Even though we may not know the exact time when the Two Witnesses begin, we are given a whole list of things to watch for and when they happen, the time is at the door. We do know that when the Two Witnesses start their ministry it will be 1260 days before they are killed by the Antichrist. We also know that three and one half days latter they will be resurrected. When that happens, we believe that the dead in Christ are resurrected also. This is when the Father in Heaven tells Jesus *"that there should be time no longer"* (Rev. 10:6). This is when the Mid-Trib Gathering happens. This is when there is no more delay for God to execute His wrath upon the Antichrist and his followers. After this event, there will be another three and one half years of great Tribulation.

We have met so many people who refuse to study these prophecies because they have been taught that no man may know the day or the hour of the Gathering to Christ. This teaching is the biggest error that keeps Christians in the dark about end time events. Because of this teaching many Christians are willingly ignorant of prophecies. *"If therefore thou shalt not watch, I will come as a thief, and thou shalt not know what hour I will come upon thee"* (Rev. 3:3). The key word is *"if."* In other words, you can know when Jesus will come for you unless you do not read prophecy and do not watch for the signs. His Gathering is not a sign-less event. The parable of the ten virgins is a study on patiently waiting and being prepared to recognize the hour of His coming (Matt. 25:1-13, see also 1 Thess. 5:4-9).

Most of Sardis is Left Behind

Read the letter to the church of Sardis,

> *... I know thy works, that thou hast a name that thou livest, and art dead. Be watchful, and strengthen the things which remain, that are ready to die: for I have not found thy works perfect before God. Remember therefore how thou hast received and heard, and hold fast, and repent.* **If therefore thou shalt not watch,** *I will come on thee as a thief, and thou shalt not know what hour I will come upon thee. Thou hast a few names even in Sardis which have not defiled their garments; and they shall walk with Me in white: for they are worthy. He that overcometh, the same shall be clothed in white raiment; and I will not blot out his name out of the Book of Life, but I will confess his name before My Father, and before His angels.* (Rev. 3:1-5 - Emphasis added).

God is saying to them, I know your deeds and you call yourselves Christians, but you are dead. Faith not put into action is dead. Furthermore, it means that if you do not watch for His return you will be left behind. God is saying to Sardis, I know you are weak but strengthen what you have and watch for Me or you will be counted among the dead.

Only a few from the church of Sardis are worthy for the Gathering because most have defiled their garments. What does that mean? We know that the Bride of Christ is clothed in the righteousness of Christ; *"For the fine linen is the righteousness of the saints"* (Rev. 19:8). So to defile ones clothes is to commit unrighteous acts, fornication with the depths of Satan. The ones who do not defile themselves will be washed clean with the blood of Jesus. Their garments will be purer and whiter than anything on earth.

> *These are they which came out of great tribulation, and have washed their robes, and made them white in the blood of the Lamb* (Rev. 7:14).

This is the blessed hope we all have. It is the same blessed hope to the overcomers found in every letter to the seven churches. The most quoted one being Revelation 3:10 because of its specific promise to keep us from the wrath of God.

Chapter 9

Understanding the Book of Revelation

The Book of Revelation is not the most important Book of the New Testament, but it is the only Book that promises a double blessing for reading it and keeping those things that are written therein. That being said, why is it then that the Book of Revelation is the least read and least understood Book of the New Testament? Perhaps it is because many people feel it is too hard to understand or that it is doomsday teaching. We think that the imminency teaching about the return of Christ is the main reason people do not read the Book. People think it does not apply to them because the church must be removed before any of what is in the Book of Revelation can happen. This idea couldn't be farther from the truth.

We will show how simple the Book of Revelation is to understand. We will show you the big picture, the purpose for the Book and what the storyline is. Most importantly, we will show you why the Book of Revelation is vital to be read and understood. One cannot fully understand what Christ did on the cross without understanding how and when Christ our Redeemer receives legal authority to have Michael remove Satan from heaven. Christ then Gathers His Bride, hears their testimony, and passes judgment on those that dwell on the earth. Christ takes physical possession of the earthly kingdoms three and one half years later, at His Triumphal Return to Earth.

What is the Purpose of the Seals?

At the beginning of the Tribulation period Jesus opens the sealed book in Heaven, which is in the spiritual realm. Christ breaks all seven seals one at a time and He opens the sealed book in Heaven. We know that your Bible probably says scroll. However, most of the Scriptures we quote are taken from the King James Version of the Bible and to be consistent, we are going with the English word *"book."* The Greek word *"biblion"* is translated only one time as "scroll," as found in Revelation 6:14, and 29 times as "book."

Whether it is a book or a scroll is not the point of importance. The important thing for you to realize is that John was weeping *"because no man was found worthy to open and to read the book, neither to look thereon"* (Rev. 5:4) until Jesus came forth. Why would John cry? It must have been evident to John that the Bride of Christ could never be brought to heaven until Satan was removed first. Heaven must be cleansed before the crowning of Christ and His Bride is brought home for the Wedding. If Jesus had not been found worthy to break the seals, then Satan would continue having his crowns of authority and dominion over the earth and its inhabitants forever.

The seals are broken one at a time in Heaven but their affects are not immediate on the earth. Things that seemingly happen instantaneously in Heaven play out over time on the earth. For example, the first seal with the rider on the white horse is the false prince that shall come and in the beginning of the Tribulation period he is selling peace and safety. Then he gains more and more power until he is on the verge of being the conqueror. That is when he is killed and appears to be brought back to life. Once indwelt by Satan mid-Trib, he is crowned as the false king of the earth and the conqueror that the first seal talked about.

The seal's affects on the earth are slow in coming but gain momentum in the second half of the Tribulation and continue until the end. However, the affects of the trumpets on the earth are quick in coming and their affects likewise stack upon the previous one until the end of the Tribulation period. See our chart:

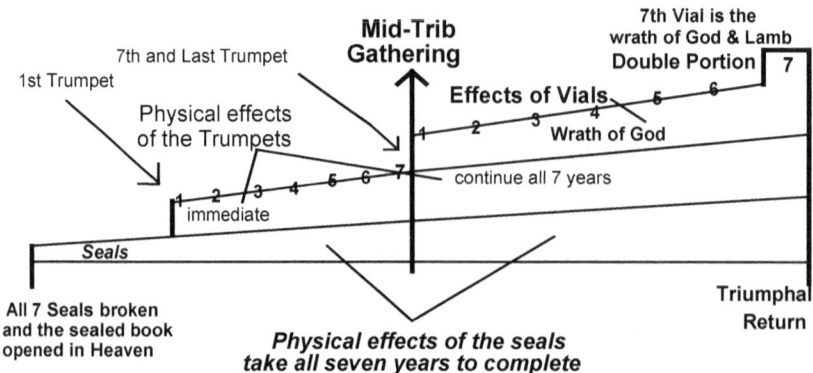

Stacking of the Seals, Trumpets and Vials

Again, remember that the seven seals are on a single book and they are broken in Heaven, but their affects encompass the whole of the seven-year Tribulation period. That means that from the time that each seal's affects are felt on the earth they will continue to the end of the Tribulation period. The overall affects stack upon one another making the conditions on earth progressively worse and worse.

Now let's look at two Old Testament examples to understand fully the importance of God's plan in the breaking of the seals on the sealed book in Heaven.

Boaz is the Foreshadow of our Kinsman-Redeemer

If a Jewish widow had no offspring at her husband's death, a kinsman-redeemer could purchase her husband's land and marry his wife in order to continue the family bloodline. An example of this is found in Ruth 3 and 4. Ruth was a widowed daughter-in-law to Naomi, a widowed Jewish woman. Boaz, as a near kinsman-redeemer had an obligation to marry Ruth to carry on the family bloodline and the right to purchase the land inherited by Ruth's deceased husband, Mahlon. Boaz agreed to marry Ruth and purchase the land. Boaz gathered the witnesses and the elders of the city to complete the transaction of the land purchase and Ruth became his wife. Boaz was a type and foreshadows Jesus Christ as our Kinsman-Redeemer.

Another example of how land was bought and sold according to Jewish *"law and custom"* is seen in Jeremiah 32:9-14. Jeremiah bought a field and he subscribed the evidence of the transaction in two documents before the court and before the witnesses. One was sealed so it could not be tampered with and the other was open or public record so all could see who owned the property. Both the sealed evidence and the open were placed in a safe place for preservation.

In Revelation 4:1-2 John is caught up to Heaven in the spirit to see the *"things which must be hereafter."* He was shown the sealed book in Revelation 5. The significance of the sealed book in Heaven is the preservation of the evidence that Jesus Christ is our Kinsman-Redeemer. It is sealed so Satan and his powers cannot tamper with it or attempt to change it. It gives Jesus Christ legal and everlasting dominion, glory, and a kingdom that shall not be destroyed (Dan. 7:14). The open evidence or public record is found in God's Will and

Testament, known to us as our Holy Bible. Only to the extent that we study the Scriptures will we know what our benefits are as joint-heirs with Christ. Therefore, *"study to show thyself approved unto God, a workman that needeth not to be ashamed, rightly dividing the word of truth"* (2 Tim. 2:15). Jesus told us that He has foretold all things that will happen so we need not be deceived (Mark 13:23, Matt. 24:25). Have you diligently studied the Scriptures to know what will happen?

The Ransom Paid

Under the New Covenant of Grace Jesus Christ came to earth to preach this good news to whosoever will believe in Him, Jew and Gentile alike. Jesus came to earth as God in the form of human flesh to pay the ransom to redeem the earth and its inhabitant's back from Satan's dominion. The purchase price was paid by Jesus' death on the cross and the presentation of His blood sacrifice in Heaven. But, as kinsman-redeemer the legal transaction will not be completed until the dominion granted by the title deed to the earth is transferred from Satan to Christ, His Bride is brought to Heaven, He marries His Bride, and He takes physical possession of the earth.

The Transfer of Dominion from Satan to Christ

Adam and Eve were originally given dominion over the earth and everything in it. However, Satan deceived them and they lost that dominion to him. Satan will continue to have legal dominion over the earth and its inhabitants until God turns that dominion over to Christ; but when does this happen? Revelation 11:15 tells us that *"the kingdoms of this world are become the kingdoms of our LORD, and of His Christ; and He shall reign for ever and ever"* at the sounding of the seventh trumpet. At that time the twenty-four elders around God's throne are worshipping God and *"saying... because thou **hast** taken to thee Thy great power, and **hast reigned"*** (Rev. 11:17 - Emphasis added). In Daniel 7 we see the little horn speaking great words against the most High and wearing out the saints *"...until a time and times and the dividing of time. But the judgment shall sit, and they shall take away his dominion..."* (Dan. 7:25-26). Therefore, legal dominion of the earth is transferred to Christ at the sounding of the seventh trumpet mid-Trib. During the war in heaven Satan is expelled and it is confirmed in Revelation 13:1 that Satan loses the seven crowns on his heads that he had in Revelation 12:3. From Daniel 7:9-10 we learn that the judgment was set and the Books were opened. Thousand thousands of angels ministered before God and ten thousand times ten thousand stood before Him (Dan. 7:10, Rev. 5:11). This is the Bride of Christ caught up to the Judgment seat of Christ. Just like the two examples from the Old Testament, this legal transaction is done before the Heavenly Court, the twenty-four elders, and the angels who are the witnesses.

The Purpose of the Courtroom Scene

In Revelation 4:1 John is told to *"Come up hither"* and see all the things that will happen in God's courtroom. The judgment court is comprised of: God, Jesus the Lamb, the seven Spirits of God better known as the Holy Spirit, the four living creatures surrounding the throne, the twenty-four elders, and the angels who are the witnesses. The first thing that the court wanted to know was; is there a legal and willing kinsman-redeemer? John was weeping until the slain Lamb, Jesus Christ, was found to be that legal and willing Kinsman-Redeemer worthy to break the seals of the title deed to earth and to marry His Bride at the Marriage Supper of the Lamb. The breaking of the seals on the sealed book bring about these and all other judgments that take place in God's courtroom in Heaven. You can read about them throughout the Book of Revelation.

The Big Picture Purpose of the Book of Revelation

God's judgment court sitting and the sealed book being opened are the scenes John describes in Revelation 4:1 - 5:14. In Revelation 12 we see that the heavenly dominion is stripped from Satan and given to Jesus Christ. Satan and his angels are banished from heaven and cast to the earth. Because he knows he has a very short time, Satan has *"great wrath"* against the inhabitants of the earth (Rev. 12:12). Revelation 7:9 describes *"a great multitude... of all nations, and kindreds, and people, and tongues, stood before the throne."* Scriptural witnesses are found in Daniel 7:10 and Revelation 5:11. *"These are they which came out of great Tribulation"* (Rev. 7:14). The Scriptural witness is found in Matthew 24:21, 29-31. At the sounding of the seventh trumpet we learn that *"the kingdoms of the world are become the kingdoms of our LORD, and of His Christ; and*

He shall reign for ever and ever" (Rev. 11:15). The 24 elders confirm this at the seventh trumpet when they fall on their faces in worship saying, *"because thou hast taken to thee Thy great power, and hast reigned"* (Rev. 11:16-17). They also say that is time to judge the dead, give rewards to the faithful and that *"Thy wrath is come"* (Rev. 11:18). Then John sees the *"sea of glass mingled with fire: and them that had gotten victory"* over the beast, his image, his mark, and over the number of his name standing on the sea of glass (Rev. 15:2). These overcomers are singing *"the song of Moses"*, *"the song of the Lamb"*, praising God and calling Jesus *"thou King of saints"* (Rev. 15:3). *"A great voice of much people in heaven"* is praising God *"for He hath judged the great whore... and hath avenged the blood of His servants at her hand"* (Rev. 19:1-2). In Revelation 19:7 *"the Marriage of the Lamb is come, and His wife hath made herself ready."* After the Marriage Supper of the Lamb, Christ takes physical possession of the earth at His Triumphal Return with *"the armies which were in heaven"* (Rev. 19:14). The Antichrist and the false prophet are *"cast alive into a lake of fire"* (Rev. 19:20). Satan is cast into the bottomless pit for a thousand years (Rev. 20:3). Christ then sets up and reigns over His Earthly Kingdom during that one thousand years, His wife ruling and reigning with Him (Rev. 1:6, 2:26-27, 5:10, 20:4, 20:6).

Why Revelation is Vital to be Read

You have the open Book contained in your Holy Bible. The sealed book in Heaven is the same as yours. Having just read from the open Book, you have learned that only the Kinsman-Redeemer is worthy to open the sealed version in Heaven, ending Satan's dominion. The Book of Revelation comforts us and gives us strength to overcome the Beast and not fall for his deceptions, worship him or his image or receive his mark. The Book of Revelation teaches us when to expect Christ and it is not in Revelation 4:1. The Gathering is after Satan is cast into the earth in Revelation 12 and Christ has received legal dominion over the kingdoms of this world in Revelation 11. Revelation 14:14-16 describes the actual Gathering of the Bride, which are both the dead and the living in Christ, by the King and His angels during the reaping of the harvest. Then in Revelation 14:13 we see a new dispensation begin by the words *"from henceforth"*.

Please remember that none of this can take place until the sealed book is opened and the opening of this sealed book brings about the trumpets, which calls the Bride home for her testimony in the Heavenly courtroom. *"The judgment shall sit"* (Dan. 7:26) issuing the verdict, so that the vials of God's wrath may be poured out upon the Antichrist and his followers. All these things are there for us to know and understand so we will not be deceived by anyone. This is just a brief overview of all the things that happen because of the provisions of the title deed to the earth contained within the sealed book.

What is the Purpose of the Trumpets?

Israel used several different types of trumpets in the Old Testament. There were metal trumpets made from silver and others from gold. Then there were the shofar trumpets fashioned from a ram's horn. Trumpets were used to signal an event or call to action. It can be a trumpet of victory or alarm. Israel used different series of blasts or bleats to signal whatever message was intended, similar to Morris Code. Israel did not have mass media like radio or television; instead used loud trumpets to communicate.

God's trumpet was sounded the first time at Mount Sinai when God established a Covenant with Israel (Ex. 19:18-20). Scripture speaks of another time the trumpet will be sounded by God in Zechariah 9:14; when Jesus shall be *"seen over them,"* revealed to Israel. In Zechariah 9:16, God protects Israel (1260 days - Rev. 12:6).

Theologians tend to focus on the seals, trumpets and vials in eschatology studies. Because of this, people miss the importance and the purpose of the Book of Revelation, which is the transference of dominion from Satan to Christ, the courtroom scene for judgment of those on earth and the new dispensation through the 144,000 mid-Trib. We are not going to get too detailed into the meaning of every trumpet or debate their relevance to Jewish traditions or feasts but think of the trumpets as judgments one would receive in our court system today. What is the purpose for the judge to issue a judgment to someone for breaking the law? It is to get them to change their behavior. We believe that the trumpets are God's call to accept Jesus Christ as Savior. We also believe there is a specific number of us that God the Father is waiting for (fullness of the Gentiles) before Christ comes at the sounding of the seventh trumpet to collect His Bride.

The affects of the trumpets in Revelation are immediate on earth unlike the seals from the sealed book, which present themselves over time, at the appointed time. Each of the first four trumpets bring about God's judgment, but is limited to a third part (Rev. 8:7-12, 9:15, 18; 12:4). Christ likened the affects of the trumpets to birth pangs of a woman in travail.

The Elect will suffer through these birth pangs until mid-Trib. Then at the appointed time, the Father in Heaven declares the Mystery of God finished. Michael the Archangel stands up and evicts Satan and his angels out of heaven. Jesus at that point legally assumes all authority, dominion, and power. Revelation 11:15, 11:17, 12:10 and 15:2-4 supports this premise. Jesus is no longer seen as just the Lamb of God, but as the King. This is evident because the one who sits on the cloud is *"like unto the Son of man"* and has a golden crown on His head as seen in Revelation 14:14.

What is the Purpose of the Vials?

When the dispensation of the Mystery is finished, then it is time for God's wrath. The great white robed multitude, which is the Bride of Christ, stands on the crystal sea mingled with fire. They are in the Heavenly Court before the Throne to give their testimonies to God after the mid-Trib Gathering (Rev. 15:1-8). Upon hearing their testimony God delivers judgment in the form of wrath. Revelation 16:5-6 describes why the vials of wrath are poured out; it is because our Lord *"hast judged thus. For they have shed the blood of saints and prophets..."* God's wrath is so terrifying that people will wish they were dead. Make no mistake, people will say that the trumpet judgments are the wrath of God, but the truth is, it is not. The wrath of God is beyond belief; it will be too horrible to even imagine. The judgments like tsunamis and earthquakes we are experiencing now are terrifying, but they are not the wrath of God. It is only going to get worse and worse until Jesus sets up His Millennial Kingdom. After the Elect are Gathered, then the wrath of God is poured out. *"For God hath not appointed us to wrath, but to obtain salvation by our Lord Jesus Christ,"* (1 Thess. 5:9). Do not be deceived by any means, the Bride of Christ will not be here for God's wrath. Faithful Christians who endure patiently until the Gathering will receive their reward by being included as the Bride of Christ.

Debunking Pre-Tribulation Theory's Chronological View

The majority of theologians read the Book of Revelation in chronological order as Pentecost explains in his doctoral dissertation, *Things to Come.*[35] They have the sudden and sign-less Rapture before the tribulation starts along with the apostasy, the Antichrist revealed and the 144,000 sealed when the tribulation period starts. Pentecost refutes the mid-Trib position by pointing out that that the Church could not enter the Tribulation period because they would convert the 144,000 becoming "saved into the church."[36] With all due respect, the 144,000 do not learn the new song until the season of the seventh trumpet, where they begin their three and one-half year ministry, so it would be hard for the 144,000 to be at the beginning of the first half of the Tribulation. Advocates of the chronology theory of the Book of Revelation insist the 144,000 minister in the first half of the Tribulation, yet they are not chronologically introduced in the Book of Revelation until the middle of the Tribulation. The pre-Tribulation Rapturists like Pentecost are seeing a piece of what we are saying when they connect all these things together in time as Scripture suggests. It is only because of their premise that when God is again dealing with Israel happens during Daniel's seventieth week. They believe Daniel's seventieth week is a seven-year period and the Tribulation happens to be that seven-year period. They are missing the split seventieth week where Christ began Daniel's seventieth week at His baptism and suspended that week in the middle of the week at the cross.

If one were to read the Book of Revelation chronologically, one would read verses that are repetitive and seemingly contradictory. An example is found in Revelation 11:7 when the beast rises out of the pit he kills the Two Witnesses. Then in Revelation 17:8 the beast rising out of the pit is mentioned again. How many beasts are there and how many times does he rise from the pit? The answer is one beast and he only rises out of the pit once. This is a prime example of the double witness, two Scriptures supporting each other. This is also a great example of why the Book of Revelation cannot be read chronologically.

Another example is when the Two Witnesses in Revelation 11:3 begin their 1260 day ministry at the beginning of the seven-year Tribulation. They are present during the first half of the Tribulation because after their resurrection there is another 42 months. In Revelation 11:15 the seventh trumpet sounds and the Two Witnesses are resurrected. Pentecost's position on the seventh trumpet is that it sounds at the end of the seven-year period.[37] Even if you truly read the Book of Revelation chronologically, then how can the seventh trumpet be anything other than mid-Tribulation, with 42-months to follow after it? Pentecost explains Revelation 11's trumpet scene, "The scene depicted is not that of a rapture, but of the revelation of Christ to the earth."[38] Pentecost is seeing the majesty aspect of the seventh trumpet in Revelation 11 and the transferring of power from Satan to Christ. He explains that Christ is revealed to Israel, but then makes the mental leap that His revealing is the Second Advent. Just think about this point for a moment; if Revelation 11 is the Second Advent chronologically, then what is Christ's Triumphal return eight chapters later in Revelation 19, His Third Advent? Of course not! Pentecost insists on interpreting the Book of Revelation chronologically as he was taught to do, but look at the inconsistencies one faces when doing so.

The Bible does not teach that the Book of Revelation must be read chronologically, but the precepts of man teaching man does; one precept built upon another until nonsense is derived.

It seems like everyone has their own pet theories and they try to interpret Scriptures to fit their premises. All we pray for is that you the reader will search the Scriptures for the truth. Read what the Word of God actually says and discern the true meaning with the Holy Spirit's guidance. We could not have said it any better than Lewis, "It must be understood, however that no doctrine rises or falls on the witness of history or of the testimony of church fathers. A valid doctrinal truth must find its authority in the words of Scripture alone."[39]

The Symphonic View

The Book of Revelation is like a master play. Each chapter tells its own story within the play, like mini plays or skits. How else would God try to explain these events concerning the Spirit World to a mere mortal? How would God explain multi-dimensional ideas? God is explaining things that happen in Heaven's time. Things that happen in Heaven do not affect earth until it is the proper time for them to do so.

There is a pattern in the Book of Revelation where something is described in Heaven spiritually and then John is shown events playing out on the earth physically. Over and over the pattern repeats. Often times the same event is described repeatedly from a different perspective or concerning different entities.

We will attempt to describe time in Heaven. God is omnipresent. God created time and placed His Creation in it. Scripture suggests time in Heaven is different from the time here on earth. One day in Heaven is like 365,000 days on earth (2 Peter 3:8 and Psalms 90:4).

One of the authors of this book had a dream that explained this using music. He heard music in Heaven, but the music did not have a beat. The music had rhythm but no time.

Another example is that the sacred name of God, (YHWH), cannot be said here on earth because it is all consonants without any vowels. In Heaven His name can be said because Heaven's time is unlike ours. We are talking about being unable to say any word that is all consonants. It cannot be done in this physical realm of time and space.

When God is showing John all these things in Heaven, He had to show him many things that are related but all happen at once. These events are taking place in Heavenly time. God had to show John one at a time so he could take it all in. God is without limits! He could have just dumped it all in John's brain, but the point is He did not. We think it is so that we the readers of the Book of Revelation can understand symphonic events.

Symphonic View of End Time Events

Please understand that a lot of these events happen simultaneously and we are trying to place them chronologically, which is impossible. However, we have them in as close to proper proximity as we understand them to be.

Pre-Tribulation Events
- The Muslim nations become increasingly jealous of Israel's wealth.
- The Israeli-Palestinian conflict leads to a pseudo peace, *"when Israel is at rest"* (Ezek. 38:11).

- Under international pressure, Israel dismantles the "wall" it has built. *"The land of unwalled villages"* (Ezek. 38:11).
- Islamic nations form an alliance against Israel and will initiate an invasion of Israel. There is some yet unknown event that triggers this war. Even now Iran is calling for the "extermination of Israel." Former President Mahmoud Ahmadinejad of Iran is denying that the holocaust of World War II ever happened and wants to declare holy war against Israel. He thinks by causing this war with Israel, it will bring about the Muslim "messiah."
- Religious war begins in the Middle East and may spread to World War III.
- Gog and Magog, modern day Russia are drawn into the conflict. God will put a hook into their jaw and drag them into this war (Ezek. 38:2-4). We do not know what that hook is yet. It could be a Russian agreement to defend Iran if attacked.
- Something happens during this first battle that changes the stalemate on the Temple Mount, making it possible for the temple to be rebuilt.
- 5/6th's of the invading Russian and Islamic armies are destroyed supernaturally and are buried in the valley of Hamon-gog in Israel (Ezek. 39:2, 11).
- Fire, nuclear war on Magog and those that dwell carelessly on the coast lands (Ezek. 39:6).
- Possible US-Russian nuclear exchange.
- Much of Europe spared from this exchange.
- It will take Israel seven years to burn the war materials (Ezek. 39:9-10). This begins at the beginning of the seven years of Tribulation.
- Gathering of Jews to Israel from every nation. It is abundantly clear God is protecting Israel from invaders. The Jews find a revived sense of pride in their religion and many move to Israel to be part of this seemingly undefeatable nation. They seek to restore the temple and return to animal sacrificing.

The Beginning of the Seven-Year Tribulation Period
- Jesus opens the seven-sealed book in Heaven. All seven seals are broken and then the book is opened. The sealed book contains

legal dominion, authority and the title deed to Heaven and the earth.

- The affects of those seals are not translated to earth instantaneously. They translate to the earth over the whole seven year time span and their affects last until the end of the Tribulation period, while accumulating to make things get progressively worse and worse (Rev. 5:1-8:5).
- The Two Witnesses, whom we believe are Elijah and Moses, start their ministry of 1260 days (Rev. 11:3).
- The church is still here.

The Rise of the false prince and still the Beginning of the Tribulation

- The false prince in Daniel 9:26-27 rises to prominence like a phoenix out of the ashes of this religious war called the Gog-Magog war that starts in the Middle East. He is also known as *"that man of sin"* from 2 Thessalonians 2:3. He is not yet revealed as the Antichrist. Hatred towards religious extremists will be at a boiling point in the world.
- The false prince will confirm a covenant with Israel. We think the covenant's purpose is to allow Israel under his auspices to rebuild the temple and re-establish the daily sacrifice (Dan. 9:26-27). This is a guess because the Scriptures do not actually say he does this. However, the temple gets rebuilt somehow.
- Construction of the temple begins in Jerusalem.
- Israel takes seven months to bury the dead from the Gog-Magog invasion. The invader's bodies lie in the valley of Hamon-gog (Ezek. 39:11-12).
- Ten days later, after the land has been cleansed, the daily sacrifices begin in the rebuilt temple. Math for this: Two halves of the Tribulation x 1260 days each = 2520 days. Then take 2520 days minus the 2300 days (from the end of the Tribulation period backwards in Daniel 8:14) = 7 months and 10 days or 220 days when using the Jewish 30-day per month calendar.
- The false prince continues to consolidate his power. He has mystery and intrigue about him. He is like a messiah figure with all the answers and the world loves him. Though he is still not revealed as a false messiah, some Christians may suspect he is.

- The mark of the beast system is set up, but is not yet mandatory. Possibly a new world currency or computer credits replacing cash. Commerce without the mark will be increasingly more difficult.

The False Prophet and the Growing Apostasy

- After the devastation of this great religious war, progressive apostasy intensifies and falling away in the church begins.
- The false prophet who is the beast that rises out of the earth is a religious leader who rises on the world scene. Some believe it will be the Pope. But whoever he is, his message is about unity of all religions and he may call it a "new age." It is not new at all. It is very old, as old as the Tower of Babel. He preaches a religion where all religions are welcome so long as your religion does not claim it is the only way to God. Anyone who believes Christ is the only way will be considered an uncompassionate, a hater and even a terrorist. This false prophet will lead astray many professing Christians from their faith. Clarification is due here. Many people will still claim to be Christian while at the same time deny His bodily resurrection, that Christ is the only way and much more. However, the Bride of Christ will not be deceived and will keep their faith under great persecution and many will be martyred. Except for the false prophet, this religious thinking and persecution of the church is already happening even now in many parts of the world. This religious war has already begun!
- The false prophet gives his allegiance to the false prince.
- The false prince uses the false prophet and his false church to rise to greater power.
- Persecution of the True Church of Jesus Christ begins slowly at first and progressively gets worse. Remember how it began with the Jews in Nazi Germany. And remember how it ended for both the Jews and Christians. Hitler also killed Christians who dared to stand against him.

Events Leading to the Middle of the Tribulation

- Trumpets begin with the first trumpet sounding (Rev. 8:7). All seven trumpets will sound by the middle of the Tribulation. Unlike the seals, the trumpet's affects on earth are translated immediately and their affects also last until the end of the

Tribulation period. Like the seals, each time a trumpet blows its affects are added to the others.

- The Two Witnesses have become a problem for the false prince, the beast coming out of the sea (Rev. 11:5-6, 11:10-12, 13:1-2).
- Sometime very close to the middle of the Tribulation God seals the 144,000 (Rev. 7:1-8, 14:1). Their ministry lasts for three and one half years during the second half of the Tribulation period.
- 30 days prior to the middle of the Tribulation the false prince or beast that rises out of the sea (Rev. 13:1) abolishes the daily sacrifice in the temple (Dan. 11:31, 12:11). He then begins the abominations, plural, that lead up to *"the consummation"* of abominations by the Antichrist just prior to mid-Trib (Dan. 9:27).
- The false prince has delusions of grandeur; he even thinks he is God (Isa. 14:13-14 and 2 Thess. 2:4).
- The false prince is assassinated or in some way receives a mortal wound. His soul goes straight to the bottomless pit (Isa. 14:15) in order that Scripture may be fulfilled. Not even Hitler or Stalin went there.
- Then there is a war in heaven and Satan is cast down to the pit (Rev. 12:7-9 and Isaiah 14:15). Satan collects the false prince, returns him to his body, and indwells him. The false prince is alive again and is now the Antichrist (Rev. 11:7, 13:3, 17:8).
- The consummation of the great apostasy may be the result of a cataclysmic event that will shake faith to its core. We believe that event to be the rising from the dead of the false prince to become the revealed Antichrist sitting in the temple and declaring to be God, just prior to mid-Trib. Many will then say, *"where is the promise of His* [Christ's] *Coming?"* (2 Peter 3:4 - Explanation added).
- The false prince being represented in prophecy as the prince of Tyrus (Ezek. 28:1-10) will after his Satanic indwelling and resurrection become the one who is represented by prophecy as the king of Tyrus (Ezek. 28:11-19). He is now the Antichrist.

Events Surrounding the Middle of the Tribulation Period
- The Archangel Michael stands up for the children of thy people (Dan. 12:1 and Rev. 12:7).

- Satan, who stood accusing the brethren of their sins, no longer has access to Heaven and the throne of God (Rev. 12:9-10).
- The entire world now wonders *"who is able to make war with him?"* (Rev. 13:4). He is the beast that ascendeth out of the bottomless pit (Rev. 11:7 and 17:8) and appears to be immortal.
- The Antichrist kills the Two Witnesses (Dan. 12:7, Rev. 11:7). He then goes to the temple and proclaims himself to be God above all others (Matt. 24:15, Mark 13:14, 2 Thess. 2:4). This is known as the *"consummation"* of abominations that cause desolation (Dan. 9:27). *"For then shall be great tribulation"* (Matt. 24:21). This is when he is revealed to Israel as the Antichrist (Rev. 13:3-8), the *"son of perdition"* (2 Thess. 2:3), *"that Wicked"* (2 Thess. 2:8), *"the king of Tyrus"* (Ezek. 28:11-19).
- The false prophet makes all people worship the image of the beast (Rev. 13:11-15).
- The economic system of the mark of the beast is implemented and is mandatory for all to have. No commerce can be done without the *"mark, or the name of the beast, or the number of his name"* (Rev. 13:17).
- The Antichrist and the false prophet seek to kill anyone who refuses to worship the Antichrist (Dan. 7:25, 12:7, 12:10, Rev. 13:7, and 13:15).

At the Gathering Mid-Trib
- *"And the dragon stood before the woman which was ready to be delivered, for to devour her child as soon as it was born"* (Rev. 12:4).
- The seventh trumpet begins to sound (Rev. 10:7).
- The trump sounds during a day of clouds and thick darkness (Zeph. 1:15-16, Amos 8:9, Matt. 24:29-31, Mark 13:24-27, Luke 21:25-28). Sign of the Son of man appears in Heaven and all the tribes of the earth mourn as they see the Son of Man coming in the clouds of Heaven. He sends *"His angels with a great sound of a trumpet"* to Gather together His Elect (Matt. 24:30-31). The seventh trump now sounds (Rev. 11:15).
- At the sound of the last trumpet, the dead shall be raised incorruptible and the living shall be changed (1 Cor. 15:52).

- *The Lord Himself shall descend from heaven with a shout, with the voice of the archangel, and with the trump of God: and the dead in Christ shall rise first: Then we which are alive and remain* [unto the coming of the Lord, verse 15] *shall be caught up together with them in the clouds, to meet the Lord in the air: and so shall we ever be with the Lord* (1 Thess. 4:16-17 - Explanation added).

- After the Two Witnesses lie in the streets for three and one half days and as the whole world watches they are resurrected, as is the Bride of Christ. All are caught up in the air to meet the Lord Jesus Christ (Rev. 11:11-12, 1 Cor. 15:51-54, 1 Thess. 4:13-17, Rev. 12:5, Matt. 24:29-31, Mark 13:24-27, Luke 21:25-28, Dan. 7:13-14, Rev. 1:7).

- *"...the mystery of God ... finished"* (Rev. 10:7).

- Great white robed multitude in Heaven (Rev. 7:9-17).

- Time to judge the dead and to give reward unto the servants the prophets, the saints, and them that fear Thy name (Rev. 11:18).

- A great earthquake occurs and a tenth of Jerusalem is destroyed (Rev. 11:13). When Christ resurrected there was an earthquake and when Christ comes for His Bride at the resurrection of the dead in Christ there will be an earthquake again.

- The woman who is believed to be Israel, having just given birth to a child, flees to the wilderness for protection from the Antichrist. She will be in God's protection for *"1260 days"* or *"a time, times, and a half time"* (Rev. 12:6, 12:14) until Christ returns to fight the battle of Armageddon.

- The dragon starts to close off all exits from Israel, only 1/3 of Israel escapes to the wilderness and 2/3 are trapped or will not go (Zech. 13:8-9). Satan through the Antichrist and false prophet kills anyone that refuses to worship him (Rev.13:15), holocaust begins.

- Israel having just seen the Lord Jesus Christ in the air will mourn for Him whom they have pierced, as for an only son (Zech. 12:10, Amos 8:10-12, Rev. 1:7).

- The end of the first half and the beginning of the second half of the Tribulation period is what Daniel calls *"time, times and dividing of time"* (Dan. 7:25). This is mid point in the Tribulation period and now there is another 42 months until the end of the Tribulation period (Rev. 13:5).

- *"Henceforth"* of Revelation 14:13 designates a new dispensation.

After the Gathering

- The Antichrist pursues the woman into the wilderness, but the earth swallows up his armies (Rev. 12:14-16).
- Now it is the time of Jacobs's trouble, but the faithful of Israel will be saved out of it (Jer. 30:7).
- The Antichrist now furious, wages war against the remnant of the woman's seed, the 144,000 and their followers (Rev. 12:17).
- It is Satan's wrath (Rev. 12:12) on those that *"keep the commandments of God and have the testimony of Jesus Christ"* (Rev. 12:17). There will be great tribulation during the last three and one half years of the Tribulation period.
- Thy wrath is come and God will destroy them that destroy the earth (Rev. 11:18). The seven *"vials of the wrath of God"* are poured out *"upon the earth"* (Rev. 16:1) during the last three and one half years (Rev. 16). These are the vials of wrath that the Elect are to be protected from (1 Thess. 5:9 and Rev. 3:10). Each vial adds to the last and a double portion is added to the seventh vial at the time of Armageddon. This double portion is *"the wrath of God"* (Rev. 16:1) and *"the wrath of the Lamb"* (Rev. 6:16). These vials are added to the affects of all seven seals and trumpets as well.
- Now the stewardship of the Everlasting Gospel is through Israel, as it was meant to be all along had they only accepted Christ in the first place (Matt. 11:14). This stewardship change is accomplished through the 144,000 (Rev. 14) who hold to *"the commandments of God and have the testimony of Jesus Christ"* (Rev. 12:17).
- The "little scroll" of Ezekiel 3:1-5 that was originally opened only to Israel is now opened to the entire world, not just Israel (Rev. 10:10-11) because of the New Covenant of Grace.
- The Antichrist will rule on earth for 42 months (Rev. 13:5).
- Marriage Supper of the Lamb takes place in Heaven (Rev. 19:6-9).

- The kings of the east see an opportunity to challenge the Christ and His kingdom. They prepare to march west to Israel to the Battle of Armageddon.
- *And the sixth angel poured out his vial upon the great river Euphrates; and the water thereof was dried up, that the way of the kings of the east might be prepared* (Rev. 16:12).
- The Triumphal Return of the Lord Jesus Christ to earth with the armies from Heaven to fight the Antichrist's army and the kings of the east at the Battle of Armageddon (Rev. 19:11 - 20:3) and all the ungodly people on the earth perish (Jude 1:14-16, Rev. 19:21).
- When Christ comes physically to earth at His Triumphal Return there will be the largest earthquake the world has ever seen (Rev. 16:17-21).

The Millennium Begins
- 45-day period to separate the sheep nations from the goat nations and setup the Earthly Kingdom (Matt. 25:31-34).

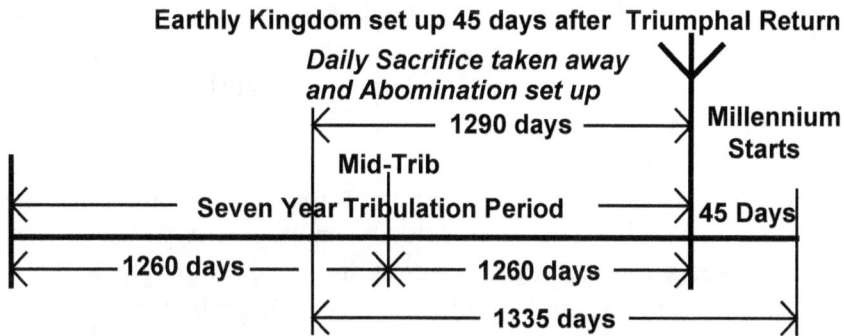

Earthly Kingdom set up 45 days after Triumphal Return

Daily Sacrifice taken away and Abomination set up

1290 days

Mid-Trib

Millennium Starts

Seven Year Tribulation Period — 45 Days

1260 days — 1260 days

1335 days

Blessed is he that makes it to 1335 days (Daniel 12:12)

- God will regenerate the planet after the Battle of Armageddon (Isa. 65:17).
- Christ will sit on His throne ruling over the entire earth for 1,000 years (Rev. 20:4, 20:6).
- Jesus Himself will be teaching God's message of salvation to those born in the Millennium. The old days of men teaching one

another to know God is over. Every person on the planet will know God and worship Him freely (Jer. 31:34, Heb. 8:11-12).
- People *"shall beat their swords into plowshares, and their spears into pruninghooks"* (Isa. 2:4, Micah 4:3).
- People will live hundreds of years, like before the flood (Isa. 65:20, 22).

At the End of the Millennium
- Satan will be let out of the pit after the 1,000 years of Christ reign on earth are completed (Rev. 20:7).
- Satan goes out to deceive the nations of the entire earth and to gather them together to do battle against the camp of the saints and the beloved city (Rev. 20:8-9).
- Fire will come down from God out of Heaven and devour Satan and his followers (Rev. 20:9).
- Satan will be cast into the lake of fire and brimstone, where the Antichrist and the false prophet were cast earlier. They shall be tormented day and night forever and ever (Rev. 20:10).
- All of the dead stand before God at the great white throne judgment. *"And whosoever was not found written in the Book of Life was cast into the lake of fire"* (Rev. 20:15). *"This is the second death"* (Rev. 20:14).

We have laid out the chronology of the master play showing verses as close to the order they actually happen as is possible. You can plainly see the verses in Revelation are not chronological. While laying out the timeline, we discovered how well written the Book of Revelation is. God showed John complex spiritual and physical events, many of which are all happening simultaneously. The Book of Revelation had to be written the way it was in order to be understood.

Conclusion of the Symphonic View
The story line or melody must have Scriptures supporting the story in depth and they are known as staffs or accompaniment. One does not have the true story line unless there are supporting accompaniments. For example, by placing the Rapture out before the Tribulation, one can find Scripture to fill various properly sounding staffs. But when all the other Scriptures that support the story line

does not sound on the right bar, all we hear is noise. If there is any conflict between Scriptures, the story line is not accurate yet. Keep looking and trying to fit the story line to all the staffs until there is no further conflict. Then you have the truth.

When we read the Book of Revelation, it repeats itself over and over as if trying to drive home a point. A point many in the church are not getting when they read the Book in chronological order. Revelation is written with much redundancy, it cannot be read chronologically. Our book is written much the same manner as the Book of Revelation. Each chapter is chronological most of the time, but different chapters talk about the same events over and over, from the perspective of the subject of that chapter. Try reading the Book of Revelation the same way. Each chapter is in chronological fashion but the chapters overlap one another. If that is still confusing to you, then picture a car accident; there are many witnesses to the accident and each chapter represents a different witness to the same event, from their perspective. That is why a Police Officer will interview all the witnesses from their visual point of view to determine how and when certain events took place as they relate to the accident. Then they piece together all the individual pieces of information to form a timeline or the overall big picture. This is over simplified to be a good explanation of the Book of Revelation, but it will be enough to help someone go down the right path of understanding and not to read the Book of Revelation chronologically. We get the impression that some theologians need to attend group therapy to recover from their addiction of reading it chronologically. It is only an addiction and it can be overcome. Just kidding!

If the Church is Gone Because of a Pre-Tribulation Rapture, Who is the Book of Revelation Written To?

This whole concept of Christians going through any part of the Tribulation period is hard for many Christians to believe. Christians have been taught that the trumpets are the wrath of God. Seminaries simply teach that the church is not mentioned in the Book of Revelation after 4:1 because of the belief that all of the Tribulation period is the wrath of God, and our promise of the *"blessed hope"* (Titus 2:13) to escape God's wrath prevents us from being in any part of the Tribulation period. This is an instance that we need to rightly divide the Word of God.

We agree with the pre-Tribbers about our *"blessed hope"* (Titus 2:13). The *"blessed hope"* is a promise we have as faithful Christians that we will be removed from the earth before *"the hour of temptation"* (Rev. 3:10), before God's wrath has come. We just do not agree with the pre-Tribbers on the timing of when the *"hour of temptation"* happens.

In no way do we want to convey that the first half of the Tribulation period is going to be easy. Just picture all the judgments that were poured out through Elijah and Moses in the Old Testament. They brought about plagues, fire from Heaven, locusts, and much more. During the first half of the Tribulation the same type of judgments will be poured out through the Two Witnesses again. In addition, the Two Witnesses will be standing in the way of the false prince, being a thorn in his side by bringing these about plagues. There will also be the affects of six trumpets to live through as well.

We have interviewed so many Christians who do not spend much time reading the Book of Revelation because they believe it does not pertain to them. Doesn't it seem strange to you that Jesus had John write the Book of Revelation if it does not pertain to the church? If it does not pertain to the church, then why write the Book of Revelation? Who is the Book written for if not the church?

Any theologian that might claim that the letters to the seven churches in Revelation 2-3 are letters for the past and has no bearing on the present cannot claim Revelation 3:10 is the *"blessed hope"* for the church now, if they want to claim that the letters are past tense. They cannot have it both ways. But, the letters are the *"blessed hope"* for us now. The letters are also a stern warning and are meant to give us hope through part of the Tribulation period. We want you to consider Revelation 2:10,

> *Fear none of these things which thou shalt suffer: behold, the devil shall cast some of you into prison, that ye may be tried; and ye shall have tribulation ten days: be thou faithful unto death, and I will give thee the crown of Life.*

Doesn't that sound like Christians can expect to go through part of the Tribulation?

When the devil is cast from heaven in Revelation 12, he will only have days to sentence us to death before the Gathering occurs. This is because God promised to shorten the days that the Satan-indwelt-Antichrist has physical dominion over the Elect (Matt. 24:22, Mark 13:20, Rev. 12:12). We need to clarify something here about Satan's dominion. Earlier in this chapter we learned that Christ will take Satan's legal dominion away in Heaven. This is true! However, Satan still retains physical possession of the earth for 42 months through the reign of the Antichrist and the ten kings, until Christ's Triumphal Return from Heaven.

The Book of Revelation is a strong warning for the church:

> *And I gave her **space to repent** of her fornication; and she repented not. Behold, I will cast her into a bed, and them that commit adultery with her **into great tribulation, except they repent of their deeds.** And I will kill her children with death; and all the churches shall know that I am He which searcheth the reins and hearts: and I will give unto every one of you according to your works. But unto you I say, and unto the rest of Thyatira, as many as have not this doctrine, and which have not known the depths of Satan, as they speak; I will put upon you none other burden. But that which ye have already hold fast till I come. And he that overcometh, and keepeth My works unto the end, to him will I give the power over the nations (Rev. 2:21-26 Emphasis added).*

> *Come hither; I will show unto thee the judgment of the great whore that sitteth upon many waters: With whom the kings of the earth have committed fornication, and the inhabitants of the earth have been made drunk with the wine of their fornication (Rev. 17:2).*

The false or apostate church is believed to be the whore who rides the beast (Rev. 17). She gives power to the beast until the beast no longer needs her. Then he kills the whore through the ten kings (Rev. 17:16).

Do you see the connection between those of the church leadership who have committed fornication with the depths of Satan? The resurrected beast rises out of the pit. Again, this happens mid-Trib when Satan is cast into the earth, into the bottomless pit (Rev. 12:9) and ascends out of the bottomless pit (Rev. 11:7, 13:3, 17:8). Our *"blessed hope"* is that those of us who have not known or fornicated with the depths of Satan will not be burdened any more.

When the Bible says, "known"; what does it mean to have known a woman? We are talking spiritually, not physically. When we make a financial deal it is common vernacular to say we are in bed together. This is the type of "known" we are talking about. This is what the Lord means by having known Satan. It could also mean to have the mark of the beast. No man may buy or sell without the mark (Rev. 13:17). Again, do you see why the Book Revelation is not chronological? Revelation 2 is talking about something in Revelation 13. They share the same time and space in the symphonic view.

Summary of the Blessed Hope

Anyway one dissects it; the church will be here when the son of perdition is here, even if only for a few days. Pre-Tribulationists are adamant that the church will not be here for any part of the Tribulation period and they use Revelation 3:10 for proof. We have shown that line of thinking to be in error. Revelation 3:10 is not the evidence they need for that.

Satan cannot indwell the false prince before Revelation 12 because he is not omnipresent. Satan is restrained in heaven until mid-Trib. The great white multitude will not be before the throne washed clean by the blood of the Lamb until after Satan is cast down from heaven. At the Gathering both the dead in Christ and the translated living are standing on the sea of glass mingled with fire before God's throne as in Revelation 15. All Christendom has the *"blessed hope"* to be removed from the earth before the great and dreadful day of the LORD. It saddens our hearts that so much bickering is going on in the church over when *"the hour of temptation"* is.

We are offering a reasonable alternative to the most popular western view in the Church, not for the purpose of dividing the Church any further, but to give hope to those who find themselves here after the Tribulation period starts. We have shown in this chapter that we still indeed have the *"blessed hope"* we were promised, even if pre-Tribbers are wrong about the timing of the Gathering.

Who is the Great White Robed Multitude and Where Did They Come From?

1290 days before the end of the Tribulation period the abomination of desolation is placed in the temple (Dan. 12:11, 11:31, Matt. 24:15, Mark 13:14). At first it is a statue of the figure of a man made of cypress and oak placed in the temple (Isa. 44:13). The false prince then switches the worship of this idol to himself and proclaims that he is God. We believe that this period of *"travailing in birth"* (Rev. 12:2) begins 30 days before the middle of the Tribulation period by the false prince.

In Daniel 6, a law or decree was signed that for 30 days no man could ask a petition of any god or any man except for the king, under penalty of death. We see this as a type or example of what the false prince will do. The false prince is killed for this and the Lord God mocks him in Ezekiel 28:9 saying, *"Wilt thou yet say before him that slayeth thee, I am God? But thou shalt be a man, and no God, in the hand of him that slayeth thee."* The false prince that rises from the dead as the Antichrist, continues as *"...the beast that was, and is not, and yet is"* (Rev. 17:8) for 42 months (Rev. 13:5). He exalts himself above God, *"so that he as God sitteth in the temple of God, showing himself that he is God"* (2 Thess. 2: 4). This Antichrist wages war against the Elect for ten days before the Gathering of the Elect, which are the True Church and faithful of Israel. These ten days are known as the days that the woman is *"pained to be delivered"* (Rev. 12:2) and during this time it is the darkest hour of the church and Israel (Matt. 24:21, Rev. 7:14, Luke 21:22-23). It will be like midnight. This time is also known as the culmination of *"a time and times and the dividing of time"* (Dan. 7:25).

The Gathering of the great white robed multitude (Rev. 7:9-17) at the sounding of the seventh and last trumpet (Rev. 11:15, 1 Cor. 15:52) is the culmination of the Mystery Dispensation that is revealed to us by Paul in his Epistles. After all, the *"Mystery of God"* is finished when the seventh angel shall *"begin to sound"* (Rev. 10:7). We believe that the Mystery is finished within days after *"the son of perdition"* (2 Thess. 2:3), the Antichrist, is revealed.

179

Using the symphonic view above, now read Revelation 7:14 in its proper context. The great white robed multitude came out of the very beginning of great tribulation caused by the Satan-indwelt-Antichrist.

> *These are they which came out of **great tribulation**, and have washed their robes, and made them white in the blood of the Lamb* (Rev. 7:14 - Emphasis added).

Possible Identities of the Great White Multitude:

- Pre-Trib theologians believe that the great white robed multitude are the Tribulation saints who became Christians and died after the Rapture, but before Christ's Triumphal Return, during the whole seven years of the Tribulation period.

- Post-Tribbers would say that they are the Christians who died as martyrs before Christ comes at the end of the Tribulation period.

- Some think that they are souls of the Bride of Christ who are waiting to be united with their Heavenly Bodies at the Gathering mid or post-Trib.

Symphonic View of When the Great White Robed Multitude is Brought to Heaven

There are many Staffs of the Master Score and a lot of instruments are playing during the great white robed multitude being brought to Heaven. When they are all being played in the proper bar of time, there is a very harmonious sound indeed. This is how one can determine the correct timing of things. Let us look at these staffs and charts concerning the great white robed multitude:

Staff 1) The great white robed multitude is mentioned between the sixth and seventh seals. The seals of the sealed book are opened one at a time. However, the affects of the seals on earth play out over time. For those in heaven, breaking the seals of the seven-sealed book in Heaven is seemingly instantaneous, but the affects of the seals on the earth build one upon another during the whole of the seven-year Tribulation period. Until Jesus opens the sealed book, nothing can happen; the trumpets cannot sound, the Gathering cannot happen,

Satan would be in Heaven forever, and creation could not ever be made perfect again. This is why John was weeping (Rev. 5:3-5).

Staff 2) Because the great white robed multitude is mentioned in the seals and the seals are being broken in Heaven, the timing of when they are physically brought to Heaven from earth is not exactly clear. Because the 144,000 are sealed for protection just before the middle of the Tribulation and that the 144,000 are mentioned almost in the same breath as the great white robed multitude, it is likely that the great white robed multitude will be in Heaven about that same time. Meaning that the great white robed multitude is in Heaven after the Tribulation period has begun and no later than mid-Trib. This eliminates the Pre-Tribulation Rapture Theory.

Great White Robed Multitude

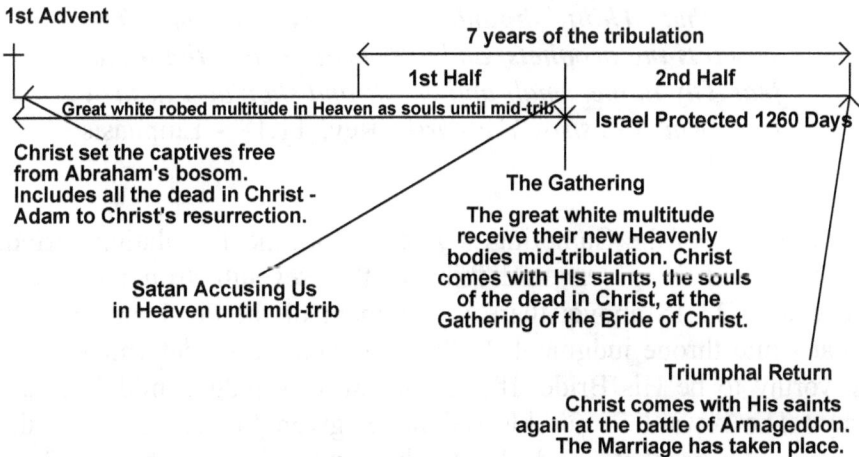

Staff 3) The fact that they are dressed in white robes is curious though. If they are souls, how can they be dressed in anything? Yet in Revelation 6:9-11 the souls of the martyred are all given white robes [see Isaiah 61:10]. Because of this, we know that souls can indeed have white robes. These souls *"of all nations, and kindreds, and people, and tongues"* (Rev. 7:9) are clearly washed by the blood of the Lamb. It is clear they are no longer spirits at the sounding of the seventh trumpet; they have Heavenly glorified bodies. The fine white linen that they are granted to wear in Revelation 19 stands in contrast

to the white robes in Revelation 7. The great white robed multitude better fits a description of the saints in Heaven awaiting their rewards and Marriage to the Lamb than a description of the martyred Tribulation saints.

Staff 4) The four angels mentioned just before the great white robed multitude were told to hold back the four winds and not harm the earth until the 144,000 had been sealed (Rev. 7:2). The 144,000 will be protected from God's wrath upon the whole earth. God's wrath starts in the second half of the Tribulation period, right after the seventh trumpet is blown.

Staff 5) There is a time of reward giving at the seventh trumpet.

> *And the nations were angry, and Thy wrath is come, and the time of the dead, that they should be judged, and* ***that Thou shouldest give reward*** *unto* ***Thy servants the prophets****, and to* ***the saints****, and* ***them that fear Thy name****, small and great; and shouldest destroy them which destroy the earth* (Rev. 11:18 - Emphasis added).

If the reward of the Gathering is given before the Tribulation period, what reward is given mid-Trib at the seventh trumpet? Read Revelation 11:18 above; there is judgment of the dead, but not the great white throne judgment. In this judgment Jesus determines who is worthy to be His Bride. If not, then who is judged mid-Trib and why? The reward is our blessed hope, given to the saints, to the servants the prophets, and also to those who fear His name. Three separate groups of people. That is a lot of reward giving in the middle of the Tribulation period. How beautiful this part of the score must sound. Think how disjointed the score would sound if this staff were placed in the wrong bar of time, way back at the beginning of the Tribulation period.

Staff 6) The next staff also has to do with the righteous dead being judged during mid-Tribulation. Christ has judged the earth and pulled out His people that are worthy just before God pours out His wrath.

"Watch ye therefore, and pray always, that ye may be accounted worthy to escape all these things..." (Luke 21:36). How do we know this is mid-Tribulation? We know, because the Two Witnesses are killed after their 1260-day ministry by the beast that ascends out of the bottomless pit, just before or at the beginning of his 42-month reign as the Antichrist. *"And after three days and an half the Spirit of Life from God entered into them* [Two Witnesses]*, and they stood upon their feet"* and they are told to *"Come up hither. And they ascended up to heaven in a cloud"* (Rev. 11:11-12). This sure sounds like the resurrection of the dead and the Gathering to Christ to us. The Gathering to Christ is clearly a resurrection and a translation of all Christ's Bride in one event, which happens at the sounding of the seventh and last trumpet. This places the timing 1260 days after the beginning and 42 months before the end of the Tribulation period, which is the middle. It is fun putting all these verses together like a tight fitting puzzle.

Staff 7) Yet another staff of the righteous dead being judged mid-Trib. The Antichrist comes on the scene mid-Trib and speaks against God.

> *And he* [false prince - Antichrist] *shall speak great words against the most High, and shall wear out the saints of the most High and think to change times and laws: they* [the saints] *shall be given into his hand until a time and times and the dividing of time* [mid-Trib]*. But the judgment shall sit, and they shall take away his* [Antichrist's] *dominion, to consume and destroy it unto the end* (Dan. 7:25-26 - Explanations added).

Staff 8) How can the saints help take away Satan's dominion, to destroy it unto the end? Well, the saints testify against all those who persecuted the Elect to this point (Rev. 15:5).

Staff 9) In Revelation 4:6 the crystal sea is without fire because judgment has not yet come. The crystal sea is empty at the beginning of the Tribulation period. At mid-Trib all those who had victory over the Antichrist, his image, his mark, and the number of his name are standing on the crystal sea mingled with fire in Revelation 15:2. They sing *"the song of Moses"..."the song of the Lamb"* and Christ is called the *"King of the saints"* in Revelation 15:3. Court begins in Revelation 15:5, where the saints of the Most High give their testimonies. Once their testimonies are heard, the wrath of God is poured out unto all them the persecuted the saints.

Staff 10) Revelation 7:14 is speaking of the mid-Trib Gathering and the white robed multitude is the Bride of Christ. The great white robed multitude has just come out of *"great tribulation"* (Matt. 24:21, Rev. 7:14) caused by Satan and his dark angels that were just vanquished from heaven and cast down to the earth. The Satan-indwelt son of perdition declares himself to be God, and the false prophet demands that everyone worship the Antichrist. The white robed multitude is then seen in Heaven holding palm branches and giving praise to God and to the Lamb. They are from all nations, kindreds, and tongues (Rev. 7:9-10). The white robed multitude *"have washed their robes, and made them white in the blood of the Lamb. Therefore are they before the throne of God, and serve Him day and night in His Temple: and He that sitteth on the throne shall dwell among them"* (Rev. 7:14-15). They will have already been justified righteous by the blood of the Lamb and will be serving God in His Temple, forever.

The 7 Years of the Tribulation

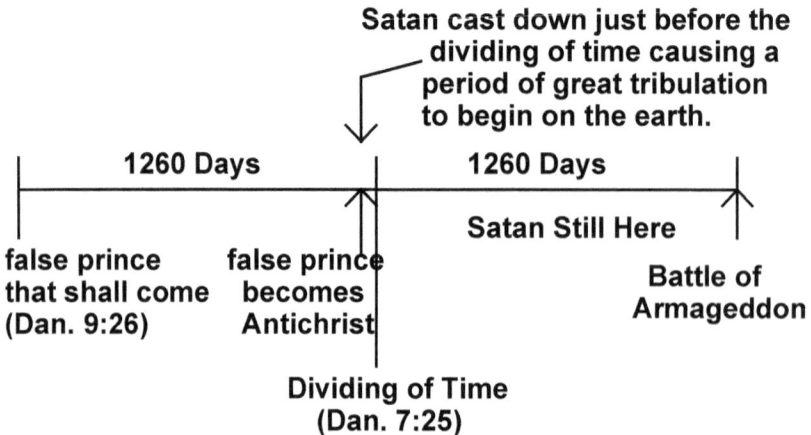

Satan cast down just before the dividing of time causing a period of great tribulation to begin on the earth.

1260 Days	1260 Days

Satan Still Here

false prince that shall come (Dan. 9:26)

false prince becomes Antichrist

Battle of Armageddon

Dividing of Time (Dan. 7:25)

If the great white robed multitude goes to Heaven before Satan is cast out, then Satan would stand before God's throne day and night still accusing them of their sins. Can you imagine the Bride of Christ in Heaven for three and one half years before Satan is finally cast out of heaven in Revelation 12:9-10? Satan is not though because *"the accuser of our brethren is cast down"* (Rev. 12:10) just prior to the Mid-Trib Gathering. When Satan is cast down from heaven, Israel is fleeing from the Antichrist and his armies. Israel gets God's protection for 1260 days (Rev. 12:6) or *"for a time, and times, and half a time, from the face of the serpent"* (Rev. 12:14 Emphasis added). Satan through the Antichrist, the false prophet and the ten kings of the earth will then have only half of the Tribulation period left. The heavens have to be cleansed before the Bride of Christ is brought before the Throne in Revelation 15. All this is part of the legal process of stripping Satan of his dominion, which started in Revelation 4 and 5. This is really strong evidence that the great white robed multitude could not have been united with their glorified bodies any sooner than the middle of the Tribulation. This is strong evidence for who the white robed multitude are and for the mid-Trib Gathering Position.

Chapter 10

Glorious Appearing vs. Triumphal Return

We will now cover a subject that is the second most important thing a Christian must know; Christ's promise to return and Gather us together in the air. It is our blessed hope. Christ's promise is a reward for those who have done the most important thing a Christian must do, have faith and belief in Jesus Christ, and accept God's gift of salvation to humanity.

Most Bible teachers and students of the Word agree with Christ's coming for His Bride in the air and His physical return to the earth. However, there is disagreement on the timing, about whether there are signs and events that must precede His return and if so, what those signs and events are. Also, is His coming for the Bride the same as His physical return to earth or are they two separate events? It is critical to rightly divide the Word of God to understand Jesus' Second Advent.

This chapter deals with the issue of the delineating Christ's Gathering of His Bride at His Glorious Appearing from His Triumphal Return on the white horse with His Wife at the end of the Tribulation period. There is much confusion in Christendom concerning these two separate events.

What is the Difference between the Glorious Appearing and the Triumphal Return?

Jesus promised that His followers would all be resurrected and anyone who is alive when He returns shall never die.

> *Jesus saith unto her, I am the resurrection, and the life: He that believeth in Me, though he were dead, yet shall he live: And whosoever liveth and believeth in Me shall never die. Believest thou this? (John 11:25-26).*

This next verse describes what is known as the Glorious Appearing. *"Looking for that blessed hope, and glorious appearing of the great*

God and Saviour Jesus Christ" (Titus 2:13). Also supported by Matthew,

> *And then shall appear the sign of the Son of man in heaven: and then shall all the tribes of the earth mourn,* **and they shall see the Son of man coming in the clouds of heaven with power and great glory.** *And He shall send His angels with a great sound of a trumpet, and they shall gather together His Elect from the four winds, from one end of heaven to the other* (Matt. 24:30-31).

And then there is another verse that describes how Jesus will come in the clouds and we will meet Him in the air.

> *For the Lord Himself shall descend from heaven with a shout, with the voice of the archangel, and with the trump of God: and the dead in Christ shall rise first: Then we which are alive and remain shall be caught up together with* **them in the clouds, to meet the Lord in the air***: and so shall we ever be with the Lord* (1 Thess. 4:16-17 - Emphasis added).

When Jesus comes for the whosoevers that believe in Him, He shall come in the clouds to Gather them in the air. When Christ receives His crown and *"the kingdoms of this world are become the Kingdoms of our LORD, and of His Christ"* (Rev. 11:15) we will receive our crown as well. We are joint-heirs to the throne of Christ. *"And when the chief Shepherd shall appear, ye shall receive a crown of glory that fadeth not away"* (1 Peter 5:4). This crown of glory is our glorified body.

Flesh and blood cannot inherit the Kingdom of God (1 Cor. 15:50). When Christ comes for us we are given new bodies. Our new bodies are flesh and bone like Jesus' body when He appeared to the Apostles (Luke 24:39). These new bodies live forever as opposed to our current bodies that physically die and decay.

Christ will not actually come to the earth and stand on the ground at His Glorious Appearing, better known as the Rapture. He does that during His Triumphal Return three and one half years later, where

Revelation 19:15 describes Christ as having a sword coming out of His mouth with which He will smite the nations. Just by Christ's word Lazarus came out of his grave; so also will His enemies fall dead by His Word at Armageddon. Most people know this Triumphal Return as the "Second Coming."

The Triumphal Return and Entry into Jerusalem

> *And Enoch also, the seventh from Adam, prophesied of these, saying, behold, the Lord cometh with ten thousands of His saints, to execute judgment upon all...* (Jude 1:14-15).

At the Triumphal Return of the Lord, Christ will physically return to earth with ten thousands of His saints. Not just 10,000, but many, many 10,000's, a limitless number indeed. He will ride a white horse (Rev. 19:11). Christ returns to the earth at the end of the Tribulation with an army from Heaven to defeat Satan and his army of malcontents at the battle of Armageddon. He then separates the sheep nations from the goat nations. Then Jesus will reign *"KING OF KINGS, AND LORD OF LORDS"* (Rev. 19:16) here on the earth, not just from Heaven. This is when He begins to rule all nations with a rod of iron (Rev. 19:15).

After the battle of Armageddon has ended Christ sits on the throne of His glory in Jerusalem. This is known as His Triumphal Entry into Jerusalem. 2000 years ago Christ entered the east gates of Jerusalem on a donkey showing His meekness. After the Tribulation period is over and Satan, the Antichrist, and the false prophet are defeated at Armageddon, Christ will enter the east gate in Jerusalem on a white horse showing His Glory. This is His real Triumphal Entry into Jerusalem.

We cannot describe these events any better than the Bible does. We have listed some Scriptures that describe the Triumphal Return:

> *And I saw heaven opened, and behold a white horse; and He that sat upon him was called Faithful and True, and in righteousness He doth judge and make war. His eyes were as a flame of fire, and on His head were many*

crowns; and He had a name written, that no man knew, but He Himself. And He was clothed with a vesture dipped in blood: and His name is called The Word of God. And the armies which were in heaven followed Him upon white horses, clothed in fine linen, white and clean. And out of His mouth goeth a sharp sword, that with it He should smite the nations: and He shall rule them with a rod of iron: and He treadeth the winepress of the fierceness and wrath of Almighty God. And He hath on His vesture and on His thigh a name written, KING OF KINGS, AND LORD OF LORDS (Rev. 19:11-16).

Which also said, Ye men of Galilee, why stand ye gazing up into heaven? This same Jesus, which is taken up from you into heaven, shall so come in like manner as ye have seen Him go into heaven (Acts 1:11).

And His feet shall stand in that day upon the mount of Olives [Triumphal Return], *which is before Jerusalem on the east, and the mount of Olives shall cleave in the midst thereof toward the east and toward the west, and there shall be a very great valley; and half of the mountain shall remove toward the north, and half of it toward the south. And ye shall flee to the valley of the mountains; for the valley of the mountains shall reach unto Azal: yea, ye shall flee, like as ye fled from before the earthquake in the days of Uzziah king of Judah: and the LORD My God shall come, and all the saints with Thee. And it shall come to pass in that day, that the light shall not be clear, nor dark* [still Triumphal Return]: *But it shall be one day which shall be known to the LORD, not day, nor night: but it shall come to pass, that at evening time it shall be light. And it shall be in that day, that living waters shall go out from Jerusalem; half of them toward the former sea, and half of them toward the hinder sea: in summer and in winter shall it be. And the LORD shall be King over all the earth: in that day shall there be one LORD, and His name one* [Triumphal Entry] (Zech. 14:1-9).

When Did Jesus Say He Was Coming?

Jesus was sitting on the Mount of Olives when some of the disciples asked Him, *"when shall these things be"* and secondly, *"what shall be the sign Thy coming?"* (Matt. 24:3). Jesus said, *"Take heed that no man deceive you. For many shall come in My name, saying, I am Christ; and shall deceive many"* (Matt. 24:4-5). There are many doctrines being taught in Christianity today. They cannot all be right. Could it be that this is in part what Christ is talking about when He says people will come in His name and will deceive many? We need to read the Bible ourselves and stop letting experts tell us what the Bible says. That goes for this book too. Do not just take our word for it, do your own research and ask the Holy Spirit to give you wisdom and understanding.

The Lord said that because the world did not have a love for the truth, He would send the world a lie to believe in. *"And for this cause God will send them strong delusion, that they should believe a lie"* (2 Thess. 2:11). We believe that this is an event caused by the false prince being raised from the dead and claiming he is God.

Christians need to pray and search their hearts for the truth in all matters. *"Therefore let us not sleep, as do others; but let us watch and be sober"* (1 Thess. 5:6). Christians need to wake from their slumber and start having a love for the truth. Some people say that they believe in the PAN theory; it will all pan out in the end. This is their excuse for not reading their Bible. We need to start reading our Bibles and know what it says about these issues. Then when the lies and deceit from the evil one comes, the true Christians will be prepared. They will recognize this man for whom he really is.

Jesus told us that when you see people claiming to be the Christ, do not believe it. Also, many people will claim they are Christians but will deny the very truth of the Bible, saying it is only partly true or it is just old stories. It cannot be understood so I believe in the PAN theory. Do not believe someone is a Christian just because they say they are. Watch for their fruit. If they do not bear good fruit or deny any part of Christ's testimony, they probably are not who they say they are. As far as people actually claiming to be Christ, true

Christians will automatically know that these people are not the true Christ because we know that when His Glorious Appearance to Gather the Elect occurs it will be instantaneous, like lightning from east to west. We will not need to hear that He is in the next room or out in the desert somewhere. When He comes to Gather the Bride of Christ, it is in an instant. No human needs to sound the alarm or announce it.

All these people that are rushing out to see the image of Christ on the side of a building should read the Olivet Discourse. Someone even paid a ridiculous amount of money on E-bay for a pancake with a likeness of Christ's image on it. Please, for Christ's sake and yours, stop looking for Christ here and there. When Christ comes for us it will be *"in a moment, in the twinkling of an eye"* (1Cor. 15:52), like lightning from east to west (Matt. 24:27) and we will be in the clouds to meet Jesus in the air. He will not be found on a pancake, on the side of a hill, or in a reflection on glass.

Jesus said that before He comes we must be on our guard; we will be handed over to the authorities and punished for our faith in Him. The Gospel will be preached to all nations. Our brothers, parents and children will betray us. We should say whatever is given to us to say in our defense because it is the Holy Spirit speaking, not us. Jesus says all men will hate you because of Me (Mark 13:13). This is when He will come. Is any of this going on right now? His return will not happen until it is. Christ's Glorious Appearing is not a sign-less event.

Are There Any Signs of Christ's Coming in the Air?

Imminency teachers say, see, another massive earthquake has just happened and here is another 100-year storm or wars and revolutions, even terrorism. See the signs of His coming. They quote the Bible referring to Luke 21:28, *"And when these things begin to come to pass, then look up, and lift up your heads; for your redemption draweth nigh."* What they are implying is that Jesus will come for us as soon as these things begin to happen. These teachers say that no further prophecy need be fulfilled for Christ to come imminently. Then why look for the signs? Many Christians do not read the Book of Revelation or study prophecy anymore simply because they have been taught that the Book of Revelation applies only to Israel, and not to the Church. This is partially due to this doctrine of imminence.

The irony of it is that the prophetic Scriptures (like Luke 21:28) are evidence of Christ's mid-Tribulation Glorious Appearing and Gathering of the saints. God gave us a list of signs to watch for found in Luke 21:8-36: religious wars, earthquakes, famine, diseases from sin, persecution of Christians, armies surrounding Jerusalem, Antichrist claiming to be God, Israel fleeing to the wilderness, sun and moon darkened. *"Men's hearts failing them for fear, and for looking after those things which are coming on the earth:* ***for the powers of heaven shall be shaken.*** *And* ***then shall they see the Son of man*** *coming in a cloud with power and great glory. And* ***when these things begin*** *to come to pass,* ***then*** *look up, and lift up your heads; for your redemption draweth nigh"* (Luke 21:26-28). That is when your redemption is at hand.

When Christ says, *"the Kingdom of Heaven is at hand"* (Matt. 4:17) it means it is near. Had Israel accepted Jesus, the Earthly Kingdom would have come three and one half years later, at the end of Daniel's seventieth week. Christ spoke of Elijah in Matthew 11:13-14, *"For all the prophets and the law prophesied until John. And if ye* [Israel] *will receive it, this is Elias* [Elijah]*, which was for to come."* This verse means if Israel would have received Christ then John the Baptist would not have been sent but rather Elijah himself would have preceded Christ. Since Israel would not receive Christ, John was sent instead, *"in the spirit and power of Elias"* [Elijah] (Luke 1:17). Elijah will still precede Christ, fulfilling the prophecy of Malachi 4:5 and Matthew 17:11 before Christ comes for His Bride. When God says the day of the Lord is at hand, it is near. When God says the day of the Lord Jesus Christ has come, it is now.

Jesus told us of many signs before His Glorious Appearing. Jesus was answering the questions posed by the disciples in the Gospels of Matthew, Mark and Luke, *"tell us, when shall these things be? And what shall be the sign when all these things shall be fulfilled?"* (Mark 13:4). When you see false-christs and false prophets performing miracles (Matt. 24:4-5; Mark 13:5-6; Luke 21:8) know that this is one of the signs that Jesus talked about. We are told to take heed that no man deceives us, but these false people will deceive many in the church. These people would deceive even the Elect if that were possible, but the true believers in Christ will not be deceived. Part of the Elect is the True Church and the Book of Revelation calls them over-comers. However, much of the church today is like the church of Laodicea mentioned in Revelation 3. Many in the church are asleep at the wheel. Jesus said He would spit them out because of their deeds. *"So then because thou art lukewarm, and neither cold nor hot, I will spue thee out of My mouth"* (Rev. 3:16). Don't you become one of them!

Signs to Watch For

We will see the temple rebuilt in Jerusalem. When you see the abomination that causes desolation standing where it does not belong in the temple (Matt. 24:15; Mark 13:14; Luke 21:20), take notice! *"That man of sin"* (2 Thess. 2:3), the false prince, will desecrate the rebuilt temple in Jerusalem and cause the daily sacrifice to cease (Dan. 11:31). This is the beginning of *"the overspreading of abominations"* (Dan. 9:27). This happens 30 days before the middle of the Tribulation (Dan. 12:11). The false prince shall continue to make it desolate, even unto *"the consummation"* of abominations (Dan. 9:27). The consummation of abominations is performed just prior to the end of the thirty-day period by the Antichrist, when he shall declare himself to be God in the temple (2 Thess. 2:4). *"But the judgment shall sit, and they shall take away his dominion, to consume and to destroy it unto the end"* (Dan. 7:26). Also see Daniel 7:9-14 and Daniel 7:21-22.

We will also see the Two Witnesses performing miracles, preparing the way for the Lord Jesus Christ to come (Rev. 11:3-6). The persecution of the Elect will help the Two Witnesses spread the Gospel of the Kingdom to all nations of the world (Matt. 24:14; Mark 13:10; Luke 21:13). We will see the Two Witnesses in Jerusalem being killed (Rev. 11:7-9).

> *But before all these, they shall lay their hands on you, and persecute you, delivering you up to the synagogues, and into prisons, being brought before kings and rulers for My name's sake. And it shall turn to you for a testimony. Settle it therefore in your hearts, not to meditate before what ye shall answer: For I will give you a mouth and wisdom, which all your adversaries shall not be able to gainsay nor resist. And ye shall be*

> *betrayed both by parents, and brethren, and kinsfolks,*
> *and friends; and some of you shall they cause to be put*
> *to death. And ye shall be hated of all men for My name's*
> *sake. But there shall not an hair of your head perish. In*
> *your patience possess ye your souls.* (Luke 21:12-19).

After the Antichrist proclaims himself to be God, some of Israel flees to the wilderness to escape, where they will be protected by God for 1260 days (Rev. 12:6, 14). Those in Judea are told to flee and those in other countries are warned not to enter therein (Matt. 24:16-21, Mark 13:14-19, Luke 21:21-24).

Another sign is when the sun and the moon are darkened and will not give off their light. The stars fall from heaven and the powers of the heavens shall be shaken (Mark 13:24-25, Luke 21:25-26). This is a picture of the *"war in heaven"* (Rev. 12:7). After this war in heaven, Satan is cast to earth just prior to mid-Trib (Rev. 12:9, 10, 12, 13). Our Scriptural support for this war in heaven mid-Trib is found in Matthew 24:29, *"And the powers of the heavens shall be shaken..."* People will say that it is the end of the world, but it will not be. It is the final labor pains while the woman is *"pained to be delivered"* (Rev. 12:2). This will be just before the coming of our Lord Jesus Christ at His Glorious Appearance to Gather His Elect, as Light against the blackened skies.

> *And then shall appear the sign of the Son of man in*
> *heaven: and then shall all the tribes of the earth mourn,*
> ***and they shall see the Son of man coming in the clouds***
> ***of heaven with power and great glory. And He shall***
> ***send His angels with a great sound of a trumpet, and***
> ***they shall gather together His Elect*** *from the four*
> *winds, from one end of heaven to the other* (Matt. 24:30-31 - Emphasis added).

The Son of man will come in the clouds with His angels to Gather the Elect. The world mourns because they now realize His promise was true and they are grieving for their losses. They are grieving the loss of so many loved-ones and because they were left behind on earth with Satan.

We need to explain what this period of great tribulation is all about. This great Tribulation period has two parts: the first part is Satan's wrath through the Antichrist. This tribulation is up to 10 days long and begins approximately six and a half days before the middle of the Tribulation period (see *Appendix - Chart B*). The Antichrist kills the Two Witnesses after they have ministered for 1260 days, during the first half of the Tribulation. The Two Witnesses resurrect after three and one half days, along with the Bride of Christ. This is when Israel recognizes The Lord Jesus Christ as the True Messiah.

> *Woe to the inhabiters of the earth and of the sea!* **for the devil is come down unto you, having great wrath,** *because he knoweth that he hath but a short time* (Rev. 12:12 - Emphasis added).

> *...for there shall be great distress in the land, and wrath upon this people* [Israel] (Luke 21:23).

> *Fear none of those things which thou shalt suffer: behold,* **the devil** *shall cast some of you into prison, that ye may be tried;* **and ye shall have tribulation ten days***: be thou faithful unto death, and I will give thee a crown of Life* (Rev. 2:10 - Emphasis added).

Even though Christians will be persecuted during the very first part of a period known as *"great tribulation"* (Matt. 24:21, Rev. 7:14), we are given a promise that *"he that shall endure unto the end, the same shall be saved"* (Matt. 24:13, Mark 13:13). The first part of this *"great tribulation"* period is for purifying and testing the faithfulness of the Elect and to provide a witness to the unbelieving world. Also see Matthew 24:9-14, Mark 13:9-20, Luke 21:12-24, Daniel 12:1. This *"great tribulation"* period begins when Satan is cast down from heaven and resurrects the false prince's body, after he is killed. The false prince then becomes the Antichrist and consummates the abominations that the false prince started. The Lord Jesus Christ appears in the air to Gather the Elect about 10 days after Satan is cast out of heaven and indwells the false prince, thereby shortening the days that the Elect are persecuted. This begins the second part of the great Tribulation period, which is a continuation of Satan's wrath through the Antichrist for 42 months (Rev. 13:5), but it also includes God's wrath poured out on the Antichrist and his followers, which is far greater. Between God's wrath and Satan's wrath, all Heaven and hell will break loose!

Who are the Elect that are Gathered from the Four Winds?

In Matthew 24:30-31, there are only a couple of possibilities for whom the Elect can be:

1. The True Church at the time of the Gathering
2. The nation of Israel

There seems to be much confusion as to when these verses take place. Ironically, both pre-Tribulation and post-Tribulation theorists agree that Matthew 24:30-31 is at the end of the Tribulation period. Because of this, we spend much time focusing on this Scripture in this book. We have two questions that might help shed light on the subject.

First Question - What do The Four Winds do?

If one has an understanding of the role and purpose of the four winds mentioned in Daniel 7, Matthew 24:31, Mark 13:27 and Revelation 7:1-3, then you would know that this event is clearly the Gathering of the Elect at His Glorious Appearing. This is not the Triumphal Return of Christ, like so many believe. Let us examine the evidence.

According to Revelation 7, we find several clues who is involved and when these events take place. We see that the four winds have the power *"to hurt the earth and the sea"* (Rev. 7:2). Four angels are *"holding the four winds of the earth, that the wind should not blow on the earth, nor on the sea, nor on any tree"* (Rev. 7:1). These angels are restraining the four winds from harming the earth, the sea, and the trees until the 144,000 are sealed in their foreheads. This places this event in the middle of the Tribulation period at or about the time of the Gathering of the great white robed multitude, or in other words, the Gathering of the Bride of Christ (Rev. 7:9-17). From this we see that the four winds are not allowed to do harm until after the servants of our God, the 144,000 are sealed for protection for their earthly ministry during the last half of the Tribulation period.

Now let us examine the Scriptures in the Gospels and see how they fit together with Revelation 7.

> *Immediately after the tribulation of those days shall the sun be darkened, and the moon shall not give her light, and the stars shall fall from heaven, and the powers of the heavens shall be shaken* (Matt. 24:29).

What event is this Scripture describing? The event that is being described is the war in heaven, where Satan and his angels are vanquished and cast down from heaven (Rev. 12: 7-12). Michael and his angels are victorious. The heavens are cleansed, making way for the Bride of Christ to be brought home for the rewarding of the saints at the Judgment Seat of Christ and to the Marriage of the Lamb.

The phrase *"immediately after the tribulation of those days",* means immediately after the 30 days of hard labor pains while the temple is being desecrated. At this point Jesus Christ is crowned King (Rev. 14:14 and 11:15). *"Now is come salvation, and strength, and the Kingdom of our God, and the power of His Christ"* (Rev. 12:10). Since Christ is not crowned King until mid-Trib, how can He come with *"power and great glory"* to Gather His Bride before mid-Tribulation? If one accepts that Matthew 24:30-31 is the Glorious Appearing and Gathering of the Bride, then one must seriously question a sudden and sign-less pre-Tribulation Rapture.

What tribulation proceeds the days when the powers of heaven are shaken in Matthew 24:29? This tribulation that immediately precedes the sun and moon darkening is called *"great tribulation"* (Matt. 24:21, Rev. 7:14; also see Dan. 12:1, Mark 13:19, Luke 21:20-24, Dan. 11:31, 12:11). This great tribulation of the Elect starts about six and a half days prior to the middle of the Tribulation period and is completed three and one half days after the middle of the Tribulation period. This is when the Two Witnesses are resurrected along with the Bride of Christ. This great tribulation is brought about by Satan through the Antichrist and lasts a total of ten days.

> *And except that the Lord had shortened those days, no flesh should be saved: but for the Elect's sake, whom He hath chosen, He hath shortened the days* (Mark 13:20).

What does it mean when Christ said He would shorten the days for the Elect sake (Matt. 24:22, Mark 13:20)? From Matthew 24:29-31 and other Scriptures we see that Jesus comes in the clouds at the sounding of the seventh and last trumpet. He sends His angels to Gather His Elect out of or from among the four winds. Let us not forget that the four winds are given power to do harm to the earth, the sea and the trees once the 144,000 are sealed for protection (Rev. 7:1-3). Therefore, God shortens the days that the Antichrist has dominion over the Elect by removing them to their respective places of protection. The 144,000 are sealed for protection to minister in the second half of the Tribulation period, the Bride of Christ is Gathered to Heaven, and the woman, the faithful of Israel, flees to the wilderness where she hath a place prepared of God to feed her there for *"a time, and times, and half a time"* (Rev. 12:14) or *"1260 days"* (Rev. 12:6). Therefore, both the True Church and the faithful of Israel are the Elect. All these things take place mid-Trib and these Scriptures all point to the same event, the *"Gathering of the Elect"* (Matt. 24:29-31). Jesus Christ comes as a thief in the night and steals His Elect out of the Antichrist's dominion! Note that we are children of the light and Christ will not come to us as a thief in the night, just to those who are in darkness.

> *But ye, brethren, are not in darkness, that that day should overtake you as a thief. Ye are all the children of the Light, and the children of the Day: we are not of the night, nor of darkness* (1 Thess. 5:4-5).

Then a Scriptural witness is found in Revelation.

> *If therefore thou **shalt not watch**, I will come on thee as a thief, and thou shalt not know what hour I will come upon thee* (Rev. 3:3 - Emphasis added).

Please rid yourself of the notion that Christians are not supposed to know when Christ will come for His Bride because He comes like a thief in the night. It is true that no one knows the hour of His return to Gather the Elect except the Father in Heaven. However, the Father in Heaven tells Jesus when to open the sealed book in Heaven and when

Jesus does this, the Tribulation period begins. Even Jesus does not know when He must open the seals. After He opens the sealed book in Heaven and the Tribulation period begins, we will know from all the signs that His return is then becoming near. Not the exact day or hour, but about three and one half years after the Two Witnesses start their ministry.

We are children of the light and will not be deceived by the Satan-indwelt-Antichrist who claims he is Christ. We know the false-christ comes before the real one does and we will not be fooled or surprised by Christ when He comes for us. So until you have seen all the signs that Christ promised, stop worrying about some sudden Rapture.

We are not predicting a year or date-setting in this book! We simply have not seen the key signs Christ said would happen before He would come. We are teaching people to look for these signs only because His return is not a sign-less event.

Second Question - When is Matthew 24:30-31 taking place?

The Symphonic Method of Scriptural Study suggests that Matthew 24:7 onward is talking about events leading up to the middle of the Tribulation period. However, both pre-Tribulationists and post-Tribulationists say that Matthew 24:31 must be talking about what they call the "Second Coming" of Christ because it takes place *"immediately after the tribulation of those days"* (Matt. 24:29), meaning after the seven-year Tribulation period is completed. What they are missing is the mid-Trib revealing of Christ to Israel at His Glorious Appearing. Why would Israel mourn for Christ, like the Scriptures say they will, if this event was His Second Advent, where they can see Him live and reign on earth in the Millennium? We think *"immediately after the tribulation of those days"* (Matt. 24:29) means at the end of the 30 days of severe labor pains (Rev. 12:2), which is at the end of the first half of the Tribulation period. This is right after the consummation of the abomination that causes desolation, and right after the great apostasy, and right after Israel flees to the wilderness. This is when the Antichrist *"opposeth and exalteth himself above all that is called God, or that is worshipped; so that he as God sitteth in the temple of God, showing himself that he is God"* (2 Thess. 2:4).

2 Thessalonians 2:1-4 tells us that our Gathering to Christ does not happen *"except there come a falling away first,"* and the son of

perdition is revealed, sitting in the temple as God. Read what Jesus said in Matthew 24:21, *"For then shall be great tribulation..."* when you see *"the abomination of desolation...stand in the holy place"* (Matt. 24:15). The abomination of desolation and Israel fleeing is the context of *"the tribulation of those days"* (Matt. 24:29). When does the abomination of desolation take place? Mid-Trib! Please check out our Scriptural witnesses: Daniel 11:31, 12:11; Revelation 12:1-12, 11:15-18; Mark 13:4-27, Luke 17:24-37, Luke 21:7-28, 2 Thessalonians 2:1-12. Please understand that Jesus Gathers His Elect after Israel builds the temple, after the persecution of Christians, after the Satan-indwelt-Antichrist proclaims himself to be God in the rebuilt temple, after there is great apostasy in the church, after the false prophet demands everyone to worship the Antichrist, and after the sun and moon have darkened. Then you will see the Son of man appear in the sky to Gather the Elect out of or from among the four winds, from one end of heaven to another. All these events take place near the sounding of the seventh and last trumpet, mid-Trib. See our chart that uses the symphonic view of Scriptures:

Melodic line: Beginning of sorrows	false prince & Tribulation starts	Temple built & Two Witnesses	false prince lives again Witnesses killed	Glorious Appearing	Wrath
staff					
2 Tim 3:1-9	Rev 5-9	Rev 11:1-2	Rev 12:10	Rev 12:5	Rev 16
staff					
Ezek 38-39	Job 41	Rev 11:3-7	Rev 11:7	Rev 11:15	Zech 14
staff					
Matt 24:7-8	Dan 9:27	Mal 4:4-5	Rev 17:8	Rev10:7	Rev 18
staff					
Mark 13:8			Rev 11:7-14	Luke 17:30	Rev 19:11-21
staff					
			Rev 13:12	Dan 12:1-2	
staff					

1 Cor 15:51-52

If there is conflict between Scriptures, one does not have the full truth yet. When using the Symphonic Method of Scriptural Study, the melodic line must change until everything is in harmony. Otherwise the orchestra is playing noise. The symphonic view is an example of the melodic line in any given bar of time. We need to remember always to keep the melodic line in mind when reading and interpreting the Scriptures. It is much easier to come up with false premises when Scriptures stand alone, out of context, or without accompaniment. Always look for at least the double witness and no conflict. Events like the Gathering of the Elect will have multiple witnesses throughout the whole of Scripture.

What is this "Rapture" So Many Are Talking About?

Nowhere in the King James Version of the Bible does the word "Rapture" appear. Roughly translated, it means to be caught up, snatched away, transformed, gathered together. The word "Rapture" comes from the Latin translation of the Greek. Most people that latch on to this word believe that it is an event that is sudden and imminent without warning or signs.

The Pre-Tribulation Rapture Theory is the belief that when the believers in Christ are gathered together in the clouds to meet Jesus, it will be a sudden, sign-less event. Jesus does not actually set foot on the earth at what they call the "Rapture" and He comes just for His Bride, the True Church. Jesus collects the Bride of Christ to join Him in the clouds and the Bride is given new Heavenly Bodies. They believe that after we are given our new bodies, we follow Jesus to Heaven, where we give an account of our lives at the Judgement Seat of Christ and join Him in the Marriage Supper of the Lamb. Then at the end of the Tribulation period, Christ returns again "with His saints" and this is what they call the "Second Coming."

Key Scriptures are often misinterpreted using an expositional method instead of using an exegesis approach to interpreting Scriptures. For example, why must the trump of God be different from the seventh trumpet sounded in Revelation 11? Pre-Trib folks say it must be different because if it is not, their theory crumbles.

Pre-Tribulation theorists must believe that Christ is not revealed to Israel at the time of the Rapture because no signs are given and the event is sudden. Obviously they must think Christ is not seen in the clouds or in the air during the Rapture. They are adamant that the Church is taken by surprise like when a thief comes, even though the Scriptures are clear that we are not of darkness to be taken as a thief.

> *But ye, brethren, are not of darkness, that that day should overtake you as a thief.* **Ye are all the children of light, and the children of the day:** *we are not of the night, nor of darkness. Therefore let us not sleep, as do others; but let us watch and be sober. For they that sleep sleep in the night; and they that be drunken are drunken in the night.* **But let us, who are of the day, be sober, putting on the breastplate of faith and love; and for an helmet, the hope of salvation. For God hath not appointed us to wrath, but to obtain salvation by our Lord Jesus Christ, Who died for us, that, whether we wake or sleep, we should live together with Him.** *Wherefore comfort yourselves together, and edify one another, even as also ye do.* (1 Thess. 5:4-11 - Emphasis added).

As the authors of this book, we say clearly that we do not believe in a sudden and sign-less Rapture, but we do believe in the Gathering of the Elect, which is preceded with many signs and is emphatically not a secret event. We believe that when Jesus is crowned King mid-Trib He will come to Gather His Bride. The Scriptures tell us that this will be a spectacular event witnessed by all the tribes of the earth (Matt. 24:30, Mark 13:26, Luke 21:27, Rev. 1:7). His Glorious Appearing will be the most major event since the cross.

Somehow pre-Tribulation theorists have failed to recognize the significance of Jesus being revealed to Israel mid-Trib. This is when Israel recognizes Jesus Christ as the True Messiah and mourns (Zech. 12:10, Rev. 1:7) because they will then recognize that they have been following the false-christ. Let us not forget that at this same time God will also take the faithful of Israel to her place of protection, away from Satan's earthly dominion for 1260 days. We believe too many theologians have focused entirely too much on the Rapture of the Church and have ignored Christ's role for Israel at the Mid-Trib Gathering of the Elect.

How Do We Know When Christ Will Come?

No one knows the day or the hour, not even the angels or the Son. Only the Father knows when it is time for Jesus to Gather the Elect (Mark 13:32). Sitting here today while writing this book we could not tell you with certainty when He is coming. However, we have just finished going over all the signs preceding His Gathering of the Elect. We can recognize the signs and know approximately when He is coming after we see these signs. For Christians to ignore this topic saying we are not supposed to know when Jesus will come is a gross misunderstanding of Scripture. Satan would love nothing more than the church to willingly fall asleep and not watch for our Lord to return (Mark 13:32-37).

If Christ's return will be an imminent or sudden and sign-less event as pre-Tribulationists would have us believe, then why is Christ telling us to watch for His Coming? If it is not the signs that we just mentioned earlier in this chapter, then what is there to watch for? Is it God's nature to keep His Bride in the dark? Does it make any sense that He would surprise His Bride, so that she would be unaware and that He would take as few as possible? Jesus warned us not to believe in or be deceived by any man that would say that Christ is here or there! Jesus has already foretold you all things that will happen before He appears in the clouds with power and great glory (Matt. 24:23-27, Mark 13:21-27, Luke 21:25-28). As children of The Light that are aware of the signs of His Coming, we should not be taken unawares (1 Thess. 5:1-11).

We have met countless people who say this whole end time prophecy stuff is a doomsday subject and they will do anything to avoid it. Some say, "we aren't supposed to know when Christ will return." These people are willingly ignorant of the prophecies. They are warned not to be.

> *Knowing this first, that there shall come in the last days scoffers, walking after their own lusts, and saying, where is the promise of His coming? For since the fathers fell asleep, all things continue as they were from the beginning of the creation. For they willingly are ignorant of, that by the Word of God the heavens were of old, and the earth standing out of the water and in the*

water: Whereby the world that then was, being overflowed with water, perished: But the heavens and the earth, which are now, by the same word are kept in store, reserved unto fire against the day of judgment and perdition of ungodly men (2 Peter 3:3-7).

In the past, every generation has promised His Coming. Now in this generation people who are *"willingly ignorant"* are saying, *"where is the promise of His coming?"* They hold on to the belief that we have evolved from primordial slime. They are fulfilling prophecy right now. In doing so, this is yet another sign that we are indeed in the end times. However, we have not yet seen the birth pangs. So far we have only seen things leading up to the beginning of sorrows.

When we see the Two Witnesses performing miracles, and the sun and the moon darken it would be fair to say our Lord's return is not a hundred years off or even a decade. Jesus said He is right at the door when this happens.

*Now learn a parable of the fig tree; When his branch is yet tender, and putteth forth leaves, ye know that summer is nigh: So likewise ye, **when ye shall see all these things**, know that it is **near**, even at the doors. Verily I say unto you, This generation* [who sees all these things] *shall not pass, till all these things be fulfilled* (Matt. 24:32-34 Emphasis added).

Some theologians read the parable of the fig tree and say, "from the time the fig tree blossoms, not one generation shall pass away." Further, they say the fig tree represents Israel's reformation as a nation in 1948 or in 1967 when Israel recaptured Jerusalem. Then they calculate how many years a generation is to try figure out when Christ will come. While their interpretation is a possibility, we think these verses mean something else. We think Christ was comparing the truth about God's natural Law, whereby, when you see the fig tree and all trees blossom you know that the season of summer is near. The Scriptural witness is, *"And He spake to them a parable; Behold the fig tree, **and all the trees**; When they now shoot forth, ye see and know of your own selves that summer is now nigh at hand"* (Luke 21:29 -

Emphasis added). Likewise, when we see all these things that Jesus foretold would happen come true, His return is not far off then. So, when you see the prophecies Christ called *"the beginning of sorrows"* (Matt. 24:8) fulfilled, the season of His return is near, even at the door. The generation that sees the temple rebuilt, the Two Witnesses performing miracles, the abomination in the new temple, and the sun and the moon darken; that generation will not pass away before all things are fulfilled. This is when His return is near, not before.

How can you say we will not be able to discern when Christ will return? It is true that no one knows the exact day or hour of His return. We do not even know that the season of summer is near yet, because we have not yet seen any of the specific signs of His Coming. What we have seen in the way of signs are signs that proceed the *"beginning of sorrows"* like wars, people claiming to be Christians and deceiving many with false teachings, ethnic wars, pestilence, and earthquake activity in diverse places (Matt. 24:4-6, Mark 13:5-7, Luke 21:8-9). Christ said that He would not come then, because *"the end is not yet"* (Matt. 24:6). Because we have only seen the signs of *"wars and rumors of wars"* and not *"the beginning of sorrows"* we know that *"the end is not yet"* (Matt. 24:6-8). But when we see the beginning of sorrows start, we know that this generation shall not pass before Christ comes for His Bride.

A key event will be the beginning of animal sacrifice in the re-built temple in Jerusalem. Approximately 1010 days after the sacrificing begins, the false prince will put an end to daily sacrifice by surrounding Jerusalem with his armies and placing a statue of a false god in the temple. [1260 days (total number days 1st half Trib) – 220 days (sacrifice begins 220 days after Tribulation starts) – 30 days (sacrifice cutoff in temple 30 days before Mid-Trib) =1010 days.] This is the first in a string of abominations. See our chart titled *The Seven Years of the Tribulation Period* in the Appendix.

Gathering the Elect

The second part of Christ's prophecy in His Gospel Discourse is about His return to Gather the Elect. This is when false prophets come and many try to deceive Christians. People betray one another and turn each other in to the government for persecution, and the love of many grows cold. The Gospel is preached to the entire world, the

Antichrist comes to the temple saying he is "God" and great tribulation comes. Those in Judea are told to flee to the mountains (Matt. 24:16, Mark 13:14). God saves the Elect from certain death when Jesus comes like lightning (Matt. 24:27), as fast as a blink of an eye (1 Cor. 15:52), at the sounding of the last trumpet (Matt. 24:29-31, Mark 13:24-27, Luke 21:25-28, 1 Thess. 4:13-18, Rev. 7:9-17, Rev. 10:7, Rev. 11:15-19, Rev. 12:5, Rev. 12:10-11; Rev. 15:2-5).

Many people reading the Gospels get the events and timing mixed up. That is why there is such confusion concerning Christ's Glorious Appearing and then His Triumphal Return. One thing people confuse the most is when the angels are called to *"gather together His Elect from the four winds, from one end of heaven to the other"* (Matt 24:31). People are gathered in the sky at the sound of the last trumpet and somehow so many theologians believe this is the Second Advent. Yet in Revelation 19 where it describes the Second Advent, no such Gathering of the Elect is mentioned. All that we are asking for is that you keep an open mind about the premise that Mathew 24:30-31 is the mid-Trib Gathering of the Elect. It will help you see these prophecies from a new prospective. All this fuss over whom the Elect are is only because so many theologians are trying to hold to the premise of a sudden and sign-less Rapture of the Bride of Christ before the Tribulation begins. If it was not for that, few would argue that the Elect must include the Bride that will be Gathered in the air and the faithful of Israel that will be Gathered to her place of protection from Satan's physical dominion on the earth during the 42-month reign of the Antichrist.

Please read about the signs of Christ's Coming in the Gospels, which we placed side by side for you on the next few pages. See where it talks about the abomination that causes desolation in the middle of the Tribulation period. Notice that the abomination of desolation is mentioned before Christ comes in the clouds of Heaven with power and great glory and before He Gathers His Elect out of or from among the four winds that intend to harm the earth and its inhabitants.

The Gospel Comparison Chart

Matthew 24	Mark 13	Luke 21	Comments
1 And Jesus went out, and departed from the temple: and His disciples came to Him for to show Him the buildings of the temple.	1 And as He went out of the temple, one of His disciples saith unto Him, Master, see what manner of stones and what buildings are here!	5 And as some spake of the temple, how it was adorned with goodly stones and gifts, He said,	2000 years ago
2 And Jesus said unto them, See ye not all these things? Verily I say unto you, There shall not be left here one stone upon another, that shall not be thrown down. 3 And as He sat upon the mount of Olives, the disciples came unto Him privately, saying, Tell us, when shall these things be?	2 And Jesus answering said unto him, Seest thou these great buildings? There shall not be left one stone upon another, that shall not be thrown down. 3 And as He sat upon the mount of Olives over against the temple, Peter and James and John and Andrew asked him privately, 4 Tell us, when shall these things be?	6 As for these things which ye behold, the days will come, in the which there shall not be left one stone upon another, that shall not be thrown down. 7 And they asked Him, saying, Master, but when shall these things be?	AD 70
And what shall be the sign of Thy coming, and of the end of the world (age)?	And what shall be the sign when all these things shall be fulfilled?	And what sign will there be when these things shall come to pass?	Asked 2000 years ago --about- the future
4 And Jesus answered and said unto them, Take heed that no man deceive you. 5 For many shall come in My name, saying, I am Christ; and shall deceive many.	5 And Jesus answering them began to say, Take heed lest any man deceive you: 6 For many shall come in My name, saying, I am Christ; and shall deceive many.	8 And He said, Take heed that ye be not deceived: for many shall come in My name, saying, I am Christ; and the time draweth near: go ye not therefore after them.	All church history
6 And ye shall hear of wars and rumors of wars: see that ye be not troubled: for these things must come to pass, but the end is not yet.	7 And when ye shall hear of wars and rumors of wars, be ye not troubled: for such things must needs be; but the end shall not be yet.	9 But when ye shall hear of wars and commotions, be not terrified: for these things must first come to pass; but the end is not by and by.	All church history

Matthew 24	Mark 13	Luke 21	Comments
7 For nation shall rise against nation, and kingdom against kingdom: and there shall be famines, and pestilences, and earthquakes, in divers places.	8 For nation shall rise against nation, and kingdom against kingdom: and there shall be earthquakes in divers places, and there shall be famines and troubles:	10 Then said He unto them, Nation shall rise against nation, and kingdom against kingdom:	Gog and Magog War Seals 1-4
8 All these are the beginning of sorrows.	**...these are the beginnings of sorrows.**	11 And great earthquakes shall be in divers places, and famines, and pestilences; and fearful sights and great signs shall there be from heaven.	**The beginning of sorrows**
9 Then shall they deliver you up to be afflicted, and shall kill you: and ye shall be hated of all nations for My name's sake.	9 But take heed to yourselves: for they shall deliver you up to councils; and in the synagogues ye shall be beaten: and ye shall be brought before rulers and kings for My sake, for a testimony against them.	12 But before all these, they shall lay their hands on you, and persecute you, delivering you up to the synagogues, and into prisons, being brought before kings and rulers for my name's sake.	Gospel of the Kingdom preached to the whole world by Two Witnesses for 1260 days, during the first half of the Tribulation period
10 And then shall many be offended, and shall betray one another, and shall hate one another.	10 And the gospel must first be published among all nations.	13 And it shall turn to you for a testimony.	
11 And many false prophets shall rise, and shall deceive many.	11 But when they shall lead you, and deliver you up, take no thought beforehand what ye shall speak, neither do ye premeditate: but whatsoever shall be given you in that hour, that speak ye: for it is not ye that speak, but the Holy Ghost.	14 Settle it therefore in your hearts, not to meditate before what ye shall answer:	
12 And because iniquity shall abound, the love of many shall wax cold.		15 For I will give you a mouth and wisdom, which all your adversaries shall not be able to gainsay nor resist.	Persecution of the Elect by the false prince for a testimony to the whole world
	12 Now the brother shall betray the brother to death, and the father the son; and children shall rise up against their parents, and shall cause them to be put to death.	16 And ye shall be betrayed both by parents, and brethren, and kinfolks, and friends; and some of you shall they cause to be put to death.	
13 But he that shall endure unto the end, the same shall be saved.	13 And ye shall be hated of all men for My name's sake: **but he that shall endure unto the end, the same shall be saved.**	17 And ye shall be hated of all men for My name's sake.	
		18 But there shall not a hair of your head perish.	
14 And this gospel of the kingdom shall be preached in all the world for a witness unto all nations; and then shall the end come.		**19 In your patience possess ye your souls.**	**Mid-Tribulation** →

(WHERE IS) **THE PROMISE OF CHRIST'S APPEARING?**

Matthew 24	Mark 13	Luke 21	Comments
15 When ye therefore shall see the abomination of desolation, spoken of by Daniel the prophet, stand in the holy place, (whoso readeth, let him understand):	14 But when ye shall see the abomination of desolation, spoken of by Daniel the prophet, standing where it ought not, (let him that readeth understand),	20 And when ye shall see Jerusalem compassed with armies, then know that the desolation thereof is nigh.	false prince stops the daily sacrifice 30 days prior to Mid-Tribulation
16 Then let them which be in Judaea flee into the mountains: 17 Let him which is on the housetop not come down to take any thing out of his house: 18 Neither let him which is in the field return back to take his clothes.	...then let them that be in Judaea flee to the mountains: 15 And let him that is on the housetop not go down into the house, neither enter therein, to take any thing out of his house: 16 And let him that is in the field not turn back again for to take up his garment.	21 Then let them which are in Judaea flee to the mountains; and let them which are in the midst of it depart out; and let not them that are in the countries enter therein to. 22 For these be the days of vengeance [by the false prince-Antichrist], that all things which are written may be fulfilled.	People in Judaea told to flee because of the persecution by false prince - Antichrist
19 And woe unto them that are with child, and to them that give suck in those days! 20 But pray ye that your flight be not in the winter, neither on the Sabbath day:	17 But woe to them that are with child, and to them that give suck in those days! 18 And pray ye that your flight be not in the winter.	23 But woe unto them that are with child, and to them that give suck, in those days!	This is **Satan's wrath** that causes **great tribulation** upon the Elect (Rev. 12:12)
21 For then shall be **great tribulation**, such as was not since the beginning of the world to this time, no, nor ever shall be.	19 For in those days shall be **affliction**, such as was not from the beginning of the creation which God created unto this time, neither shall be.	23 ...for there shall be **great distress** in the land, and **wrath** upon this people. 24 And they shall fall by the edge of the sword, and shall be led away captive into all nations:	God shortens the days that Satan has power over the Elect, by Gathering the Bride of Christ to
22 And except those days should be shortened, there should no flesh be saved: but for the Elect's sake those days shall be shortened.	20 And except that the Lord had shortened those days, no flesh should be saved: but for the Elect's sake, whom He hath chosen, He hath shortened the days.	...and Jerusalem shall be trodden down of the Gentiles, until the times of the Gentiles be fulfilled.	heaven and protecting the woman [Israel] for 1260 days (Rev. 12:6,14)

Matthew 24	Mark 13	Luke 17	Comments
23 Then if any man shall say unto you, Lo, here is Christ, or there; believe it not. 24 For there shall arise false Christs, and false prophets, and shall show great signs and wonders; insomuch that, if it were possible, they shall deceive the very Elect.	21 And then if any man shall say to you, Lo, here is Christ; or, lo, He is there; believe him not: 22 For false Christs and false prophets shall rise, and shall show signs and wonders, to seduce, if it were possible, even the Elect.	23 And they shall say to you, See here; or, see there; go not after them, nor follow them.	Don't be deceived by this <u>man</u> who <u>claims to be</u> "God"
25 **Behold, I have told you before.** 26 Wherefore if they shall say unto you, Behold, He is in the desert; go not forth: behold, He is in the secret chambers; believe it not.	23 **But take ye heed: behold, I have foretold you all things.**		**Jesus has already told us all things that you need to know to not be deceived.**
27 For as the lightning cometh out of the east, and shineth even unto the west; so shall also the coming of the Son of man be.		24 For as the lightning, that lighteneth out of the one part under heaven, shineth unto the other part under heaven; so shall also the Son of man be in His day.	
28 For wheresoever the carcass is, there will the eagles be gathered together.		37 Wheresoever the body is, thither will the eagles be gathered together	Do you read His Word?

Matthew 24	Mark 13	Luke 21	Comments
29 Immediately after the tribulation of those days shall the sun be darkened, and the moon shall not give her light,	24 But in those days, after that tribulation, the sun shall be darkened, and the moon shall not give her light,	25 And there shall be signs in the sun, and in the moon, and in the stars; and upon the earth distress of nations, with perplexity; the sea and the waves roaring; 26 Men's hearts failing them for fear, and for looking after those things which are coming on the earth:	30 days leading up to Mid-Tribulation (Dan. 12:11)
... and the stars shall fall from heaven, and the powers of the heavens shall be shaken:	25 And the stars of heaven shall fall, and the powers that are in heaven shall be shaken.	...for the powers of heaven shall be shaken.	Satan and his angels cast down from heaven Mid-Tribulation

211

Matthew 24	Mark 13	Luke 21	Comments
30 And then shall appear the sign of the Son of man in heaven: and then shall all the tribes of the earth mourn, and they shall see the Son of man coming in the clouds of heaven with power and great glory.	26 And then shall they see the Son of man coming in the clouds with great power and glory.	27 And then shall they see the Son of man coming in a cloud with power and great glory.	Gathering of the Bride of Christ to the Heavenly Kingdom
31 And He shall send His angels with a great sound of a trumpet, and they shall Gather together His Elect from the four winds, from one end of heaven to the other.	27 And then shall He send His angels, and shall gather together His Elect from the four winds, from the uttermost part of the earth to the uttermost part of heaven.	28 And when these things begin to come to pass, then **look up**, and lift up your heads; for your redemption draweth nigh.	**Mid-Tribulation**

Matthew 24 & 25	Mark 13	Luke 21	Comments
Matthew 24:32-35 Parable of the trees. **Matthew 24:36-51 - 25:1-30** Parables showing only faithful is admitted to Kingdom of Heaven. **Matt. 25:31** "When the Son of man shall come in His glory, and all the holy angels with Him, then shall He sit upon the throne of His glory [at His Triumphant Return to earth]:"	**Mark 13:28-31** Parable of the trees is in the context of "heaven and earth shall pass away" after the 1000 year reign of Jesus Christ over the Earthly Kingdom. **Mark 13:32-37** Instructions on how to prepare for the Gathering of the Bride to Christ and a command to watch for His return.	**Luke 21:29-33** Parable of the trees. All things will be fulfilled in the new heaven and earth. **Luke 21:34-36** A command to watch and pray always, that you may be accounted worthy to escape all these things that shall come to pass, and to stand before the Son of man.	Instructions about Gathering to Christ at Mid-Trib. Answer to Matthew's third question, when is "the end of the age?" (Matt. 24:3)
32 And before Him shall be gathered all nations: and He shall separate them one from another, as a shepherd divideth his sheep from the goats: 33 And He shall set the sheep on His right hand, but the goats on the left. 34 Then shall the King say unto them on His right hand, Come, ye blessed of My Father, inherit the Kingdom prepared for you from the foundation of the world:	**Mark does not speak of Jesus' Triumphant Return to set up the Earthly Kingdom in the Olivet Discourse, only the signs leading up to Gathering of the Bride of Christ.**	**Luke does not speak of Jesus' Triumphant Return to set up the Earthly Kingdom, only the signs leading up to the Gathering of the Bride of Christ.**	Christ's Triumphal Return to Earth at the end of the Tribulation period Christ's 1000 year reign over the Earthly Kingdom

Notice that Matthew 25 is the only Gospel that talks about the Triumphal Return when Christ physically comes back to earth as KING OF KINGS AND LORD OF LORDS. This is in part why theologians say that Matthew's Gospel is the "Gospel of the King."

With the three Gospels that deal with this subject side by side, it is much easier to understand when things will happen. Here is a point to look at when you do the side-by-side comparison of Matthew 24:30-31, Mark 13:26-27 and Luke 21:27-28. If this is the Triumphal Return like many believe, then where is the Rapture mentioned in Matthew, Mark and Luke? Once again, Matthew is the only one of the Gospels that even talks about the Triumphal Return of Christ at the end of the Tribulation period, found in Matthew 25:31-46. Therefore, since Matthew 25:31-46 describes the Triumphal Return, how can Matthew 24:29-31 be the Triumphal Return? It clearly is not the Triumphal Return, but a description of His Glorious Appearing and Gathering of the Bride of Christ.

Why Must Christians Endure Trials and Tribulations?

Let us imagine for a moment that you were God and you love all your children. These children are suffering on earth and some of them do not know you as their true Father. You have the power to remove them all at any time you want to from the earth, but if you do, many of them who did not accept Jesus as Lord would absolutely never do so. Wouldn't you wait until the last possible moment? Wouldn't you have them all endure patiently while waiting for their brothers to accept Jesus like Revelation 3:10 says? Read about the fifth seal in Revelation 9:1-11; the consequences for removing them too soon would be that some of God's children might not know Him because they did not endure long enough. Life was too easy for them to need God. *"The Lord is not slack concerning His promise, as some men count slackness; but is longsuffering to us-ward, not willing that any should perish, but that all should come to repentance"* (2 Peter 3:9). Think about it. If God spared all of us from any trials or tribulations, when would we drop to our knees and thank God for what we have? It is not that God doesn't want us to have the easy life; what Father would not want that for his children? However, He does not want those things for us at the expense of our eternal salvation. He loves us too much for that.

Chapter 11

The Gathering

Our Blessed Hope is His Glorious Appearing

In the last chapter we discussed the difference between the Gathering of the Bride in the air at His Glorious Appearing and the Triumphal Return of the Lord to the earth to physically rule and reign. We hope this chapter will dispel much of the confusion concerning the timing of these two events.

Believe in whatever you believe, but please know and understand why you believe in it. The main thing is that you believe Christ will return for His Bride before He returns to earth with His Wife.

Our belief is obvious in this chapter and is based on our own research. Your belief should be based on Scripture and not what someone else told you. Some of the hardest things we have had to overcome in doing the research for this book was the previous teachings about eschatology and all the pre-conceived ideas that came with them. All the authors of this book were brought up in the United States and were taught the Pre-Tribulation Rapture Theory; it was ingrained into us. Chances are you have been ingrained in it as well. Most religious organizations in America today teach the pre-Tribulation Rapture position, which is a theory. Our Mid-Trib Gathering Theory and all other Rapture theories are just those, theories! If you get nothing else from this book except this point, then we have somewhat succeeded. No one scholar has all the answers. Trust in the Word of God and not in man's interpretation of the Word.

On the other hand, we have seen people mentally shut down when they discover that what was taught to them is different from what they are now hearing from us. Please do not shut down mentally! You need to read the Word of God for yourself and be diligent in your studies, allowing the Holy Spirit to lead you where He may in your studies. Do not let someone else tell you what the Bible says and means without reading it for yourself, confirming what you believe. In our society we so often refer to an expert to tell us what the problem is and then offer a solution. Not so with the Bible. God wants you to read it. Many people will perish because of a lack of knowledge about the Word of God.

Exhibits Supporting the Mid-Tribulation Gathering Position

We have a mountain of evidence that suggests that Christ's Gathering of His Bride is mid-Tribulation. Let us explore the evidence of these Exhibits numbered Mid-1 through Mid-43.

Daniel Split the Tribulation Period

Mid-1) Daniel 7:25 divides the Tribulation period into two halves.

> *And he* [the false prince - Antichrist] *shall speak great words against the Most High, and shall wear out the* **saints** *of the Most High, and think to change times and laws: and they shall be given into his hand* **until** *a time and times and* **the dividing of time** (Dan. 7:25 - KJV - Emphasis and explanation added).

From the moment we are born again we become saints in the spirit realm and no longer sinners, even though our sin-flesh is still condemned to die. Daniel 7:25 says that the *"saints"* of the Most High are persecuted by the false prince - Antichrist. This persecution must be during the first half of the Tribulation because the saints are given unto him *"until"* the dividing of time. According to the Strong's Concordance, the definition of *"the dividing of time"* is found in # 6387, (Chaldean) p^{e}l-ag; *"a half -- dividing."*[40] Because Daniel clearly means there are three and one half years after the dividing of time, Daniel clearly intended to divide time equally. Daniel 9:27 and Daniel 12 gives us the idea that what he is dividing is a week of seven-years.

Michael stands up for the *"children of thy people"* in Daniel 12:1. We believe that the Elect are the children of thy people. Daniel is asking the question, *"how long shall it be to the end of these wonders?"* (Dan. 12:6).

> *That it shall be for a time, times and* **an half** [Strongs # 2677 - half, middle, mid (-night), midst, part, two parts[41]]; *and when he* [the false prince - Antichrist] *shall*

have accomplished to scatter the power of the holy people, all these things shall be finished (Dan. 12:7 - Emphasis and explanation added).

"A time, times and half a time" is three and one-half Jewish years or 1260 days. The scattering of the holy people does not happen until the Two Witnesses are killed, after they prophesy 1260 days (Rev. 11:3, 7). The Mystery is finished or completed when the seventh angel is about to sound at the middle of the Tribulation period (Rev. 10:7).

Why would so many Scriptures point to the middle of the Tribulation period known as the Day of Christ if there is a sudden and sign-less pre-Trib Rapture? His Glorious Appearance mid-Trib is the main event in end time prophecies. The cross is infinitely as important but lacks the fireworks spectacular that His Glorious Appearance will have. The cross was a dark day in history that brings much joy and happiness once one understands its significance. Christ's Glorious Appearing will be the darkest hour for the Elect and will bring much sorrow and mourning for those left behind. Can you imagine the darkest hour in earth's history, when the sun and moon will not even give off their light? Then, Christ comes as The Light of the world, like lightning from east to west. He reveals Himself to all the tribes of the earth right after receiving His crown and legal dominion over the kingdoms of this world. Wouldn't you mourn for Him if you were left behind with the Antichrist and God's wrath? We cannot emphasize enough how significant His Glorious Appearance is to the world mid-Trib. When He returns to Heaven with His Bride, then the rest of the world has to make a choice; choose Christ or the Antichrist. Those who choose the Antichrist will die at Christ's Triumphal Return during the battle of Armageddon.

Daniel's Split Seventieth Week

Mid-2) In our Chapter about *"Daniel's Seventieth Week"* we have given a strong argument for the splitting of Daniel's seventieth week. There were sixty-nine weeks *"unto Messiah the Prince"* (Dan. 9:25). Christ confirmed the New Covenant with Jew and Gentile for one week. In the middle of that seventieth week, Christ was crucified because of Israel's rejection of the Messiah and His Covenant. The stewardship of the Gospel was given to the Gentiles (the Mystery).

The stewardship of the Gospel will change back to Israel through the 144,000 when the second half of the split week starts up again. The Gathering of the Bride will be mid-Trib because the Mystery of God is finished at the sounding of the seventh trump (Rev. 10:7).

Saints Persecuted Until Mid-Trib

Mid-3) It does not get much clearer than this. The saints are given into his hand until mid-Trib or the dividing of time.

> *And he* [the false prince - Antichrist] *shall speak great words against the Most High, and shall wear out the saints of the Most High, and think to change times and laws:* **and they** [the saints] **shall be given into his hand until a time and times and the dividing of time** [mid-Trib] (Dan. 7:25 - Emphasis and explanation added).

What happens to the saints mid-Trib? If it is not the Gathering at Christ's Glorious Appearing, then what? Why are the saints given into the false prince - Antichrist's hand only until the dividing of time mid-Trib?

This point shows the persecution of the saints until time is divided. We will be given into the hand of the false prince for approximately three and one half years (*"prince of Tyrus"* is a type or an example in Ezek. 28:2). After that amount of time Daniel 12 and Revelation 13:5 makes it clear that when the son of perdition has accomplished to scatter the power of the holy people, he will rule on the earth three and one half years or 42 months. The son of perdition is also known as the Antichrist (*"king of Tyrus"* is a type or an example in Ezek. 28:12). This is evidence for a mid-Trib Gathering of the saints and the splitting of Daniel's seventieth week. Jacob's trouble is three and one half years long and is only during the second half of the Tribulation period, after the fullness of the Gentiles ends (Rom. 11:25-27) at mid-Trib. This is strong evidence for a mid-Trib Gathering of Christ.

Mid-Trib Resurrection in Daniel 12:2

Mid-4) The angel Michael shall stand up for *"the children of thy people"* (Dan. 12:1). When does Michael actually do this? During the war in heaven Michael and his angels fight the dragon and his angels. Satan and his angels are vanquished and cast down from heaven (Rev. 12:7-9). Then the abomination that causes desolation happens (Rev. 12:12-13, Matt. 24:15, Mark 13:14). Now that we have established that Michael stands up during mid-Trib, read Daniel 12:2; *"and many of them that sleep in the dust of the earth shall awake."* Doesn't that sound like a resurrection to you? This is evidence that the resurrection of the dead happens in the middle of the Tribulation period.

Philadelphia Church Promised To Be Kept From The Hour Mid-5) The church of Philadelphia is told,

> *Because thou hast kept the word of My patience, I also will keep thee from the hour of temptation, which shall come upon all the world, to try them that dwell upon the earth* (Rev. 3:10).

In fact, in all the letters to the seven churches we are given promises to *"he that overcometh"* (Rev. 2 and 3). We ask, what are all the churches overcoming if not the first half of the Tribulation? What are they asked to be patient through? We theorize that the letter was giving comfort to the church of Philadelphia in their past history. We also need to look at all the letters to the seven churches as prophecies that give comfort and warnings to the future as well.

In reviewing the Philadelphian letter, when in history has the hour of temptation come upon the whole world? Never in history has this happened. We believe that *"the hour of temptation"* is a 42-month period of time that the Satan-indwelt-Antichrist lives and reigns on the earth. We believe the temptation will be that the entire world will have to choose whom to worship, the raised Antichrist or the resurrected Lord Jesus Christ. We believe that the *"strong delusion"* (2 Thess. 2:11) sent by God is the false prince that appears raised from the dead as the Antichrist, and that the entire world will worship him except for those whose names are written in the Lamb's Book of Life (Rev. 13:8). This brings us to our conclusion that the church at present is being comforted by knowing that they will be kept from the *"hour,"* (Rev. 3:10, 14:7, 17:12, 13:5) a 42 month period of temptation to worship the Antichrist that will come upon the whole world. And, the church of Philadelphia will endure patiently through something that has not happened yet, the first half of the Tribulation period of 1260 days.

There are Still Souls in Heaven after Revelation 4:1

Mid-6) There are souls in Heaven asking God, how much longer until You avenge our blood? They are told,

> *And white robes were given unto everyone of them; and it was said unto them, that they should rest yet for a little season, until their fellowservants also and their brethren, that should be killed as they were, should be fulfilled* (Rev. 6:11).

There are still souls in Heaven without their Heavenly Bodies well after Revelation 4:1, but before the seventh and last trumpet is blown. The souls that die before the Gathering are resurrected with the Bride of Christ. They receive their glorified Heavenly bodies and are transformed with the living into incorruptible flesh and bone beings at the mid-Trib Gathering.

Those souls that are killed after the dispensation change in Revelation 14:13, *"from henceforth,"* will be resurrected after they have rested for a little season. Their blood is fully avenged when God judges the great whore according to Revelation 19:2.

John is Weeping after Revelation 4:1

Mid-7) Why would John be weeping in Revelation 5 if the Rapture had already happened in Revelation 4:1? John knew that unless someone could break the seals and open the book that the Gathering could not happen and the Bride would be eternally separated from God. Satan could not be cast out of heaven, nor could the Mystery be finished and God could never restore creation back to its perfect condition. Nothing could happen unless the sealed book could be opened and John knew it.

The problem for the pre-Tribulationists in reading the Book of Revelation chronologically is that it disproves the Pre-Tribulation Rapture Theory. Say what, you are wondering. If you truly read the Book of Revelation chronologically, it disproves the pre-Tribulation gathering of the Bride. Yet, when doing the research for this book we found that numerous pre-Tribbers boldly claim that the Book of Revelation must be read chronologically.

Using the Symphonic Method of Scriptural Study, building a timeline of events and scrutinizing Scriptures looking for any possible conflicts, one finds many conflicting issues while trying to read the Book of Revelation chronologically.

How can the Rapture of the church happen before Christ opens the seven-sealed book in Heaven? It is like putting the cart before the horse. Until that book is opened, nothing can begin to happen; that is why John was crying when no one was found worthy to break the seals on the book. Satan would continue accusing us of our sins in Heaven forever and ever if that book could not be opened. All seven seals must be broken and the book opened before the first trumpet can sound. When all seven trumpets have sounded, then and only then can the vials be poured out from Heaven. It all starts when Jesus opens the sealed book in Heaven.

Revelation 4:1 does mention something that sounded as if it was a trumpet blast, but it specifically says that the sound is a voice *"talking with me"* (Rev. 4:1). This *"great voice, as a trumpet"* is the voice of the *"Alpha and Omega"* of Revelation 1:10-11 and *"the first voice"* that John heard. To reach for a meaning that what John heard was a trumpet blast would be putting words in his mouth. Revelation 4:1 does not mention any trumpet blast or anyone being translated to meet Jesus in the air. For sure, John was not translated into his flesh and bone body, or in other words, his glorified body. But, 1 Corinthians 15:52 does mention these things *"at the sounding of the last trumpet, the dead in Christ shall be raised and the living shall be changed."* So again, how is it possible for the church to be raptured to the heavens and be in Heaven before the sealed book is opened or before the trumpets are sounded? The resurrection happens at the sounding of that last trumpet, after Satan is cast down.

Pre-Tribulationists say that the last trumpet must be another trumpet other than the seventh and last trumpet in Revelation; but how can we be Gathered at the sound of the last trumpet if there are seven more trumpets to be blown during the Tribulation? Where is the Scriptural evidence to support that notion? Our whole book is based on literal interpretation of Scripture supporting Scripture. We cannot find Scripture that supports multiple sets of trumpets being blown in the end times.

The Scriptures would not be so difficult to understand if people would just read them and take them for what they say. Why must the last trumpet announcing the Glorious Appearing and Gathering of the Bride to Christ be something other than the last trumpet in Revelation? They say it must be because of the premise that some sudden and sign-less Rapture happens before the Tribulation period. Get rid of that premise and these trumpet issues become clear.

Who Comes First - Elijah or Christ?

Mid-8) Most of the church thinks that Christ's return is imminent. Why? Christ said that Elijah must come first. So if anything, Elijah's return is imminent, not Christ's. When we see Elijah proclaiming the coming of Christ, then we will know that Christ's return is near.

The disciples asked Jesus why the Jewish scribes said that Elijah must comes first. Jesus said, *"Elias* [Elijah] *truly shall first come, and restore all things"* (Matt. 17:11). Notice Jesus was alive when He said this so He was talking about the future. Jesus was talking about Elijah coming as one of the Two Witnesses during the first half of the Tribulation period.

> *And I will give power unto My two witnesses, and they shall prophesy a thousand two hundred and threescore days* [1260 days] (Rev. 11:3).

The Two Witnesses proclaim that the Kingdom is coming until mid-Trib.

> *And when they* [Two Witnesses] *shall have finished their testimony, the beast that ascendeth out of the bottomless pit* [Antichrist] *shall make war against them, and shall overcome them, and kill them* (Rev. 11:7).

> *And after three days and an half the Spirit of Life from God entered into them* [Two Witnesses], *and they stood on their feet; and great fear fell upon them which saw them. And they heard a great voice from heaven saying unto them, "Come up hither." And they ascended up to*

heaven in a cloud; and their enemies beheld them (Rev. 11:11-12).

The dead in Christ are caught up to Heaven along with the Two Witnesses when they are resurrected, and the faithful living will be changed and caught up in the clouds to meet Jesus in the air (1 Thess. 4:13-18). Most people know this event as the "Rapture," but we call it His Glorious Appearing and Gathering of His Bride. This event takes place mid-Trib.

The Mystery started with Elijah and will end with Elijah
Mid-9) When Moses and Elijah were standing with Jesus after the transfiguration, Peter, James and John asked Jesus why the scribes said that Elijah must come before He does (Matt. 17:1-13). Jesus said that Elijah truly shall come before Me and restore all things (Matt. 17:11). But Elijah had come already and Israel knew him not. He was killed and so likewise also the Son of man shall suffer the same way (Matt. 17:12). Then the disciples knew Jesus was talking about John the Baptist. John had come in the spirit and power of Elijah (Luke 1:17).

> *For all the prophets and the law prophesied until John. And if ye shall receive it, this is Elias* [Elijah], *which is to come* (Matt. 11:13-14).

Since the Law and the Prophets prophesied until John the Baptist, it can be said that a New Covenant of Grace started when John baptized Jesus. Since John came in the spirit of Elijah before the Mystery started, doesn't it make sense that the real Elijah comes before the Mystery will end? The Mystery is finished at the mid-Trib Gathering of the Bride to Christ.

Our point is that Elijah must come before Christ does. Elijah dies and then is resurrected mid-Trib, just as Christ comes in the air. We are not looking for the sudden coming of Christ yet because we are still waiting for Elijah to come as Christ promised he would. The Mystery is finished when Elijah and all the dead in Christ resurrect in the days of the voice of the seventh angel (Rev. 10:7). The Mystery is the Bride of Christ, brought about by the stewardship of the Gentiles preaching the Gospel of Christ's death, burial and resurrection to whosoever believes. This is strong evidence supporting the mid-Trib position.

Two Witnesses Represent Israel and the Church

Mid-10) The *"Two Witnesses"* are *"the two olive trees"* representing Israel, *"the two candlesticks"* representing the church and they will prophesy for 1260 days (Rev. 11:3-4). Elijah must come before Christ (Matt. 17:11). Not only does Elijah come before Christ, but Elijah is also here for 1260 days until mid-Trib (Rev. 11:3). So why would someone believe that Christ comes before Elijah comes or before Elijah is caught up to Heaven mid-Trib? Christ is warning the church of Ephesus to repent or *"I will come unto thee quickly, and will remove thy candlestick out of his place, except thou repent"* (Rev. 2:5). After Christ removes Moses and Elijah mid-Trib, it will be too late for those from the church of Ephesus who did not repent by then. The opportunity to be the Bride of Christ will have been removed from them, when there is *"time no longer"* (Rev. 10:6).

The Two Witnesses are representative of and minister to both Israel and the church until they are killed. Moses represents the righteous dead in Christ and Elijah represents the living in Christ. When Christ resurrects the dead and translates the living in Christ, He takes all of them to Heaven in their glorified bodies. This includes *"the two candlesticks"* (Rev. 11:4), Elijah and Moses, that are caught up together with the Bride of Christ to Heaven mid-Trib.

The Mid-Trib Gathering of the Two Witnesses

Mid-11) Elijah comes before the *"great and dreadful day of the LORD"* (Mal. 4:5), which is God's wrath. The wrath of God is not poured out until after the Two Witnesses, Moses and Elijah, are ascended to Heaven in the middle of the Tribulation.

> *Behold, I will send you Elijah the Prophet before the coming of the great and dreadful day of the LORD: And he shall turn the heart of the fathers to the children, and the heart of the children to their fathers, lest I come and smite the earth with a curse* (Mal. 4:5-6).

Malachi 4:6 is a warning that whoever does not follow Elijah will be cursed with Jehovah's wrath. Elijah will come before Christ just as He promised (Matt. 17:11). This then infers that anyone that follows Elijah shall escape God's wrath that is poured out in the second half of the Tribulation period. We believe the people that follow Elijah will be kept from the hour of temptation via the Gathering of the Bride to Christ at His Glorious Appearance and those of Israel that escape into the wilderness to seek God's protection while the Antichrist reigns for 42 months (Rev. 12:6, 12:14, 13:5).

If one believes in a pre-Tribulation sudden and sign-less Rapture, then one must believe that resurrection of the Bride of Christ is separate from the mid-Trib resurrection of the Two Witnesses. The Scriptures conflict with this theory. If there is a resurrection of people from the True Church before the Tribulation, another resurrection of the Two Witnesses during mid-Trib, then there are multiple Raptures and multiple resurrections of the dead that are separate parts of the Bride of Christ. Where in the Bible does it promise this? Is not the entire Bride of Christ Gathered at once? Not all pre-Tribulationists claim to believe in multiple resurrections or Raptures, but placing events like these on a timeline symphonically can show the conflicts of a premise.

Pre-Tribulation Theory

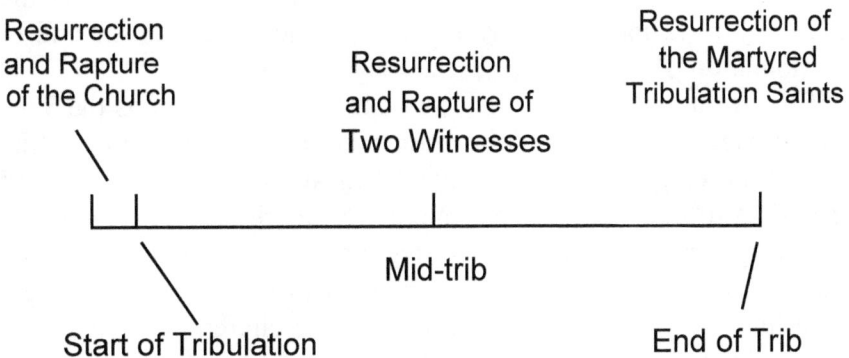

Resurrection and Rapture of the Church

Resurrection and Rapture of Two Witnesses

Resurrection of the Martyred Tribulation Saints

Mid-trib

Start of Tribulation

End of Trib

Pre-tribbers must believe in multiple raptures of the Bride. This doesn't have Scriptural support.

Who Comes First, the Son of Perdition or
Christ to Gather His Bride?

Mid-12) Who comes first, the false-christ or Jesus Christ for His Bride? According to 2 Thessalonians 2:3 when the false prince dies and is raised from the dead, *"the son of perdition"* or Antichrist comes first. Satan always tries to steal God's thunder and glory. Satan often appears in a godly form to deceive. The false prince rising from the dead, declaring himself to be God in the temple and becoming the Antichrist is no different (Rev. 13:3). This leader has many names found in Scripture and dies from a mortal wound.

Before his fatal wound his names are: *"the prince that shall come"* (Dan. 9:26), *"prince of Tyrus"* (Ezek. 28:1-10), *"beast"* who rises *"out of the sea"* (Rev. 13:1-4) and *"that man of sin"* (2 Thess. 2:3).

After the Antichrist rises from the dead and is indwelt by Satan, his names are: *"son of perdition"* (2 Thess. 2:3), *"king of Tyrus"* (Ezek. 28:12-18), *"beast"* who rises *"out of the bottomless pit"* (Rev. 11:7, 17:8), *"that Wicked"* (2 Thess. 2:8), *"that Antichrist"* (1 John 2:18), and *"the beast that was, and is not, and yet is"* (Rev. 17:8). The Antichrist is a mirror image or an imitator of Jesus Christ (Rev. 1:18).

Satan wants to steal God's glory by bringing about the pseudo-christ before Christ comes to Gather the Elect mid-Trib. By bringing the false prince's soul out of the pit and restoring it to his body, the false-christ is seemingly immortal. He even sits in the temple and declares he is God. This man is the beast that rises out of the bottomless pit mid-Tribulation (Rev. 11:7, 17:8). He continues as the Antichrist for 42 months (Rev. 13:5), from the middle to the end of the Tribulation period.

If the resurrection of the Bride of Christ, also known as the True Church, were prior to the Tribulation period it would be in conflict with Scripture. 2 Thessalonians 2:1-12 makes it clear that the false prince rises from the dead to become the Antichrist before the coming of our Lord Jesus Christ. The resurrection of the righteous dead and our Gathering together to Christ in the air will not happen until there is a falling away or the great apostasy of the church and the son of perdition is revealed (2 Thess. 2:1-3). The revealing of *"that Wicked"* (2 Thess. 2:8) cannot happen until Satan is cast out of heaven mid-Trib. Because of this, the resurrection of the True Church cannot happen until mid-Trib. *"And for this cause God shall send them a strong delusion, that they should believe a lie"* [the lie is that the man of sin raised from the dead is God and should be worshipped] (2 Thess. 2:11).

> *The beast that thou sawest was, and is not; and shall ascend out of the bottomless pit, and go into perdition: and they that dwell on the earth shall wonder...when they behold the beast that was, and is not, and yet is* (Rev. 17:8).

The beast that rises *"out of the sea"* in Revelation 13:1 is the same beast in Revelation 17:8 that *"was"*. The beast or *"that man of sin"* (2 Thess. 2:3) is a world leader who will gain almost total control of the world by mid-Trib. This world leader is killed and becomes the beast that *"is not"* (Rev. 17:8). Then Satan is cast down from heaven into the earth (Rev. 12:9). Satan indwells the body of *"that man of sin"* (2 Thess. 2:3) and becomes the beast that shall ascend *"out of the bottomless pit"* (Rev. 11:7), *"and all the world wondered after the beast"* (Rev. 13:3). The *"son of perdition"* is revealed (2 Thess. 2:3, 8). He becomes the beast that *"yet is"* (Rev. 17:8), also known as the Anti-christ and takes total control of the world. God sends the world a *"strong delusion"* (2 Thess. 2:11). We put all these verses together so you would see the connection and timing of these events symphonically describing a single mid-Trib event. Remember that Revelation cannot be read in chronological order. Many verses are describing the same event over and over from different viewpoints. Revelation 17:8 and Revelation 13:3 are doing just that. With these Scriptures organized like we have done for you, how could anyone say the son of perdition is revealed before the Tribulation period? That just would not fit symphonically.

According to the Book of Daniel, does the Antichrist's kingdom or Christ's Heavenly and Earthly Kingdoms Come First?

Mid-13) In Daniel 2 the king had a dream of a statute representing seven successive earthly kingdoms that has had and will have dominion over the earth. God helped Daniel to interpret the dream. King Nebuchadnezzar was said to be the head of gold representing the first kingdom. The second kingdom was that of Media-Persia represented by the chest and arms of silver. The third kingdom represented by the belly and thighs of brass was Greece. The fourth kingdom was Rome, represented by the legs of iron.

The fifth kingdom is represented by *"**the feet and toes**, part of potter's clay, and part of iron, **the kingdom shall be divided"** (Dan. 2:41 - Emphasis added). This kingdom is the beginning of the dividing of truth and lies, the dividing of political entities, and ends at the mid-Trib dividing of time or change of dispensation. This is the kingdom that the false prince raises to power in. This fifth kingdom is also divided from the sixth kingdom by the death of the false prince. After Satan indwells the false prince at his death and it appears that he rises from the dead, this is when the son of perdition, "the Antichrist" is revealed. The false prince will be a mere-evil-mortal-man in the fifth kingdom and becomes the Satan-indwelt-man referred to by many as the Antichrist in the sixth kingdom of the statute dream.

The sixth kingdom is represented by *"the toes of the feet"* (Dan. 2:42). The ten toes of the feet refer to the ten kings that rule under the Antichrist (Rev. 17:12) during his 42 month reign in the last half of the Tribulation period (Rev. 13:5).

> *And **in the days of these** [ten] **kings shall the God of heaven set up a Kingdom,** which shall never be destroyed... Forasmuch as thou sawest that the **Stone** [Jesus Christ] was cut out of the mountain without hands, and that it brake in pieces the iron, the brass, the clay, the silver, and the gold...* (Dan. 2:44-45 - Emphasis added).

This stone cut out of the mountain without a human hand represents the seventh and final kingdom that is setup by God. Jesus Christ is that Stone (Rom. 9:33, 1 Cor. 10:4). His dominion is an everlasting dominion and a kingdom that shall never be destroyed (Dan. 7:14, 2:44). This is a basic description of the statute and the kingdoms that are represented by it.

Now let us look at the timing of when these earthly kingdoms are set up as related to their chronological order.

> *Then was the iron, the clay, the brass, the silver, and the gold, broken to pieces together... that no place was*

found for them: and the Stone that smote the image…
filled the whole earth (Dan. 2:35).

These Scriptures show that Christ's Kingdom is the last earthly kingdom *"and the Kingdom shall not be left to other people, but it shall break in pieces and consume all these kingdoms, and it shall stand for ever"* (Dan. 2:44). That means that the false prince's kingdom and the Antichrist's kingdom must come chronologically before Christ's Earthly Kingdom according to the king's statute dream in Daniel 2.

We see the same chronological order with a more detailed description of when dominion is transferred to Christ and when He receives His Heavenly and Earthly Kingdoms given in Daniel 7.

In Daniel 7:17-18 we see an example of the four beasts coming chronologically before Christ's Heavenly Kingdom.

> *These great beasts, which are four, are four kings, which shall arise out of the earth. But the saints of the Most High shall take the Kingdom, and possess the Kingdom for ever, even for ever and ever* (Dan. 7:17-18).

Once Christ's Heavenly Kingdom starts it lasts forever!

Daniel 7:19-22 tells us the same thing. Daniel was asking for the interpretation of the fourth beast with the ten horns and that little horn that had eyes and a mouth speaking great things.

> *I beheld, and the same* [little] *horn made war with the saints, and prevailed against them;* **Until** *the Ancient of days came, and* **judgment was given to the saints** *of the Most High;* **and the time came that the saints possessed the Kingdom** (Dan. 7:21-22 - Emphasis added).

Once again we see that Christ's Heavenly Kingdom comes after the fourth beast kingdom and after the little horn has risen to power. Please notice that it said the little horn was prevailing against the saints until God and His Heavenly Court passed judgment in favor of the saints and the time came that the saints possessed the kingdom.

In the interpretation given to Daniel in Daniel 7:23-28, we see the chronological order given very plainly. The fourth beast is the fourth kingdom that arises. It is *"diverse from all kingdoms, and shall devour the whole earth, and shall tread it down, and break it in pieces"* (Dan. 7:23). This breaking it in pieces by the false prince brings about or causes the ten horns or ten kings of the fourth kingdom to arise. These are the same ten kings talked about in Revelation 17. *"And another* [the little horn or Antichrist] *shall rise after them"* (Dan. 7:24). From Daniel 7:12 we see that *"the rest of the beasts... had their dominion taken away: yet their lives were prolonged for a season and a time."* This little horn subdues the dominion of the three beasts or kings of Daniel 7 that co-exist with the fourth beast when he first comes to power. In order for the little horn or Antichrist to have complete world dominion, anyone opposing him will have to have their national sovereignty taken away or give it up voluntarily. That does not necessarily mean these nations will cease to exist as people groups. Thus the ten kings that receive power with the Antichrist *"have one mind, and shall give their power and strength unto the beast"* (Rev. 17:13). Remember that according to Revelation 13, the false prophet is also symphonically part of the fourth beast kingdom of Daniel 7.

Daniel goes on to say that this little horn speaks…

> *great words against the Most High, and shall wear out the saints of the Most High… and they* [the saints] *shall be given into his* [little horn or Antichrist's] *hand **until a time and times and the dividing of time. But the judgment shall sit,** and they* [God, Jesus, 24 elders and angels (Rev. 4 and 5)] *shall **take away his** * [little horn or Antichrist's] ***dominion,** to consume and to destroy it unto the end* (Dan. 7:25-26 - Emphasis added).

In Daniel 7:7-8 we find a description of the fourth beast with the little horn rising up as the Antichrist. Immediately following in verse 9 there is the connecting phrase, *"I beheld till the thrones were cast down."* Verses 10-14 goes on to describe *"one like the Son of man came with the clouds of heaven."* The Scriptural witness to this is found in Revelation 1:7; *"Behold, He cometh with clouds; and every eye shall see Him, and they also which pierced Him: and all kindreds of the earth shall wail because of Him."* Thousand thousands of angels minister unto the Ancient of days *"and ten thousand times ten thousand stood before Him: the judgment was set, and the Books were opened"* (Dan. 7:10). The Books that are opened are more than just the sealed book talked about in Revelation 5. This probably includes the Book of Life and the Books of Rewards for the saints. This sure sounds to us like the Gathering of the Bride to the Heavenly Kingdom and *"the judgment seat of Christ"* that Paul talked about in Romans 14:10 and 2 Corinthians 5:10.

So, when does Jesus Christ begin to reign as King by receiving dominion over the earth and its inhabitants? This question requires a careful examination of Daniel 7:14, Daniel 7:27 and a two-part answer.

> *And there was given Him* [Son of man] ***dominion, and glory, and a kingdom, that all people, nations, and languages, should serve Him****: His dominion is an everlasting dominion, which shall not pass away, and His Kingdom that which shall not be destroyed* (Dan. 7:14 - Emphasis and explanation added).

> *And the kingdom and dominion* [in Heaven], ***and the greatness of the kingdom under the whole heaven*** [earthly kingdom], *shall be given to the **people of the saints** of the Most High, Whose kingdom is an Everlasting Kingdom, and **all dominions*** [both Heavenly and earthly] *shall serve and obey Him* [Son of man] (Daniel 7:27 - Emphasis and explanation added).

Pay close attention to the order given in Daniel 7:14; first the Son of man is given *"dominion,"* then *"glory,"* and lastly a *"kingdom."* The reason this question requires a two-part answer is because Jesus Christ ultimately receives two Kingdoms. Part 1: A Heavenly Kingdom, and three and one half years later, Part 2: An Earthly Kingdom.

Part 1: A Heavenly Kingdom

From all the Scriptures above we see that Satan's dominion is beginning to be stripped from him when *"the judgment was set, and the Books were opened"* (Dan. 7:10). The first book opened is the sealed book in Heaven (Rev. 5:1-10). The opening of this sealed book in Heaven's courtroom is the beginning of the legal process of transferring all dominion to Jesus Christ. As our Kinsman-Redeemer, Jesus paid the ransom price by dying and presenting His blood as a sacrifice on the altar in Heaven. Jesus Christ spiritually broke the curses caused by Satan over the earth and its inhabitants on the cross. However, physical death caused by sin in our flesh and blood bodies and the curses on the earth are still in affect today. Satan still retains dominion through the title deed to the earth and its inhabitants until that dominion is legally transferred to Christ by God's judgment court. The Books being opened and God's judgment court sitting in Daniel 7 are the very scenes John described in Revelation 4:1-5:14. This legal transaction for His Bride will not be completed by Jesus Christ as our Kinsman-Redeemer until: the dominion granted by the title deed to the earth is transferred from Satan to Christ (Rev. 11:15-19), Satan and his angels are banished from heaven (Rev. 12:1-17), Christ's Bride is brought to the Heavenly Kingdom (Rev. 7:9-17, 15:1-8), the rewards are given to the faithful (Rev. 11:18) and Christ marries His Bride (Rev. 19:1-9).

The Scriptures in Daniel 7 describe *"the little horn"* as speaking or taking action against the most High and His saints *"till"* or *"until"* God's court passes judgment, stripping Satan of his legal dominion in heaven and giving that dominion to Christ and His saints. In Revelation 12:9, Satan and his angels are cast out of heaven, thereby cleansing the heavens for the Gathering of the Bride to the Heavenly Kingdom. In the next verse it says, *"Now is come salvation, and strength, and the Kingdom of our God, and the power of His Christ: for the accuser of our brethren is cast down"* (Rev. 12:10). According to Revelation 11, *"the kingdoms of this world are become the kingdoms of our LORD, and of His Christ; and He shall reign for ever and ever"* at the mid-Trib sounding of the seventh trumpet (Rev. 11:15). The twenty-four elders confirm this at the seventh trumpet by saying, *"because Thou hast taken to Thee Thy great power, and hast reigned"* (Rev. 11:17). At the sounding of the seventh trumpet, Jesus Christ has received all *"dominion"* in Heaven (Rev. 11:15-18, 12:1-12), *"glory"* at His Glorious Appearing to Gather the Bride in their glorified bodies away from the Antichrist (Matt. 24:29-31, Mark 13:26-27), and a *"kingdom"* when as a King with a single crown He takes His Bride back to the Heavenly Kingdom (Rev. 11:15, 17; 12:10, 14:14-16). This completes the dispensation of the Bride of Christ and *"the Mystery of God"* being *"finished"* as He declared to the prophets (Rev. 10:6-7). According to the prophet Daniel, this also completes the time *"they* [the saints] *shall be given into his* [little horn or Antichrist's] *hand"* at the dividing of time (Dan. 7:25).

Part 2: An Earthly Kingdom

The new dispensation reverts back to Israel and starts the second half of Daniel's seventieth week at mid-Trib. The 144,000 are preaching the Everlasting Gospel to Jew and Gentile alike (Rev. 10:8-11). The 144,000 were sealed just before the Gathering of the white robed multitude to the Heavenly Kingdom (Rev. 7).

Just like the Heavenly Kingdom, the Earthly Kingdom follows the same pattern of *"dominion, and glory, and a kingdom"* (Dan. 7:14).

Christ asserts His dominion over the Antichrist on earth by protecting the woman for 1260 days (Rev. 12:6) or *"a time, and times, and half a time"* (Rev. 12:14) during last half of the Tribulation period. This protection starts at the Gathering of the Elect (Matt. 24, Mark 13), which includes the Bride of Christ being Gathered to the Heavenly Kingdom and the Elect from Israel being Gathered to their place of protection. They are protected the whole 42 months that the Antichrist reigns on earth (Rev. 13:5) with the ten kings of Revelation 17. All living converts and overcomers on the earth after the Gathering of the Bride are to repopulate the earth in the Earthly Kingdom during the Millennium. Those who go into the Heavenly Kingdom receive glorified bodies, whereas those going into the Earthly Kingdom have flesh and blood bodies.

Christ is glorified when He comes from Heaven riding on a white horse with many crowns on His head. The armies of Heaven are clothed in fine linen, white and clean. They also are riding on white horses as Christ is (Rev. 19:11-14).

Christ takes physical possession of the earth at His Triumphal Return to earth. The Antichrist and the false prophet are thrown into the lake of fire. *"The dragon, that old serpent, which is the Devil, and Satan"* is cast into the bottomless pit and shut up there till the thousand years are fulfilled (Rev. 20:1-3). This is when Christ reigns as KING OF KINGS AND LORD OF LORDS over all the Earth. All these events contained within the sealed book in Heaven take seven years to be fulfilled.

These are things that *"the great God hath made known to the king* [Nebuchadnezzar] **what shall come to pass hereafter"** (Dan. 2:45 - Emphasis and explanation added). In Revelation 1:19 John was told to *"write the things which thou hast seen, and the things which are, **and the things which shall be hereafter.**"* Revelation 4:1 tells us that John was told to *"Come up hither, **and I will show thee things which must be hereafter.**"* This just goes to show that God is the author of all Scripture and that in order to determine the timing of events you have to use all of Scripture to find the truth. Most importantly it shows us that the *"little horn"* (Dan. 7:8, 8:9), also known as the *"son of perdition"* (2 Thess. 2:3) or the *"Antichrist"* (1 John 2:18, 22), rises to world power chronologically before the mid-Trib Gathering of the Bride of Christ to God's throne.

Chronology of the Olivet Discourse

Mid-14) Christ is revealed in Matthew 24. Most of Matthew 24 and much of Matthew 25 is leading up to the middle of the Tribulation. Theologians speak of these verses as the Olivet discourse. The disciples asked Jesus three questions in Matthew 24:3: (1) *"When shall these things be?"* (2) *"And what shall be the sign of Thy coming?"* (3) *"And the end of the world* [age]*?"* Matthew 24:7 through Matthew 25:31 deals with the second question and Matthew 25:31-46 deals with the last question. Actually Matthew 25:31 has a double fulfillment; *"When the Son of man shall come in His glory; and all the holy angels with Him, then shall He sit upon the throne of His glory."* It has a double fulfillment because Christ comes in His glory mid-Trib with the angels to Gather the Bride and again at His Triumphal Return three and one half years later.

Christ spiritually claimed the throne at the cross and He is now *"Messiah the Prince"* (Dan. 9:25), *"the Prince of Life"* (Acts 3:15), *"a Prince and a Saviour"* (Acts 5:31) and *"the Prince of the kings of the earth"* (Rev. 1:5). As we write this book Christ is presently acting as our High Priest (Heb. 3:1, 6:20, 8:1). Christ will not legally become King or take physical dominion of His Heavenly Kingdom until He is crowned mid-Trib. Christ receives all legal dominion just before He brings His Bride to Heaven. Then three and one half years later He takes physical dominion over His earthly kingdom and sits on His throne as KING OF KINGS AND LORD OF LORDS over the entire earth. This takes place after His Triumphal Entry into Jerusalem, at the beginning of the Millennium.

Try reading Matthew 24:7-25:31 with the idea that these verses are leading up to the mid-Tribulation period and Matthew 25:31-46 as the Triumphal Return at the end of the Tribulation period. If after reading Matthew 24:15-25:31 you concur with us that these events are indeed mid-Trib, then this is one more piece of evidence that His Glorious Appearing and Gathering happens mid-Trib.

Why isn't the Gathering Mentioned Early On in Christ's Prophetic Discourse?

Mid-15) Why didn't Christ mention the Gathering of the Elect early on in His prophetic discourse if the Pre-Tribulation Rapture Theory is correct? This was Christ's answer to the questions *"when shall these things be? And what sign will there be when these things come to pass?"* (Luke 21:7). Christ did not say He was Gathering the Elect before all these things He mentioned. After Christ's list of things that will be signs that signal His Coming, Christ said, *"And then shall they see the Son of man coming in a cloud with great power and great glory"* [as a King] (Luke 21:27). This verse is a little more evidence that in Matthew 24:30-31 Christ is talking about a mid-Trib event, not an event before the Tribulation period begins and that Matthew 25:31-46 is His Triumphal Return at the end of the Tribulation period. Then Christ says in Luke 21:36, *"Watch ye therefore, and pray always, that ye may be accounted worthy to escape all these things that shall come to pass, and to stand before the Son of man."* If you are accounted worthy you will stand before the judgement seat of Christ and escape God's wrath during the last three and one half years of the Tribulation period.

"And when these things begin to come to pass, then look up, and lift up your heads; for your redemption draweth nigh" (Luke 21:28). Your redemption as an individual better fits the mid-Trib Gathering than the Triumphal Return of Christ at the end of the Tribulation period. This verse is also often used as evidence for the Pre-Tribulation Rapture Theory. However, Christ said that you would see

the Son of man coming **after** you see these things begin to happen. He said the time is near or close, even at the door. Christ does not come until His list of signs is fulfilled. Then, at that time, they will see the Son of man coming in the clouds.

Christ's Gathering is Imminent after Signs Listed in Matthew 24

Mid-16) The Olivet discourse tells us when the Gathering is.

> *Now learn a parable of the fig tree; When the branch is yet tender, and putteth forth leaves, ye know that summer is nigh: So likewise ye, **when ye shall see all these things**, know that **it is near**, even at the doors* (Matt. 24:32-33 - Emphasis added).

Even after seeing all the things Jesus spoke of in the Olivet discourse, **Jesus said it is near, still not here yet**! Symphonically some of the signs to watch for are: the temple being rebuilt on the Temple Mount, animal sacrifice re-instituted, the Son of Perdition claiming he is God after coming back from the dead, the sun and moon are darkened. When you shall see all these things take place, then His Gathering is imminent. Then you shall see the Son of man coming in a cloud with great power and glory (Mark 13:26).

Peace and Safety in Israel

Mid-17) When all the enemies of Israel are dead after the Gog and Magog war and Israel starts to burn the weapons as fuel for seven years, then a new peace will arise. A peace unlike anything that has ever existed since Israel became a nation in 1948. An unknown leader will arise and will confirm a covenant. Israel will say, finally, peace and safety and when they do, sudden destruction will come mid-Trib. The desolation will come that is spoken of in Daniel 12:11.

> *But as the days of Noe* [Noah] *were, so shall also the coming of the Son of man be. For as in the days that were before the flood they were eating and drinking, marrying and giving in marriage, until the day that Noe entered into the ark, And knew not until the flood came, and took them all away; so shall also the coming of the Son of man be* (Matt. 24:37-39 - Explanation added).

Noah's ark was the instrument used by God to save His people from His wrath and is an example of the Gathering of the Elect. The Gathering will cause the Bride to escape the wrath of God and protect the faithful of Israel from the Antichrist for 42 months. Israel will have no idea that the flood is about to come, like in the days of Noah. Except this time, the flood that comes is in the form of war. When Satan has been cast down from heaven, he indwells the false prince by raising his dead body. This Antichrist will force himself upon the world and with the help of the false prophet cause all people of the world to worship the Antichrist as "God." The entire world wonders after the Antichrist saying, *"who can make war against him?"* (Rev. 13:4). The Antichrist's armies will surround Israel in the middle of the Tribulation period, during the time of desolation (Luke 21:20). Then the holocaust begins. This is the flood that Christ is talking about.

> *And the serpent cast out of his mouth water as a flood after the woman, that he might cause her to be carried away of the flood. And the earth helped the woman, and the earth opened her mouth, and swallowed up the flood which the dragon cast out of his mouth* (Rev. 12:15-16).

As the wrath of Satan begins, Christ comes for the Elect like a thief in the night and steals them away from Satan. *"And then **they** shall see the Son of man coming in a cloud with power and great glory"* (Luke 21:27 - Emphasis added). The *"they"* must be Israel, thereby revealing Christ to Israel mid-Trib. *"They"* that mourn for Christ and flee to the wilderness for protection are what we call the faithful of Israel. They are protected *"for a time, times, and half a time from the face of the serpent"* (Rev. 12:14). The dragon has 42 months *"to continue"* through the Antichrist (Rev. 13:5) after he loses his armies in pursuit of the faithful of Israel, like Pharaoh did in the Exodus. This definitely is a mid-Trib event. The rest of Israel is cut off and the remaining Jews shall be led away captive in all nations in another holocaust (Luke 21:24).

Israel Blinded to the Mystery until Mid-Trib
Mid-18) First, the Mystery is clearly the Bride of Christ and the Gentile stewardship of the Gospel message. The Mystery of God is

finished at the Gathering of the Bride of Christ in the air mid-Trib.

Secondly, Romans 11 is talking about how God cut off the natural branches, which is Israel, from the olive tree. And if He did that to Israel, how much more is He willing to cut off the grafted in branches, which is the church, if we deserve it. Then Romans 11 goes on to explain that we should not to be ignorant of *"this mystery... that blindness in part has happened to Israel, until the fulness of the Gentiles be come in"* (Rom. 11:25). The Mystery will be kept hidden from Israel until the fullness of the Gentiles has come in mid-Trib.

The fullness of time, the fullness of Gentiles and the times of the Gentiles are all separate issues. *"The fullness of time"* is when Christ was baptized (Gal. 4:4). *"The fullness of the Gentiles"* comes in mid-Trib (Rom. 11:25). *"The times of the Gentiles"* (Gentile Nations) are fulfilled at the battle of Armageddon, after 42 months of treading upon the holy city (Luke 21:24, Rev. 11:2). This is also when the Millennium begins. In Scripture things often sound similar and are easily confused. In this point we are concerned with the fullness of the Gentiles when the Mystery of God is finished at the seventh trumpet (Rev. 10:7), at the change of dispensation (Rev. 14:13).

Jesus is that ruler that shall come from Bethlehem, *"whose goings forth have been from old, from everlasting"* (Micah 5:2). Jesus existed before He was born into His flesh and blood body.

> *Therefore will He give them* [Israel] *up, Until the time that she which travaileth hath brought forth: Then the remnant of His brethren shall return unto the children of Israel* (Micah 5:3).

Christ gave up Israel until the time she travails. The woman, Israel does not travail until Revelation 12:2 at mid-Tribulation. Then as a witness to this, Micah 5:5-6 tells us that this is when the Assyrian shall come into our land and tread in our palaces. The Assyrian is the Antichrist. Revelation 11:1-2 is our Scriptural witness to when the Holy city shall be tread under foot for 42 months in the second half of the Tribulation period. Micah then speaks of a mid-Tribulation battle where the land of Israel is lost to the Assyrian, but the people of Israel are delivered from him. We believe this is the woman going into the wilderness for protection in Revelation 12:6, 14 and Jeremiah 30:7.

In Micah 5:3, we saw Christ giving up Israel until mid-Tribulation and now in Matthew Christ says,

> *O Jerusalem, Jerusalem, thou that killest the prophets, and stonest them which are sent unto thee, how often would I have gathered thy children together, even as hen gathers her chickens under her wing, and ye would not? Behold your house is left unto you desolate. For I say unto you, Ye shall not see Me henceforth, till ye shall say, Blessed is He That cometh in the name of the Lord* (Matt. 23:37-39).

Israel would not be gathered and that is why her house was left desolate for two thousand years. Our point has to do with the last sentence. Israel will not see Christ from henceforth until mid-Trib, when they see Him in the clouds. Then they will see Him whom they have pierced and mourn for Him as an only son (Zech. 12:10). This is when Israel starts worshiping Christ, during the three and one half-year period in the second half of the Tribulation.

We need to tie the desolation of the house of Israel to one more mid-Trib event. The house of Israel is again made desolate by the Antichrist when the abomination that causes desolation happens. The Antichrist proclaims he is God in the temple in Jerusalem. Once again Israel goes into captivity. Once again there is a holocaust, but this time the faithful of Israel will be protected. Christ reveals Himself to Israel and the ones that follow Him are saved. Christ is Gathering His flock under His wing to protect them from the 42 months of great tribulation. The ones that stay in Israel are put into captivity and many die in the holocaust. It is Matthew 23:37-39 all over again. It will be like hell on earth because of the wrath of Satan through the Antichrist and from the wrath of God poured out on the Antichrist's kingdom.

Christ Is Revealed Mid-Trib
When the Bridegroom is Taken Away From Israel
Mid-19) When Christ comes for His Bride He is revealed to the whole world (Rev. 1:7, Luke 17:24, 17:30). Israel will see Him whom they pierced and mourn for Him as an only son (Zech. 12:10). If Christ is revealed at the so-called Rapture, how can it be a secret?

And if Christ is revealed before the Tribulation period, then why does Israel build the temple and begin animal sacrifice? Christ ended animal sacrifice (Dan. 9:27, Heb. 10:10, 10:12). If Israel mourned for Christ before the Tribulation period they would certainly not spite Him and negate His ultimate sacrifice by offering mere animal sacrifices instead. No, they would bow down and worship Christ as their true Messiah. Neither would Israel seek a covenant with any leader other than Christ, especially some reprobate influenced by Satan who claims to be God.

Christ is revealed in Matthew 24:29-31, 2 Thessalonians 1:3-12 and Revelation 1:7. These verses cannot be at the end of the Tribulation period because it leaves no time for Israel to mourn for Christ. Israel will be with Him forever when He comes at His Triumphal Return. Israel will mourn for Christ when He is revealed to them and then taken away from them at the mid-Trib Gathering of the Elect. Read Matthew 9:15,

> *And Jesus said unto them, Can the children of the bridechamber mourn, as long as the bridegroom is with them? but the days will come, when the Bridegroom shall be taken from them, and then they shall fast.*

The Bridegroom cannot be taken away from Israel before the Tribulation period begins because Israel will be sacrificing animals in the rebuilt temple until the abomination of desolation happens. Matthew 24:29-31 makes it clear that Christ is revealed *"immediately after"* the Antichrist claims he is God in the temple mid-Trib. Neither can the Bridegroom be taken from Israel at the end of the Tribulation period because Christ is not leaving again after His Triumphal Return. This is strong evidence for the mid-Tribulation revealing of Christ to Israel. Christ is revealed at His Glorious Appearing (2 Thess. 1:4-11) when He Gathers His Bride in the air (1 Thess. 4:13-17).

Christ Revealed Just Before the Mid-Trib Wrath of God

Mid-20) When is the Son of man revealed? Luke 17:28-30 is explaining that God's wrath will be like it was when Lot went out from Sodom. After Lot went out, the wrath of God poured down on Sodom. These verses are referring to *"them which be in Judaea flee* *into the mountains"* as in Matt. 24:16-18. When Israel sees the abomination of desolation, they should flee to the mountains and not look back, like when Lot went out from Sodom.

> *But the same day that Lot went out of Sodom it rained fire and brimstone from heaven, and destroyed them all. Even thus, shall it be in the day when the Son of man is revealed* (Luke 17:29-30).

When does the wrath of God begin? The same day that Israel flees from the Antichrist. Christ is revealed moments before the wrath of God is poured down from Heaven, just like when it rained fire and brimstone onto Sodom. Keep in mind that Luke 21:25-30 is when Christ is answering the question, what will the signs of your coming be? He obviously is not talking about His Triumphal Return because Israel goes into protection in the middle of the Tribulation, not after the Tribulation is over. God protects the faithful of Israel for 1260 days (Rev. 12:6, 12:14). Matthew 24:30-31 is mid-Trib. The Son of man is revealed with His Glorious Appearance on the same day that those in Judea flee into the mountains. Conversely, His Triumphal Return happens at the end of the Tribulation period. They are two separate events separated by three and one half years.

Christ Revealed Mid-Trib

Mid-21) A time of peace and safety will come to Israel after the Gog and Magog war against Israel. Most of the Islamic and Russian enemies of Israel will have been killed by the war that the Islamic nations helped start. So Israel will live in peace like never before since 1948, when they first reformed the nation of Israel.

> *But as the days of Noah were, so shall also the coming of the Son of man be. For as in the days that were before the flood they were eating and drinking, marrying and giving in marriage, until the day that Noah entered the ark, and knew not until the flood came, and took them all away; so shall also the coming of the Son of man be* (Matt. 24:37-39).

The first half of the Tribulation period is a time of relative peace for Israel. Israel is happy with whatever arrangement was made with the false prince, at first. However, the son of perdition is not yet revealed to Israel. The son of perdition is revealed when the false prince is killed, brought back to life and the Satan-indwelt-man declares himself to be God in the temple! Israel is mortified when she sees the fulfillment of the abomination of desolation that Daniel prophesied about.

Immediately after those days of tribulation, Christ will be revealed to Israel in the clouds and Israel mourns for Him as an only son (Zech. 12:10). They mourn for Him because they did not believe Him when He came the first time, 20 centuries ago.

> *Even thus shall it be in the day when the Son of man is revealed. In that day, he which shall be upon the housetop, and his stuff in the house, let him not come down to take it away: and he that is in the field, let him not return back. Remember Lot's wife* (Luke 17:30-32).

It continues to explain the concept of those people who are left behind when Jesus comes in the clouds. When Israel sees the abomination of desolation, let no man hesitate, run for the hills to save your life.

This verse is strong evidence for a mid-Tribulation coming of the Lord. When the abomination happens and Judea flees to the wilderness, Christ is revealed to Israel. He is revealed because of His Glorious Appearing to Gather the Elect, which are both His Bride and the faithful of Israel. The Bride will be Gathered into the clouds and He will Gather the faithful of Israel into the wilderness for their protection. In fact, all the tribes of the earth see Christ when He appears in the clouds (Matt. 24:30, Rev. 1:7).

Christ Comes When Time Has Run Out

Mid-22) When there is time no longer and the Mystery of God is finished, the seventh angel is about to sound his trumpet. *"Time no longer"* (Rev. 10:6) does not mean the end of time or the end of the world. *"Time no longer"* means that there will be no more delay before the dispensation of the Mystery is finished. We strongly believe this is the Glorious Appearing and Gathering of His Bride.

And one said to the man clothed in linen, which was upon the waters of the river, How long shall it be to the end of these wonders? And I heard the man clothed in linen, which was upon the waters of the river, when he held up his right hand and his left hand unto the heaven, and sware by Him That liveth forever that it shall be for a time, times and a half; and when he [Antichrist] shall have accomplished to scatter the power of the holy people, all these things shall be finished (Dan. 12:6-7).

Now compare Revelation 10:5-7.

*And the angel which I saw stand upon the sea and upon the earth lifted up his hand to heaven, and sware by Him That liveth for ever and ever, Who created heaven, and the things that therein are, and the earth, and the things that therein are, and the sea, and the things which are therein, **that there should be time no longer**: But in the days of the voice of the seventh angel, when he shall begin to sound, the mystery of God should be finished, as He hath declared to His servants the prophets (Rev. 10:5-7 - Emphasis added).*

We believe that Daniel's *"all these things shall be finished"* and Revelation's *"time no longer"* are the same reference. Their meaning is synonymous. Interestingly, some say Christ will come at the end of time, which they say is at the end of the Tribulation period. We are saying that this is a prime example of how one can read Scripture and not grasp God's intent.

When the seventh angel sounds the trumpet there is time no longer, thus ending one dispensation and bringing in the new dispensation. Daniel 7:25 confirms that there is a new dispensation by *"dividing of time"* (KJV). That is when Christ comes in the air, at the sound of this last trumpet (1 Thess. 4:16-17 and 1 Cor. 15:51-52). The Mystery of God is finished mid-Trib.

Michael Stands Up for the True Church Mid-Trib
Mid-23) Why does Michael stand up for the True Church in the

middle of the Tribulation period (Rev. 12:7) if the True Church is truly gone before the Tribulation period begins?

> *And at that time shall Michael stand up, the great prince which standeth for* **the children of thy people** [True Church]*: and there shall be a time of trouble, such as never was since there was a nation even to that same time: and at that time* **thy people** [Israel] *shall be delivered* [to wilderness for 1260 days (Rev. 12:6, 12:14)], *everyone that shall be found written in the Book* (Dan. 12:1 - Emphasis added).

This is huge! Who are thy people? Israel is thy people. Who are the children of thy people? The Mystery that comprises the True Church is *"the children of thy people"* (Dan. 12:1). What is this time of trouble such as never was? This is the time of Jacob's trouble during the second half of the Tribulation. *"Alas! For that day is great; so that none is like it: It is even the time of Jacob's trouble; But he shall be saved out of it"* (Jer. 30:7). The "he" that Jeremiah is talking about is the Jews that are delivered because they are written in the Book of Life. These people are distinct from those in Revelation 17:8 who are not written in the Book of Life and are not delivered.

Our point is that Michael stands up for the True Church, which is the Mystery of God, when he stands up for the children of thy people. Revelation 12 makes it clear that Michael does not stand up for the Mystery of God until just prior to the middle of the Tribulation period. This makes it impossible for the True Church to be gone until the beginning of the second half of the Tribulation period. It is no coincidence that *"the Mystery of God"* is *"finished"* mid-Trib when the seventh trumpet shall begin to sound (Rev. 10:7).

Jeremiah 30:3 is promising that Israel will again be brought into captivity in the days of Jacob's trouble, and then God promises to return them to their land later. We believe that Israel will continue as a nation through the 42 months of protection in *"the wilderness"* (Rev. 12:6, 14), but the landmass known as Israel will be encompassed by armies and conquered by the Antichrist mid-Trib. In Jeremiah 30:10 we see that Israel shall return to their land when Christ will *"make a full end of all nations"* (Jer. 30:11). This happens at the time of His Triumphant Return to end all wars at Armageddon.

Satan is in Heaven until Mid-Trib

Mid-24) Satan stands before the throne of God accusing the brethren day and night of all their sins until he is cast out of heaven in the middle of the Tribulation period (Rev. 12:10). How is it possible that the Bride of Christ is suddenly raptured pre-Trib and stands in front of the Throne of God while Satan is still accusing them of their sins day and night in front of that same Throne? Satan still has access to the Throne of God even today and will continue to until he is thrown out of heaven. We cannot be with the Lord until Satan is permanently removed from heaven and he is not cast out of heaven until mid-Trib. This is yet another huge point supporting the mid-Trib Gathering of the True Church after Satan is cast out of heaven. This is one of the simplest and most powerful points supporting the mid-Trib Gathering of the Bride of Christ.

Revealing the Antichrist Mid-Trib

Mid-25) The great restrainer in 2 Thessalonians 2 is holding back the son of perdition until it is time for him to be revealed.

> *Let no man deceive you by any means: for that day shall not come,* [Day of the Lord Jesus Christ at His Glorious Appearing] *except there come a falling away first, and that man of sin be revealed, the son of perdition* [the Antichrist]*; who opposeth and exalteth himself above all that is called God, or that is worshipped; so that he as God sitteth in the temple of God, showing himself that he is God* (2 Thess. 2:3-4 - Explanation added).

> *And now ye know what withholdeth that he might be revealed in his time. For the mystery of iniquity doth already work: **only he who now letteth will let, until he be taken out of the way. And then shall that Wicked be revealed**, whom the Lord shall consume with the spirit of His mouth, and shall destroy with the brightness of His coming: **Even him, whose coming is after the working***

> *of Satan with all power and signs and lying wonders* (2
> Thess. 2:6-9 - Emphasis added).

These Scriptures clearly show that the son of perdition is what must
be revealed, but who or what is the son of perdition? Satan entered
into Judas in John 13:27 and Jesus referred to Judas as *"son of
perdition"* (John 17:12). This was because Satan indwelt Judas. The
son of perdition is Satan indwelt in human flesh. Since Satan is not
cast out of heaven until the middle of the Tribulation period, then the
great restrainer will not allow the son of perdition to be revealed until
the middle of the Tribulation period. This happens when he declares
himself to be God in the Holy of Holies in the rebuilt temple.

> *Son of man, say unto the prince of Tyrus... Because thine
> heart is lifted up, and thou hast said, **I am a God, I sit in
> the seat of God, in the midst of the seas**; yet thou art a
> man, and not God* (Ezek. 28:2 - Emphasis added).

> *Wilt thou yet say before him that slayeth thee, I am God?
> but thou shalt be a man, and no God, in the hand of him
> that slayeth thee* (Ezek. 28:9).

Examine the differences between the prince of Tyrus and the king of
Tyrus:
1) The prince of Tyrus claims to be God and is killed for it. Then this
   prince is thrown into the sides of the pit (Isa. 14:12-19). Also see
   Ezekiel 28:1-10.

2) The king of Tyrus walked in the garden of Eden, is the anointed
   cherub, and was perfect from the day he was created until iniquity
   was found in him (Ezek. 28:12-19). The king of Tyrus is clearly
   talking about Satan and is a type of the Satan-indwelt Antichrist.
   The king of Tyrus claims to be God in the temple after being
   raised from the dead.

The son of perdition is not the prince of Tyrus, but the king of Tyrus.
He is not the man who rises to power, but is the man who is raised
from the dead and is indwelt by Satan as the Antichrist. The king of
Tyrus is the Antichrist that stands in the temple of God in Jerusalem

and proclaims himself to be God (2 Thess. 2:4). This is the abomination that causes desolation (Matt. 24:15, Mark 13:14). This is the very definition of what it means to reveal the son of perdition.

The great restrainer does not allow the son of perdition to be revealed until Satan is cast out of heaven in the middle of the Tribulation period (Rev. 12:10). That is when it will be possible for an angelic being that was created and does not have the power of omnipresence like God has to be able to indwell a human body. Satan cannot be in heaven and indwell this body at the same time. Therefore, the Antichrist cannot be present on earth before the Tribulation period or until just prior to the mid-Trib *"great tribulation"* (Matt. 24:21, Rev. 7:14). Also, the Gathering to Christ cannot be before mid-Trib, thereby debunking the imminency of Christ's return. The whole second letter to the Thessalonians is debunking the imminency of Christ's return.

> *Let no man deceive you by any means: for **that day*** [Gathering to Christ] *shall not come, **except there come a falling away first, and** that man of sin **be revealed, the son of perdition*** (2 Thess. 2:3 - Emphasis added).

When Does Salvation Come?

Mid-26) Revelation 12 is all future tense because everything from Revelation 4:1 onward is a description of God's court passing judgment *"hereafter"* or future to John's time. All of the judgments contained in the sealed book are future. Once the sealed book is opened in Heaven, it takes seven years on earth for all the provisions of the title deed to take place. Revelation 12 is just one of the many scenes of God's judgment being carried out against Satan and his principalities and powers.

- The woman is Israel who is with child, travailing in birth, and pained to be delivered. This is in the future.
- Satan is cast down from heaven. A future event.
- The dragon tries to devour the child as it is being born. A future event.
- The woman gave birth to a man-child who was to rule the world with a rod of iron. A future event. Although many theologians try

to say this is in the past, our point is this, how can this be Christ in the past when all other verses surrounding it are pointing to the future? See Isaiah 66:7-8 and "Mid-27 Exhibit."

- The man-child is caught up to Heaven at the Gathering! It is future because Satan tries to devour the child in the future, not 2000 years ago.
- Beast goes after the remnant of Israel. This is a future event.
- *"Now is come salvation, and strength, and the Kingdom of our God, and the power of His Christ: for the accuser of our brethren is cast down..."* (Rev. 12:10). It says here that salvation will come mid-Trib when our accuser is no longer in Heaven. A future event.

How could someone get the idea Christ's return is imminent from this verse. Just because people from every generation got it in their heads that His return was imminent does not make it true. If Christ taught that His return was imminent way back then, He would have deceived His followers and that is not possible because God does not lie (Titus 1:2, Heb. 6:18). Christ simply did not teach it, nor did His disciples.

True Church Born at the Mid-Trib Gathering
Mid-27) All those who say that the man-child in Revelation 12 is past tense are taking the verse out of context. Jesus was delivered before the woman travailed, before her pain.

> *Before she travailed, she brought forth; Before her pain came, she was delivered of a man-child* [Jesus] (Isa. 66:7 - Explanation added).

There are 2000 plus years between Isaiah 66:7 and 66:8.

> *Who hath heard such a thing? who hath seen such things? Shall the earth be made to bring forth in one day? or shall a nation be born at once? For as soon as Zion travailed, she brought forth her children* (Isa. 66:8).

Zion is the woman and she travails in Revelation 12. The child in Revelation 12 is not Christ being born, but is the Bride of Christ, the

Mystery of God, the saints taking possession of the Heavenly Kingdom (Dan. 7:18, 22, 27).

There are 2000 plus years between Jesus the child that Zion brought forth before her pain and when Zion is in travail with her children in Isaiah 66:8 and Revelation 12. Isaiah 66:8 does not say man-child again but it does say, *"she brought forth her children"*, *"the children of thy people"* (Dan. 12:1), the True Church. We believe that Revelation 12 is referring to the Bride of Christ when it says "the man-child." Notice that the child is caught up to Heaven like the Gathering of the Bride mid-Trib.

Also supporting the premise of the Gathering being mid-Trib is Isaiah 66:4. It appears that the delusions in Isaiah 66:4 are very similar to 2 Thessalonians 2:11. We believe that the *"strong delusion"* that is mentioned in 2 Thessalonians 2:11 is that man of sin being raised from the dead to become the Antichrist.

Man-Child is the Bride of Christ

Mid-28) The man-child in Revelation 12 is the True Church. Read about the man-child in the chapter titled *"Israel"* for a detailed explanation of why the man-child is the Bride of Christ. Together with Christ we will rule all the nations with a rod of iron (Rev. 2:26-27, 5:8-10, 20:6, 21:7). *"And her child was caught up unto God, and to His throne"* (Rev. 12:5). Presuming that the child is the Bride of Christ, then this must be when the True Church is Gathered. Why was not such a statement associated with Revelation 4:1? The verse where John is told to *"Come up hither and see"* is a far cry from the True Church being *"caught up unto God."* It is so obvious that the Rapture did not happen back in Revelation 4:1.

Many theologians believe that the man-child is Christ. However, it does not make any sense to have the Bride of Christ suddenly raptured in Revelation 4:1 and then have Christ as the man-child caught up to Heaven again mid-Trib. Especially in light of the woman fleeing into the wilderness immediately after the man-child is caught up to Heaven. The man-child could not be the man-child two thousand years ago as some theologians would espouse because the woman is protected for 42 months, making this a mid-Trib event. Get rid of the pre-Trib Rapture notion and this issue is resolved. Christ is the Bridegroom, we are the Bride, and we are caught up to Heaven together at His Glorious Appearing mid-Trib.

Christ the Bridegroom Comes at Midnight

Mid-29) Satan is cast down from heaven in the middle of the Tribulation period (Rev. 12:9-12). This will be the darkest hour for Israel and the Bride of Christ. Because the True Church is still here when Satan is cast down from heaven, it would be late in the eleventh hour for the Bride and Israel, even midnight. Satan tries to devour the True Church but fails to do so (Rev. 12:4-5). Jesus comes like a thief in the night and steals the True Church away from Satan. Satan through the Antichrist also goes after the woman, Israel, but God supernaturally protects the woman for 1260 days (Rev. 12:6, 14). This also supports the premise this event happens mid-Trib.

> *While the bridegroom tarried, they all slumbered and slept. And **at midnight** there was a cry made, **Behold, the Bridegroom cometh;** go ye out to meet Him* (Matt. 25:5-6 Emphasis added).

What is the middle of the Tribulation period? Midnight! When does the Bridegroom come for His Bride, the True Church? Midnight! When does God supernaturally protect Israel? Midnight! All these things take place mid-Trib.

Christ Has One Crown at the Glorious Appearance and Many Crowns at the Triumphal Entry into Jerusalem

Mid-30) When Christ comes for His Bride during His Glorious Appearing, He is a King with one golden crown (Rev. 14:14).

> *Now is come salvation, and strength, and the Kingdom of your God, and the power of His Christ: for the accuser of our brethren is cast down, which accused them before our God day and night* (Rev. 12:10).

Christ has received the Kingdoms that Satan had just lost. Satan is thrown into the earth (Rev. 12:9). When he rises out of the bottomless pit, he now indwells *"that man of sin"* (2 Thess. 2:3) and thus becomes the Antichrist. Then the Antichrist kills the Two Witnesses (Rev. 11:7). After three and one half days, the Two Witnesses rise from the dead and are caught up to Heaven along with the Bride of Christ (Rev. 11:11-12). They do this at the sounding of the seventh trumpet.

> *And the seventh angel sounded; and there were great voices in heaven, saying, The kingdoms of this world are become the Kingdoms of our LORD, and of His Christ; and He shall reign for ever and ever* (Rev. 11:15).

At the sounding of the seventh trumpet Jesus collects what is rightfully His. The debt or ransom was paid at the cross. The demise of Satan's dominion was set in motion 2000 years ago. At the breaking of the seals Christ is given legal *"dominion, and glory, and a kingdom..."* (Dan. 7:14). Jesus is crowned King at the sounding of the seventh and last trumpet mid-Trib (Rev. 11:15, 12:10).

Matthew 24:30 is talking about the Glorious Appearance and it says Jesus will appear in the sky with great power and glory. He comes as the King. He comes with full legal dominion and authority. He will issue judgment on the world and He will remove from Satan's dominion all that are accounted worthy (Luke 21:36).

This point is concerning the time span of Revelation 14. Note that Christ has one golden crown in Revelation 14:14. He received this crown when He received His kingdoms in Revelation 11:15 and Revelation 12:10. Christ thrusts in His sickle at the Gathering, also called the harvest *"and the earth is reaped"* (Rev. 14:16).

Immediately after this mid-Trib Gathering, another angel *"gathered the vine of the earth, and cast it into the great winepress of the wrath of God"* (Rev. 14:19). *"For the hour of His judgment has come"* (Rev. 14:7). God's wrath is not 60 minutes long. This Scripture is referring to a 42-month period, which is the duration of the Antichrist's reign (Rev. 13:5). God's wrath is poured out on the Antichrist and his kingdom for the whole 42 months that the Antichrist thinks he is in control of the entire world. The ten kings on the earth give their kingdoms unto the Antichrist for one-hour or 42 months (Rev. 17:12) until the words of God shall be fulfilled (Rev. 17:17).

> *And the winepress was trodden without the city, and*
> *blood came out of the winepress, even unto the horse*
> *bridles, by the space of a thousand and six hundred*
> *furlongs* (Rev. 14:20).

God's judgments in the Book of Revelation manifest spiritually in Heaven before they happen physically on earth. Please notice that Revelation 14:20 is seen spiritually in Heaven by John but happens physically at Jesus' Triumphal Return during Armageddon. The double witness to this Scripture is when Christ *"treadeth the winepress of the fierceness and wrath of Almighty God"* in Revelation 19:15. John also saw the wrath of the Lamb spiritually in Heaven during the sixth seal, but it does not take place physically on earth until Armageddon. The action goes back and forth between Heaven and earth throughout the Book of Revelation. That is why it is so important to see where the action is taking place in order to determine when an event will happen in the Book of Revelation.

From all this we see that Christ's Spiritual Kingdom is established when the heavens are cleansed by the removal of all things evil from Heaven. This takes place mid-Trib when Satan and his angels are cast down to the earth, thereby cleansing Heaven in preparation for the Bride to be Gathered.

Jesus is already crowned King when He Gathers the Two Witnesses and the Bride of Christ to His Heavenly Kingdom and protects the faithful of Israel from the Antichrist's dominion for the last 42 months of the Tribulation period on earth. Immediately after the Gathering of the Elect, God's wrath is poured out on those that ignored or rejected Christ's invitation of eternal life through the Two Witnesses. This wrath of God culminates at the battle of Armageddon with Christ coming with the armies of Heaven to destroy evil from the earth. This cleanses the earth for Christ's earthly reign.

Christ comes to earth to set up His Millennial Kingdom at His Triumphal Return *"...and on His head were many crowns"* (Rev. 19:12). This is shortly after the Marriage Supper of the Lamb. By showing that Christ had the one crown at mid-Trib, and many crowns at His Triumphal Return illustrates the fact that these are two separate events and that His Glorious Appearing is mid-Trib.

More Evidence Christ is King at the Gathering Mid-Trib

Mid-31) At the Gathering, Christ has *"a golden crown"* (Rev. 14:14). We know this verse is a mid-Trib event because of the verses leading up to it and after it:

- *"The hour of judgment has come"* (Rev. 14:7).
- *"The wine of the wrath of God is poured out"* (Rev. 14:10).
- *"Here is the patience of the saints"* (Rev. 14:12).
- The new dispensation in *"henceforth"* (Rev. 14:13).
- In Revelation 15:2-3, *"them that had gotten victory over the beast"* are praising the *"King of saints."*

This is the fulfillment of the blessed hope in Revelation 3:10, *"Because thou hast kept the word of My patience, I also will keep thee from the hour of temptation."* Revelation 14 is proclaiming that this is when the hour has come. When this hour or 42 month period has come, Jesus only has the one crown and He received this crown in Revelation 11:15. God has taken the legal dominion of the kingdoms of this world away from Satan (Rev. 12). Christ has one crown at the mid-Trib Gathering. When Christ returns at the end of the Tribulation period as KING of KINGS and LORD of LORDS He will have *"many crowns"* (Rev. 19:12).

Jesus is no longer just the Lamb of God, but now He has received all legal authority as King. Christ will then have all the power and the authority as the Son of God. By Revelation 15:3, He has already passed judgment on the world and removed all those accounted worthy to be the Bride of Christ during His Glorious Appearing and Gathering of the Elect.

Food for thought; it is possible that the seven thunders are the multitudes of the souls that have been waiting in Heaven to receive their Heavenly Bodies at the Gathering. The seven thunders are shouting because now they know the time has come. Christ is assuming all authority in Heaven and on earth mid-Trib. We think the reason John was told not to write what the seven thunders said is because it would possibly give away the exact time of the Gathering. Again, we on earth are not to know the hour, but we are given signs to be watchful for so we are not taken by surprise when He comes. No one can predict for certain when Christ will come, but that does not make His return imminent either. When we see Elijah proclaiming

Christ in Jerusalem we will know His return is within a few years. When we see the animal sacrifice ceasing in the temple in Jerusalem caused by one who says he is God, we will know His return is within a month. When sun and moon have darkened and we see Elijah and Moses lying dead and the whole earth rejoicing over their deaths, we know His return is three and one half days away. Then, and only then, will Christ's return be imminent.

The Gathering at the Last Trumpet Mid-Trib

Mid-32) The Glorious Appearing happens at the sounding of the last trumpet. How many last trumpets can there be and when is the last trumpet sounded? The seventh and last trumpet is sounded at the middle of the Tribulation period when the Two Witnesses are resurrected from the dead and are caught up to Heaven. There is no Scriptural evidence for another set of trumpets sounding. At the sounding of the last trumpet, the dead in Christ shall be raised and the living shall be changed (1 Cor. 15:52). When we are resurrected we are transformed into our Heavenly flesh and bone bodies. From then on, we will live in our glorified bodies. This is another huge point for a mid-Trib Glorious Appearing to Gather the Elect out of or from among the four winds waiting to harm the earth and the sea (Rev. 7:1-3, Matt. 24:30-31, Mark 13:26-27).

A New Dispensation Mid-Trib – Point 1

Mid-33) *"Thou art righteous, O Lord, Which art, and wast, and shalt be, because Thou hast judged thus"* (Rev. 16:5). Because Jesus has judged, past tense, now the vials of wrath can be poured out on the world. Notice that this Scripture is not near Revelation 4:1. It is written right after the Gathering mid-Trib, when the wrath begins. There has to be a dispensation change after the Gathering of the Bride to Christ. If Revelation 4:1 is the sudden Rapture, then where in Scripture is there evidence of a new dispensation before mid-Trib?

> *Here is the patience of the saints: here are they that keep the commandments of God, and the faith of Jesus. "...Blessed are the dead which die in the Lord **from henceforth** [from now on]: Yea, saith the Spirit, that*

they may rest from their labours; and their works do follow them" (Rev. 14:12-13 - Emphasis added).

It is clear from these Scriptures that God has a new dispensation for the earth. The context of these Scriptures are mid-Tribulation and not associated with any events at or near Revelation 4:1.

Before Christ's sacrifice on the cross, atonement for sin was possible by animal sacrifice through faithful works and obedience to God's commandments. The message of salvation was through Israel, but Israel rejected Christ during His earthly ministry. After Christ's death and resurrection, salvation became possible by faith through grace taught through the Mystery. That Mystery is the relationship between Christ and His Bride, which includes Messianic Jews and Gentiles alike. The Mystery is finished mid-Trib at the time of His Glorious Appearing and Gathering of the Elect. After the Gathering, the message of salvation will be through the stewardship of the 144,000 Jews from Israel. They will be proclaiming the Everlasting Gospel to the world by holding to the commandments of God and to the testimony of Jesus.

A few thoughts supporting this dispensational change:
1) Because prophecy tells us that Israel will rebuild the temple and will begin animal sacrifice in the first half of the Tribulation, they will not hold to the testimony of Jesus at that time. Israel certainly will not mourn for Christ until they see Him in the air during His mid-Trib Glorious Appearing. This is after the son of perdition is revealed and after the abomination of desolation.
2) If there were a sudden Rapture before the Tribulation period began, the new dispensation would have to start then. Otherwise, there would be no dispensation for several years until mid-Trib when the new dispensation starts in Revelation 14:13.
3) Why isn't this new dispensation *"from henceforth"* (Rev. 14:13) mentioned near Revelation 4:1?
4) The new dispensation is mentioned during the mid-Trib harvest, just before the angel told the Son of Man to *"thrust in Thy sickle and reap"* (Rev. 14:15). This dispensation change is also clearly before the end of the Tribulation period.

New Dispensation Mid-Trib – Point 2

Mid-34) There is a new economy or dispensation that starts in the middle of the Tribulation period. We found Scriptures suggesting that the time of Jacob's trouble does not start until the second half of the Tribulation; it is a period of 42 months. Yet many in the church believe a new dispensation starts at the beginning of the Tribulation period before the time of Jacob's trouble. Or they say Jacob's trouble is seven years long, negating Daniel's split seventieth week and Daniel 12:1-2.

Many scholars see what we see connecting the new dispensation to the beginning of Jacob's trouble because the *"mystery of God is finished."* The problem is, so many believe Jacob's trouble is seven years long, not three and one half. Scripture tells us that the Mystery Dispensation goes through and up to the time of Jacob's trouble.

> *But in the days of the voice of the seventh angel, when he shall begin to sound, the **mystery of God should be finished**, as He hath declared to His servants the prophets* (Rev. 10:7 - Emphasis added).

Since the Mystery is finished (dispensation change) at the moment the seventh trumpet is sounded, when is the sounding of the seventh trumpet? If one tries to place the seventh trumpet at the end of the Tribulation period, then God's wrath mentioned at the seventh trumpet (Rev. 11:18), the time of Jacob's trouble and the 1260 days that the woman is protected (Rev. 12:6) have no length of time to run their course at all, so this would make no sense. Yet there are a vast number of theologians who place the seventh trumpet at the end of the Tribulation period. These theologians must overlook or dismiss this fact somehow to make their theory viable.

We are back to the Symphonic Method of Scriptural Study again. If there is conflict between Scriptures because the timing of an event does not synchronize with the story line, it is not truth. If Jacob's trouble is linked to God's wrath and God's wrath does not start until the seventh trumpet, then Jacob's trouble must be three and one half years long, because the only place the seventh trumpet synchronizes symphonically is mid-Trib.

Some might say, Jacob's trouble is concurrent with all seven trumpets. And many believe all seven trumpets take seven years to sound thereby making Jacob's trouble all seven years. Symphonically this does not fit because of the 42-month reign of the Antichrist after the seventh trumpet has sounded and the woman being protected for 1260 days starting in the days of the seventh trumpet. But the most important reason it is not symphonic is that the time of Jacob's trouble cannot overlap the Mystery Dispensation. We hearken back to a dispensational view that The Church Age and The Age of Law cannot co-exist in the same dispensation. In chapter two we dispel dispensationalism the way it is commonly understood, but the idea that Jacob's trouble and the Mystery cannot co-exist in the same dispensation is similar. The Mystery is the Bride of Christ; and the Mystery is finished just as the time of Jacob's trouble begins mid-Trib.

The Mystery Dispensation is how God deals with the message of salvation through the stewardship of the Mystery, which is the Bride of Christ. Once the Mystery is finished, then the message of salvation reverts back to being through the stewardship of Israel. The Mystery is finished during the middle of the Tribulation at the sounding of the seventh and last trumpet (Rev. 10:7). Then the time of Jacob's trouble begins (Jer. 30:4-7), transferring one dispensation to another.

Points supporting the premise that the time of Jacob's trouble is 42 months:
- Israel is being smooth talked by a messiah-like person who comes in his own name (John 5:43) during the first half of the Tribulation period. Israel is at peace when they are surrounded by armies (Luke 21:20) just before the middle of the Tribulation. Israel is being persecuted after Satan is cast out of heaven (Rev. 12:13). Another Holocaust will take place after Israel recognizes the son of perdition. Two thirds of Israel will not escape his wrath (Zech. 13:8). *"Alas! For that day is great, so that none is like it: it is even the time of Jacob's trouble;* **but he shall be saved out of it"** (Jer. 30:7 Emphasis added). One third does escape (Zech. 13:8-9) and is protected by God *"for a time, and times, and half a time"* (Rev. 12:14) or *"1260 days"* (Rev. 12:6).

- The two olive trees are representing Israel and the two candlesticks are representing the church on earth for the first half of the Tribulation period. The time of Jacob's trouble begins when the two olive trees and the two candlesticks, which we believe are Elijah and Moses, and the Bride of Christ are Gathered to Heaven and the faithful of Israel is protected. The time of Jacob's trouble concerns the two thirds of Israel that does not believe Christ is the Messiah after the mid-Trib Gathering.

- Michael stands up *"and there shall be a time of trouble, such as never was since there was a nation even to that same time"* (Dan. 12:1). Michael stands up mid-Tribulation with 42 months left before Christ's Triumphal Return (Rev. 12:6-9).

- Read our section in this book about *"Daniel's Split Week."* This is really strong evidence that the time of Jacob's trouble is only 42 months.

After the Mid-Trib Revealing of Christ,
The 144,000 Start Their Ministry

Mid-35) We see that the beast and the economic system of the mark will tempt the saints in Revelation 14:9-19, *"If any man worship the beast or his image, and receive his mark in his forehead, or in his hand, The same shall drink of the wine of the wrath of God."* This is confirmed in Revelation 15:3, *"...and them that had gotten the victory over the beast, and over his image, and over his mark, and over the number of his name, stand on the sea of glass, having the harps of God."* The Scriptures above suggests that we will have to refuse to take the mark and refuse to worship the beast before we are Gathered to meet Christ in the air. In Matthew 24:29 *"Immediately after the tribulation of those days"* is referring to a short period of time when the Antichrist has been revealed and is persecuting the saints. Perhaps *"those days"* are just 30 days or less when the mark of the beast will be required and the sun and moon darken before the Gathering (Matt. 24:29, Rev. 9:2).

Need more evidence? Read Daniel 7:25, the false prince shall wear out the saints until mid-Trib. In Revelation 2:22, those in the church who commit adultery economically or spiritually with Satan will see the second half of the Tribulation period and will experience God's wrath. *"Behold, I* [Jesus] *come quickly: hold that fast which thou hast, that no man take thy crown"* (Rev. 3:11). The false prince is a man. Do not let him take your crown.

Christ is the Lamb in Revelation 14:4 and is still the Lamb in Revelation 14:10. In Revelation 14:13, there is a change in dispensation and in Revelation 14:14 Christ has His crown. He is then the King. This is confirmed in Revelation 15:2-3 where *"them that had gotten the victory over the beast, and over his image, and over his mark, and over the number of his name"* are praising the *"King of saints."* Do you see His Glorious Appearing for His Bride in there? Why would Christ come for His Bride before He is crowned King?

Now let us look at how this affects the 144,000 and their ministry. Going back to Revelation 11:7, when the Two Witnesses have finished their 1260 day ministry, the Antichrist is allowed to kill them. Daniel 12:11 is talking about when the abominations (plural) are set up, it would be another 1290 days before the end of the Tribulation period. The Tribulation period is two halves of 1260 days. So there is a 30-day window prior to the revealing of Christ for the abominations to happen. The 144,000 are sealed in Ezekiel 9 by the angel with the inkhorn. This happens in that 30-day window when all the abominations are occurring. When the Two Witnesses are killed and their ministry is finished, the 144,000 are learning the Everlasting Gospel proclaimed by the angel in Heaven.

Our whole point is about stewardship change and the 144,000 who begin their ministry at mid-Trib. They learn the Everlasting Gospel before the Gathering, before Christ is revealed by only a few days. After His Glorious Appearance we see a new dispensation or change in stewardship, *"Blessed are the dead which die in the Lord from henceforth"* (Rev. 14:13). Then the 144,000 start preaching that Gospel in the second half of the Tribulation period.

In Revelation 14:14 Christ is no longer the just Lamb. He is then the King, the Lion of the tribe of Judah. He is the King with a sickle to Gather His Elect out from among the four winds that are intending to do harm on the earth. From henceforth, Christ will require acceptance of His grace and obedience by not denying Him. Satan requires worship and obedience or die. Both are demanding an answer to "who is your master?" Everybody must choose whom he or she will serve. That choice will either have eternal rewards or eternal consequences.

**The Mystery is Finished Mid-Trib – 144,000 Begin Ministering
Mid-36)** More evidence that a new dispensation starts in the middle
of the Tribulation:

> *In the days of the voice of the seventh angel, when he
> shall begin to sound* [the seventh and last trumpet], ***the
> mystery of God should be finished***, *as He hath declared
> to His servants the prophets* (Rev. 10:7 - Emphasis and
> explanation added).

In Revelation 10:8-11, John is told to eat the little book. The angel
said unto John, *"thou must prophesy again before many peoples, and
nations, and tongues, and kings"* (Rev. 10:11).

Ezekiel is told to eat a little book in Ezekiel 2:8 through 3:6.
Unlike John, Ezekiel is told to prophesy to Israel only. Ezekiel is told
not to prophesy unto all nations, peoples, and tongues.

When the Mystery of God is finished and John is told to prophesy
again to all peoples, and nations, and tongues, and kings, this is the
beginning of a new dispensation. This new dispensation is the
message of salvation through the stewardship of Israel once again,
like it was when Ezekiel first ate the little book. Except now, Israel
has the message of grace through Christ. They have the Everlasting
Gospel to preach.

God's grace does not end at the Gathering. The 144,000 Jews lead
this new evangelical mission after the seventh trumpet. The dragon
will be wrought with fury against the woman because God protects
Israel from him, so the dragon pursues the remnant of her seed, which
are the 144,000 (Rev. 12:17). *"And the remnant of Jacob shall be
among the Gentiles in the midst of many people"* (Micah 5:8). Again,
the purpose of the 144,000 is to preach to all the nations, peoples, and
tongues. Read our section in this book called *"The Remnant of Israel,
the 144,000."*

When is the Resurrection Earthquake Mentioned?
Mid-37) When Christ was resurrected it was a type or foreshadow of
the resurrection we call the blessed hope. This is also known as His
Glorious Appearing to Gather His Bride. Look at the chart and see
that at the moment of His resurrection a large earthquake happened.

The veil in the Temple separating the Holy of Holies from the inner court was torn from top to bottom, signifying that there is no need for it any longer. From that moment on Christ is *"The Way, The Truth, and The Life"* (John 14:6).

> *And the graves were opened; and many bodies of the saints which slept arose, and came out of the graves **after His resurrection,** and went into the holy city, and appeared unto many. Now when the centurion, and they that were with him, watching Jesus, saw the earthquake, and those things that were done, they feared greatly, saying, "Truly this was the Son of God"* (Matt. 27:52-54 - Emphasis added).

Symphonic View of the Earthquake

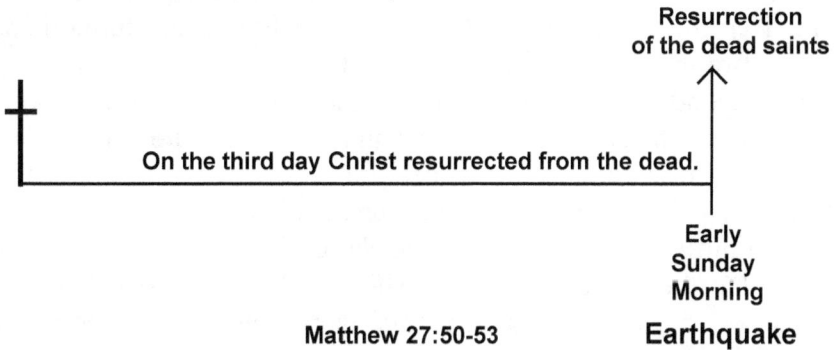

**Resurrection
of the dead saints**

On the third day Christ resurrected from the dead.

**Early
Sunday
Morning**

Matthew 27:50-53   **Earthquake**

Since at the first resurrection there was an earthquake and the first resurrection is the type for the one to come, we should expect another earthquake when we are Gathered to Christ. Where in Scripture does it show another earthquake and mention the resurrection of the dead? Revelation 11:12-13 tells us the Two Witnesses are told to *"come up hither"* and *"the same hour was there a great earthquake"* at the seventh and last trumpet (Rev. 11:15). Not after the seventh trumpet, but at the mid-Trib sounding of the seventh trumpet the Two Witnesses are resurrected and reward is given *"unto Thy servants the prophets, and to the saints, and them that fear Thy name"* (Rev. 11:18).

If there is a sudden and sign-less Rapture at Revelation 4:1, why does it not mention a resurrection of the dead then? Why does it not mention the rewarding of the saints then? Why does it not mention an earthquake then? Is it not curious? Perhaps the premise that the Rapture at Revelation 4:1 is all wrong and when those things **are mentioned later in the Book of Revelation** they are actually describing the Gathering of the Elect in the clouds.

Mid-Tribulation Anger at God Because of His Wrath

Mid-38) The world is not angry with God until His wrath begins mid-Tribulation. In Revelation 11:18, the nations of the world become angry with God. Curious, if the pre-Tribbers are right and the whole seven years are the wrath of God, why are the nations waiting to become angry until mid-Tribulation? Could it be that the first half of the Tribulation period is not God's wrath? Could it be that the first 1260 days of the Tribulation are birth pangs separating the soil types for the Harvest of the Bride of Christ? Through immense turmoil and trials by fire the Bride will stand with Christ. It will not be anything like the second half of the Tribulation though. The wrath of God is beyond comprehension. Let us not paint a rosy picture for the first half of the Tribulation period either. First nuclear war and massive volcanic activity, earthquakes and tsunamis followed by a burning mountain hitting the earth, perhaps an "asteroid," and the atmosphere so dark that the sun cannot shine. This is what the first half of the Tribulation brings to the world, yet the world only curses God in the second half.

The *"42 Months"* in Revelation 13 is equal to *"The Hour"* in Revelation 3 and Revelation 17

Mid-39) The Satan-indwelt son of perdition is not revealed until Revelation 13 and only has 42 months to reign before Christ's Triumphal return. To understand this point you need to know that there is a distinction between *"that"* mere mortal, evil *"man of sin,"* *"the prince that shall come"* (Dan. 9:26), and the Satan-indwelt *"son of perdition"* (2 Thess. 2:3-12), *"the Antichrist"* (1 John 2:18, 20). Satan comes to earth about ten days before Christ does and the church suffers the wrath of Satan through the Antichrist a very short time before Christ comes to Gather His Bride. The Bride of Christ is promised to escape God's wrath. It is not promised to escape any or all persecution. When Satan is cast to the earth and into the bottomless pit, he has approximately 10 days to persecute the Elect through the Antichrist before the Gathering (Rev. 2:10) and 1260 days (Rev. 12:6, 12:14) before Christ defeats him at His Triumphal Return to earth (Rev. 19:11- 21).

Please figure 1260 days divided by 30 days per month equals 42 months. The Scriptural witness to the 42 months is found in Revelation 13:5, *"and power was given unto him to continue forty and two months."* Revelation Chapters 12, 13, and 17 are all talking about the same time frame. In Revelation 13:3-5 the Antichrist is given 42 months to continue, but to continue from what? To continue from being *"that man of sin"* that is killed, raised from the dead and indwelt by Satan as *"the son of perdition"* (2 Thess. 2:3), better known as the Antichrist.

The Philadelphia church is promised to be kept from *"the hour of temptation,"* from the Antichrist's 42-month reign of terror. We derive the meaning of the English word *"hour"* to be 42 months. The English word *"hour"* in the Greek is **"hora** {ho'-rah} [Strong's Concordance *#5610*, definition]; apparently a primary word; an "hour" (literal or figurative): — *day, hour, instant, season, ×short, [even-] tide, (high) time."*[42] From the definition you can see that the meaning of the English word hour can range from an *"instant"* all the way to a *"season."* You have to use the Scripture context to determine the proper meaning. Here are the Scriptures that support the premise that *"the hour"* (Rev. 3:10) is 1260 days or 42 months:

> *Because thou hast kept the word of My patience, I also will keep thee from **the hour** of temptation, which shall come upon all the world, to try them that dwell upon the earth* (Rev. 3:10 – Emphasis added).

> *And the ten horns, which thou sawest, are ten kings, which have received no kingdom as yet; but receive power as kings **one hour** with the beast* (Rev. 17:12 - Emphasis added).

That *"one hour"* is the same as the 42 months. It is illogical that these kings received their power for sixty minutes.

The fact that *"the hour"* (Rev. 3:10, 17:12) is 42 months or three and one half years long is evidence supporting the idea that the Bride of Christ is removed from great tribulation (Rev. 7:14, Matt. 24: 21, Dan. 12:1) caused by the Satan-indwelt-Antichrist in the middle of the Tribulation period. The Bride of Christ is removed just before the wrath of God is poured out on the Antichrist and his kingdom for 42 months (Rev. 13:5).

Court is Now in Session!

Mid-40) After the Glorious Appearing and Gathering of the Bride mid-Trib, the courtroom will be open and all the saints who were persecuted for Christ's namesake are asked to give their testimony in the Temple (Rev. 15:5).

> *And when He had opened the fifth seal, I saw under the altar the souls of them that where slain for the word of God, and for **the testimony** which they held: and they cried with a loud voice, saying, How long, O Lord, Holy and True, dost thou not judge and avenge our blood on them that dwell on the earth?* (Rev. 6:9-10 - Emphasis added).

> *Vengeance is mine; I will repay, saith the Lord* (Rom. 12:19).

After the courtroom session our Lord God Almighty will reach a verdict. The seven angels come out of the Temple carrying seven vials of God's wrath. They then pour out the wrath of God onto the earth, which judges the Antichrist and his followers.

In Revelation 15:5 we have the courtroom scene. In Revelation 16:5 we have the judgment past tense, *"because Thou hast judged thus."* Revelation 16:5 partially fulfills the fifth seal in Revelation 6:9-10. Scriptural witnesses are found in Revelation 18:20, and 19:2 where it says, *"... for He hath judged the great whore, which did corrupt the earth with her fornication, and hath avenged the blood of His servants at her hand."*

The Temple in Heaven is closed until the mid-Trib sounding of the seventh trumpet (Rev. 11:19). We find it very insightful when considering the majestic aspect of the courtroom scene taking place in

Heaven, when Christ receives His crown and inherits the kingdoms of the earth described in Revelation 11:15. Once crowned, Christ immediately brings His Bride to Heaven (great white robed multitude). Then the Father opens the Temple doors, which were closed back in Revelation 4, beginning the court hearings and the judgment seat of Christ. All the Saints give their testimony and the Father instructs the angel to begin dispensing the first bowl of His wrath, while Christ our advocate gets all the Saints cases dismissed.

How could there be a sudden and sign-less Rapture before the Tribulation period if the Temple in Heaven is closed for the first 1260 days of the Tribulation period? This would mean the Bride is kept in waiting while Satan is still in heaven accusing them of their sins day and night. And, if one holds the premise that the seventh trump is at the end of the Tribulation period, when would there be time for this courtroom scene to unfold? This is exactly the kind of conflict in Scripture that arises when the timing of an event is placed in the wrong bar of time symphonically. The only place the sounding of the seventh trumpet and the courtroom scene playing out in Heaven could be played in perfect harmony is mid-Trib.

Once the Temple in Heaven is opened mid-Trib John sees,

> *...a sea of glass mingled with fire: and them that had gotten the victory over the beast, and over his image, and over his mark, and over the number of his name, stand on the sea of glass, having the harps of God. And they sing the song of Moses the servant of God,* [see Duet. 31- 32] *and the song of the Lamb* (Rev. 15:2-3).

John is told to *"come up hither"* in Revelation 4:1 and he is shown things that must be *"hereafter."* He is shown the sea of glass like unto crystal before the throne of God (Rev. 4:6). In Revelation 15:2 the sea of glass is full of overcomers who have the victory over the beast. The overcomers are singing the song of Moses and the song of the Lamb (Rev. 15:3). Back in Revelation 4:6 the overcomers are omitted and not mentioned with the sea of glass. So how can anyone say that when John is told to *"come up hither"* in Revelation 4:1 that this is a sudden and sign-less Rapture before the Tribulation starts? Where are all the overcomers of the seven churches? They are found in Revelation

15:2. If these overcomers who *"had gotten victory over the beast"* at the sounding of the seventh trumpet are not the Bride of Christ; then who are they? This is yet another point for a mid-Trib Gathering of the Bride to Heaven. Look at all the neat things one can dig up out of Scripture. Too many Christians do not read the Book of Revelation and they miss all this good stuff.

Sounds Too Good To Be True

Mid-41) Why is it so easy for modern Christians to believe that God will not expect them to endure some trials or tribulations? When in history has God ever made it easy for His true and faithful followers? Look at the example that the Apostle Paul gave in 2 Thessalonians 1:3-12. And, do not say Noah! He was not spared trials and tribulations. He was laughed at and ridiculed while he built the ark. Noah was spared the wrath of God though. The Book of Revelation makes it very clear that the wrath of God is poured out in the second half of the Tribulation (Rev. 15:1, 16:1-18:24). Christ even said that when He comes for the church it would be like the times of Noah (Matt. 24:37-39). How can anyone get pre-Trib out of these verses?

> *And when these things begin to come to pass, then look up, and lift up your heads; for your redemption draweth nigh* (Luke 21:28).

Many Bible scholars are claiming that this verse is talking about the imminent return of Christ. However, they may be taking the verse out of context. They focus on the word *"begin"* and imply that when these things begin to happen, the Rapture happens. Even though the Scriptures say that when you see these things begin to happen, you know that the time for His Coming is near. That does not mean that some sudden Rapture will happen before all these signs are revealed. It means that the signs will happen in quick succession or in a short period of time before Christ is revealed at His Glorious Appearing and Gathering of His Bride.

Christ Comes When We Least Expect It

Mid-42) Most Christians believe that Christ is returning for the church either before or after the Tribulation period. Christ said that

He would come when people are not expecting Him. He said *"Be ye therefore ready also: for the Son of man cometh at an hour when ye think not"* (Luke 12:40). Since most expect Christ to gather His Bride before or after the Tribulation period, then isn't it likely that He would return mid-Trib when most people do not expect Him?

Multiple Last Trumpets

Mid-43) This one is for pre-Tribulationists still stuck on the idea that the trumpet blast that calls us home is not to be confused with the seventh trumpet in Revelation. Let us look at the facts:

- One might believe that Matthew 24:30-31 is talking about the end of the Tribulation period. These verses in Matthew say Christ will come in the clouds with angels at the sound of a trumpet to Gather the Elect out of or from among the four winds and from one end of heaven to the other. If these verses are truly what they call the "Second Coming," then there must be another trumpet blast other than the seven trumpets. There is no mention of this trumpet in the Book of Revelation or anywhere else that we can find. Where is their Scriptural support for this? It is clear to us that the seventh and last trumpet not only has Scriptural witnesses but also symphonically fits the mid-Trib Gathering of the Elect, as well.

- In 1 Corinthians 15:52, the resurrection and translation of the saints happens at the sounding of the last trumpet.

- Revelation does mention seven trumpets. The last trumpet is the seventh one. This trumpet is very clearly sounded during mid-Trib. Revelation 11:15 through 12:12 tells us when the seventh trump is sounded and it has 42 months following it (Rev. 13:3-5).

Look at all that happens at the seventh trumpet in Revelation: Michael stands up for *"the children of thy people"* (Dan. 12:1-2) at the war in Heaven (Rev. 12:1-8). Satan is cast down from heaven (Rev. 12:9-13). Time of the dead that they should be judged, Thy servants the prophets and the saints and them that fear Thy name are rewarded, the nations were angry with God and God's wrath has come (Rev. 11:15-18). The faithful of Israel, the woman, is under God's protection for 42 months (Rev. 12:6, 14). All these things happen during mid-Tribulation.

When trying to discern from Scripture a meaning or an understanding, be careful not to spiritualize the Word of God. Take the Word of God literally and do not try to make the Word have meaning beyond the instrument. It appears as though this is exactly what pre-Tribulationists have done here with the last trumpet. What do you think, are they spiritualizing the trumpet of God? Using the Symphonic Method of Scriptural Study, are there three last trumpets or one?

See our chart comparing the last trumpet in **Pre-Trib View** vs. **Mid-Trib View**:

Pre-Trib View

The last trumpet is not to be confused with the seventh trumpet in Revelation.

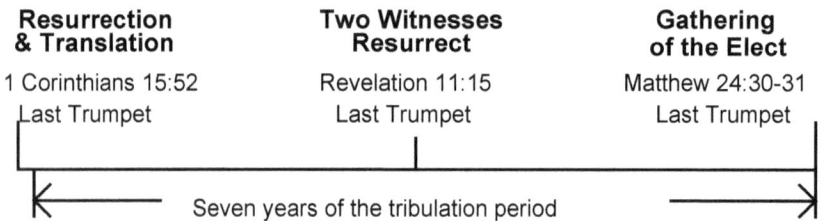

Resurrection & Translation	Two Witnesses Resurrect	Gathering of the Elect
1 Corinthians 15:52	Revelation 11:15	Matthew 24:30-31
Last Trumpet	Last Trumpet	Last Trumpet

Seven years of the tribulation period

To believe in the Pre-Trib theory one must believe that there are multiple last trumpets.

Mid-Trib View

Seventh and Last Trumpet
Mid-Tribulation

Seven years of the tribulation

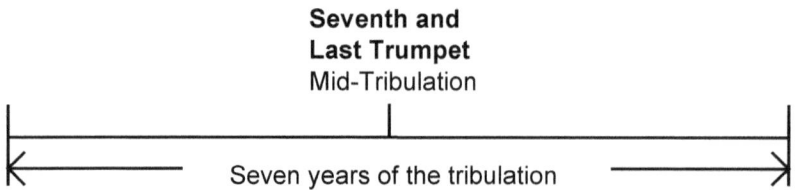

All three verses happen in one event:
1 Corinthians 15:52
Revelation 11:15
Matthew 24:30-31

Which one do you believe makes more sense?

Chapter 12

The Pre-Tribulation Rapture Theory

The Pre-Tribulation Rapture Theory

Pre-Tribulation Rapture is based on an exegesis or literal interpretation of Scripture whenever possible. The premise holds a segregationist view of the Church and Israel, that they are two separate groups of people. This view does not believe in replacement theology whereby the Church replaced Israel, but rather does believe in a dispensational view of where God dealt with salvation through Israel until the cross and now in the present age God deals through the Church. Once the Church is removed God will once again deal with salvation through Israel. We like the phrase "Parenthetical View" to describe the pre-trib belief that God first used the age of Law, then the current age of Grace, followed by the age of Law again. Adherents to this theory also believe that this present age is the mystery and that this mystery form of the Kingdom must be completed before God will resume the program He started through Israel.

Exhibits Supporting the Pre-Tribulation Rapture Theory

In this section we will first give the Pre-Tribulation Rapture View and then give our rebuttal according to the Mid-Tribulation Symphonic View. We have read volumes of books and listened to theologians preach about various Rapture theory points and yet we struggled to come up with ten points that support the Pre-Tribulation Rapture Theory. If the point does not stand on its own in support of the position, it is discarded.

Blessed Hope

Pre-1) The Blessed Hope and the Glorious Appearing are two separate events.[43] *"Looking for that blessed hope, and the glorious appearing of the great God and our Saviour Jesus Christ"* (Titus 2:13). The Blessed Hope is that there is a sudden and imminent

Rapture before the Tribulation period. At the end of the Tribulation period the Lord comes back again and this is known as the Glorious Appearing of the Lord, which is the Second Coming. In this pre-Tribulation Rapture theory, one must interpret Matthew 24:30-31 as being the Second Coming. Christ comes with power and great glory in those verses.

The blessed hope is that we will be removed from the earth before the hour of temptation. According to Larkin, the hour of temptation is at least seven years long.[44] Because pre-Tribbers believe all seven years are "the hour of temptation," they believe that our blessed hope is that all Christians will be removed from the earth before the seven years of Tribulation period begin. Revelation 3:10 promises us to be kept from *"the hour of temptation,"* so we must be removed from the earth before that temptation.

Rebuttal

Earlier in this book we have shown that the hour of temptation is 42 months long. So we shall be kept from that three and one half year period of God's wrath on earth, thereby fulfilling our Lord's promise to us in Revelation 3:10, 1 Thessalonians 1:10 and 5:9-10. This is our blessed hope.

Tim LaHaye is a brother in Christ and we love him for it. We give Tim LaHaye and Jerry Jenkins thanks for co-authoring the "Left Behind" series and bringing much awareness to the world about the Gathering of the Bride to Christ.

Tim LaHaye believes that the Rapture and the Glorious Appearing are separate events. LaHaye does not see that there are two Glorious Appearances of our Lord Jesus Christ, the first being mid-Trib and the second at the end of the Tribulation period. It is easy to understand why, because at the Triumphal Return our Lord has many crowns (Rev. 19:12). But what he is missing is that Matthew 24:30-31 is the Gathering of the Elect; the Bride of Christ to Heaven and the faithful of Israel to her place of protection for 1260 days or a time, times and half of a time (Rev. 12:6, 12:14). At the Gathering, Christ has one crown on His head (Rev. 14:14). He is the King when He comes for His Bride, but when is He crowned King?

And the seventh angel sounded; and there were great

> *voices in heaven, saying, The kingdoms of this world are*
> *become the Kingdoms of our LORD, and of His Christ;*
> *and He shall reign for ever and ever* (Rev. 11:15).

The timing of this verse is definitely mid-Trib because the Two Witnesses were just caught up to Heaven after 1263 ½ days and Satan will have just been cast down from heaven (Rev. 12:10) having 42 months to live and reign through the Antichrist on earth (Rev. 13:5). Pre-Tribbers like to say that the Book of Revelation must be read chronologically. So chronologically Christ is crowned King at the seventh trumpet mid-Trib. It is also mid-Trib symphonically because of the 42 months Satan has on the earth after being cast down from heaven. Satan is bound and cast into the bottomless pit at Christ's Triumphal Return at the end of the Tribulation period.

It is right to distinguish the Blessed Hope from the second of Christ's two Glorious Appearances. When the Lord Jesus Christ first appears to us it will be a Glorious Appearing because He will be the King coming for His Bride at the middle of the Tribulation period, immediately after He is crowned King in Heaven (Rev. 11:15, 12:10, 14:14, 15:3). All the tribes of earth shall mourn for Him at His Glorious Appearing in the Heavens during the Gathering of the Elect according to Matthew 24:30-31 and Revelation 1:7. Matthew 25:31-34 is the second Glorious Appearing and is what we call His Triumphal Return to Earth.

Events after the Rapture

Pre-2) According to pre-Trib theorists, only the pre-Trib position allows enough time for the Judgment seat of Christ and the Marriage Supper of the Lamb. Tim LaHaye points out that these two time-consuming events will happen after the Rapture. He concludes that only the pre-Trib position allows enough time for these events.

> Two very significant, time-consuming events await the church after the rapture and before the glorious appearing. At the Judgment Seat of Christ (Rom. 14:10 and 2 Cor. 5:10), every Christian will give account of himself to God for the deeds done in the flesh (a judgment described in detail in 1 Cor. 3:9-15).

According to 1 Corinthians 4:5, this judgment occurs after the rapture. The Wedding and Marriage Supper of the Lamb (Rev. 19:7-9) follow the Judgment Seat of Christ, just prior to the glorious appearing.[45]

Rebuttal

LaHaye hits a home run with this point for systematically dismantling the post-Trib position. However, he has laid out the groundwork for supporting the mid-Trib position. We could not have said it better ourselves.

First, every Christian will give an account of themselves at the Judgment Seat of Christ. LaHaye points out that this judgment occurs after the Rapture. But where in Scripture does it describe the timing of the actual judgment. At the seventh trumpet in Revelation 11:18 it says, *"and the time of the dead, that they should be judged, and that Thou shouldest give reward unto Thy servants the prophets, and to the saints, and them that fear Thy name."* Also in Revelation 14:7, *"the hour of judgment is come."* And in Revelation 15:5, *"...and, behold, the Temple of the tabernacle of the testimony in heaven was opened."* This is when all Christians are to give account or *"testimony"* in the Temple. The Temple in Heaven is closed until this time of testimony. After the testimony of the saints, the wrath of God is poured out because the Lord *"hast judged thus"* (Rev. 16:5).

Second, the Marriage Supper of the Lamb in Revelation 19:7-9 is just before the Triumphal Return of Christ at Armageddon. Symphonically both of these events are after mid-Trib and before the end of the Tribulation period. LaHaye's point is strong evidence supporting the mid-Trib position.

If there were a sudden and sign-less Rapture pre-Trib, the saints would be in Heaven while Satan is still there accusing us of our sins until the heavens are cleansed. However, Satan is cast out of heaven just prior to mid-Trib. God's wrath begins immediately after the Bride is Gathered at the mid-Trib sounding of the seventh trumpet. LaHaye's point just does not fit the pre-Trib position as well as it does the mid-Trib position.

Christ must come before the Antichrist is Revealed

Pre-3) On Glenn Beck's 03/02/2007 cable television show, Glenn interviewed Tim LaHaye. Tim said that Christians would not be here to see the Antichrist because we will be raptured before the Tribulation period begins. Hal Lindsey agrees, he claims that there is a short interim period between the Rapture and the signing of the peace treaty.[46]

Dwight Pentecost expounds on why there must be a period of time between the Rapture and the coming of the Antichrist.

> Again, Revelation 13:7 makes it clear that all who are in the seventieth week are brought into subjection to the Beast and through him to Satan, who gives the Beast his power. If the church were in this period she would be subjected to Satan, and Christ would lose His place as Head, or He, Himself, because of His union with the church, would be likewise subjected to Satan's authority. Such a thing is unthinkable. Thus it is concluded that the nature of the church and the completeness of her salvation prevent her from being in the 70th week.[47]

Satan is restrained by the great restrainer until it is time for the restrainer to be taken out of the way. Pentecost espouses a pre-Tribulation Rapture of the Bride and that the Holy Spirit Himself is that Restrainer. Pentecost is also saying that the Holy Spirit must be removed from the earth to allow the Satan-indwelt-Antichrist to be revealed.

> Thus, this ministry of the Restrainer, which will continue as long as His temple is on the earth and which must cease before the lawless one can be revealed, requires the pre-tribulation rapture of the church, for Daniel 9:27 reveals that the lawless one will be manifest at the beginning of the week.[48]

Clearly in the pre-Trib position there is a paradox; on one hand Pentecost holds the position that the church and Satan cannot be on the planet at the same time for the reason described in his quote above and on the other hand there is 2 Thessalonians 2. Pentecost writes,

The work of the Restrainer in 2 Thessalonians 2. The Thessalonian Christians were concerned for fear that the Rapture had already taken place and they were in the day of the Lord. The persecutions that they were enduring, as referred to in the first chapter, had given them the basis for this erroneous consideration. Paul writes to show them that such a thing was impossible. First, he shows them in verse 3 that the day of the Lord could not take place until there was a departure. Whether this departure be a departure from the faith or a departure of the saints from the earth, as already mentioned in verse 1, is beside the point here.[49]

Rebuttal

It may be beside the point in Pentecost's book, but it is very much the point in ours. There are many problems with how pre-Tribbers have interpreted 2 Thessalonians 2. We will discuss these problems individually and how those interpretations conflict symphonically with Scriptures as a whole.

Choosing the word "departure" to replace what the King James Version of the Bible interpreted as *"a falling away"* and the Strong's Exhaustive Concordance defines as *"defection from truth"* or *"apostasy"*[50] is like going to a thesaurus or a Greek Lexicon and choosing any English word that best suits one's point just because it has the same root word meaning. The Greek language is a much more precise language than English is and that is like putting the cart in front of the horse.

The teachings of men seems to be more relevant than Scripture among parts of the Eschatological society, in that we have heard many well known teachers who have jumped on the bandwagon with the word "departure" as apposed to *"falling away"* (KJV) or *"rebellion"* in the NIV. These teachers must have derived their source from the works of previous men such as Dwight Pentecost because in looking at the root word, one would conclude that "departure" should not even be a choice to translate the original Greek word *"Apostasia"*. Let us look at the definitions from the Strong's Exhaustive Concordance of the Bible:

646. **Apostasia,** *ap-os-tas-ee'-ah;* feminine of the same as *647; defection* from truth (properly the state) ["apostasy"]: — falling away, forsake.[51]

647. **Apostasion,** *ap-os-tas'-ee-on;* neuter of a (presumed) adjective from a derivative of *868;* properly something *separative,* i.e. (special) *divorce:* — (writing of) divorcement.[52]

868. **Aphistemi,** *af-is'-tay-mee;* from *575* and *2476;* to *remove,* i.e. (active) *instigate* to revolt; usually (reflexive) to *desist, desert,* etc.: — depart, draw (fall) away, refrain, withdraw self.[53]

575. **Apo,** *apo';* a primary particle; "*off,*" i.e. *away* (from something near), in various senses (of place, time, or relation; literal or figurative): — (×here-) after, ago, at, because of, before, by (the space of), for (-th), from, in, (out) of, off, (up-) on (-ce), since, with. In composition (**as a prefix**) it usually denotes *separation,* ***departure,*** *cessation, completion, reversal,* etc. (Emphasis added).[54]

2476. **Histemi,** *his'-tay-mee;* a prolonged form of a primary, *stah'-o* (of the same meaning, and used for it in certain tenses); to *stand* (transitive or intransitive), used in various applications (literal or figurative): — abide, appoint, bring, continue, covenant, establish, hold up, lay, present, set (up), stanch, stand (by, forth, still, up). Compare *5087.*[55]

Both *"apostasia"* and *"apostasion"* are derived from the root word *"aphistemi",* which means: *"desist, desert, etc."*[56] According to the definition of Strong's #868, *"aphistemi"* is a compound Greek word; *"apo",* Strong's #575, used as a prefix, and *"histemi",* Strong's #2476.[57] *"Apo"* **when used in composition as a prefix** usually denotes "separation, **departure,** cessation, completion and reversal."[58] For someone to say that the original Greek word used must be reduced to its root word, then further reduced only to the root word's prefix, and then derive some obscure meaning beyond the obvious is deliberate. Especially when the Greek word *"apostasia"* was also used in Acts 21:21, where Paul is being accused by the Jewish religious leaders of religious apostasy when teaching the Gentiles to *"forsake"* God's Law of circumcision given to Moses. Why not take the literal definition that is given for *"apostasia"*, which is *"defection* from truth (properly the state) ["apostasy"]. *"*[59] Especially in light of the fact that there is the Greek word *"analusis"* that has the definition of *"departure"* according to the Strong's Concordance *#359.*[60] Since there is a Greek word for "departure," then why did Paul not use that Greek word if departure was what he really meant?

The way Pentecost would have us read and understand this Scripture is; *"Let no man deceive you by any means; for **that day** [**the day of the LORD** (Jehovah's wrath)] shall not come, except there come **a falling away** [**a departure** (the pre-Tribulation Rapture)] **first**, and that man of sin be revealed, the son of perdition* [then the Antichrist is revealed]*"* (2 Thess. 2:3 - Emphasis and explanation added). This is changing the context of the Greek word *"apostasia"* from defection from truth or apostasy to mean the pre-Tribulation Rapture of the church. It is also changing the context of *"the day of Christ"* (2 Thess. 2:2-KJV) from meaning the day of *"the coming of our Lord Jesus Christ"* and *"our gathering together unto Him"* (2 Thess. 2:1), to mean *"the day of the LORD"* (the day of Jehovah's wrath) as found in the Old Testament. What pre-Trib theologians have failed to see or have purposely ignored is that the term *"the day of our Lord Jesus Christ"* (1 Cor. 1:8) is clearly in the context of the Gathering of the saints to Christ. In addition to this, *"the day of Christ"* (Phil. 1:10, 2:16, 2 Thess. 2:2), *"the day of the Lord Jesus"* (1 Cor. 5:5, 2 Cor. 1:14), and *"the day of Jesus Christ"* (Phil. 1:6) are all in the same context of the Gathering to Christ. Therefore, the meaning of *"the day of the Lord"* in 2 Thessalonians 2:2 as found in some versions of the Bible is clearly not the pouring out of Jehovah's wrath, as pre-Tribbers try to claim. To change the overall context of 2 Thessalonians 2 conflicts with the Scriptural witnesses and with Scripture as a whole.

Let's go back to the Scripture and put this erroneous consideration to bed.

*Now we beseech you brethren, by **the coming of our***

> ***Lord Jesus Christ,*** *and by* ***our gathering together unto***
> ***Him,*** *That ye be not soon shaken in mind, nor by word,*
> *nor by letter, as from us,* ***as that the day of Christ is at***
> ***hand,*** *Let no man deceive you by any means: for* ***that***
> ***day*** *shall not come, except there come a falling away*
> ***first, and*** *that man of sin* ***be revealed, the son of***
> ***perdition,*** *who opposeth and exalteth himself above all*
> *that is called God, or that is worshipped;* ***so that he as***
> ***God sitteth in the temple of God,*** *showing himself that*
> *he is God* (2 Thess. 2:1-4 - Emphasis added).

Verse one set the subject, the topic, and the reason for writing this consolatory letter to the Thessalonians. The subject is the Lord Jesus Christ and the topic is the Gathering of the Bride to Christ. These verses clearly mean that the day Christ comes for His Bride will not happen until there is *"a falling away"* or apostasy in the church, *"that man of sin"* the false prince is killed, appears to rise from the dead, and is revealed as the Satan-indwelt-Antichrist. Satan indwelling the dead body of the false prince takes place just prior to mid-Trib, after Satan is banished from heaven, thereby revealing the Antichrist, *"the son of perdition"* (2 Thess. 2:3) shortly before the mid-Trib Gathering of the saints to Christ. Matthew 24 also makes it very clear that the abomination of desolation in verse 15 occurs before the Gathering of the Elect in verses 29-31 and is the Scriptural witness to the fact that the Antichrist is revealed before the Gathering of the saints to Christ.

Look at the lengths which men have gone to make you believe their pre-Tribulation theory is factual. And for so many men to espouse the same slanted diatribe is suspicious. We promise you that we have not obscured the truth in our book, like was done here by some pre-Tribbers. We talk about the symphony in Scripture and they are playing musical chairs with Scripture words, just to make their view sound better.

Pentecost also takes liberty by interjecting the pre-Tribulation theory's dogma into Revelation 13:7. Let's read the verse,

> *And it was given unto him* [false prince] *to make war*
> *with the saints, and to overcome them: and power was*
> *given him over all kindreds, and tongues, and nations.*

Revelation 13:7 does not make it clear about the distinction between the false prince and the Satan-indwelt-Antichrist. Pentecost does not see that distinction or Daniel's split seventieth week. In the first half of the Tribulation period the false prince is a mere-evil-mortal-man who is killed near mid-Trib. After the false prince appears to rise from the dead, he is then the Antichrist, *"the son of perdition"* (2 Thess. 2:3). It is an assumption by most theologians that a so-called "peace treaty" is signed by the Satan-indwelt-Antichrist as opposed to the false prince. It is even an assumption that there is a peace treaty. Daniel 9:27 does not mention peace or treaty, only that *"he would confirm a covenant with many."* But we have already exhausted this subject in earlier chapters.

Pentecost makes an astute observation, he writes, "If the church were in this period she would be subjected to Satan...".[61] We happen to agree with his observation to a point, after all this is what Scripture says, *"And it was given unto him to make war with the saints, and to overcome them"* (Rev. 13:7). This period he writes about is at or near mid-Tribulation. Pentecost is one who believes that the Book of Revelation is written chronologically. Let us assume it is chronological. Revelation 13:7 is in the middle between Revelation 4:1 and Revelation 20:1. So if the Church were in this period, the Church would be in the middle of the Tribulation period. In fact Revelation 13:5 proves that this period is mid-Trib symphonically because the beast has 42 months to continue. Continue from what you might ask. He continues from his death as the false prince, a mere evil-mortal-man and coming back to life as the Satan-indwelt-Antichrist. He continues as the Antichrist after Satan is cast down from heaven (Rev. 12:7-10).

Pentecost goes on to say, "...Christ would lose His place as Head, or He, Himself, because of His union with the church, would be likewise subjected to Satan's authority. Such a thing is unthinkable."[62] Why would Christ be subjected Satan's authority when Christ at this point in time will have stripped Satan of his crowns and real authority? Christ receives all legal authority in Heaven when Satan is cast down into the earth just before mid-Trib (Rev. 12:7-10).

As far as being in union with Christ, we are betrothed to Christ and are now one in Christ spiritually. When we are Gathered to Heaven we will become one flesh and receive our glorified bodies that never die. The legal consummation happens at the Marriage to the Lamb in Heaven. When Christ says we are now one body in Him, He means spiritually. When we are born again our sin flesh does not crawl back into the womb to be born again; our spirit is born again or spiritually conceived by the Holy Spirit when He seals our spirit. *"Now this I say, brethren, that flesh and blood cannot inherit the Kingdom of God; neither doth corruption inherit incorruption"* (1 Cor. 15:50). These flesh and blood bodies that we are now in are corruptible and are of sin nature. These bodies we are now in will never see the Kingdom of God unless they are made incorruptible flesh and bone or glorified. So the idea that Satan cannot have a position of power over our sinful flesh and blood bodies through the Antichrist and the ten kings of the earth is a misnomer. While Satan has limited authority over our sinful flesh and blood bodies, he has no authority over our spirit. Can you see that there is no promise that our sinful flesh will inherit the Heavenly Kingdom (1 Cor. 15:50)? We hope you see the error in Pentecost's logic as being non-Scriptural.

Therefore, when Satan is banished from heaven to the earth, he will have no real authority like he had in heaven. In Revelation 13:3 and 13:12 the beast is killed and comes back to life. When he comes back to life, he is Satan-indwelt. When Satan indwells the false prince he is still another Antichrist having human authority over Christians, as has always been the case. The only power Satan would have over us is the power humanity yields to him through the Antichrist and his ten kings. He will have the power to persecute us and subject us to his earthly powers, but how is that any different from Caesar having power over the Jews in Christ's day? Think logically for a moment. Throughout all Christianity Christians have been subjected to world authority and persecution for Christ's namesake. All world leaders who have persecuted and subjugated Christians and denied Christ are antichrists. Do not get caught up in the Hollywood version of this Antichrist. Anyone who denies Christ is an antichrist. Either one is with Christ or is against Him (see 1 John 2 and 4). Christ is not a way; He is the only way to Heaven!

The Antichrist's kingdom is established before Christ's kingdom in Matthew 24 and Mark 13. Christ does not appear in the clouds with His angels to Gather the Elect (Matt. 24:29-31, Mark 13:24-27) until after the abomination of desolation stands in the holy place (Matt.

24:15, Mark 13:14). In Daniel we read, *"I beheld, and the same horn made war with the saints, and prevail against them; until the Ancient of days came, and judgment was given to the saints of the Most high"* (Daniel 7:21-22). The Ancient of days gives judgment to the saints at the Gathering by removing them from Satan's physical dominion through the Antichrist's political, religious, and economic system on the earth. Then we read,

> *And he* [false prince - Antichrist] *shall speak great words against the Most High, and shall wear out the saints of the Most High, and think to change times and laws: and they* [saints] *shall be given into his hand until a time and times and the dividing of time* (Dan. 7:25).

The false prince, and very briefly the Antichrist through the ten kings, will have the ability to persecute the saints until mid-Trib. This sounds an awful lot like Revelation 13:6-7,

> *And he opened his mouth in blasphemy against God, to blaspheme His name, and His tabernacle, and them that dwell in heaven. And it was given unto him to make war with the saints, and to overcome them: and power was given him over all kindreds, and tongues, and nations* (Rev. 13:6-7).

We have established that Satan is restrained in heaven until it is time for the restrainer to be taken out of the way, thereby revealing the Satan-indwelt-Antichrist. Revelation 12:1-9 places Satan still in heaven until just before mid-Trib, so how can there be a sudden and sign-less Rapture before the Tribulation period begins?

Let's bring it home. Clearly we have shown from 2 Thessalonians 2:1-17 that the day Christ comes for His Bride will not happen until there is the great apostasy or *"falling away"* in the church and *"the son of perdition"* is revealed (2 Thess. 2:3). This man is revealed as *"that Wicked"* (2 Thess. 2:8) by claiming he is God in the earthly temple (2 Thess. 2:4), at the abomination of desolation when he stands in the holy place (Matt. 24:15, Mark 13:14). The abomination of desolation clearly happens before Christ comes with His angels at the Gathering of the Elect (Matt. 24:29-31, Mark 13:24-27). And finally, Satan is not omnipresent like God is. Satan is restrained in heaven until mid-Trib, when he is cast into the earth (Rev. 12:7-12). Since most people think the great Restrainer is probably the Holy Spirit, He does not allow the revealing of the Satan-indwelt-Antichrist until mid-Trib. Therefore the evidence we have brought to light requires that no sudden and sign-less Rapture can happen before the Tribulation begins. The pre-Trib sudden and sign-less Rapture conflicts with Scripture. We have shown you the lengths that pre-Tribbers have gone in attempting to satisfy the paradox. On one hand, they believe that Satan and the church cannot be on the planet at the same time, and on the other hand 2 Thessalonians 2:1-4 clearly says *"the son of perdition"* will come declaring to be God in the earthly temple **before** Christ Gathers His Bride. Daniel 2:31-45, 7:2-27, 9:27, 11:31, 12:11; Matthew 24, and Mark 13 also bear witness that the Satan-indwelt-Antichrist stands in the Holy Place in the earthly temple **before** Christ Gathers the Elect.

Past, Present and Future

Pre-4) One must read the Book of Revelation chronologically to understand the Pre-Tribulation Rapture Theory. Before the seals are opened, before the trumpets are sounded, John is told *"come up hither, and I will show thee things which must be hereafter"* (Rev. 4:1). This verse is believed by pre-Tribulationists to be the Rapture. Everything else after Revelation 4:1 is considered to be after the Rapture. Here is what Hal Lindsey has to say about this subject:

> **The Things Which You Have Seen...**
> This covers Chapter 1 where John describes the risen Lord Jesus' appearance to him and the phenomena that occurred during that visitation. It is described in the past tense.
> **The Things Which Are...**
> This describes Chapter 2 and 3.
> **The Things Which Shall Take Place after These Things...**
> This third division of the Book's Divinely given outline is clearly intended to convey things that will happen

after the events covered by the first and second divisions.[63]

Lindsey goes on to explain the Greek verbs used and clearly defines the three divisions of the Book of Revelation according to his interpretation. He concludes that after Revelation 4:1's *"Come up here, and I will show what must take place after these things"* that John is caught up to Heaven to see things that are future to our present time, even now. Then Lindsey writes, "John is actually representative of the whole church in Heaven. It is a preview of the Rapture and what we will see in Heaven when we get there."[64]

Rebuttal

Everything after Revelation 4:1 is future tense according to Hal Lindsey and we agree with his assessment. We also agree with his view that all seven letters to the churches have prophetic value, as well as historic value. However, we do not agree that John is representative of the church in Heaven. Scripture does not say that or even imply that.

Why do so many latch onto Revelation 4:1 where it says *"Come up hither, and I will show thee things which must be hereafter"* as being the Gathering of the church as apposed to Revelation 11:12, *"And they heard a great voice from heaven saying unto them, 'Come up hither.' And they ascended up to heaven in a cloud...?"* When John is told to come up and see the future in Revelation 4:1, there is no mention of the dead being raised or John being caught up in a cloud. Conversely, the Two Witnesses in Revelation 11 are raised from the dead, are caught up in a cloud, and brought to Heaven at the sounding of the trumpet. Our Scriptural witnesses say,

> *For the Lord Himself shall descend from heaven with a shout, with **the voice of the archangel**, and with **the trump of God**: and **the dead in Christ shall rise first**: Then we which are alive, and remain, shall be **caught up together with them in the clouds**,* to meet the Lord in the air: and so shall we ever be with the Lord (1 Thess. 4:16-17 - Emphasis added).

*And then shall appear the sign of the Son of man in heaven: and then shall all the tribes of the earth mourn, and **they shall see the Son of man coming in the clouds of heaven** with power and great glory. And **He shall send His angels with a great sound of a trumpet, and they shall gather together His Elect** from the four winds, from one end of heaven to the other* (Matt. 24:30-31 - Emphasis added).

Which one sounds more like the Gathering to you, Revelation 4 or Revelation 11?

Furthermore, where could one derive the conclusion that John is representative of the church. Lindsey does not show his homework on that point. The Two Witnesses on the other hand are representative of the church and Scripture supports this premise. *"These are the two olive trees, and the two candlesticks, standing before the God of the earth"* (Rev. 11:4). First, the olive tree always represents Israel and second, the two candlesticks represent the church. Read Revelation 1:20, *"...the seven candlesticks which thou sawest are the seven churches."* In addition, Elijah never died just like those who will be the Bride of Christ that are still alive when the Gathering occurs. Perhaps the other Witness is Moses and is like those that are the dead in Christ and resurrect at the Gathering.

Who Moved the Lamps?

Pre-5) Hal Lindsey makes another great point for pre-Trib. We can tell from his writing that he definitely loves the Lord.

When the apostle John is caught up to heaven in Revelation Chapter 4, he sees seven lamps of the fire burning before the throne of God (verse 5). Those seven lamps first appeared on the earth in Chapter 1, verses 12 through 20. In verse 20 they are identified as the seven symbolic churches. I [Hal Lindsey] believe that these seven lamps are the church, which has just been raptured into heaven. Here they are called the seven spirits of God because John is emphasizing that the Spirit indwells the churches.[65]

Through our exhaustive research into the pre-Trib position we have struggled to find ten stand-alone points favoring their position. This is one of the better ones. It is easy to see how one could come to this conclusion by looking at these verses as stand alone Scripture. Hal Lindsay equates these *"seven lamps of fire burning before the throne, which are the seven Spirits of God"* (Rev. 4:5) as the raptured church in Heaven. He believes this because John is emphasizing that the Holy Spirit indwells the seven churches.

Rebuttal

Do these verses really mean that the seven lamps of fire burning before the throne represent the Church that is indwelt by the Holy Spirit and is in Heaven because of the Rapture as Hal Lindsay ascribes? First we look at the relationship of the lamps to the candlestick and then we will answer the question with a summary. Let us look at the whole of Scripture for double witnesses and conflicts to establish the relationship of the candlestick to the lamps.

John is not the first one to be shown Heavenly things. Centuries before John lived, Moses was shown the complete tabernacle in Heaven, including the candlestick, for a pattern of what he was to build here on earth (Exodus 25:9, 25:31-40; Num. 8:4, Heb. 8:5, 9:19-24).

The Pattern of the Candlestick and Lamps

Throughout the Old Testament when the candlestick, singular, was mentioned, the lamps, plural, are mentioned as being thereof or upon. *"The pure candlestick, with the lamps thereof..."* (Exodus 39:37). *"...and thou shall bring in the candlestick, and light the lamps thereof"* (Exodus 40:4). Also read Exodus 25:37, 37:17 and 37:23. Moses was instructed *"and he put the candlestick in the tent of the congregation...and he lighted the lamps before the LORD; as the LORD commanded Moses"* (Exodus 40:24-25). From these patterns we see that there is a distinction between the candlestick and the lamps, yet they work in unity with one another. These seven lamps of the candlestick were lit before the LORD in an earthly tabernacle patterned after the one in Heaven, the one John saw in Revelation and Moses saw in Exodus.

According to all that I show thee, after the pattern of the tabernacle, and the pattern of all the instruments thereof, even so shall ye make it (Exodus 25:9).

Who serve unto the example and shadow of heavenly things, as Moses was admonished of God when he was about to make the tabernacle: for, "See," saith He, "that thou make all things according to the pattern showed to thee in the mount" (Heb. 8:5).

And this work of the candlestick was of beaten gold, unto the shaft thereof, unto the flowers thereof, was beaten work: according unto the pattern which the LORD had showed Moses, so he made the candlestick (Num. 8:4).

Moses' candlestick was to be a single piece of beaten gold to form the center shaft and its six branches with all its ornamentation, but the seven lamps were made separate. However, in order for there to be light outside the veil of the Holy of Holies in the earthly tabernacle, the candlestick and the seven lamps that sat thereon had to function as a unit. The lamps need the candlestick to hold them to provide the light.

Under the Old Covenant we see God the Father as sitting upon the mercy seat within the Holy of Holies and the seven lamps to be representative of the Holy Spirit. We see the candlestick of beaten gold as a representation of Jesus Christ, who would be *"wounded for our transgressions"* and *"bruised for our iniquities"* (Isa. 53:5).

The pattern is repeated when king David was shown the pattern and he gave it to Solomon with instructions how to build everything for the Temple and their intended use (1 Chron. 28:11, 28:12, 28:19). *"Moreover the candlesticks with their lamps, that they should burn after the manner before the oracle, of pure gold:* (2 Chron. 4:20). *"... and the candlestick of gold with the lamps thereof, to burn every evening"* (2 Chron. 13:11). *"He shall order the lamps upon the pure candlestick before the LORD continually"* (Lev. 24:4). We see that the seven lamps are to burn as a continual ordinance before the LORD. However, Judah failed to keep the commandments of God and keep the lamps burning all night or offer burnt offerings in the Holy place unto the God of Israel. In Jeremiah 52 we read that the candlesticks and all the Temple articles, minus the Ark of the Covenant, were carted off to Babylon. Israel going into captivity was their punishment for not obeying God and not worshipping Him wholeheartedly.

We found a third example of the candlestick pattern or what we would call a triple witness. In Zechariah 4 we read about how Zechariah was awakened from his sleep by an angel who showed him a vision.

> *And I said, I have looked, and behold **a candlestick** all of gold, with a bowl upon the top of it, **and his seven lamps thereon**, and seven pipes to the seven lamps, which are upon the top thereof: And **two olive trees** by it, one upon the right side of the bowl, and the other upon the left side thereof* (Zech. 4:2-3 - Emphasis added).

It is clear from all these examples of the candlestick that the candlestick is possessor or holder of the lamps. We also see this from the language of *"and his seven lamps"* (Zech. 4:2, Num. 4:9). This candlestick in Zechariah 4 is unique from the candlesticks of the Old Covenant in that there are two olive trees, one on each side of the bowl. It is interesting to note that the two olive trees are the *"two anointed ones that stand by the Lord of the whole earth"* (Zech. 4:14). We believe them to be the Two Witnesses of Revelation 11. *"These are the two olive trees, and the two candlesticks standing before the God of the earth"* (Rev. 11:4). Zechariah only saw the two olive trees and not the two candlesticks that John saw in Revelation 11 because the message of salvation was intended to be through Israel. When Israel rejected the message and the Messenger of the New Covenant of Grace, the dispensation of the Mystery began. Under the New Covenant of Grace and the Mystery Dispensation, the Two Witnesses as the olive trees will minister unto Israel and as the candlesticks they will minister unto the church during the first 1260 days of the Tribulation period (Rev. 11:3). This is to prepare the True Church for the coming Heavenly Kingdom and Israel for the coming Earthly Kingdom.

Zechariah was shown this prophetic vision of a candlestick and his seven lamps with the two olive trees representing a New Covenant of Grace many years before that Covenant was confirmed. Jesus began to confirm that New Covenant of Grace at His Baptism. Three and one half years later He presented Himself as the once for all time blood sacrifice in Heaven (Dan. 9:27, Heb. 8:6, 9:12, 9:15, 9:22-28, 10:9-18). The veil in the Temple was ripped from top to bottom after Jesus' death on the cross, signifying that we now as individuals have access to the Holy of Holies in Heaven through Jesus Christ and Holy Spirit (Heb. 9:8, 9:24). After Christ's victory on the cross and His bodily resurrection from the dead, *"the Messiah the Prince"* confirmed that New Covenant of Grace *"with many"* (Dan. 9:25, 27). He became *"the Prince of Life, whom God hath raised from the dead"* (Acts 3:15). He also became *"a Prince and a Saviour, for to give repentance to Israel, and forgiveness of sins"* (Acts 5:31). Jesus Christ stands as a Lamb that has been slain in the midst of the Throne in Revelation 5. He is the only acceptable sacrifice to God as Kinsman-Redeemer for our sins. Christ will be the only one found worthy to break the seals of the sealed book in Heaven and is presently *"the Prince of the kings of the earth"* (Rev. 1:5).

When Revelation 4:5 is read literally, it clearly states that the seven lamps of fire burning before the throne are the seven Spirits of God or the seven-fold Spirit of God.

> *And out of the throne proceeded lightnings and thunderings and voices: and there were* **seven lamps of fire** *burning before the throne,* **which are the seven Spirits of God** (Rev. 4:5 - Emphasis added).

The double witness of this is found in Revelation 1:4-6 where we see the Trinity represented as God the Father, Jesus Christ, and the Holy Spirit as *"the seven Spirits which are before His throne"* (Rev. 1:4). The attributes of *"the spirit of the LORD"* are defined in Isaiah 11:2. Also, **"in the midst of the throne... stood a Lamb** *as it had been slain,* **having seven horns and seven eyes, which are the seven Spirits of God** *sent forth into all the earth"* (Rev. 5:6 - Emphasis added). This seven-fold Spirit is the Holy Spirit!

When read literally, Revelation 1:20 clearly states that *"the seven candlesticks which thou sawest are the seven churches."* It is clear from Revelation 1:13 that *"one like unto the Son of man"* is *"in the midst of the seven candlesticks"* and the Scriptural witness to this is found in Revelation 2:1. Jesus Christ is the True Candlestick, who is the possessor or holder of these seven lamps of fire burning before the Throne in Heaven.

Under the New Covenant of Grace we see God the Father as sitting on the Throne in the Holy of Holies in Heaven throughout the Book of Revelation. The Holy Spirit is represented by fire throughout the New Testament and seen before the Throne as seven lamps of fire by John in Revelation 4:5. John sees Jesus Christ as being in the midst of the candlesticks or churches in Revelation 1:13. From the rest of the New Testament we see Jesus as Head of the Body of Christ, as being one with the True Church, and the espoused Bridegroom to the Bride of Christ. Faithful believers are individual members of the Candlestick, who is Jesus Christ in Heaven. Our bodies become the new Temples in which the Candlestick still holds the continual flame, which is the Holy Spirit. That Candlestick will stand before the Throne of God with its individual fires of the Holy Spirit burning, as evidenced by overcomers standing on the sea of glass being mingled with fire, praising God and calling Jesus *"thou King of saints"* (Rev. 15:3). What a blazing light that will make before the Throne of God in Heaven's Holy of Holies.

Symphonic View of the Lamps

Symphonically the seven churches are still here on the earth in Revelation 4. In Revelation 4:5 there are only the seven lamps of fire burning before the Throne, which we are clearly told are the seven Spirits of God, representative of the Holy Spirit. The sea of glass like unto crystal is without fire and empty of the overcomers in Revelation 4:6. However, in Revelation 15 there are clearly overcomers standing on the sea of glass mingled with fire.

In Revelation 4:4 the twenty-four elders are clothed in white raiment and have gold crowns on their heads. The symphonic timing of the twenty-four elders receiving their crowns cannot be before the rewards are given at the mid-Trib sounding of the seventh trumpet. The white linen is granted at the Marriage Supper of the Lamb and is clearly given after the Gathering of the Bride to Christ mid-Trib.

According to the American Standard Version and in the Greek

manuscript, Revelation 4:9-10 is future tense.

> *And **when** the living creatures **shall** give glory and honor and thanks to Him that sitteth on the throne, to Him that liveth for ever and ever, the four and twenty elders **shall** fall down before Him that sitteth on the throne, and **shall** [Greek says "will"] worship Him that liveth for ever and ever, and **shall** [Greek says "will"] cast their crowns before the throne* (Rev. 4:9-10, ASV - Emphasis and explanation added).

To understand the timing of Revelation 4:10, you have to go to the courtroom scene that is in Heaven in Revelation 19.

> *For true and righteous are His judgments: for He hath judged the great whore which did corrupt the earth with her fornication, and hath avenged the blood of His servants at her hand. And again they said, Alleluia. And her smoke rose up for ever and ever. And the four and twenty elders and the four beasts fell down and worshipped God that sat on the throne...* (Rev. 19:2-4).

At the Marriage Supper of the Lamb (Rev. 19:6-10) the Bride of Christ physically becomes one with Christ and Christ receives all the crowns of His Bride. This is evidenced by Christ having *"many crowns"* in Revelation 19:12 as apposed to having a single crown when He Gathers His Bride in Revelation 14:14. Symphonically the timing of when the four beasts fall down in worship to God and the 24 elders cast their crowns are at the Marriage Supper of the Lamb. These are the crowns that are cast before the Throne in Revelation 4:10. Therefore, what John sees in Revelation 4:1-11 symphonically covers the entire seven-year time span of the Tribulation period.

Another thing that one must keep in mind is that God in His infinite wisdom has placed double witnesses within the Book of Revelation, proving that His words are a true and faithful witness of events that will take place. That means that there are at least two Scriptures talking about the same event. The first is spiritually seen in Heaven and the second is the physical action taking place on earth.

That is why it does not make any sense when trying to read the Book of Revelation chronologically.

Also, many do not understand that Satan still has dominion over the earth until the Father says it is time for Jesus to take away Satan's crowns. This process does not start until the seals of the sealed book are broken in Heaven. Satan presently is not allowed to roam the earth physically as he did up until the cross (John 12:24-31, Rev. 12:9-10). When the great restrainer (2 Thess. 2:6-8,) is taken out of the way and Satan is stripped of his dominion, he realizes that he has lost. But Satan does not leave heaven without a fight, he and a third of the heavenly host fight a war in heaven with Michael and the good angels. Satan loses; he and the dark angels are cast to the earth to roam freely, but without dominion this time. Satan's only dominion will be through the Antichrist and the ten king's governments. All this happens when the sun and moon are darkened, just days before the seventh and last trumpet sounds. And when the seventh angel sounds that trumpet, *"...The kingdoms of this world are become the Kingdoms of our LORD, and His Christ; and He shall reign for ever and ever"* (Rev. 11:15). An everlasting dominion is clearly given to Jesus Christ at the sounding of the seventh trumpet (Dan. 7:13-14, Rev. 11:15-19, 12:10-12).

Symphonically the whole Book of Revelation has a story line. We find most people get confused trying to understand the sealed book, the trumpets and the vials. They also fail to see whether the action is taking place in Heaven or on earth. A majority of the Book of Revelation is about the courtroom scene in Heaven that starts in Revelation 4. Each individual judgment takes place in Heaven and afterward its effects are felt on earth at its appointed time. What is manifested in the physical realm always starts in the Spiritual Realm. When the sealed book is opened in Heaven, it affects are felt on earth throughout the entire seven-year Tribulation period. The breaking of the seals starts the process of Jesus Christ stripping Satan's dominion. The heavens are cleansed when Satan and his angels are cast out of heaven just before mid-Trib. Jesus is crowned King at the sounding of the seventh trumpet. He resurrects the Two Witnesses and all the faithful dead, and Gathers His Bride. The Temple of the tabernacle of the testimony in Heaven is opened, the judgment seat of Christ is set and court is in session for the saints. The rewards are given *"unto Thy servants the prophets, the saints, and them that fear Thy name"* (Rev. 11:18). Immediately upon Christ's judgment, the angels start to pour out the vials or bowls of God's wrath upon the earth. Christ marries His Bride and the Marriage Supper of the Lamb begins. Christ then comes back to earth with the armies of Heaven. He makes swift work of defeating the Antichrist and the false prophet by casting them into the lake of fire. All the armies of the ten kings are slain with the sword that proceeds out of Christ's mouth. Satan is thrown into the bottomless pit and chained there for one thousand years. Christ will have successfully taken physical possession of the earth and begins establishing His governmental rule over the earth for a thousand years.

Summary of the Seven Lamps

Now we are going to answer the question of Who Moved the Lamps. Hal Lindsay is saying that the seven lamps of fire burning before the throne represent the church that is indwelt by the Holy Spirit and is in Heaven because of the sudden and sign-less Rapture. Let us take a look at how this assumption conflicts with Scripture in many profound ways.

1) According to the Old Testament pattern of the real one in Heaven, **there are always seven lamps on one candlestick**. The seven candlesticks in Revelation 1:20 clearly are the seven churches, not the seven lamps of fire burning before the Throne. If these seven churches indwelt by the Spirit and raptured to Heaven were the seven lamps of fire as Hal Lindsey states, there would be 49 lamps of fire burning before the Throne and not seven lamps (7 candlesticks, which are churches x 7 lamps per candlestick = 49 lamps).

2) We also saw from the Old Testament pattern that the candlestick and the lamps are two distinct entities that function in unity. Moses' candlestick was to be a single piece of beaten gold to form the center shaft and its six branches with all its ornamentation, but the seven lamps were made separate. Jesus Christ is the True Candlestick, who is the possessor or holder of these seven lamps of fire burning before the Throne in Heaven. The seven lamps of

fire burning before God's Throne *"are the seven Spirits of God"* (Rev. 4:5 and 5:6; also compare Rev. 1:4). This is clearly the Holy Spirit, not the church that is indwelt by the Holy Spirit and taken to Heaven as Hal Lindsey claims.

3) Jesus is Head of the Body of Christ and the espoused Bridegroom to the Bride of Christ. Just as Jesus Christ as the true Candlestick in Heaven is the holder or possessor of the Holy Spirit, our bodies on earth are individual members of that Candlestick that become the many individual Temples that hold the Holy Spirit, which is the continual flame. In Revelation 4:6 John is shown *"a sea of glass like unto crystal"* before the throne. It is empty of overcomers and there are only seven lamps of fire burning. However, in Revelation 15 individual members of the true Candlestick stand before the Throne of God with their individual fires of the Holy Spirit burning, as evidenced by overcomers standing on the sea of glass being mingled with fire, praising God and calling Jesus *"thou King of saints"* (Rev. 15:3). These victorious overcomers in Revelation 15 are clearly standing on the sea of glass before the throne of God after Jesus has been crowned King at the seventh trumpet (Rev. 11:15, 12:10, 14:14), after the dispensation change (Rev. 14:13), after the harvest of the earth (Rev. 14:14-16). Choosing between either Revelation 4 or Revelation 15, which set of Scriptures sound more like the Gathering of the Bride to Christ to you? Where are the overcomers of the seven churches that were talked about in Revelation 2 and 3 shown in Revelation 4? It conflicts with Scripture that the seven lamps of fire burning before the throne is the Spirit-indwelt church that has been raptured to Heaven in Revelation 4.

4) The seventh trumpet is where the 24 elders, who are represented by the servants the prophets under the Old Covenant and the saints under the New Covenant, receive their rewards (Rev. 11:18). How is it possible that the 24 elders *"cast their crowns before the throne"* in Revelation 4:10 before they receive them as their reward at the seventh trumpet in Revelation 11? How is it possible for the 24 elders to cast their crowns before the throne in

Revelation 4:10 when Christ has not yet received His own crown until Revelation 14:14? How is it possible for the 24 elders to be arrayed in white linen before the Marriage Supper of the Lamb? That is when they are granted to wear *"fine linen, clean and white"* (Rev. 19:8). Therefore, what John sees in Revelation 4:1-11 symphonically covers the entire seven-year time span of the Tribulation period.

5) The Two Witnesses will minister unto Israel as the olive trees and they will minister unto the church as the candlesticks during the first 1260 days of the Tribulation period (Rev. 11:3). We are told that the seven candlesticks in Revelation 1 are the seven churches. So, how can the Two Witnesses minister unto the church for 1260 days of the Tribulation period if the church is already in Heaven because of the pre-Tribulation Rapture in Revelation 4? It is obvious that they cannot. Another major conflict for the church being in Heaven in Revelation 4.

6) In addition to that, the Two Witnesses who are representatives of Israel and the True Church are clearly resurrected and caught up to Heaven after their 1260-day ministry in Revelation 11. Where are the resurrection of the dead and the Gathering of the Elect in Revelation 4?

7) As individuals we now have access to the Holy of Holies in Heaven through Jesus Christ and Holy Spirit (Heb. 9:8, 9:24). Jesus invites *"whosoever believeth in Him"* (John 3:16) into God's Throne room because *"the Messiah the Prince"* (Dan. 9:25) has already confirmed the eternal blood Covenant of Grace *"with many"* (Dan. 9:27). He became *"the Prince of Life, whom God hath raised from the dead"* (Acts 3:15) and *"a Prince and a Saviour, for to give repentance to Israel, and forgiveness of sins"* (Acts 5:31). Christ is presently *"the Prince of the kings of the earth"* (Rev. 1:5). Christ has not yet been crowned King! Satan still has dominion over the earth until the Father says it is time for Jesus to take away Satan's crowns. This process does not start until the seals of the sealed book are broken in Heaven (Rev. 6:1 - 8:1). When Christ is crowned King, Satan loses his crowns (Rev. 13:1). Satan and the dark angels are cast to the earth and the

heavens are cleansed (Rev. 12). How could the seven lamps of fire burning before the throne in Revelation 4:5 be the raptured church standing in Heaven before the seals are broken and the heavens cleansed? How could the raptured church be in Heaven before Christ is crowned King and given dominion? An everlasting dominion is clearly given to Jesus Christ at the sounding of the seventh trumpet (Dan. 7:13-14, Rev. 11:15-19, 12:10-12).

All these things clearly place the timing of the Gathering to Christ mid-Trib; not Revelation 4 as Hal Lindsey ascribes.

Pentecost's View of Daniel's Seventieth Week

Pre-6) Pentecost holds to the precept that Daniel's seventieth week has not yet begun. He concludes the entirety of the Tribulation period being seven-years is the seventieth week. In Pentecost's thesis, he encompasses the nature, the scope and the purpose of the seventieth week.[66]

The Nature - the Tribulation period consists of Divine judgment and Divine wrath upon the earth.

The Scope - "there can be no question that this period will see the wrath of God poured out upon the whole earth." Pentecost goes on to explain that this period is the time of Jacob's trouble, a period not meant for the church. He sites Daniel 9:24, *"Seventy weeks are determined upon thy people and upon the holy city..."* He concludes that,

> ...since every passage dealing with the tribulation relates it to God's program for Israel, that the purpose of the scope of the tribulation prevents the church from participating in it.[67]

The Purpose - "the Scriptures indicate that there are two major purposes to be accomplished in the seventieth week."

Pentecost says, "the first purpose is stated in Revelation 3:10, *'I also will keep thee from the hour of temptation...'* " Pentecost implies that the *"hour"* is the seventieth week, which is the seven-years of the Tribulation. This period is to judge those that dwell on the earth and not the church.

Secondly he writes, "the second major purpose of the seventieth week is in relation to Israel." In Malachi 4:5-6 it is stated that Elijah will come before the great and terrible day of the LORD. This is to prepare Israel for the Second Coming of the Lord Jesus Christ. To support this he sites Matthew 11:14 and then he concludes that John's ministry

> was a ministry to prepare the nation of Israel for the coming of the King. It can be concluded then that Elijah, who is to come before the great and terrible day of the LORD, can have only one ministry: that of preparing a remnant in Israel for the advent of the Lord. It is evident that no such ministry is needed by the church since she by nature is without spot or wrinkle or any such thing, but is holy and without blemish.
>
> These two purposes, the testing of the earth dwellers, and the preparation of Israel for the King, have no relation to the church whatsoever. This is supporting evidence that the church will not be in the seventieth week.[68]
>
> ### The Unity of the Seventieth Week -
> "While all would agree, on the basis of Daniel 9:27; Matthew 24:15; and Revelation 13, that the week is divided into two parts of three and one-half years each, yet the nature and character of the week is one, permeating both parts in their entirety."[69]

Through this logic Pentecost determines that it would be impossible for the church to be present during the first half of the Tribulation period.

Rebuttal

We could pick apart Pentecost's thesis six ways till sundown, but to reduce redundancy we will limit it to a two-point rebuttal.

First, Daniel's seventieth week is not synonymous with the Tribulation period; that is an assumption by Pentecost. The root of which comes from a misnomer that the seventieth week in Daniel 9:27 is the Tribulation period. The verse does not say that. When we read Daniel 9:24-27, we see that *"Messiah the Prince"* (Dan. 9:25) is clearly the subject of the whole passage and the *"He"* in verse 27. We are sure of this.

> *Know therefore and understand, that from the going forth of the commandment to restore and to build Jerusalem* **unto Messiah the Prince** *shall be seven weeks, and threescore and two weeks...* [7 weeks + 62 weeks = **69 weeks completed**] (Dan. 9:25 - Emphasis and Explanation added).

Jesus Christ came as *"Messiah the Prince"* at His Baptism and from that time on the seventieth week began in Jerusalem two thousand years ago. There is no mention in Scripture of any gap in time between the sixty-ninth and the seventieth week. Christ came suddenly to His Temple and was *"the Messenger of the Covenant"* (Mal. 3:1) or *"New Testament"* (Matt. 26:28, Mark 14:24, Luke 22:20, 1 Cor. 11:25, Heb. 9:15) between God and man. Christ began to confirm the Covenant with many, Jew and Gentile alike, for one week or seven-years (Dan. 9:27). Jesus Christ, as the True Image of God, began the seventieth week. In the midst of the seventieth week, Messiah, the Anointed One (Dan. 9:24-26, Luke 4:18, Acts 10:38) was cut off, put to death. The earthly kingdom would have come at the end of the seventieth week had Israel not rejected Christ. Because Israel did reject the message and the Messenger of the Covenant, that message was given to the Gentiles *"until the fullness of the Gentiles be come in"* (Rom. 11:25) at the mid-Trib Gathering of the True Church. Therefore, the second half of Daniel's seventieth week still needs to play out for Israel and the 144,000 during the second half of the Tribulation period. Upon completion of the seventieth week, the earthly kingdom will finally come.

Besides being Messiah the Prince when He came, He was *"that Prophet"* (Deut. 18:15, 18; John 6:14, Acts 3:23) and He was *"the Lamb of God"* (John 1:29, 1:36). Animal sacrifice was required until

Jesus Christ *"the Lamb of God"* was crucified; after that any animal sacrifice would be an abomination to God. So in the midst of Daniel's seventieth week concerning God's plan, Christ caused the need for the animal sacrifice and the oblation to cease. Christ prophesied that because of the overspreading of abominations Jerusalem would become desolate (Matt. 24). Daniel writes, *"and **the people** of the prince that shall come shall destroy the city and the sanctuary"* (Dan. 9:26 - Emphasis added). Israel holding to the Mosaic Law and the Jewish traditions rejected their Messiah and continued sacrificing animals. Israel openly opposed Paul's gospel of grace under the New Covenant, thereby committing abominations until the city and its temple were made desolate in 70 AD.

On the other hand, Daniel 9:27 has a double fulfillment. Meaning that *"he"* can and should also be interpreted as *"**the prince that shall come"*** (Dan. 9:26 - Emphasis added). This *"prince"* is a mere evil-mortal-man that places an image of a god in the temple that should be worshipped near mid-Trib. This false prince is a mirror image of *"Messiah the Prince"* (Dan. 9:25), Jesus Christ. Just because this false prince copies Christ with a seven-year covenant in Satan's mirror image plan does not mean that the entire seven years of Tribulation period is Daniel's seventieth week. It only means that Satan through the false prince and the Antichrist is a copycat and a fraud.

Christ fulfilled the Scriptures that began Daniel's seventieth week 20 centuries ago. Then Christ was crucified in the middle of the week, which leaves only three and one half years of Daniel's seventieth week to be completed from God's perspective. However, there are still seven years to be completed from Satan's perspective. The first three and one half years are Satan's plan for humanity to accept the false prince as the messiah. The last three and one half years are Satan's plan for humanity to worship the Antichrist as God and the Antichrist to act as the counterfeit ruler of the whole earth. All seven years are Satan's mirror image of God's plan for Daniel's seventieth week.

The whole pre-Trib theorem is based on a supposition that the *"he"* of Daniel 9:27 is not Christ and must only apply to the Antichrist, thereby the seventieth week must not have begun yet. These theorists have built an entire theology based on this foundational supposition. Take away that supposition and everything Pentecost has written about the seventieth week concerning the nature, the scope, and the purpose becomes meaningless.

Secondly, Pentecost claims that Elijah comes preparing Israel for the King before the great and terrible day of the LORD, the time of Jacob's trouble and God's Wrath. There are two obvious observations we need to point out about this precept.

1) Elijah must come before the great and terrible day of the LORD (Jehovah) because Scripture says this in plain language. If we suppose that the entire seven-years of the Tribulation period is "the day of the LORD" as Pentecost does,[70] then we should be looking for Elijah before the Tribulation period. In fact, because Elijah comes to prepare Israel before the day of the LORD, we should expect him to come quite some time before the Tribulation begins. Otherwise Israel would have no time to prepare.

We believe that one of the Two Witnesses is Elijah. In fact, the Book of Revelation clearly tells us that the Two Witnesses' ministry is 1260 days long before the beast that rises out of the bottomless pit kills them. The beast does not rise out of the bottomless pit until Revelation 11:7 and 17:8, which is in the season of the seventh-trumpet mid-Trib. Since these verses are clearly mid-Trib, Scripture does not support the notion that Elijah comes before the Tribulation period begins. And since Elijah definitely comes before the great and terrible day of the LORD, then we know beyond reasonable doubt that the great and terrible day of the LORD is not seven years long. Pentecost's position that the church is exempt from the first half of the Tribulation is found baseless in fact.

2) Concerning Malachi 4:5-6 Pentecost writes, "The prophet states that the ministry of this Elijah was a ministry to prepare the people for the King who was shortly to come."[71] We take issue with his statement. Nowhere does Malachi mention the "coming King." Furthermore, the insertion "King" into what Malachi actually wrote is another misnomer. It clearly demonstrates the pre-Trib dogma imposed upon Scripture. If John the Baptist *"in spirit and power of Elias"* [Elijah] (Luke 1:17) was preparing the way for the King, then why is it that when John was given his opportunity to be Christ's witness did he announce Christ as *"the Lamb of God"* (John 1:29, 36) and not the King? It is because Christ had the role of *"the Lamb"* when He came to Jerusalem at His first Advent; He was *"that Prophet"* (John 6:14, Acts 3:23), Christ was *"the Messenger of the Covenant"* (Mal. 3:1), and He was *"Messiah the Prince"* in Daniel 9:24-27.

Christ came as an heir to be King (Zech. 9:9 & Matt. 21:4-5). He came not as a conqueror, but came meek and lowly, knowing He was to be the Sacrificial Lamb for the world. His role for us now is as the High Priest. We no longer need earthly priests to convey our prayers to God because Christ is our High Priest. Jesus Christ is presently *"a Prince and a Saviour"* (Acts 5:31) and *"the Prince of the kings of the earth"* (Rev. 1:5). To this day He still has not received all authority as the King. Christ will be crowned King in Heaven (Rev. 14:14, 11:15) before He comes for His Bride at His Glorious Appearance. This will be His coming in the clouds, when He has the angels with Him Gathering the Elect out from among the four winds mid-Trib (Rev. 14:14-16, Matt. 24:29-31 and Rev. 7).

No Church in Revelation

Pre-7) According to pre-Tribulation theorists, the word "church" is not mentioned after Revelation 4:1 until the end of Revelation in 22:16. There must be a reason why the church is not mentioned during the Tribulation period, which pre-Tribber's say are the seven years of Jacob's trouble.[72] In all the verses spanning the entire Tribulation period in the Book of Revelation, the church is not mentioned even once. The obvious explanation for this is that the sudden and sign-less Rapture happens before the Tribulation period begins.

Rebuttal

We surmise that this is one of the strongest arguments supporting the Pre-Tribulation Rapture Theory; it has to be because practically every author we have ever read teaches this.

To illustrate how untenable their point is we would like to point out that 1 Thessalonians is Paul's letter to the Thessalonians explaining the Gathering of the Bride to Christ. The very letter that explains the Gathering event that removes the church from the earth does not mention the word "church" except in the salutation. Furthermore, the very section of Scripture (1 Thess. 4:13-18) that the pre-Tribbers use as the sudden and sign-less Rapture in Revelation 4, the word "church" is not used either. The fact that the word "church" is not mentioned after Revelation 3:22 until the end of Revelation is a valid point, but no more important than the church not being mentioned in Paul's letter to the Thessalonians, and that point is meaningless. It does not prove the church is absent from the first half of the Tribulation period. However, it is obvious that in Paul's letter to the Thessalonians that the faithful of the True Church, which is the Bride of Christ, is talked about. Likewise, the Bride of Christ is talked about after Revelation 3:22 by using other words such as: *"great multitude ... with white robes"* (Rev. 7:9-17), *"the mystery of God"* (Rev. 10:7), *"child that was caught up unto God"* (Rev. 12:5), *"the saints"* (Rev. 11:18, 14:12), and *"them that had gotten the victory over the beast... his image...his mark...the number of his name"* (Rev. 15:2). Obviously the faithful of the True Church is mentioned through these other names after Revelation 4:1.

Trumpet of God is Different Then the 7th Trumpet

Pre-8) One must believe that a single trumpet is sounded at the sudden and sign-less Rapture. The Lord Himself descends from Heaven when the trump of God is sounded. The pre-Tribulationists say that *"the trump of God"* from 1 Thessalonians 4:16 could not be the same as the trumpet sounded in the Tribulation period. The trumpet of God gives blessings to the Bride of Christ and calls us all home to be with our Father in Heaven. Tim LaHaye says, "By no stretch of one's imagination could the seventh trumpet be called the trumpet of blessing sounded in 1 Thessalonians 4:16-18."[73] That trumpet of wrath in Revelation 11 brings wrath upon all those non-believing people that dwell on the whole earth and does not bring any blessings. This pre-Trib view believes that there are no blessings given during the Tribulation period at the sounding of the seventh and last trumpet.

We have a two-part rebuttal

1) The single trumpet point is easily refuted with 1 Corinthians 15:52, *"the last trumpet"* verse. If the Gathering happens at the sound of the last trump, then there must be at least one other trumpet that sounded before the last one can sound. The pre-Trib folks are adamant that there is only one trumpet sounded for the sudden and sign-less Rapture. How can the Rapture happen at the last trumpet if no other trumpets are sounded before the Rapture? In order to have a last trumpet there needs to be at least one trumpet prior to the last one. We cannot find any Scriptural witnesses to their premise. The Pre-Trib Rapture Theory has some serious conflicts because of this point.

2) While this "no blessings" point is often sited by theologians as evidence for a pre-Tribulation Rapture, there seems to be conflict with the blessings in Revelation 11:18. Yes, it says in plain language that rewards are given at the seventh trumpet. Why would rewards be given in the middle of the Tribulation period if there were a sudden and sign-less Rapture three and one half years earlier? It is because the Gathering is mid-Trib at the seventh and last trumpet of God.

Imminency

Pre-9) All one needs to do is look at 1 Thessalonians to know that the early church was expecting Christ to come in their day. In fact, throughout all church history are examples of people who believed in the doctrine of imminence.

Often when we read about this supposed doctrine, the scholars and authors we read are using strong tone like the imminent return of Christ is a fact and you must believe it. Of course the Rapture can happen at any moment and is a sign-less event. If the return of Christ is not a sign-less event, then imminency is destroyed and any Rapture theory that destroys imminency is heresy.[74] The doctrine of imminence forbids the participation of the church in any part of the 70th week.

Rebuttal to the supposed doctrine of imminency

Why would the sudden and sign-less pre-Trib Rapture theorists even use the words "doctrine of imminency" or "imminent" to describe the glorious event of the Gathering of the Elect? The definition of "imminency" in Webster's Dictionary is: *"something imminent; impending evil, danger, etc."*[75] Webster's definition of "imminent" is: *"likely to happen without delay; impending; threatening: said of danger, evil, misfortune, etc."*[76] From these two definitions we see an impending evil or danger that is likely to happen without delay. These definitions do fit the false prince who rises to world power and becomes the Satan-indwelt-Antichrist mid-Trib. He always copies God's plan and is the mirror image of Jesus Christ in an evil way, attempting to deceive people into thinking he is the true God. He does this by appearing to rise from the dead like Jesus Christ did and declaring to be God in the temple just days prior to mid-Trib. At that time the false prophet causes people to worship this Antichrist as the true God, **before** Jesus Gathers His Elect. The appearing of this false prince better fits the definition of "imminency" because of the *"impending evil"* that is *"likely to happen without delay"* than the appearing of Christ to Gather His Bride.

Christ told us to watch for fearful sights and great signs of His coming from Heaven to redeem us (Luke 21:10-11, 25-28). This is a partial list of signs that need to come to pass before we are told to lift our heads looking for our redemption: Elijah comes before the great and dreadful day of the LORD [Jehovah] (Mal. 4:5, Matt. 17:10-13, Mark 9:11-13), the Two Witnesses prophesy for 1260 days (Rev. 11:3), Christians will betray one another (Matt. 24:9-13, Luke 21:12-19), the son of perdition will proclaim he is God in the new temple (2 Thess. 2:3-4), Israel flees into the wilderness for protection (Rev. 12:14), and the sun and moon darken (Luke 21:25-26, Mark 13:24, Rev. 6:12-13). And then you shall see the Son of man coming in a cloud with power and great glory. *"And **when these things** begin to come to pass, **then** look up, and lift up your heads; for your redemption draweth **nigh"*** (Luke 21:28 Emphasis added). The lack of imminency is well illustrated in Luke 21:28. Christ prophesied that all these things would take place before the redemption occurs. When the list of things that are stated just prior to Luke 21:28 becomes recent historic facts, then we are supposed to look up because our redemption is drawing near. Near does not mean it is here yet. So if we are to look for a list of things to happen before our redemption is near; then how is our redemption imminent before the list of things has begun to happen? How then is the Rapture imminent at this very moment in time?

Christ knows all things (John 21:17). He knew for example that He would be crucified in time for the Passover. He knew that He would be betrayed and by whom. He knew He would rise again in three days. He knew things only God or a prophet of God could know.

After He first ascended to the Father in Heaven, Christ appeared on several occasions to further instruct His disciples. Christ said,

> *Go ye therefore, and teach all nations, baptizing them in the name of the Father, and the Son, and of the Holy Ghost: Teaching them to observe all things whatsoever I have commanded you: and, lo, I am with you alway, even unto the end of the world. Amen* (Matt. 28:19-20).

Jesus told the disciples to go into all the nations. When He did this He had to have known that it would not be accomplished in their lifetimes. He had to know it would take two thousand years to accomplish this goal. Even today it could be argued that we have not accomplished the Great Commission. How can Christ's return be imminent until we have accomplished the Great Commission? To believe in the imminency teaching by Christ would require one to believe that Christ deceived two thousand years worth of disciples into believing His return is imminent. He did not teach us to watch the sky until His return. He taught us our redemption is near and to look up at the sky when we see the abomination of desolation in the temple in Jerusalem. Read Acts 1:11; *"Why stand ye gazing up into heaven?"* The angel was telling the disciples that Jesus would one day return in like manner. He did not tell them to stand watching the sky for His imminent return. Our Scriptural witness is found in Acts 1:6-8,

> *When they therefore were come together, they asked of Him, saying, Lord, wilt thou at this time restore again the Kingdom to Israel? And He said unto them, It is not for you to know the times or the seasons, which the Father hath put in His own power. But ye shall receive power, after that the Holy Ghost is come upon you: and ye shall be witnesses unto Me both in Jerusalem, and in all Judaea, and in Samaria, and unto the uttermost part of the earth.*

Then the disciples watched as Jesus was taken up in a cloud to Heaven. Jesus knew these men would not witness for Christ in East Asia and the Americas. They did not even witness to most of their own continent. Christ meant that through the disciple's efforts they would be witnesses to *"all nations"* (Matt. 28:19), unto the uttermost part of the earth on His behalf.

Since God never lies (Titus 1:2, Heb. 6:18) or deceives us, why do so many people believe Christ taught the disciples His return is imminent? Why do people believe He taught them to expect His sudden return in their first-century lifetime? This belief in imminency since the first century is a half-truth. When we read writings supporting imminency, the author invariably site the "saints of old" as the reason to believe. In other words, the belief in the imminent return of Christ is based upon how other men have interpreted the Scriptures. Yes some of these men actually knew at least one disciple personally. But does this make imminency a fact?

Let us go back in time. Paul came to your village for two full weeks, for a total of three Sabbaths (Acts 17:1-13). Could Paul impart all his knowledge of Christ's teachings in that short period of time? Now you were really convicted by Paul to be a Christian convert. You begin to preach and outreach to others about Christ. Paul hears some of the things being taught and decides he needs to send you a letter, an Epistle correcting some of the erroneous thinking and teaching going on in your fledgling church (1 Thessalonians). So you make the changes in your church and correct the things Paul told you to do.

A little while later someone deceives your church by saying Christ has already come and that you missed it. Paul hears about this and has to write you another letter (2 Thessalonians). This letter tells you that you are not to let anyone deceive you. Christ's return to Gather the Elect will not happen until there is the great apostasy in the church, and the son of perdition is revealed by rising from the dead and declaring himself to be God in the new temple of God in Jerusalem (2 Thess. 2:1-4).

At this point, part of your church finally understands and the other part of your church still believes Christ is coming at any moment. One of these members that believe in imminency may have actually met Paul. Does the fact that this man believed in imminency make imminence a fact? We think that Lewis answers this well, "It must be understood, however that no doctrine rises or falls on the witness of history or of the testimony of church fathers. A valid doctrinal truth must find its authority in the words of Scripture alone."[77]

Present imminency believers look upon the saints of old as being infallible and that they had a better understanding than we possibly could today because they knew an apostle or someone an apostle taught first hand. Except 2 Thessalonians proves that the people of Thessalonica were deceived. Even though the leaders in Thessalonica had met Paul and knew his teachings first hand, the church thought they missed the Gathering. Paul quickly dispels that thinking in the first century with his second letter to the Thessalonians.

Not everyone in the early Church believed Christ was coming in his or her lifetime, Paul sure did not. Here is what Paul taught: In 1 Thessalonians 4:13-18, Paul was giving hope to the brothers and sisters in Christ,

> *But I would not have you to be ignorant, brethren, concerning them which are asleep* [dead], *that ye sorrow not, even as others which have no hope. For if we believe that Jesus died and rose again, even so them also which sleep in Jesus will God bring with Him* (1 Thess. 4:13-14 - Explanation added).

These Scriptures are clearly in the context of the Gathering of the Bride to Christ. Also 2 Thessalonians 2 clearly told the early Church that Christ would not come until the son of perdition is revealed. In modern day vernacular, we think Paul was saying do not worry about Christ's imminent return.

Imminency teaching is based upon man's traditions of someone else's interpretation of the Epistles. Imminency was not taught by Christ so it cannot be true, even if the early church got it in their heads like some people in Thessalonica did. The conclusion is that Christ did not teach it. Search your heart, is it a fact? Some people in every generation thought His return was imminent. Obviously they were wrong.

The generation that says Christ is not coming is the generation that He returns to. We are definitely hearing people say He is not coming, even now. We have not seen all the signs of His coming yet, so His return is soon, but not imminent. One of these signs is the apostasy of the church. We believe there is a terrible war before the Tribulation period in the Middle East, the Gog/Magog nuclear war and this speeds up this progressive apostasy. It is so bad the world will say it is Armageddon. Many in the church will walk away because they have been lulled into believing that they will not have to live through any of this end time stuff. They believe they will be kept from any tribulation like nuclear war. Wrong! The church is promised to be kept from God's wrath. This war is not even close to God's wrath.

We believe that the great apostasy will be caused by the Antichrist rising from the dead and declaring to be God in the earthly temple just prior to mid-Trib. Then the false prophet will demand all people of all religions to worship the Antichrist only! This may cause many marginal Christians to lose faith.

Having read some of the prophecies of Christ listing things that still need to be fulfilled before His Gathering of the Bride, how can any theologian hold to the supposed doctrine of imminency?

Seminary Teaches the Pre-Trib Rapture Theory as Fact

Pre-10) The biggest point in favor of the Pre-Tribulation Rapture Theory is that most scholars believe in the theory as fact. If everyone believes in it, then it must be true. The sudden and sign-less Rapture theory and imminence are inseparable issues. Since some Christians in the first century believed in the imminent return of Christ, then they must have believed no further prophecy need happen before His return. Since His return was imminent then, His return must be before the Tribulation period because of all the prophecies therein. The fact that His coming is before the Tribulation period proves His coming is imminent. All other theories that place the Rapture within the Tribulation period destroy imminency, so they must be false.

Rebuttal

Their logic is circular. We mention this circular logic because many scholars use this logic to try to prove the Pre-Trib Theory.

The Pre-Tribulation Rapture Theory as it exists today has been around since about the early to mid-eighteen hundreds. What is really impressive about this theory is that almost everyone believes in it. After all, that is why it is taught as fact, even doctrine. When one reads about the Pre-Tribulation Rapture in eschatology books, one invariable will read as proofs other scholar's opinions on the theory. Just because many other scholars believe this theory, it must be true.

Have we gotten to the point where we will listen to the traditions of men rather than read the Word of God?

A very high percentage of the Seminaries in the United States require this theory to be studied. To be a Priest, Reverend or Pastor in almost every major denomination one must believe in this theory as fact, even pledge to it.[78] Therefore, pre-Trib Rapture scholars and teachers do not need to prove that the Pre-Tribulation Rapture Theory is a fact, it is assumed. By no means is there harmony in the ranks though. But few dare to step out with their concerns about conflicting Scriptures with respect to the Pre-Tribulation Rapture Theory.

Does it seem right that our clergy cannot entertain the idea that there might not be a sudden and sign-less Rapture before the Tribulation period or explore the possibility that there could be a Gathering of the Bride mid-Trib? Well they can, but not while they are working for the establishment. "Go start your own church and preach that stuff, but not here!" It is as if the Pre-Tribulation Rapture Theory and the belief in the imminent return of Christ have become sacred untouchable doctrines. The virgin birth is doctrine. The resurrection of the body is doctrine. Who made a theory doctrine? Many scholars having doctorates in theology cannot even agree that there is a sudden and sign-less Rapture, let alone make imminency or the Pre-Tribulation Rapture Theory doctrines.

There are some denominations that also espouse the Post-Tribulation Rapture Theory. However, we are not aware of any major denominations that espouse the Mid-Trib Gathering Theory. Not even one! Wouldn't it be sad that if after everything was all said and done that the Mid-Tribulation Gathering Theory was the right one? Almost the entire church will have gotten it wrong!

Chapter 13

The Left Behind

Who Will Miss the Gathering?

It is a requirement to be a faithful Christian to be included in the reward known as the Bride of Christ. *"That if thou shalt confess with thy mouth the Lord Jesus, and shalt believe in thine heart that God hath raised Him from the dead, thou shalt be saved"* (Rom. 10:9). However, not all who confess Christ are the Bride of Christ. Pentecost writes, "The rapture will remove, not all who make a profession of faith in Christ, but only those who have been born again and have received His life."[79] Pentecost sees that some so-called Christians will be left behind. Larkin agrees and he writes, "But one of the surprises of that day will be that so many professing Christians, and among them many ministers and Christian workers, will be left behind, while some who were not known to be Christians will be missing."[80] The LORD is not willing that any should perish, but all should come to repentance (2 Peter 3:9). Obviously people are left behind, but it is not God's will that they are. It is because humanity is rejecting the truth about Jesus Christ.

The Scriptures suggest that as much as 50% of Christendom is left behind. Matthew 24:40-41 says that when two people are working, one will be taken and the other left behind. Luke 17:33-36 says when people are sleeping, one is taken and one is left behind. Matthew 25:1-12 talks about the ten virgins; the five wise are taken and five foolish are left behind. All these verses have a common theme; 50% are left behind. Out of six to seven billion or so people on the planet, there are about two billion people that claim to belong to some form of Christendom. From this, we know that the Scriptures do not mean 50% of the world population is removed by the Gathering. Logic dictates 50% of Christendom is left behind and if one billion Christians are removed at the Gathering, then about 85% of the world population will be left behind.

Why are some left behind? Well, it has to do with the parable of the four soil types (read Matt. 13:1-9 and Luke 8:5-18). The thorny soil type represents Christians that are caught up with the cares of the world. Instead of being obedient to the Holy Spirit in doing God's work and producing good fruit from their labor, they pursue their own selfish desires. Some of you reading this are ready to rebuke us saying WORKS, WORKS! We are not even coming close to saying works will earn one's way into Heaven. *"For by grace are ye saved through faith; and that not of yourselves: it is the gift of God"* (Ephes. 2:8). However, being included as the Bride of Christ at the Gathering of the Bride and having eternal salvation are not synonymous with one another. Faith offers salvation through Christ and faith must come first. True faith automatically causes works to follow, but works by itself does not bring you to faith or earn your way to Heaven. Faith in Jesus Christ is what saves us and we are rewarded for the works we do for Him. If we confess Christ before men on earth, Christ said He would confess us before the Father and His angels (Matt. 10:32-33, Luke 12:8-9, Rev. 3:5). Therefore, *"faith without works is dead"* (James 2:20, 26) means one is left behind when Christ comes for His Bride.

In understanding the parable of the four soil types, one must ask why there is even the third, thorny soil type, if not for justification-salvation through Christ. In the first soil type the fowls devour the seed before it took root. The rocky soil type hears but does not accept the free gift of salvation into their heart. If the thorny soil type does not accept the free gift of salvation-justification with roots in Christ, then how is the thorny soil type different from the rocky soil type. Both hear the word and embrace it, but the rocky soil type never accepts the free gift of justification, which is being sealed by the Holy Spirit. The thorny soil type must have roots to produce fruit. However, the thorns are sapping the nourishment for growth of the mature fruit, thus it is imperfect fruit. This is not pleasing to the Lord. The thorny soil is a type of the five foolish virgins. They are warm and not hot. Their fruit is imperfect because of their selfish desires and not allowing the Holy Spirit full control of their lives. This is why Christ spits them out when He comes for His Bride.

The good soil type represents Christians who first have faith in Christ, securing their eternal salvation, and then also striving to become sanctified in the Lord. They have a close personal relationship with God through Christ, allowing the Holy Spirit to cultivate their soil, keeping it thorn free and well nourished. This fruit is pleasing to the Lord. This good fruit is required to be included as the Bride of Christ and is a type of the five wise virgins.

This whole argument is not about works to get to Heaven. It is about taking action to mature in Christ to become His Bride, after receiving His free gift of salvation-justification. It is about striving to become as close to sanctification as is fleshly possible. Christ was completely sanctified without sin, blameless when He hung on the cross. We are to be Christ-like by allowing the Holy Spirit total reign.

Now that you know what these parables like the ten virgins and the four soil types mean, you need to ask yourself some questions. Am I ready for Christ if He came now? Do I have enough oil? Am I bearing good fruit for the Lord? How should I live my life, knowing that a lack of action on my part may prevent me from escaping the wrath of Antichrist during his 42-month reign of terror? Ask the Holy Spirit to come in and fill you up with the anointing oil that Christ was speaking of. Christ commanded us to,

> *Watch ye therefore, and pray always, that ye may be accounted worthy to escape all these things that shall come to pass, and to stand before the Son of man* (Luke 21:36).

The promise of being Gathered at His Glorious Appearing requires us to take action; we must watch and pray always that we may be counted worthy to go with Christ when He comes as the Bridegroom. We must also be vigilant in looking for His Gathering so we will not be deceived by the false-christ. We must never deny Christ's name, even under the threat of severe persecution, even unto death.

What Will It be Like for Those Left Behind?

Those who are left behind will know that people have been Gathered; maybe even people they know personally will be gone. The Christians from the thorny soil type already believe in Christ, but now find themselves left behind. They will be confused and may even feel betrayed. These Christians need to know it is their fault for not reading the Word of God and for not receiving nourishment from Christ often enough to bear good fruit. The left behind people should know that aliens did not take the ones who disappeared, but rather Jesus has taken them to be His Bride in Heaven. They have longed to be with the Lord and it is their will to be with Him. If you are reading this after the Gathering, it was because of your refusal to fully accept Christ that you were left behind. Do not blame your loved ones for having gone and left you behind. It is your fault, not theirs.

All hope is not lost for you if you were left behind. Accept the Lord Jesus Christ's free gift of salvation. You still have a chance to have eternal life because of Christ, but you can never be part of the Bride. The message of salvation through grace is still being offered to you. Seek out one of the 144,000 Jewish messengers of God or ask the Lord into your heart and repent of your sins.

There will be a price to be paid for being a Christian during this great Tribulation period. One should expect to give their life for Christ's namesake. If you should be put into a situation to renounce Christ, do not do it! Take death over pledging allegiance to the Antichrist and his economic mark system because death ensures your eternal life with the Lord. By choosing to worship the Antichrist, that worship will only ensure both physical and spiritual death! *"Whosoever shall seek to save his life shall lose it; and whosoever shall lose his life shall preserve it"* (Luke 17:33).

We think this verse also concerns Christians prior to the Gathering because the persecution of Christians does not end at the Gathering. At the time of the Gathering it is just the beginning of Satan's persecution of the earth and on everyone not willing to take his mark or worship him. God's wrath will also be poured out on the Antichrist and his kingdom right after the Gathering of the Elect. The Elect consists of the Bride of Christ that is taken to Heaven and the faithful of Israel, which is taken to the wilderness for 1260 days to protect them from the Antichrist and his ten kings. The faithful will be the righteous flesh and blood that goes into the Earthly Kingdom set up by Jesus after His Triumphal Return to earth.

The times ahead for the ones left behind are indeed tumultuous. Not only is all hell breaking loose, but all Heaven is too. If one takes the mark, worships the beast, or his image, one loses their salvation or eternal life with God and their fleshly life as well. We know the Antichrist promises that the mark will protect anyone who receives it, but this is a lie. God promises to inflict additional suffering on anyone who worships the Antichrist, his image or his mark system.

It will also be a miraculous time, meaning miracles will happen on a daily basis during the period of God's wrath. God is not willing that you should suffer. If you are His and you are an overcomer, God will provide hidden manna, which is food from Heaven (Rev. 2:17). God can sustain you through this time, if it is His will for you.

What is Promised to Those Martyred After the Gathering?

When Satan is banished from heaven, he attempts to have physical dominion over the earth through the Antichrist and the false prophet. The false prophet will attempt to deceive the people on the earth into worshipping the Antichrist as God and causes people to take the mark, both for economic and political reasons. The Satan-indwelt-Antichrist will attempt to physically put to death anyone who does not worship him as God. The severe labor pains of the woman begin the persecution that starts ten days before the Gathering of the Elect and continues for 42 months. This ten-day period before the Gathering of the Elect affects the Bride of Christ and the woman who is protected for 1260 days. The 42-month period affects those that are left behind after the Gathering of the Elect. The harvest of the earth includes the Gathering of the Elect and also the Gathering of those left behind into *"the great winepress of the wrath of God"* (Rev. 14:19). This is all one event that happens at the seventh trumpet.

> *Blessed are the dead which die in the Lord from henceforth: Yea, saith the Spirit, that they may rest from their labours; and their works do follow them* (Rev. 14:13).

In Rev. 14:13 *"from henceforth"* is clearly a dispensation change at the harvest of the earth (Rev. 14: 14-19). The harvest starts with the Gathering of the Elect and the effects continue until Jesus sets up the Millennial Kingdom on earth. The Bride of Christ will receive their glorified (spiritual) bodies and are taken to the spiritual dimension in Heaven for rewards (Rev. 11:18). This Gathering at the harvest of the earth begins the 42-month *"time of Jacob's trouble; but he shall be saved out of it"* (Jer. 30:7). The faithful of the woman (Israel) are protected on the earth by the Godhead for *"1260 days"* (Rev. 12:6) or *"a time, times, and half a time, from the face of the serpent"* (Rev. 12:14). These protected people are still in their flesh and blood (physical) bodies for the purpose of repopulating the earth during the Millennial Reign of Christ. Israel will also become the head of nations during the Millennium.

The clusters of the vine of the earth are also Gathered at the harvest of the earth (Rev. 14:17-19). These clusters of the vine are those people that are left behind after the Elect are taken to their respective places of protection and starts immediately after the Elect are protected from God's wrath. Of this group of people that are left behind, there are two classes. They are as follows:

1) Those people *"whose names are not* (or) *were not written in the Book of Life"* (Rev. 13:8, 17:8).

2) Those people that will be *"they which are written in the Lamb's Book of Life"* (Rev. 21:27). There are two divisions in this class and they are broken down as follows:

   A) The first division is the people that God supernaturally protects through the last 42 months of the Tribulation period. This is during the time that the Antichrist and the false prophet are reigning. These people will go into Jesus' Earthly Kingdom as flesh and blood bodies if they are alive when Jesus has established His 1000-year reign.

   B) The second division will be martyred for their testimony of Jesus, the Word of God, and refusal to worship the beast or his image, and refusal to received his mark in or upon their foreheads or hands. This division will have their name written in the Book of Life because they fear God and for their stand in Christ. They are the ones that receive the promise of resurrection and reigning with Christ as priests for a thousand years in Revelation 20:4-6. Perhaps these are the friends of Bridegroom. However, this division is not part of the Bride of Christ. This resurrection of the Tribulation martyrs takes place approximately three and one half years after the mid-Trib resurrection of the dead and translation of the living in Christ at the Gathering of the Bride to Christ.

Christ physically comes to earth to setup His 1000-year reign as KING OF KINGS AND LORD OF LORDS. The beast and the false prophet will be *"cast alive into a lake of fire burning with brimstone"* (Rev. 19:20). An angel comes down from Heaven, binds Satan and casts him into the bottomless pit so he can no longer deceive the nations *"till the thousand years should be fulfilled: and after that he must be loosed a little season"* (Rev. 20:3). This is the context of when the Heavenly Court pronounces the reward to *"the souls of them"* who have been slain *"for the witness or testimony of Jesus and for the Word of God"* (Rev. 20:4, 6:9). This is the answer to *"the souls of them"* under the altar in the fifth seal as to *"How long, O Lord, Holy and True, dost Thou not judge and avenge our blood on them that dwell on the earth?"* (Rev. 6:10). White robes were given to them and they were told to *"rest yet for a little season, until their fellowservants also and their brethren that should be killed as they were, should be fulfilled"* (Rev. 6:11). There is a direct correlation between the souls of the fifth seal and the souls that did not take the mark or worship the Antichrist that are beheaded.

> *Blessed and holy is he that hath **part** in the first resurrection: on such the second death hath no power, but they shall be priests of God and of Christ, and shall reign with Him a thousand years* (Rev. 20:6 – Emphasis added).

This resurrection in Revelation 20:6 is part of the first resurrection of the righteous dead that began three and one half years prior, at the Gathering of the Bride. This is only a part of the whole resurrection of the righteous dead. It started with Christ as the first fruits two thousand years ago, then the resurrection of the Bride of Christ that occurred at the seventh and last trumpet mid-Trib. It is evident from the above Scriptures that there is a resurrection of souls into glorified bodies that happens at the setting up of the Millennium as well.

"But the rest of the dead lived not again until the thousand years were finished" (Rev. 20:5). The rest of the dead is not resurrected until the 1000 years are finished. This includes all the unrighteous dead from the time of Adam to the end of the Millennium and all the dead from the Millennium period that are righteous.

What is Beyond the Tribulation Period?

The Millennium:

There will be a regeneration of the earth after Armageddon. Part of Jesus' work on the cross as Kinsman-Redeemer is the breaking of the curses put on the earth at Adam and Eve's fall. The last curse to be broken is death at the end of the Millennium. If one survives until the Millennium, one will live hundreds of years like people did in the days before Noah's flood. There will be no more wars or terrorism. The earth will be restored to a state similar to that before the flood when the Lord Jesus Christ takes physical possession of the earth. This will be "the day of the Lord Jesus Christ" that started with the mid-Trib Gathering of the Bride of Christ and extends to the end of the Millennium. 2 Peter 3:8 says, *"that one day is with the Lord as a thousand years, and a thousand years as one day."* This Millennium is 1,000 years long (Rev. 20:2-7) and Christ will sit on His throne as KING of KINGS and LORD of LORDS over all the earth.

During the Millennium God completely fulfills the Abrahamic and Davidic Covenants through the New Covenant of Grace that Christ offered to Israel during His earthly ministry. Satan is loosed on the earth to deceive the nations after the 1,000 years are expired. Once Satan is loosed it is unclear how long he is allowed to deceive the nations. Is he loosed for a few years or a few days? We do not know. The Bible is unclear on this subject.

Matthew is the only one of the four Gospels to even describe what follows Armageddon [the millennial reign] and none of the Gospels talk about the battle itself.

> *When the Son of man shall come in His glory, and all the holy angels with Him, then shall He sit upon the throne of His glory: And before Him shall be gathered all nations: and He shall separate them one from another, as a shepherd divideth his sheep from the goats: And He shall set the sheep on His right hand, but the goats on His left. Then shall the King say unto them on His right hand, "Come, ye blessed of My Father, inherit the Kingdom prepared for you from the foundation of the world"* (Matt. 25:31-34).

Jesus starts to separate the sheep nations from the goat nations in the first days of the Millennium. This happens over a 45-day period.

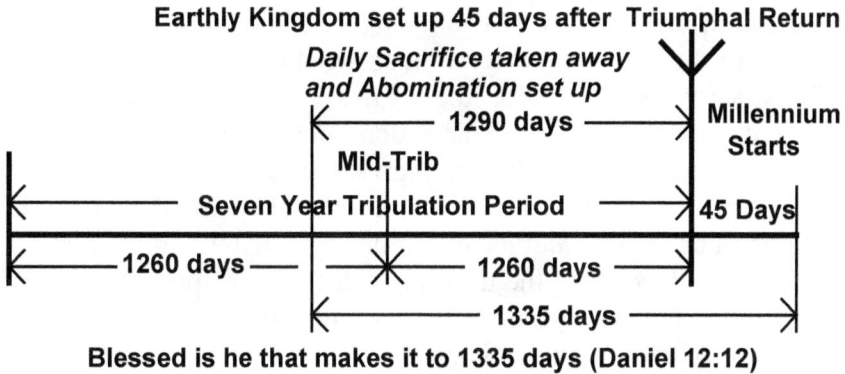

Earthly Kingdom set up 45 days after Triumphal Return

Daily Sacrifice taken away
and Abomination set up

← 1290 days →	**Millennium Starts**

Mid-Trib

← Seven Year Tribulation Period → | **45 Days**

← 1260 days — | → 1260 days → |

← 1335 days →

Blessed is he that makes it to 1335 days (Daniel 12:12)

God gathers Israel from the nations and then He sets king David over them after the Millennium begins. Read Ezekiel 37:21-22. The Lord GOD makes them one nation in the land of the mountains of Israel. The two kingdoms, Israel and Judah shall be united as one.

> *And David My servant shall be king over them; and they all shall have one shepherd: they shall also walk in My judgments, and observe My statutes, and do them. And they shall dwell in the land that I have given unto Jacob My servant, wherein your fathers have dwelt; and they shall dwell therein, even they, and their children, and their children's children forever: and My servant David shall be their prince forever* (Ezek. 37:24-25).

David is king over Israel during the millennial period, but Jesus is the KING of KINGS over all the kings of the earth. After the thousand years have expired, David is their prince forever and ever.

Let us talk about the big picture of God's plan to restore creation since iniquity was found in Lucifer. God created humanity to replace Lucifer and the heavenly host that had fallen. Satan was told in Genesis, that from the seed of the woman Christ would come. This is what the struggle in the Bible is all about. Satan has tried to kill off

317

humanity and the bloodline leading up to Christ. Then Satan tried killing Christ and finally succeeded, unwittingly sealing his own doom. Since then, Satan has been restrained in heaven, having limited powers on earth through demonic influences. When Satan is loosed on earth in the near future he will once again try to kill off humanity, starting with the Christ followers. Satan would succeed at killing off all Christianity, however, for the Elect's sake God shortened the number of days Satan would have dominion over them. God will remove the Elect from Satan's dominion at the seventh trumpet.

God wants to dwell among us like He did with Adam in the Garden of Eden. Since iniquity was found in Lucifer, sin resulting in death was introduced into the universe. All the pain and suffering, all wars, all of human history, including Christ having to die on the cross was a result of this iniquity. Satan lied to Eve and he succeeded in tempting Adam and Eve. When they sinned, they were condemned to die because the wages of sin is death. When Jesus died on the cross, He made atonement for sin for everyone by His once for all sacrifice. It has been God's plan all along to set things right in the universe and restore His creation through Christ. He will live among us on earth during the Millennium and His Bride will live and reign with Him. This is when people beat their swords into plowshares and spears into pruning hooks (Micah 4:3). Christ wants to live among us because He loves us and simply wants us to love Him back.

Satan is locked up in the pit after Armageddon and will stay there until he is released at the end of Christ's 1,000-year reign. After the 1,000 years have expired Satan is allowed to deceive the nations and bring about war once again. When Satan deceives the people of the world and draws them into battle, God defeats him forever. Satan is then cast into the lake of fire, where the false prophet and the Antichrist already are, to be tormented day and night forever and ever.

Chapter 14

The Great White Throne Judgment

The elementary things of this earth will be destroyed by fire and a new heaven and a new earth will replace it. This earth will be forever.

And I saw a great white throne, and Him that sat on it, from Whose face the earth and heaven fled away; and there was found no place for them (Rev. 20:11).

And I saw the dead, small and great, stand before God; and the Books were opened: and another Book was opened, which is the Book of Life: and the dead were judged out of those things which were written in the Books, according to their works (Rev. 20:12).

Notice that *"the Books"* of works is differentiated from *"the Book of Life."* Those, whose name is written in the Book of Life, are given a pass. They still go before the Judge but no case is heard. The case is dismissed. The blood of the Lamb has expunged all the works of evil from *"the Books."* Those, whose names are not found written in the Book of Life, must have their case heard before the God. No amount of good works will save them from their iniquities. They are guilty and await their second death in the lake of fire.

And the sea gave up the dead which were in it; and death and hell delivered up the dead which were in them: and they were judged every man according to their works. And death and hell were cast into the lake of fire. This is the second death. And whosoever was not found written in the Book of Life was cast into the lake of fire (Rev. 20:13-15).

Chapter 15

Future of the Church

On Sunday Mornings My Church Does Not Talk About It, So Why Should Christians Be Concerned About the Gathering or End-times Prophecy?

We hear some people say, "oh, that is doomsday stuff and I am not listening." Being ignorant of the law does not make an excuse. Being ignorant of what Christ warned us about in Revelation 3:14-22 does not make an excuse either. The Lord is going to leave the lukewarm church members behind. That does not sound very good to us, how about you? Many people want to go on living their lives in denial that these are the ends of times. Christ warned us to be watchful and vigilant so we will not be left behind. We were warned in advance not to be lukewarm for the Lord. It does not matter how many good deeds one has done or that one attends church every Sunday. All that matters is that one is accounted worthy at the time of the Gathering.

> *And the Lord make you to increase and abound in love one toward another, and toward all men, even as we do toward you: to the end He may stablish your hearts unblameable* [accounted worthy] *in holiness before God, even our Father, at the coming of our Lord Jesus Christ with all His saints* (1 Thess. 3:12-13).

If one is not part of the Bride of Christ, then one is just another Laodicean church member looking for good business contacts or whatever the motive is for going to church. Some in the church will have been justified through Christ and others will have never known Christ. He is only coming to get His Bride; all others will be left behind. What could be more important than teaching this concept from the pulpit? Yet, too many churchgoers have never heard that Christ is coming for His Bride, only that He is coming at the end of time or something vague.

John's letters to the seven churches in Revelation 2:1 - 3:22 are letters to actual churches in his time. However, we believe these letters are also describing the church throughout its history on earth. In this way the letters are prophecy. Much of the church today is like the church of Laodicea, talked about in John's letter in Revelation 3:14-22. In this particular letter, the Lord acknowledges that the congregation's deeds are neither cold nor hot. Then the Lord says that because the congregation is *"lukewarm, and neither cold nor hot, I will spue thee out of My mouth"* (Rev. 3:16). He is going to leave them behind at the Gathering. One caveat, Christ does not judge us corporately; He judges us on an individual basis. This is why we need to talk about the Gathering and prophecy from the pulpit. We have personally met too many Christians who have never heard anything about the Gathering or any mention of being caught up in the air to meet Jesus in the twinkling of the eye. Anyone who reads his or her Bible will know about this promise from our Lord. However, large sects of the church are not encouraging people to read their Bible, leaving it up to the clergy to impart the truth therein. Obviously this trickle down style of imparting God's truth is not working because too many Christians do not know what we are talking about when we tell them about the Gathering. Often they are people that grew up in a Christian home.

You need to read the Bible every day if you can. Make time for it by getting up early and taking fifteen minutes to use the concordance in the back of your Bible to find topics you are interested in. Get in the Word and let God speak to you through His Word. It will change your life. Reading your Bible and studying prophecy will strengthen your love for the Lord and after all, that is the greatest commandment Christ gave to us (Matt. 22:38). He said, *"Thou shall love the Lord thy God with all thy heart, and with all thy soul, and with all thy mind"* (Matt. 22:37). Then He said, *"and the second is like unto it, Thou shalt love thy neighbor as thyself"* (Matt. 22:39).

What Can I Do to Prepare for Christ's Gathering?

First and foremost you must have faith in Jesus. Secondly, Jesus told us to pray always that we may be accounted worthy to escape His wrath. You should become a strong Christian. Have a strong appetite for God's Word. Have a love of the truth.

> *Of Whom we have many things to say, and hard to be uttered, seeing that ye are dull of hearing. For when for the time ye ought to be teachers, ye have need that one teach you again which be the first principles of the oracles of God; and are become such as have need of milk, and not of strong meat. For the one that useth milk is unskilful in the word of righteousness: for he is a babe. But strong meat belongeth to them that are of full age, even those who by reason of use have their senses exercised to discern both good and evil* (Heb. 5:11-14).

You can prepare for His Gathering by starting to eat meat. Stop being satisfied with the milk that they serve every Sunday in our Laodicean churches of today. Start having a hunger for God's wisdom and knowledge. Pray for it. Become more mature in the Word of God and hunger for the meat therein.

We often referred to Hebrews 5:12 as we were writing this book because the Lord had given us a seven course meal to eat, with new understanding about various Scriptures. Just when we were so full from eating the Word of God and were satisfied, we would get a fuller understanding, even bigger than the last.

Start to study Bible prophecy so when world events happen before your eyes, you are satisfied in knowing the truth about the events you are witnessing, as you will not find the truth on television or any traditional media source about the upcoming prophecy events.

Here are a few prophecies that you should know:
- War with Russia and its allies like Iran against Israel is in our near future.
- Elijah is coming before Christ, to proclaim the return of Christ to Gather the Elect.
- An economic and political system that involves ten regions around the globe will begin. Nations will gradually lose their sovereignty to be part of the ten units, regions, sectors or whatever it is going to be called under the new political system. Many more major world events are soon to happen.

- Something placed on or in one's hand or forehead will allow one to purchase things. Do not get this implanted on or in your hand. Even if getting this mark does not require you to renounce Christ when it first becomes available, it soon will.

It is all in the Bible, just waiting for you to discover the verses. If you have the knowledge of these Bible verses, you will be well prepared for Christ's return. You will not be surprised when He comes and He will not come as a thief in the night for you.

The most important thing we can do to prepare for His Gathering is to do His will now. He commanded all His followers to make disciples of each other, baptizing each other in the name of the Father, and the Son, and the Holy Spirit. Many evangelism ministries are very successful in bringing people to Christ. This is a good thing, but then many of these people are going out the back door as fast as their replacements are coming in the front door. This is a problem. We have heard that as many as 80% of all new Christians turn from their Christian walk in just a few years. Christ taught us to make disciples, who then make disciples, and so on. The people who become disciples of Christ almost never leave. This is our mission and purpose in life as a Christian. Every aspect in our Christian lives should be centered on this mission. Our worship, our tithing, our evangelism, our works, everything should support this mission.

We are not bashing evangelists. What we are saying is that once someone has been given milk for the first time and is brought to Christ, we need to guide them and nurture them along in the Word of God, pastor them, and feed them the meat of God's Word. We should make disciples of them so they can go to others and do the same. This requires faith with Bible study and constant prayer. The ultimate goal for these new disciples is to have a spirit filled walk in life.

Chapter 16

Salvation

This chapter delves into how to become a believer in Christ. It also addresses common questions and beliefs of many Christians, new and old.

What Is Salvation?

Before we are born again and become a new creation in Christ, we live according to the flesh, a prisoner of sin. *"Wherefore, as by one man* [Adam] *sin entered into the world, and death by sin; and so death passed upon all men, for that all have sinned"* (Rom. 5:12). So the first Adam brought sin into the world and into his flesh body. We are his descendents and have inherited his sin nature down through the generations, for in Adam all will die (1 Cor. 15:22).

Christ is the *"last Adam"* (1 Cor. 15:45). Through Him we have been purchased for a price (Matt. 20:28, Mark 10:45, 1 Tim. 2: 5-6). Because Christ rose from the dead, all will live (1 Cor. 15: 21-23), the righteous and the unrighteous (Dan. 12:2, Rev. 20:4-5). Only Christ justifies us before God so we can have God's gift of salvation.

Salvation is to live with Christ for eternity and to inherit the promised Kingdom, as opposed to being separated from Him forever. Those Christians who are the Bride of Christ will be before the throne of God and they shall not hunger or thirst anymore (Rev. 7:15-17). If you are found wanting by the Lord when the Gathering occurs, you will be left behind. But that does not mean the Lord has forsaken you. Being left behind is an opportunity to get right with the Lord and do His work for once in your life. However, you may be asked to give your life for Christ's sake if you are left behind.

Only you know in your heart whether you have accepted Jesus or not. Many people go through the motions pretending to be people of God, but they are only fooling other people. A phony believer will never fool God. One cannot behave like a Christian to become one. One must have faith in Jesus to become a Christian.

> *Verily, verily, I say unto thee, Except a man be born again, he cannot see the Kingdom of God* (John 3:3).

> *That which is born of flesh is flesh; and that which is born of Spirit is spirit* (John 3:6).

All men have fallen short of God's Law and stand condemned. Only by faith in Christ can we be set free from the bondage and yoke of God's Law.

> *He that believeth on Him* [Jesus Christ] *is not condemned: but he that believeth not is condemned already, because he hath not believed in the name of the only begotten Son of God* (John 3:18).

God's Contract with You

You need to ask yourself one question; do you think God would lie to you? Really, would God tell you something that is not true? Scripture tells us that it is *"impossible for God to lie"* (Heb. 6:8, also see Titus 1:2). God gave each one of us a two-part contract, and it is up to us to accept it or reject it. This is in fact why we are placed on the earth, to know the Lord and love Him as He loves us. The first part of God's contract with us is:

> *For God so loved the world, that He gave His only begotten Son, that whosoever believeth in Him should not perish, but have everlasting life. For God sent not His Son into the world to condemn the world; but that the world through Him might be saved* (John 3:16-17).

> *Behold, I stand at the door, and knock: if any man hear My voice, and open the door, I will come in to him, and will sup with him, and he with Me* (Rev. 3:20).

God has done His part, now it is up to you to open the door and let Him in. Then the second part of God's contract with us is:

That if thou shalt confess with thy mouth the Lord Jesus, and shalt believe in thine heart that God hath raised Him from the dead, thou shalt be saved. For with the heart man believeth unto righteousness; and with the mouth confession is made unto salvation (Rom. 10:9-10).

Attaining Salvation

This is a simple thing to do. Trust in Jesus Christ as your personal Savior and have faith in Him. Then ask for forgiveness of your sins and ask for the Holy Spirit to enter you and seal your spirit that you may be born again, not of flesh but in spirit. Publicly confess your faith in Christ by simply standing in front of people "proclaiming" that you are a Christian is good enough. Baptism is not a requirement for salvation, but it is a symbol of being born again in your spirit. Christ told us to baptize each other as He had done. He is our example and this practice is part of publicly accepting Christ.

The Bible says that the only way to have eternal life is through Jesus. This invitation is open to anyone; no matter what they have done, where they have come from or what religion or denomination they were raised to be. Just accept the contract God gave us and salvation is yours!

The Salvation Prayer

My Father in Heaven,
Thank you for sending Your Son for my sins.
I am a sinner not worthy of Love, yet You still love me.
I ask Jesus to come into my heart and to reside there forever.
I ask the Holy Spirit to enter me so I may be born again in spirit.
Please forgive me of my sin as I forgive others who wrong me.
Lord, let Your Will and not mine rule all my life.
Lord, I am nothing without You.
In Jesus name I pray.
Amen!

☺

What is Justification?

When you say this prayer and truly mean it in your heart, you have salvation. We call it justification by faith, which means: the act

327

by which a sinner is freed through faith from the penalty of his sin and is accepted by God as righteous.

> *Therefore being justified by faith, we have peace with God through our Lord Jesus Christ: By Whom also we have access by faith into this grace wherein we stand, and rejoice in hope of the glory of God* (Rom. 5:1-2).

> *Knowing that a man is not justified by the works of the law, but by the faith of Jesus Christ, even we have believed in Jesus Christ, that we might be justified by the faith of Christ, and not by the works of the law: for by the works of the law shall no flesh be justified* (Gal. 2:16-17).

Being justified is being born again. You become a new person after receiving the free gift of salvation through Christ by His justification of you before the Father. Though your flesh body is of sin nature, your spirit and soul are born again, made new without sin or blemish. The Holy Spirit then resides within your spirit.

> *What? know ye not that your body is the Temple of the Holy Ghost which is in you, which ye have of God, and ye are not your own? For ye are bought with a price: therefore glorify God in your body, and in your spirit, which are God's* (1 Cor. 6:19-20).

God Dwells Inside You

When you accept Jesus as your personal Savior, the Holy Spirit enters you just as God entered the Holy of Holies in Solomon's Temple in Israel. Except now the Holy Spirit enters your body instead of entering an earthly temple built by human hands. Think about that for a minute, God resides within you. You are God's Temple now. God is not in some far off place where you need to face east to worship Him. He knows your every thought and prayer even before you say it. Once you really grasp that God is indwelt inside you, ask yourself; what things are now possible in the name of Jesus? Praise the Lord daily for everything in your life. Amen!

328

What is Sanctification?

Sanctification is the ongoing process of purification and being free from sin. When one accepts the free gift of justification, spiritually something amazing happens inside you. The sinful nature of the old man inside you must die so that the new man may be born again spiritually (Rom. 6:1-14).

> *For if we have been planted together in the likeness of His death, we shall be also in the likeness of His resurrection: Knowing this, that our old man is crucified with Him, that the body of sin might be destroyed, that henceforth we should not serve sin. For he that is dead is free from sin* (Rom. 6:5-7).

Just because we are free from sin spiritually does not mean our flesh body is free from sin. We actually have to turn from sin and the ways of the old sin nature. Without God this would be impossible, but when we became this new creation, the Holy Spirit entered us and sealed us.

There are three parts to each one of us: the spirit, the soul or the mind, and the physical body. Our spirit becomes one with the Holy Spirit when we are justified by Christ and we are sealed by the Holy Spirit. Our minds become renewed through hearing the word of God (Rom. 12:2, Ephes. 4:23). However, our physical flesh body is still inherited from the first Adam; it is still sinful flesh. When we bring the mind and the spirit into agreement, the flesh body is brought into a spirit filled walk. The spirit is pure and is always ready, but the mind being part of the sinful flesh body is weak. In this way, the spirit and the flesh body are at enmity with each other. The battlefield is in the mind. This is where the struggle between the old man and the new man happens. With time and constant renewing of the mind with God's word, one matures and grows by walking according to the Spirit. This is called a spirit filled walk and it is part of the sanctification process that is never finished until we are resurrected or made incorruptible.

But I Was Taught We Are Not Under the Law

Many Christians are taught wrongfully that we are not under God's Law reciting Romans 6:14, *"For sin shall not have dominion over you: for ye are not under the law, but under grace."* While it is true sin has no dominion over us, we need to ask; who are we in Christ? Are we the old man condemned to death or the new man with hope in salvation? However, the flesh body we live in while on earth is still condemned to die, even after we have been born again. Our sinful flesh bodies will never see the Kingdom of Heaven. So Romans 6:14 could not be referring to our flesh body being free from sin, but rather our born again spirit and soul.

If we went on living our lives obeying the flesh, thinking our flesh body was above God's Law, we would have the equivalent of having license to sin. On the contrary, the sins we do in this flesh body have consequences in the flesh. *"What shall we say then? Shall we continue in sin, that grace may abound? God forbid. How shall we, that are dead to sin, live any longer therein?"* (Rom. 6:1-2).

So what does it mean *"ye are not under the law"* if it does not mean I have license to sin? The key to understanding this concept is in understanding who we are in Christ once we are born again. Are we sinners or are we saints? The next time someone says you are a sinner, you can inform him or her you are a saint, not a sinner. You are royalty. In fact when you are born again in the spirit, you become a foreigner to earth; you are ambassadors for Christ. Spiritually you are justified by Christ, but your flesh body is not yet. Only when we are resurrected from the dead are we fully sanctified. Our flesh body will be transformed from corruptible and made incorruptible, and this mortal body transformed to immortality. The Bible describes this by saying,

> *So also is the resurrection of the dead. It is sown in corruption; it is raised in incorruption: It is sown in dishonour; it is raised in glory: it is sown in weakness; it is raised in power:* ***It is sown a natural body; it is raised a spiritual body.*** *There is a natural body, and there is a spiritual body* (1 Cor. 15:42-44).

Since this flesh and blood body will never see the Kingdom of God, I am something other than this flesh vehicle I reside in. I am more than what meets the eye. My spirit was dead to God, but now I am born anew and live in Christ and Christ lives in me. I am no longer spiritually under the yoke of God's Law, but my flesh body is and is condemned to die because of it. However, my soul will never die, but have everlasting life. Therefore, we need to develop a spirit filled walk so we do not fulfill the lusts of our flesh body.

> *This I say then, Walk in the Spirit, and ye shall not fulfil the lust of the flesh. For the flesh lusteth against the Spirit, and the Spirit against the flesh: and these are contrary the one to the other: so that ye cannot do the things that ye would. But if ye be led by the Spirit, ye are not under the Law* (Gal. 5:16-18).

We will have peace and harmony with God when we walk in the Spirit. He helps us to live fulfilled lives, free from our past failures. Walking in the Spirit makes it possible to live a fruitful life and share that life with others who want what you have.

Becoming the Bride of Christ

The Bride of Christ produces mature fruit and is from the good soil type. The good soil type represents Christians who first have faith in Christ, securing their eternal salvation, and then also striving to become sanctified in the Lord. They have a close personal relationship with Jesus Christ, allowing the Holy Spirit to cultivate their soil, keeping it thorn free and well nourished. They renew their mind in the Word of God and spend time in communication with their loving Heavenly Father. This fruit is pleasing to the Lord Jesus Christ. One should mature in Christ and become part of the Bride of Christ. The Bride will escape God's wrath and inherit the Heavenly Kingdom.

The Great Commission

> *Go ye therefore, and teach all nations, baptizing them in the name of the Father, and of the Son, and of the Holy Ghost: Teaching them to observe all things whatsoever I have commanded you: and, lo I, am with you alway, even unto the end of the world. Amen* (Matt. 28:19-20).

And he that taketh not his cross, and followeth after Me, is not worthy of Me (Matt. 10:38).

Then said Jesus to those Jews which believed on Him, **If ye continue in My word***, then are ye My disciples indeed; And ye shall know the truth, and the truth shall make you free* (John 8:31-32 - Emphasis added).

These are the disciples that wrote this book: Bob Anderson, Gregory Gilmore, Israel Gilmore, and Duane Klebs. We testify that we are Holy Spirit led and wrote these things as He willed us to write. We do not claim to be prophets of God. We know the Bible is truth and that the truth has set us free. And if you let Him, the Truth will set you free too. Amen!

Appendix

Important

Charts

on next

pages!

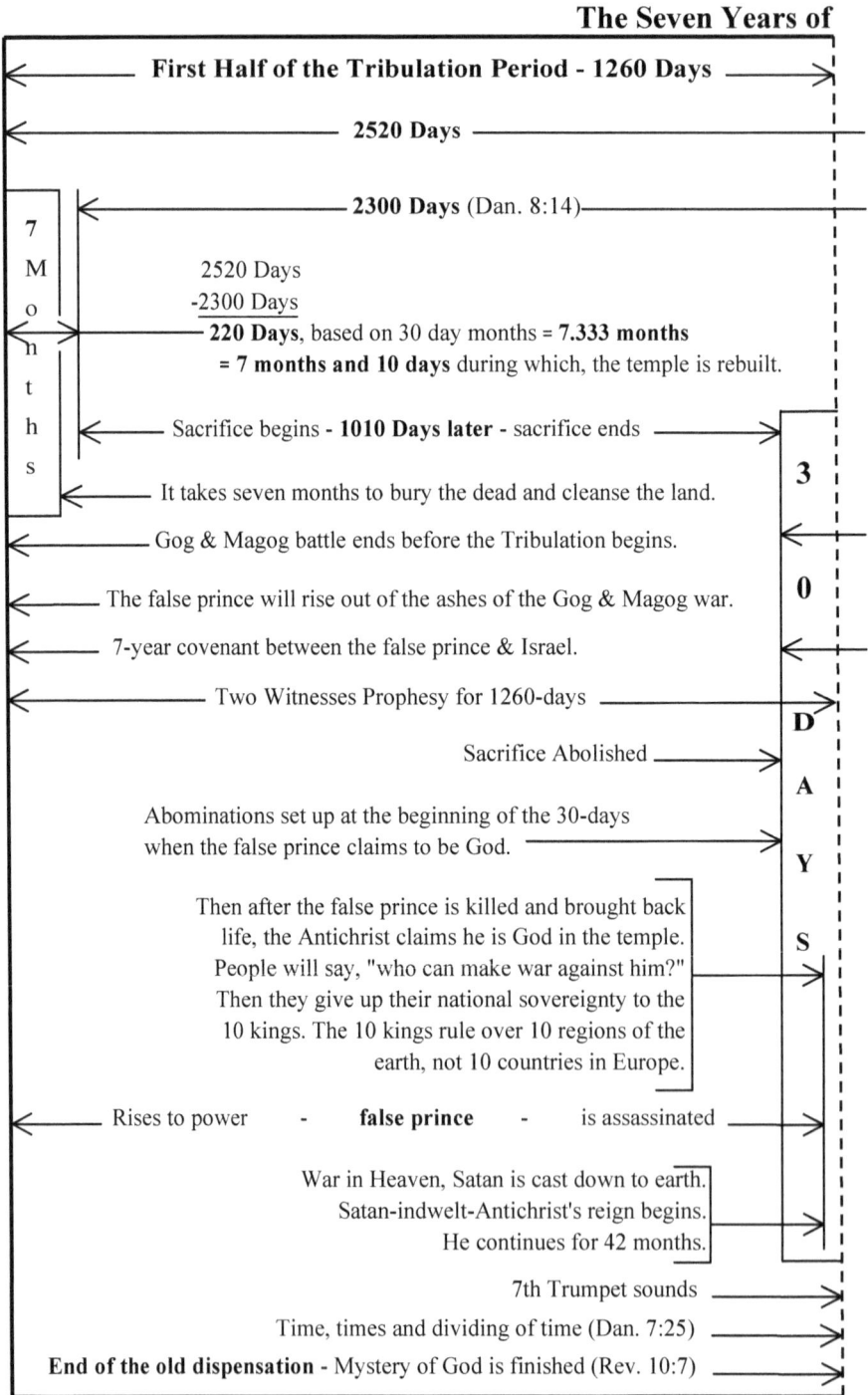

The Seven Years of

First Half of the Tribulation Period - 1260 Days →

2520 Days

2300 Days (Dan. 8:14)

7
M
o
n
t
h
s

2520 Days
-2300 Days
220 Days, based on 30 day months = **7.333 months**
= **7 months and 10 days** during which, the temple is rebuilt.

Sacrifice begins - **1010 Days later** - sacrifice ends

It takes seven months to bury the dead and cleanse the land.

Gog & Magog battle ends before the Tribulation begins.

The false prince will rise out of the ashes of the Gog & Magog war.

7-year covenant between the false prince & Israel.

Two Witnesses Prophesy for 1260-days

Sacrifice Abolished

Abominations set up at the beginning of the 30-days
when the false prince claims to be God.

Then after the false prince is killed and brought back
life, the Antichrist claims he is God in the temple.
People will say, "who can make war against him?"
Then they give up their national sovereignty to the
10 kings. The 10 kings rule over 10 regions of the
earth, not 10 countries in Europe.

Rises to power   -   **false prince**   -   is assassinated

War in Heaven, Satan is cast down to earth.
Satan-indwelt-Antichrist's reign begins.
He continues for 42 months.

7th Trumpet sounds

Time, times and dividing of time (Dan. 7:25)

End of the old dispensation - Mystery of God is finished (Rev. 10:7)

3
0
D
A
Y
S

The Tribulation Period

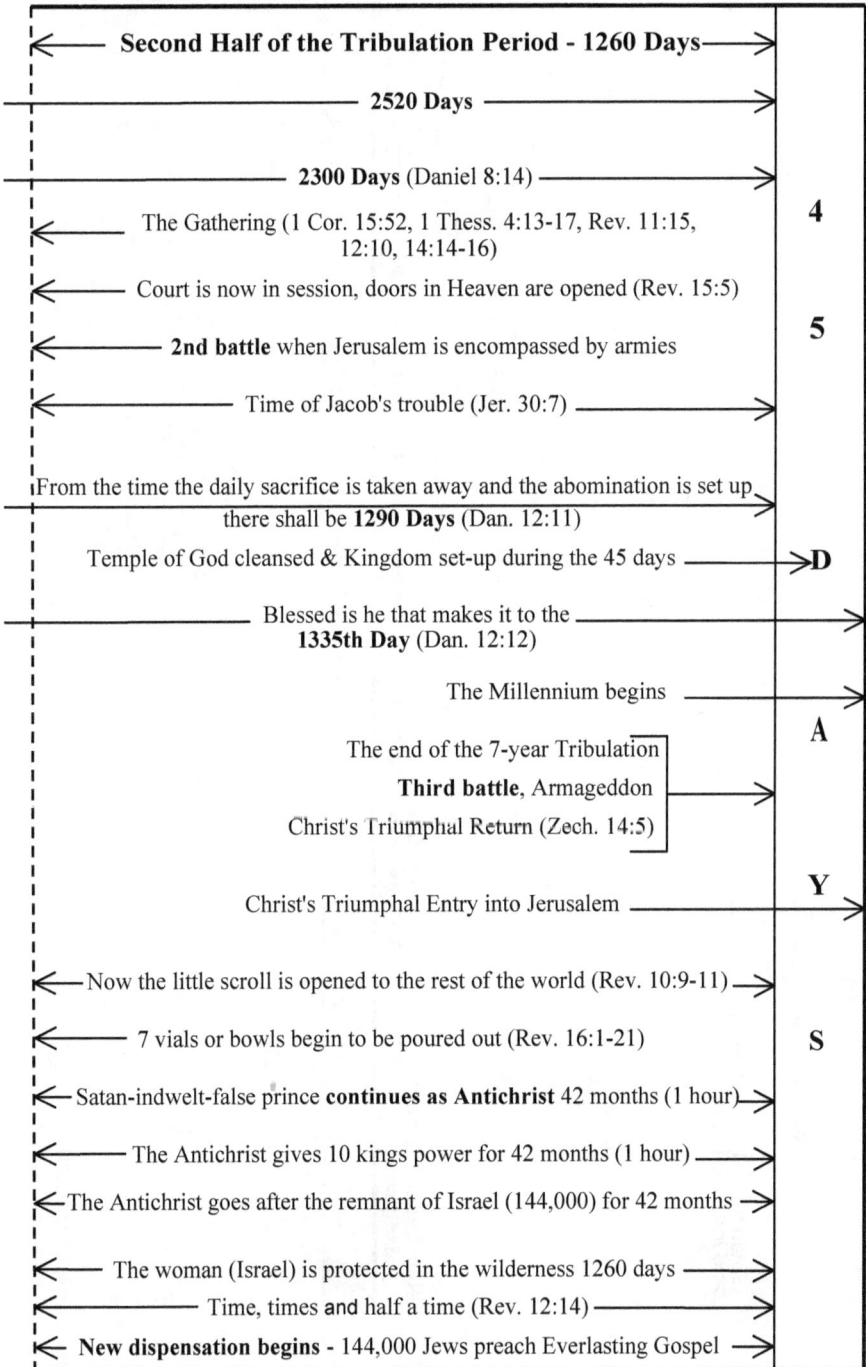

←——— **Second Half of the Tribulation Period - 1260 Days**——→

←—————————— **2520 Days** —————————→

←————————— **2300 Days** (Daniel 8:14) —————————→

←——— The Gathering (1 Cor. 15:52, 1 Thess. 4:13-17, Rev. 11:15, 12:10, 14:14-16) **4**

←——— Court is now in session, doors in Heaven are opened (Rev. 15:5)

←——— **2nd battle** when Jerusalem is encompassed by armies **5**

←——— Time of Jacob's trouble (Jer. 30:7) —————→

From the time the daily sacrifice is taken away and the abomination is set up, there shall be **1290 Days** (Dan. 12:11)

Temple of God cleansed & Kingdom set-up during the 45 days ——→**D**

————————— Blessed is he that makes it to the ——————→
1335th Day (Dan. 12:12)

The Millennium begins ———————→

The end of the 7-year Tribulation **A**

Third battle, Armageddon ——→

Christ's Triumphal Return (Zech. 14:5)

Christ's Triumphal Entry into Jerusalem ——————→ **Y**

←—Now the little scroll is opened to the rest of the world (Rev. 10:9-11)—→

←——— 7 vials or bowls begin to be poured out (Rev. 16:1-21) **S**

←—Satan-indwelt-false prince **continues as Antichrist** 42 months (1 hour)→

←——— The Antichrist gives 10 kings power for 42 months (1 hour)——→

←—The Antichrist goes after the remnant of Israel (144,000) for 42 months→

←——— The woman (Israel) is protected in the wilderness 1260 days ———→

←——— Time, times and half a time (Rev. 12:14)———→

←— **New dispensation begins** - 144,000 Jews preach Everlasting Gospel →

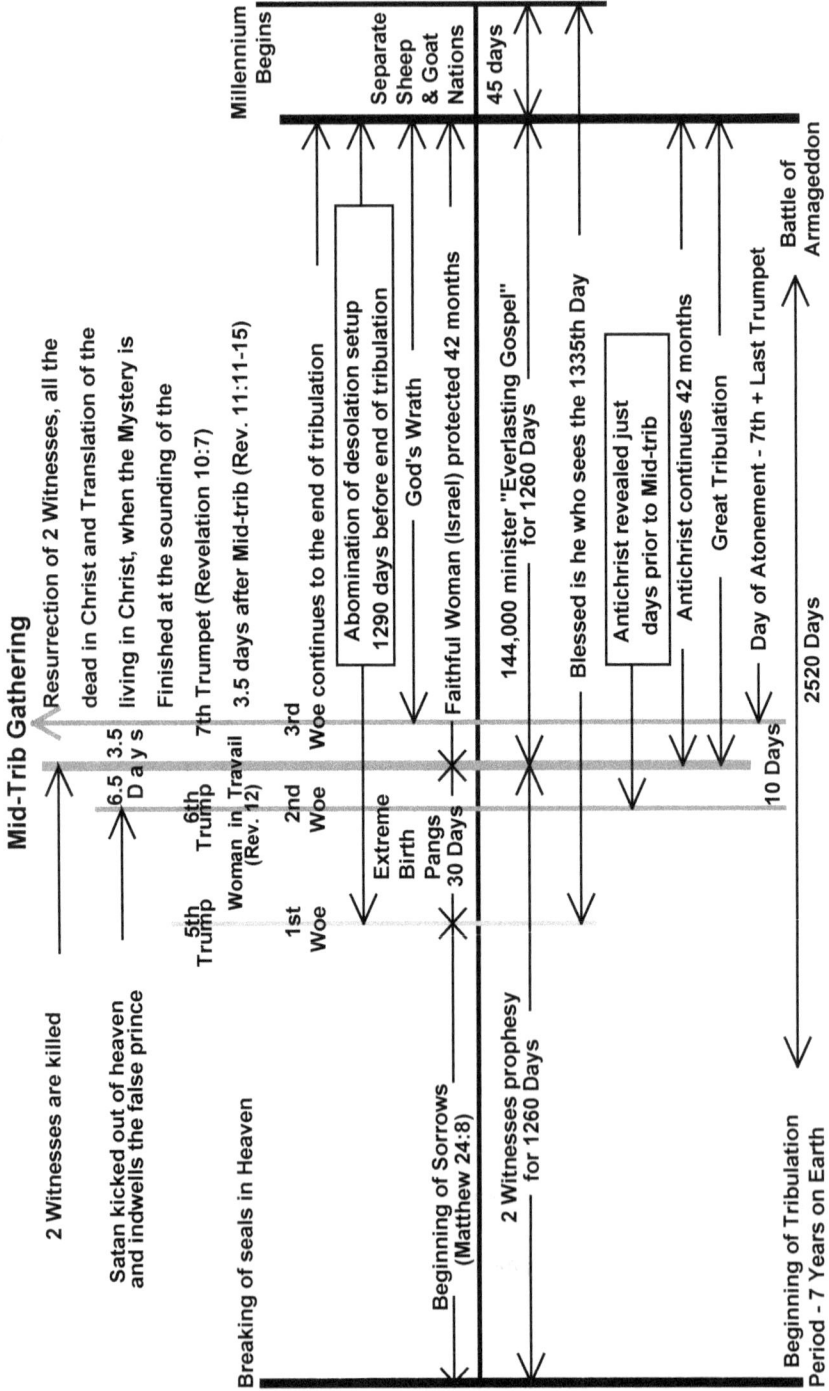

Appendix – Chart B

Mid-Trib Gathering

- Millennium Begins
- Separate Sheep & Goat Nations
- 45 days

- 2 Witnesses are killed
- Satan kicked out of heaven and indwells the false prince
- Breaking of seals in Heaven

- Resurrection of 2 Witnesses, all the dead in Christ and Translation of the living in Christ, when the Mystery is Finished at the sounding of the
- 7th Trumpet (Revelation 10:7)
- 3.5 days after Mid-trib (Rev. 11:11-15)
- Woe continues to the end of tribulation
- Abomination of desolation setup 1290 days before end of tribulation
- God's Wrath
- Faithful Woman (Israel) protected 42 months
- 144,000 minister "Everlasting Gospel" for 1260 Days
- Blessed is he who sees the 1335th Day
- Antichrist revealed just days prior to Mid-trib
- Antichrist continues 42 months
- Great Tribulation
- Day of Atonement - 7th + Last Trumpet
- Battle of Armageddon
- 2520 Days

- 5th Trump
- 6.5 3.5 Days
- 6th Trump
- Woman in Travail (Rev. 12)
- 7th Trump
- 1st Woe
- 2nd Woe
- 3rd Woe
- Extreme Birth Pangs 30 Days
- 10 Days

- Beginning of Sorrows (Matthew 24:8)
- 2 Witnesses prophesy for 1260 Days
- Beginning of Tribulation Period - 7 Years on Earth

Chart C
Symphonic View of Daniel's Split Week

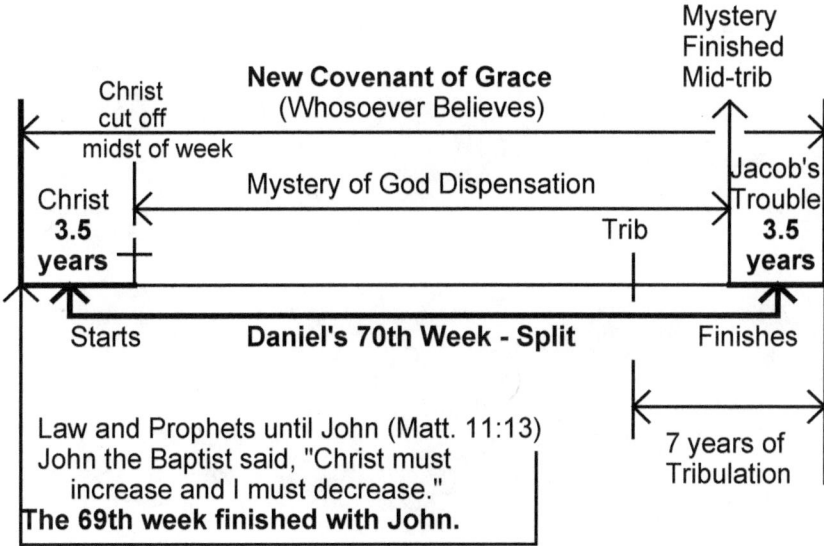

Mystery
Finished
Mid-trib

Christ
cut off
New Covenant of Grace
(Whosoever Believes)

midst of week

Mystery of God Dispensation

Christ
**3.5
years**

Jacob's
Trouble
**3.5
years**

Trib

Starts   **Daniel's 70th Week - Split**   Finishes

Law and Prophets until John (Matt. 11:13)
John the Baptist said, "Christ must
    increase and I must decrease."
The 69th week finished with John.

7 years of
Tribulation

Chart D
Symphonic View of the Mystery of God

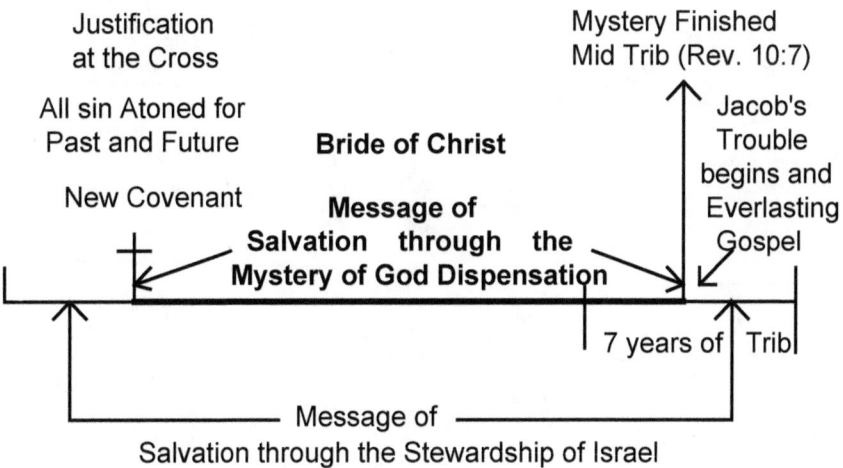

Justification
at the Cross

Mystery Finished
Mid Trib (Rev. 10:7)

All sin Atoned for
Past and Future

Bride of Christ

Jacob's
Trouble
begins and
Everlasting
Gospel

New Covenant

**Message of
Salvation   through   the
Mystery of God Dispensation**

7 years of Trib

Message of
Salvation through the Stewardship of Israel

337

Endnotes

1. Clarence Larkin, *The Greatest Book on Dispensational Truth in the World* (Glenside, PA.: Rev. Clarence Larkin Est., 1920), 20.
2. Hal Lindsey, *Vanished into Thin Air* (Beverly Hills, CA.: Western Front Ltd., 1999), 168-169.
3. Clarence Larkin, *The Greatest Book on Dispensational Truth in the World* (Glenside, PA.: Rev. Clarence Larkin Est., 1920), 21.
4. Hal Lindsey, *Vanished into Thin Air* (Beverly Hills, CA.: Western Front Ltd., 1999), 283.
5. Hal Lindsey, *Late Great Planet Earth* (Grand Rapids, MI.: Zondervan Publishing House, 1970), 151-152.
6. Hal Lindsey, *Vanished into Thin Air* (Beverly Hills, CA.: Western Front Ltd., 1999), 168.
7. Clarence Larkin, *The Greatest Book on Dispensational Truth in the World* (Glenside, PA.: Rev. Clarence Larkin Est., 1920), 149 1/2.
8. Hal Lindsey, *Vanished into Thin Air* (Beverly Hills, CA.: Western Front Ltd., 1999), 168-169.
9. Ibid., 169.
10. Clarence Larkin, *The Greatest Book on Dispensational Truth in the World* (Glenside, PA.: Rev. Clarence Larkin Est., 1920), 40.
11. Ibid., 38-41.
12. Hal Lindsey, *Vanished into Thin Air* (Beverly Hills, CA.: Western Front Ltd., 1999), 265-267.
13. Clarence Larkin, *The Greatest Book on Dispensational Truth in the World* (Glenside, PA.: Rev. Clarence Larkin Est., 1920), 16.
14. Hal Lindsey, *Vanished into Thin Air* (Beverly Hills, CA.: Western Front Ltd., 1999), 110.
15. Hal Lindsey, *Late Great Planet Earth* (Grand Rapids, MI.: Zondervan Publishing House, 1970), 105.
16. Jack Van Impe, *JVI Television Show*, March 22, 2006.
17. Hal Lindsey, *Vanished into Thin Air* (Beverly Hills, CA.: Western Front Ltd., 1999), 288.
18. Hal Lindsey, *Late Great Planet Earth* (Grand Rapids, MI.: Zondervan Publishing House, 1970), 111.

19. Tim LaHaye, *The Rapture* (Eugene, Ore.: Harvest House Publishers, 2002), 58-59.

20. J. Dwight Pentecost, *THINGS TO COME – A Study in Biblical Eschatology* (Grand Rapids, MI.: Zondervan Publishing House, 1979), 194-195.

21. Hal Lindsey, *Vanished into Thin Air* (Beverly Hills, CA.: Western Front Ltd., 1999), 203.

22. Wikipedia.org., "VeriChip," http://en.wikipedia.org/wiki/Veri Chip (accessed November 23, 2013).

23. Wikipedia.org., "Supercomputer," http://en.wikipedia.org/wiki/ Supercomputer (accessed November 14, 2013).

24. Truth or Fiction.com., "Beast of Belgium," http://www.truthor fiction.com/rumors/b/beastofbelgium.htm (accessed November 14, 2013).

25. Joel C. Graves, *Gathering Over Jerusalem* (Maitland, FL.: Xulon Press, 2003), 88.

26. Duane Nicol, *Prevail Magazine.org.*, December 2007, http:// www.prevailmagazine.org/the-return-of-the-twelfth-imam/ (accessed November 23, 2013).

27. Hal Lindsey, *Late Great Planet Earth* (Grand Rapids, MI.: Zondervan Publishing House, 1970), 151-152.

28. J. Dwight Pentecost, *THINGS TO COME – A Study in Biblical Eschatology* (Grand Rapids, MI.: Zondervan Publishing House, 1979), 250.

29. David Allen Lewis, *PROPHECY 2000: Rushing To Armageddon* (Green Forest, AR.: New Leaf Press), 171-259.

30. Ibid., 171.

31. Ibid., 186-209.

32. Ibid., 259.

33. Wikipedia.org., "2004 attempt to revive the Sanhedrin," http://en.wikipedia.org/wiki/2004_attempt_to_revive_the_Sanhe drin (accessed November 7, 2013).

34. Tim LaHaye, *The Rapture* (Eugene, Ore.: Harvest House Publishers, 2002), 53.

35. J. Dwight Pentecost, *THINGS TO COME – A Study in Biblical Eschatology* (Grand Rapids, MI.: Zondervan Publishing House, 1979), 187-188.

36. Ibid., 185.

37. J. Dwight Pentecost, *THINGS TO COME – A Study in Biblical Eschatology* (Grand Rapids, MI.: Zondervan Publishing House, 1979), 186.
38. Ibid., 186.
39. David Allen Lewis, *PROPHECY 2000: Rushing To Armageddon* (Green Forest, AR.: New Leaf Press), 213.
40. James Strong, *Strong's Exhaustive Concordance of the Bible* (Madison, NJ., 1890; 43rd Printing, Nashville: Abingdon Press, 1984), Hebrew and Chaldee Dictionary #6387, 94.
41. Ibid., Hebrew and Chaldee Dictionary #2677, 42.
42. James Strong, *Strong's Exhaustive Concordance of the Bible* (Madison, NJ., 1890; 43rd Printing, Nashville: Abingdon Press, 1984), Greek Dictionary of the New Testament *#5610*, 79.
43. Tim LaHaye, *The Rapture* (Eugene, Ore.: Harvest House Publishers, 2002), 78.
44. Clarence Larkin, *The Greatest Book on Dispensational Truth in the World* (Glenside, PA.: Rev. Clarence Larkin Est., 1920), 16.
45. Tim LaHaye, *The Rapture* (Eugene, Ore.: Harvest House Publishers, 2002), 124.
46. Hal Lindsey, *Vanished into Thin Air* (Beverly Hills, CA.: Western Front Ltd., 1999), 212.
47. J. Dwight Pentecost, *THINGS TO COME – A Study in Biblical Eschatology* (Grand Rapids, MI.: Zondervan Publishing House, 1979), 200.
48. Ibid., 205.
49. Ibid., 204.
50. James Strong, *Strong's Exhaustive Concordance of the Bible* (Madison, NJ., 1890; 43rd Printing, Nashville: Abingdon Press, 1984), Greek Dictionary of the New Testament *#646*, 15.
51. Ibid., Greek Dictionary of the New Testament *#646*, 15.
52. Ibid., Greek Dictionary of the New Testament *#647*, 15.
53. Ibid., Greek Dictionary of the New Testament *#868*, 17-18.
54. Ibid., Greek Dictionary of the New Testament *#575*, 14.
55. Ibid., Greek Dictionary of the New Testament *#2476*, 38.
56. Ibid., Greek Dictionary of the New Testament *#868*, 17-18.
57. Ibid., Greek Dictionary of the New Testament *#2476*, 38.
58. Ibid., Greek Dictionary of the New Testament *#575*, 14.
59. Ibid., Greek Dictionary of the New Testament *#646*, 15.

60. James Strong, *Strong's Exhaustive Concordance of the Bible* (Madison, NJ., 1890; 43rd Printing, Nashville: Abingdon Press, 1984), Greek Dictionary of the New Testament *#359*, 11.

61. J. Dwight Pentecost, *THINGS TO COME – A Study in Biblical Eschatology* (Grand Rapids, MI.: Zondervan Publishing House, 1979), 200.

62. Ibid., 200.

63. Hal Lindsey, *Vanished into Thin Air* (Beverly Hills, CA.: Western Front Ltd., 1999), 275-277.

64. Ibid., 277-278.

65. Ibid., 225.

66. J. Dwight Pentecost, *THINGS TO COME – A Study in Biblical Eschatology* (Grand Rapids, MI.: Zondervan Publishing House, 1979), 194-199.

67. Ibid., 196.

68. Ibid., 198.

69. Ibid., 198.

70. Ibid., 197-198.

71. Ibid., 198.

72. Ibid., 194-195.

73. Tim LaHaye, *The Rapture* (Eugene, Ore.: Harvest House Publishers, 2002), 115.

74. J. Dwight Pentecost, *THINGS TO COME – A Study in Biblical Eschatology* (Grand Rapids, MI.: Zondervan Publishing House, 1979), 310.

75. David B. Guralnik, Editor in Chief, *Webster's New World Dictionary, Second College Edition* (Cleveland - New York: William Collins + World Publishing Co., Inc., 1974), 702.

76. Ibid., 702.

77. David Allen Lewis, *PROPHECY 2000: Rushing To Armageddon* (Green Forest, AR.: New Leaf Press), 213.

78. Ibid., 212.

79. J. Dwight Pentecost, *THINGS TO COME – A Study in Biblical Eschatology* (Grand Rapids, MI.: Zondervan Publishing House, 1979), 199.

80. Clarence Larkin, *The Greatest Book on Dispensational Truth in the World* (Glenside, PA.: Rev. Clarence Larkin Est., 1920), 13.

www.ingramcontent.com/pod-product-compliance
Lightning Source LLC
Chambersburg PA
CBHW060244100426
42742CB00011B/1631